The Lesbian Parenting Book

A Guide to Creating Families
and Raising Children

D. Merilee Clunis, Ph.D.

G. Dorsey Green, Ph.D.

SEAL PRESS

Published by Seal Press
An Imprint of Avalon Publishing Group Incorporated
161 William Street, 16th Floor
New York, NY 10038

Cover design by Kate Thompson
Cover photographs by Dana Schuerholz
Text design by Clare Conrad

Library of Congress Cataloging-in-Publication Data
Clunis, D. Merilee
    Lesbian parenting : a guide to creating families and raising children /
D. Merilee Clunis and G. Dorsey Green.
    Includes bibliographical references and index.
    1. Lesbian mothers. 2. Gay parents. 3. Children of gay parents. 4. Parenting.
I. Green, G. Dorsey. II. Title
HQ75.53.C58   1995   649'.1—dc20   95–14905
ISBN 1-878067-68-0

Printed in the United States of America
10   9   8   7   6   5   4

Distributed to the trade by Publishers Group West
In Canada: Publishers Group West Canada, Toronto, Ontario
In the U.K. and Europe: Airlift Book Company, Middlesex, England
In Australia: Banyan Tree Book Distributors, Kent Town, South Australia

ACKNOWLEDGMENTS

When we first met in 1982, one of us wanted to write about lesbian couples and the other one wanted to write about parenting and children. We decided early on in our friendship that we would like to work together; our first book, *Lesbian Couples*, was published in 1988. Four years later Faith Conlon of Seal Press asked us to consider writing a book about lesbian parents. Little did she know that she was helping us complete our original dream.

This book project and its authors received much help and support from many directions. Seal Press's faith in us and their vision of a parenting book for lesbians are the foundation on which we have relied for the last three years.

We are indebted to a number of people for broadening and adding depth to our perspectives about parenting and about lesbians who parent. Thanks to Susan Barrett, Jean Catellani, Theresa Clark, M. Kiser, Patricia Matthews, Margaret Schonfield, Lin Skavdahl, Ann Stever, Stephanie Van Dyke, Lynn Waddington, Susan Waller and Clare Wey-Driscoll. We are also grateful to professional colleagues in medicine, law, social work and psychology whom we interviewed or who evaluated the manuscript for accuracy in specific content areas. They are Mimi Acosta, Susan Barrett, Laura Brown, Jeff Gold, Teresa Jones, Kim Kendall, Suzy Myers, Susan Petcoff, Maria P.P. Root, David Springer, Barbara Wechsler and Leanne Wilson.

Towards the end of the process we hired Nancy Brandwein, an independent editor, whose direct commentary and editorial suggestions helped us reorganize the manuscript. Cathy Johnson provided copy editing direction to produce a more coherent, consistently written book. Ann Stever helped organize and type the footnotes and bibliographies. Stacy Lewis was the production wizard who ensured that the book reached its final form.

We thank again our editor, Faith Conlon, whose vision, direction and editing kept us going when we would rather have taken long vacations from the project. Faith has an amazing capacity for being both supportive and calming when all else seems crazy. We are extremely grateful for her steady hand at the tiller of Seal Press.

Dorsey thanks Margaret Sorrel, without whom she would never have had their two sons. Thanks to Don and Barry for being the main men in my sons' lives. I am grateful to Ethan and Brendan for providing a reality check for all my wonderful theories. I am indebted to Ann Stever for sharing the beginning of our dating relationship with this book writing project and grateful to her for being an additional parent support for my sons while I was busy at the computer. Most of all, I thank Merilee for once again being a challenging, forgiving and humorous co-author. My writing is better for her and my parenting of my sons is deepened and improved because of her insights.

Merilee thanks her family—who made it all possible. My partner, Margaret Schonfield, brought children into my life and taught me almost everything I know about parenting. This book is as much hers as mine. Lise and Noah unfolded, providing on-the-job training in the awesome challenges and pleasures of family life. I feel very grateful for the support, course correction and co-learning opportunities that my family—individually and collectively—continues to offer. I also want to express my thanks to Dorsey for taking the lead with this project and for her solid presence, unflagging good humor and grace under pressure.

To the children

CONTENTS

Introduction: Navigating the Journey of Lesbian Parenting　　　3

Section One: Our Lives as Lesbian Families　　　9

1　*We're Here: Our Unique Families*　　　11

What's It Like Being in a Lesbian Family? / *Structure and Language* / *Coming Out* / The Strengths of Our Families / *A Challenge to Sexism* / *Egalitarian Arrangements* / *More Room at the Table* / *A Wide Support Network* / *A Broader Perspective* / "Family Values" of the Future

2　*Starting Out: Alternative Insemination, Foster-Parenting and Adoption*　　　19

Children—To Have or Not to Have / Pregnancy via Alternative Insemination / *An Insemination Prep Talk* / *A Word About HIV and AIDS* / *The Great Lesbian Sperm Chase* / *A.I. with a Known Donor* / *Romancing the Syringe: At-Home Insemination* / Getting Pregnant the Old-Fashioned Way / When You Can't Conceive / Foster-Parenting / *Loving and Letting Go* / Adoption / *Crossing Ability, Cultural and Racial Lines* / *Agency Adoption* / *Foster-Adopt Programs* / *Independent Adoptions* / *International Adoptions* / How Do I Know if I Like Having Children in My Life?

3　*Branches on Our Family Tree: Partners, Fathers, Siblings and Others*　　　41

What's In a Name? / *Beyond Our "Job Descriptions"* / Fathers and Other Men in Our Lives / *Fathers via Marriage* / *Donors: Anonymous or Known?* / *Fathers via Chosen Family* / *Father Fantasies* / *Male Role Models* / *Changing Relationships* / Extended Family: From "Goddess-Parents" to Grandparents / The Significance of Siblings / New Visions

4　*Coming Out to Our Children and Families*　　　60

Defining Our Terms: Coming Out, Heterosexism and Homophobia / The Advantages of Coming Out to Our Children / *Intimacy vs. Secrecy* / *Open Communication* / *Self-Esteem* / The Risks of Coming Out to Our Children / How to Come Out to Children / *"But What's a Lesbian?"—Coming Out to Young Children* / *"What If She Hates Me?"—Considerations with Adolescents* / *Coming Out to Adult Children* / Full Circle: Coming Out to Our Family of Origin / *When Lesbian Becomes Parent* / *When Parent Becomes Lesbian*

5 *Engaged Parenting: Communication and Conflict Resolution*   **81**
Caring Communication / *Listening So Children Will Talk* /
Talking So Children Will Listen / Setting Limits / Resolving
Conflicts Constructively / *Parents as Models* / *Resolving
Conflicts with Young Children* / *Sibling Rivalry* / *Resolving
Conflicts with Adolescents* / The Tradition of Family Meetings /
When to Get Help

6 *Helping Our Children Through Loss and Divorce*   **108**
The Stages of Grief / *Supporting Your Child Through the Grieving
Process* / Helping Your Child Face Death / *Death of a Child* /
Divorce / *Navigating Divorce: The Challenges for Parents* / *What
Divorce Does to Kids* / *Telling Your Child About Divorce* / *Lesbian
Divorce*

7 *Confronting Racism and Building Rainbows*   **126**
How Racist Are We? / *Defining Our Terms* / How Racism
Affects Individuals / How Racism Affects Families / *Thinking
About Adoption and Race* / *Living in an Interracial Adoptive
Family* / *"You Picked Me Out!": How Children Perceive Race and
Adoption* / *Interracial Couples with Children* / Raising Bias-Free
Children / *Building Self-Esteem and Positive Racial Identity* /
Confronting Racist Comments / *When Your Child Practices Racism* /
When Your Child Experiences Racism / *Walking Our Talk*

8 *Celebrating Our Lives: New Family Traditions*   **146**
Reclaiming Rituals and Building Traditions / *Everyday Rituals* /
Earthly Delights / *Holiday Celebrations* / *Spur-of-the-Moment
Gatherings* / *Birthdays and Rites of Passage* / *While We're Apart* /
Death / Creating Your Family Traditions

Section Two: Parenting Our Children as They Grow   **159**
9 *At the Very Beginning: Pregnancy and Childbirth*   **161**
Great Expectations / *A Pregnancy Preview* / *Getting Support* /
A Word for Adoptive Parents-to-Be / *Days in the Lives of Pregnant
Lesbians* / Childbirth / *Getting Quality Prenatal Care* / *Birthing
Issues for the Pregnant Mother* / *. . . And Her Partner* / *Labor
Preparation: From Birthing Classes to Popsicle Supplies* / *Giving
Birth at a Hospital* / *At a Birthing Center* / *A Home Birth* /
Miscarriage and Stillbirth

10 *Your New Baby: The First Eighteen Months*   **178**
Development Guideposts / *Newborn to Six Months: Pee, Poop, Tears . . . and Smiles* / *Six to Eighteen Months: Learning Through Movement* / Parenting Issues / *Who Does What?* / *Family and Friends: Help or Hindrance?* / Out in the World

11 *Parenting the Toddler: Eighteen Months to Thirty-Six Months*   **192**
Development Guideposts / *Physical Skills* / *Cognitive Advances* / *Psychological/Social Development* / Parenting Issues / *Becoming Independent* / *"I Go Potty!"* / *The Gentle Art of Discipline* / *She Said . . . She Said: Being Consistent as a Couple* / *Support Groups and Play Groups* / Out in the World / *Toddler "Outings"* / *Out at Work* / Couple Time

12 *The Emerging Child: Three to Six Years*   **208**
Development Guideposts / *Spirals of Change* / *Physical Skills* / *Cognitive Advances* / *Emotional/Social Development* / *Gender and Sexuality* / Parenting Issues / *Moms as Mirrors* / *The "Why" Years* / Out in the World / *Structured Enviroments: Preschool and Kindergarten* / *Religious Groups* / *International and Interracial Adoptions* / Time Out for Relationships / *You and Your Partner* / *Educating Your Extended Family*

13 *Logic and Rules; Fairness and Morals: Six to Ten Years*   **226**
Development Guideposts / *The Logical Child* / *Rules and Moral Reasoning* / *Emotional/Social Development* / *Physical Skills* / *The Playing's the Thing* / Parenting Issues / *Playing by the Rules* / *Values—Yours, Mine and Ours* / Out in the World / *Sports* / *School* / *Sex Education* / *Moving and Making Friends*

14 *The Journey of Adolescence: Not Necessarily a Nightmare*   **244**
Four Myths About Adolescence / A Development Overview / *Early, Late or on Time* / *Skills: Now You See Them, Now You Don't* / Raising Boys . . . Raising Girls / *The Damaging Messages Our Daughters Hear* / Putting Your Own Adolescence in Perspective / Shifting the Parenting Gears / *Engaged Parenting . . . Adolescent Style*

15 *On the Road to Adulthood: Ten to Fourteen Years*   **260**
Development Guideposts / *Physical Changes* / *Sexual Awakening* / *Intellectual and Moral Development* / *Emotional Growth* / Is This Problem Serious? / *Serious Problems* / Parenting Issues / *Separation and Independence* / *School and Socal Life: Get Involved or Steer Clear?*

16 *Independence and Identity: Fourteen to Eighteen Years*   **286**
Development Guideposts / *Intellectual and Moral Development /*
Emotional Growth / *The Social Scene* / *The Golden Age of Friend-*
ship / Parenting Issues / *Is Your Teen's Having a Job Good or Bad? /*
Sex, Drugs and Rock 'n' Roll / Is This Problem Serious? / *Drug*
and Alcohol Problems / *Academic Slide* / *Other Behavior Problems*

17 *Stepping into New Roles: Our Adult Children*   **312**
Family Occasions: Fun or Fearful? / Meeting Your Child's
Partner / The Challenge of Weddings / From Moms to
Grandmoms / Hey, Mom, I'm Home Again

Notes   325

Selected Biblography   331

General Bibliography   339

Resources   357

Appendices: 361

  A: Second-Parent Adoption   361

  B: Alternative Insemination and Infertility Workups   363

  C: Sample Parenting Agreement   367

Index   369

About the Authors   379

THE LESBIAN PARENTING BOOK

Introduction:

Navigating the Journey of Lesbian Parenting

When you set out to have a child or find yourself joining a ready-made family, it is wise to have both dreams and road maps for the journey: dreams for envisioning and realizing a family unit not mirrored by mainstream culture, and road maps to turn to when the ride gets bumpy and you find yourself wondering, "Now what?" Raising children is a meandering journey, full of surprise, discovery and change. As a parent, you'll need to be ready to shift gears for the inevitable transitions that family life brings. The developmental stages that children go through in themselves guarantee changes. Fate also has a way of adding its own surprises. You may find yourself on a different road than planned if you decide to change jobs, or move to another state where you do not have friends, or if you unexpectedly lose your partner and become a single parent. Your entire map may change as time, emotional and financial demands veer off in new directions.

Lesbian parenting is a unique journey, marked by love—our own and that of our communities—as well as by lack of assistance from the world around us. But it is no longer a lonely or isolated trip. When we started our own parenting journeys in the 1970s and 1980s, there was very little written and few visible role models available for lesbian parents. We ventured out—along with our children—with little support or understanding from other than those who knew us personally. Thankfully that has changed. National magazines and newspapers now feature stories about lesbian families and more than a dozen books of interest to gay and lesbian parents have been published. More academic research which explores the ramifications of living in lesbian-headed families is being published. Adoption agencies have sponsored workshops for prospective gay and lesbian adoptive parents and Health Maintenance Organizations (HMOs) have established informational groups for lesbians considering parenthood. Courts are reexamining their negative assumptions about lesbian parents and their children and in some parts of the country non-legal lesbian parents can become legal parents through second-parent adoptions.

While there are still not enough resources specifically for lesbian parents, anyone who peruses parenting sections in bookstores risks being overwhelmed by the hundreds of books on parenting. Some discuss month-by-month development from infancy to toddlerhood or year-by-year from three to six and beyond. There are books on rearing children of color, gifted children, children with disabilities and adolescents. Some advise how to raise girls, others focus on raising boys. There are books for adoptive parents and foster parents as well as countless books on parenting skills and approaches. How is a parent to choose? Particularly since one of the features of parenting in this day and age is a shortage of time.

Our goal in writing *The Lesbian Parenting Book* was to offer road maps and suggestions which speak to both the lesbian and the parenting parts of being a lesbian parent. We wanted to address issues and challenges which are specific to lesbian parents—mothers, partners and others involved in parenting roles with children. That's the lesbian part. We also wanted to distill useful information about child development as well as what we have found to be the best principles and practices of child-rearing. That's the parenting part. We are well aware that much of the day-to-day parenting has little to do with being a lesbian. On the other hand, the reality of being a *lesbian* parent informs the whole picture of parenting and family life—and sometimes it becomes the main feature.

Although every family is unique, certain features make lesbian-headed families distinct from those headed by a heterosexual parent or parents. And then within lesbian-headed families, there are features which can make these families very different from each other. For example, some lesbian parents are biological (therefore legal) mothers while others have no biological connection to the children in their family and hence no legal rights. While many lesbian mothers had their children in the context of a heterosexual relationship, many others have adopted, given birth or become involved in parenting children after they have come out as lesbians. Some lesbian parents have had to deal with the fall-out from a heterosexual divorce, such as shielding the children from an angry, homophobic ex-spouse; others are now navigating their way through a lesbian divorce. Some lesbian-headed families include additional unrelated adults as part of a close extended family. A number of lesbian parents have incorporated a previously unknown donor into their family. Each of these situations has particular challenges which we address.

Partly because we ourselves have had different personal experiences, we are well aware that lesbian parenting comes in a variety of flavors. While we are both psychologists, both white, middle-class and self-employed, our family situations are different.

Dorsey is the mother of two sons, Ethan and Brendan, both of whom were born into an out lesbian family. She shares the parenting of the children with her ex-partner, Margaret. They each have lovers who have jumped in as extra "moms." Two men the boys call their "Dads" are combination "fathers-uncles" and have nurtured Ethan and Brendan since birth. A large group of friends, biological family and the local Quaker meeting round out Brendan and Ethan's extended family. Dorsey's family illustrates transitions and changing forms, and what we describe in the book as a "lesbian-first family."

Merilee's situation is an example of another kind of lesbian family. Children came into Merilee's life when she met her partner Margaret. Lise and Noah, now well into their twenties, were nine and seven years old at the time. Family living arrangements varied over the years. Initially, the kids lived with their father and stepmother and spent weekends and vacations in Seattle with Margaret and Merilee. When they were twelve and fourteen, that situation switched when they moved to Seattle and spent vacations with their dad. As the partner of a lesbian mother, Merilee's parenting role and title has been an ongoing question with changing answers. What has not changed is the love, connection and commitment to family.

This book represents the lessons we—and our children—have learned from personal experience. We have also tried to represent the distilled wisdom of our friends, our colleagues, our clients and the many books and resources on parenting we have consumed.

The book is organized into two sections which we hope will allow for easy access to the information that is the most relevant to you. In the first section we discuss topics that are common to lesbian families, such as coming out, the role of our partners as well as the question of men in our children's lives, and dealing with difficult issues such as racism and divorce. We also describe how to develop "engaged parenting" skills. We believe that in order to successfully apply engaged parenting skills, parents must first understand their children. Thus, in the second section of the book we use a child development framework—offering a chapter-by-chapter overview of each age—to provide a road map of the typical changes you can expect as your child matures.

If you are thinking about having or adopting a child, for example, you will be particularly interested in the information on alternative insemination in Chapter 2, on adoption in Chapters 2 and 7, and in the material on pregnancy and childbirth in Chapter 9. If you are the parent of a thirteen-year-old adolescent girl, turn to Chapter 5 for communication and conflict resolution skills, Chapter 14 for reassurance and Chapter 15 for the developmental road map of early adolescence. If you are a new partner in a multiracial lesbian family with a toddler and a sixteen-year-old, you will find relevant information about parenting roles in Chapter 3, about multiracial families in Chapter 7, about toddlers in Chapter 11 and about middle and late adolescence in Chapter 16.

Our hope is that this book will provide recognition and support to lesbian parents. We want to acknowledge those of you who are translating your dreams and visions of lesbian family into a proud reality. We also want to provide practical information, ideas and suggestions to help you navigate your way in the journey of becoming parents and raising your children.

We do not think of this book as the only parenting resource you will ever need. We do not even attempt to cover all of the possible topics, nor every topic in the depth which it deserves. What we have tried to do is highlight those areas which we thought would be pertinent to most lesbian parents, and to address other topics more briefly. Although we hope the book speaks to your situation, we anticipate that many of you will need more detailed information. At the end of the book, we provide two bibliographies and a resources section which may assist you.

Good parenting is one of the greatest gifts you can give to the world, to your children and to yourself. As you take the lessons learned from surviving in a heterosexist world and empower your children to live differently, you give the gift of rising above bigotry and of celebrating diversity. As we move into the twenty-first century, the world will need women and men who know in their hearts and souls that difference is not to be feared, it is to be celebrated. Your children are these women and men and you are their teachers.

D. Merilee Clunis and G. Dorsey Green
Seattle, Washington
June, 1995

I

OUR LIVES AS LESBIAN FAMILIES

1 We're Here:

Our Unique Families

Lesbian families are everywhere. We live in cities, towns, suburbs and the country. We attend Little League games, religious services and parent-teacher conferences. We change dirty diapers, comfort our children when they have an "owie," ride out the storms of adolescence and beam with pride at graduations.

And we have always done so. Yet, because of homophobia and the very real threat of losing custody of our children, lesbian families have been invisible—until recently.

Some researchers estimate that between one and five million children in the United States have lesbian mothers who came out after having their children. Increasingly, lesbian families have become more visible. Lesbian mothers have been willing to stand up for their right to be who they are and to fight back in custody battles. In addition, starting in the late 1970s and early 80s there has been a baby boom among visible lesbians, particularly in some of the larger, lesbian-friendly urban areas in the United States. A *Newsweek* magazine article estimated that by 1990, five to ten thousand lesbians had children after coming out.

That's a lot of lesbian families!

◆ ◆ ◆

What's It Like Being a Lesbian Family?

Structure and Language

In the seventh grade, Dorsey's son Ethan had an assignment to draw a family tree. First he had to define his family. For sure he wanted his two moms, his brother, his three dads and his grandparents. When he tried to sketch it out he realized he had to identify who was his biological mother, his other mother, his brother who shared the same family but had a different biological mother, his biological father and his two "chosen family" dads whom he had known from birth. Then he wondered about his half-sister in Kansas. She was his biological father's daughter from a previous marriage. He had written to her in Kansas but never seen her. Should he try to fit her in the picture? The "family tree" just didn't work so he decided to call the whole thing his family bramble bush. He liked that.

As Ethan discovered, the images and words commonly used to describe families do not fit ours—or the words don't exist at all. We have to make them up.

Our chosen families represent a very different approach to kinship than the idealized myth of the "nuclear family" or the reality of the extended family which is characteristic of many ethnic cultures. As lesbian families, we challenge the very foundation upon which the notion of family has been based, namely heterosexuality. Blood relationships and legal ties are not the defining factors for inclusion in our families. Or at least they are not the only factors—and are often not the primary ones. For instance, partners in a lesbian family are of the same gender and not allowed to be legally married. Children may be biologically related to one parent and not the other; or may be the biological child of one parent and adopted by the other; or may be co-parented by a number of unrelated people. The biological father may be actively involved or purposefully unknown, while other men take on the parenting role of "dad." Our families also may include other members such as ex-partners and friends whose kinship is based on mutual agreement to be there for each other. These chosen lesbian families often have a complex array of relationships.

Coming Out

Twenty-year-old Lise introduced Merilee to different people as "my

*mother's partner" or "my other mother" or "my mother's friend " or just
"Merilee" all within the space of six months. It depended on what Lise
described, with her dry sense of humor, as "the circumstances."*

Children in lesbian families, as well as the adults, have to deal with
coming out or not, how out to be and to whom. The "circumstances"
may be awkward or smooth, heavy or light, humorous or deadly serious—but they are always there.

Some circumstances, such as the threat of losing custody of your
children, may lead you and your partner to remain closeted until the
children are grown. Or perhaps your situation is that you were already out before deciding to have children and currently live in a lesbian-friendly environment. These circumstances may find you dis-
playing pictures of your lesbian family on your desk at work and
marching in the Lesbian/Gay Pride March every year.

Lesbian parents, and parents-to-be, face coming out decisions in an
ongoing way:

- You want to tell your parents that you are a lesbian *and* that you
  and your partner are planning to have a baby.
- Another mother on the playground asks if your son looks like his
  father—and you have no idea because his father was an unknown
  donor.
- Your child's first-grade teacher calls to let you know that when the
  children were asked what they wanted to be when they grew up,
  your daughter responded that she wanted to be a lesbian.
- You have been living with your lover and her ten-year-old daughter for a year when a business acquaintance asks if you have children.
- You wonder whether to cross out "father" on the junior high school
  form and write in "other mother" or "co-parent" or leave it blank.
- Your five-year-old announces to the grocery store cashier that the
  ice cream is for a birthday party for her other mother.

Of course not all coming out stories about lesbian families have
happy endings, or middles or even beginnings. Some lesbians grapple
for years with defining who they are in relation to children to whom
they have no biological or legal tie. Some get embroiled in bitter cus-

tody fights with their male (or female) ex-partners while others suffer the pain of being rejected by their own children, or by their partner's children, because of their lesbianism.

Yet mothers continue to come out and lesbians continue to create families and raise children. Why? Because many of us already have, or want to have, children in our lives. Because we increasingly believe that we have a right to be here—alive, visible and accepted for who we are. And because we want the same opportunities as anyone else to experience the joys, the challenges and the sorrows of parenthood and family life.

The Strengths of Our Families

Kathy and her partner Nance are members of the Quaker meeting in town. The meeting held a Celebration of Commitment for them eleven years ago and since then had happily welcomed the arrival of each of their two children. Kathy and Nance are quite aware that their willingness to be out has invited the meeting's members to take them seriously as individuals and as a lesbian family.

Today, the two women arrive with a cake to share with everyone. They are celebrating that they have each been able to adopt the other's biological child, thus making each of them a legal parent of both children. The whole meeting cheered and some cried. The presence of this couple had challenged the membership to change its collective views about lesbians and lesbian parents. Today it is all worth it as the community shares the joy.

While we don't claim that lesbians do a better job of parenting than anyone else, we do think that our families have particular strengths because they are lesbian families.

Lesbian families are pioneers. Lesbians have challenged cultural beliefs and norms by combining lesbian with "parent" and with "family." Possibilities which most of us never even dreamed of as we were growing up are seen as "normal" by children in lesbian families. Lesbian parents are designing new and unique family structures which redefine the description of who a parent is and what a family looks like.

Not having models can be difficult. However, we think it gives lesbian families certain advantages over traditional heterosexual families. These advantages include more egalitarian relationships, a broader perspective, a more flexible and fluid concept of family and the opportunity for greater sharing of parenting responsibilities and more varied role models for children.

A Challenge to Sexism

In a heterosexual, two-parent family, the gender niches are typically clear to the family and to the world around them. Mothers are often in charge of the emotional and relationship aspects of family life while fathers concentrate on the physical aspects.

Women-headed families challenge the sexism about roles which is so common in our culture and often embedded in our unconscious. Because there is no father to fix the leaking faucet, cook on the barbecue or mow the lawn, women share all the chores—and the fun. In lesbian families, the roles are usually more fluid than in heterosexual families. Each woman likely takes responsiblity for both the physical and the emotional well-being of the family.

Children in lesbian families learn that women are capable of doing non-traditional as well as traditional kinds of work. This can free girls to choose what they want to do based on talent and interest rather than cultural expectations. It can prepare heterosexual boys to share their lives with equally strong, and gentle, female partners.

Egalitarian Arrangements

In addition to sharing household and breadwinning responsibilities, many lesbian families also view childcare-related activities differently. In heterosexual families there is a tendency for both parents to assume that the woman will be the primary caretaker for the children and the family. Some believe that the woman is the *only* one who can do that job. Then, because it is "women's work," the role of nurturer and caretaker has less value than the breadwinner role.

Who does what in lesbian families is not defined by gender, biology or legal responsibility but rather by interest, practicality and mutual decision. It has been well documented that lesbians approach dealing with money, household tasks and roles in a much more egalitarian way than other kinds of couples—straight or gay.[1] This strength allows for better communication and much greater flexibility in taking care of the parents' needs as well as those of the children in the family.

More Room at the Table

The concept of family is more elastic in lesbian families. This allows for parenting responsibilities to be distributed over a number of adults. For children this means that a variety of different adults have a clear presence and specific role in their lives.

> Pat had agreed to be an "aunt" to Tracy's daughter, Anna. This translated into Pat taking care of Anna every Tuesday afternoon. Initially it was always at Tracy's house but over time Anna began to spend time at Pat's house as well. This went on for two years until the adults thought that Anna was ready for an overnight. Pat and Anna spent the afternoon playing as usual. After dinner, when it was time for bed Anna cried for her mom. Pat held her and reminded her that she'd see Tracy in the morning. Anna fell asleep clutching her favorite stuffed animal. She woke up in the morning, happy and ready to play again with Auntie Pat.

These arrangements are to everyone's advantage. Tracy gets breaks, which probably improves her parenting overall. Anna discovers that she has another adult on whom she can rely. And Pat is able to give love and care to a child without needing to be a full-time parent, a role she does not want.

A Wide Support Network

Most lesbians have learned the benefits of building a community of support. Developing an extensive support network of friends and chosen family is sometimes a response to being rejected by one's biological family of origin or to the reality of living in a homophobic world. Whatever the reasons, once it is developed, this support system not only serves as psychological buffer and protection but also has very practical advantages. Thus lesbian parents frequently have other adults in their support community who happily babysit, take their children on outings or spend time with them in a variety of ways. Some of these people will come and go; others will be around for the duration.

Lesbian families and support systems are often an intricate and changing tapestry of chosen, legal, biological, current and historical relationships. Having these examples of a wide and fluid chosen family and a large community of support can encourage our children to develop an extensive network of friends.

A Broader Perspective

There is a different awareness and view of the world that comes from being a member of a minority group. Being lesbian in a heterosexual world means that you have at least two perspectives. You can see the world from the heterosexual perspective, because that is the majority view that everyone learns. You also have a lesbian perspective and perhaps even a third perspective, such as being a woman of color or being Jewish, for example. Having more than one way to see the world gives us a different consciousness, and hopefully, a broader and more compassionate perspective.

Our children reap the benefit of our experience in being part of a lesbian family. They can come to understand prejudice, homophobia, racism and all the other "isms" for the hateful and limiting blinders that they are. Differences become a positive rather than a negative.

For an assignment for a college speech class, Noah's topic was "Children of Gay and Lesbian Parents." He pointed out that his mother's homosexuality led him to be more open, not only to gays and lesbians, but to all people. In addition, he thought he was less likely to generalize or stereotype others. For him, differences make people interesting. He concluded: "My mother's lifestyle has made me more open with my family, with myself and with other people in ways that might not have been possible in a purely heterosexual environment."

As lesbians, we *have* to learn to value ourselves because the world so often devalues us. These are often painful lessons, learned at considerable cost. The reward is that they can enrich our own and our children's lives.

"Family Values" of the Future

Our families have embraced new visions and have created new structures. Like all families we are challenged to incorporate all the enormous and small changes that can go with family life—kids outgrowing their shoes in three months, a divorce, a teenager getting his driver's license, moving, getting involved with a new lover, a friend ill with AIDS.

Especially in these times of high-speed change, parents need to design flexible yet solid family structures and to approach parenting challenges with consistency and creativity. We encourage you to keep experimenting until *your* system works; don't worry that it may not look like anyone else's. Remember, your solution of today could be a role model in ten years.

Lesbians have shown amazing adaptability, flexibility and responsiveness in creating families. You may be the forerunners of the parents and families of the future as the world gets more complicated and diversity is more honored. So as you go about the business of creating your family and raising your children, remember to appreciate the strengths that being a lesbian family brings with it.

2 Starting Out:

Alternative Insemination, Foster-Parenting and Adoption

Children—To Have or Not to Have?

Children alter your life forever. If you choose to bear, foster-parent or adopt a child or simply to become an "aunt" to a friend's child, you are linking your life to a youngster, opening your world to hers or his. You will never be the same. How do you go about making such a life-changing decision?

Perhaps you have already worked through the pros and cons of having a child in your life. If so, bear with us as we list some of the questions lesbians need to address when considering becoming a parent. We also highly recommend that you read at least one of the books in the Selected Bibliography on lesbian families as well.[1]

- Do you want a child, or do you simply like the *thought* of having children? Spend time with children and with parents as you consider this question. If it is the fantasy of having children you are enamored with and not the realities of child-rearing, you will find out quickly as you spend time with children and their parents. (We discuss activities you can do to get a feel for parenting at the end of this chapter.)

- Do you have enough time, support and money to have a child?

- How will your work be affected by raising a child?

- Are you going to be a single parent, part of a couple that parents, a co-parent or one of an extended network of co-parents?

- Do you want to bear a child, adopt one, foster-parent or be the partner of a parent? A lesbian couple is the only kind of couple who may have the option of deciding who bears or does not bear a baby. One woman may not want to be the biological parent, or both may want to be pregnant. Some women prefer to adopt or foster-parent children.

- If you are interested in adoption or foster-parenting, are you patient enough and sure enough of yourself to endure the likely homophobia and daunting red tape of social service agencies?

- If you are in a relationship or want to be, have you thought through how a child will affect the relationship? No one can predict exactly how children will affect a couple's relationship, but they will affect it. For some women their relationship is their highest priority and they would rather not risk upsetting it.

- If you are partnered, do you and your partner agree about the legal relationships of the biological and non-biological parents? This may include doing a second-parent adoption to ensure that the non-adoptive or non-biological mother is legally a parent of the child. (See Appendix A for more information on second-parent adoptions.)

- If you are partnered, have you and your partner discussed or worked through potential trouble spots such as parenting styles, individual needs for control and discipline and differing cultural and family backgrounds?

- Have you thought about how having a child affects your being out in the world as a lesbian? When you have children you lose control of who knows you are lesbian, and you may not be in a position to or want to take that risk.

- Do you have support from your lesbian community for your choice to parent? Some lesbians may feel you have abandoned the cause if you choose to have a child. If your community feels this way, have you considered how that will affect you?

- Are you prepared to cope with the effects of heterosexism and homophobia on your child? Homophobia takes on new meaning when it is directed at your child.

- Have you considered the impact of racism on your family? While racism affects us all, interracial families face more complex challenges.

- Have you thought about the pros and cons of raising a son as compared to a daughter?

- Do you want men involved in a conscious way with your child? If so, what are you willing to do to have that happen? Parents cannot control who is in their child's life, but you *can* make some philosophical decisions and begin the child's life with those in place. As the child grows up, she will gradually take control over who is important to her.

- If you have a disability do you automatically assume you should not parent? If so, we encourage you to think how your disability might affect parenting, rather than reject it out of hand.

- Have you thought about raising a child who has a disability? What strengths do you bring to this and what issues are likely to be problems for you?

- Have you considered alternatives to parenting, such as coaching or being an "aunt" to a friend's child?

As you decide whether to become a parent, it is important to remember that you do not have to be Super Mom to prove to the world that you are as good as or better than the traditional notion of mother. Lesbians can be regular mothers and be good enough!

These questions will spark lively discussions between you and your partner, friends and perhaps other members of your family. You will not be able to answer all of them. Yet know that having doubts does not mean you should abandon the idea of raising children. The key is to be aware of your doubts and to know which of them you can live with. Sometimes bringing a child into your life will be the only way you can put some of those doubts to rest!

But how do you bring that child into your life? By becoming pregnant? By adopting? By foster-parenting? The rest of this chapter explores the options.

Pregnancy via Alternative Insemination

One day Vanessa's four-year-old son asked her how a man got the sperm into the woman's body. She answered that there were several ways, and he asked for the easiest. She started to say, "Most people think the easiest way is when the man puts his penis into the woman's vagina," but he interrupted by shaking his head and said, "Tell me the other one." Vanessa replied that the man puts his sperm into a jar, and the woman... "Oh," he said, "Then she puts the jar into her vagina."

When we were young, our parents or friends told us "the facts of life." Then there was only *one* set of facts—only *one* way of getting pregnant. Today, a woman who wants to have a child can take advantage of new methods: alternative (or artificial) insemination, intrauterine insemination, in vitro fertilization, ovum donation and surrogate motherhood.

If you would like more detailed information about the various methods of insemination we refer you to Appendix B in the back of the book. We have included descriptions and some cost and time estimates for the physician-assisted techniques. It is particularly useful information if you are having difficulty conceiving.

Alternative insemination is the process of transferring a man's semen to a woman's vagina without intercourse. Although the terms "artificial insemination" and "alternative insemination" are used interchangeably, we have chosen to use alternative insemination, or A.I. Because the simplest way to get pregnant—heterosexual intercourse—is not desirable to most lesbians, alternative insemination is usually the method of choice.

The experience of trying to get pregnant is something like riding a roller coaster. You live your life in two-week cycles—first preparing for insemination, inseminating and then waiting to see if you are pregnant. Lesbians trying to get pregnant by A.I. have a heightened sense of these ups and downs because the act of fertilization is an unusual event in their day—there is no way to get pregnant by just rolling over and having sex with your regular partner. Be prepared with good support and humor relief as you work on getting pregnant.

An Insemination "Prep Talk"

Before you inseminate, keep a record of your basal body temperature (BBT) to determine when you ovulate. To do this you need a basal body thermometer which measures temperature in tenths of a degree.

Take your temperature first thing in the morning, before you get up, and keep a daily record over a period of six months so you can maximize the chances of recognizing the best time to inseminate. Generally speaking, when your temperature rises after a sharp drop, you have ovulated. Using this chart you can make informed guesses as to the most likely times you will ovulate during the month. You can then arrange to have donors, physicians or sperm banks on alert during those times.

Other ovulation indicators are changes in vaginal fluids, or mucus, and size of the cervical os or opening. When you ovulate your vaginal mucus changes consistency: it becomes more viscous and a little stringy, stretching between your fingers as they are pulled apart. You need to look at and feel the mucus during other parts of your cycle so you will recognize the change when you ovulate. Your cervical os also changes slightly at ovulation, widening and softening. Again, you or your partner need to look at the cervix before ovulation so you will recognize the changes. You can do this using a speculum, flashlight and mirror if by yourself, or you can ask a friend or partner to use the speculum and look for you.

Ovulation predictor kits measure an increase in the luteinizing hormone, which signals that ovulation will occur in the near future. The kits, which are available in drugstores, alert you that you will ovulate within either twelve to twenty-four hours and others predict ovulation within twenty-four to thirty-six hours, depending on the product. Because the predictor kit gives advance warning, it may be helpful if you are trying to arrange for A.I.

Most lesbian mothers who have used A.I. have given birth to boys, perhaps because they chose the temperature method to determine their time of ovulation. When you use this method, you will have usually ovulated before insemination. Sperm bearing the Y, or male, chromosome move faster and die sooner. Thus, if the egg has already been released, the Y-bearing sperm is the more likely to reach it first. If you use a predictor kit to determine ovulation, you often inseminate before ovulation. This tends to favor the slower, longer-living X (female) chromosome-bearing sperm.

A Word About HIV and AIDS

Before the advent of AIDS most lesbians used semen donated by gay and bisexual men. Now, the prevalence of AIDS makes it potentially very dangerous to use semen from gay, bisexual and heterosexual men with unknown or unsafe sex histories. Most health care experts say that evidence of HIV infection can take as long as six months or more to show up. Thus, sperm banks have instituted a policy of screening blood from a donor and then testing the blood from the same donor after six months to ensure that he has not converted to HIV-positive status in that time. We recommend careful screening of your prospective donor's sexual history and checking with health care specialists about HIV antibody testing to ensure safety, regardless of your donor's sexual orientation. Although only a few women have been infected with HIV from alternative insemination, it has happened.

The Great Lesbian Sperm Chase

Once you have decided to get pregnant by alternative insemination, you need sperm. Easier said than done! It can be surprisingly difficult to find men who are willing to donate their sperm, and sperm banks can be very expensive if you have to inseminate over a long period of time. The following sections should help you find a source and site for your A.I.

Sperm Banks

Sperm banks are expensive and charge a fee for each insemination and additional office visits. Some facilities may also require you to buy home pregnancy tests to determine if you are pregnant. You could have monthly costs beginning at two hundred dollars. Be well aware of what it could cost you to inseminate, and be sure you are prepared to pay.

Sperm banks vary in terms of what they ask of recipients. Before making an appointment, determine what the sperm bank requires in information and fees, whether it inseminates single and lesbian women and what its rate of successful pregnancies is. Depending on the sperm bank, you may have some choice about genetic characteristics of the donor and be able to check medical histories to maximize the chances for a healthy child.

Sperm banks test donor semen for disease and then freeze it. Frozen sperm is generally not as vigorous as fresh sperm, so it may take longer for you to conceive.

Some sperm banks require that you inseminate on their premises, others may give you the choice of taking the sperm home. Some places use a plastic cup which they, or you, place over the cervix after insemination to ensure the sperm maximum access to the cervical os. This procedure is uncomfortable, and you may feel more secure having a practiced staff person perform it. Some banks will ship frozen sperm to your physician or directly to you. Ask in advance who inseminates the woman, where it can be done and any other questions you have about the actual insemination itself.

Most states consider that a man legally gives up his parental rights when he donates sperm through a sperm bank. Some sperm banks give you more information about the donor once you have conceived or borne the child, but others give out no information beyond the medical and genetic characteristics you saw initially. If having more access to a donor is important to you, ask the available sperm banks what their respective policies are about donor history and check with an attorney about how contact with a donor can affect parental rights.

Physician's Office

A physician's office may offer several advantages over a sperm bank as a source and site for A.I. When you are inseminated in a physician's office you can use fresh or frozen sperm, although some physicians use only frozen, which has been checked for HIV infection. In many states, men who donate through a physician are considered to have given up their legal rights to paternity as well.

Especially in large urban areas, you may be able to find a physician who is lesbian or supportive of a lesbian's right to have children, in which case you can be inseminated in the physician's office as an out lesbian; if you are in a couple your partner may be allowed to attend and even do the actual insemination. Contact a local lesbian group, ask friends who have used physicians for insemination, or contact one of the groups in our Resources section for possible referrals.

Mail-order cryogenic banks (storehouses of frozen semen) mail frozen sperm to physicians in different parts of the country, allowing women in areas where there is no sperm bank or donor to use A.I. to get pregnant.

◆　◆　◆

A.I. with a Known Donor

During the first wave of the lesbian baby boom, many lesbians used sperm from a donor unknown to them but known to an intermediary. Women used unknown donors because they did not want to risk a donor's changing his mind and wanting contact with his child; lesbian couples often used them to reinforce the non-biological mother's role as the second, rather than the third, parent. Since the AIDS epidemic, however, there has been a decrease in the use of unknown donors. Here we discuss A.I. with a known donor. If you are interested in using a donor of any kind, we recommend strongly that you evaluate this option with your physician and use the following ideas only as suggestions, to be modified as necessary by consultation with a health care professional.

The man should get a thorough medical examination including an evaluation for any sexually transmitted diseases such as AIDS, chlamydia, syphilis and gonorrhea. He should also have a semen analysis to make sure his sperm is viable. You could ask that the donor's sperm be frozen (by a sperm bank) for six months, after which the donor would be again tested to ensure that he is still HIV-negative.

The advantage of using a known donor is obvious: you know who the person is—his health, his family history, his physical, mental and emotional characteristics. He might even be amenable to contact in the future if your child decides she or he wants to meet their biological father. The primary disadvantage is that the donor could attempt to gain visitation or custody rights after the child is born. Courts in the United States have given conflicting rulings when these cases have been tried. Their rulings depended on whether the court considered the donor to be a father or a donor. Fathers usually get full parental rights, while donors are seen as having waived their paternal rights. If you do not want to share parenting with a donor, find out what the laws are in your state that pertain to sperm donor rights. This may mean that you should inseminate at a physician's office and it certainly means that you need to get a known donor to sign attorney-prepared documents in which he specifically waives any parental rights he might have.

◆　◆　◆

Romancing the Syringe: At-Home Insemination

Carol was moving quickly to the point of orgasm. Her partner, Susan, knew exactly the right spot and rhythm to bring her lover to that delicious place. Then Susan stopped and said, "Time to inseminate, my love." Carol moaned and laughed. She looked around the room at the burning candles and listened to the soft background music. The mood was definitely right, but the syringe in her vagina somehow didn't fit the ambiance.

Most of us grew up with some sort of romantic fantasy of getting pregnant and having children with our spouse. Alternative insemination is definitely not romantic in the usual sense. However, many couples create rituals and / or incorporate lovemaking into the process. This is infinitely easier when inseminating at home, but do not necessarily rule it out if insemination is planned at a sperm bank or physician's office.

Once the health of your donor has been confirmed, you can begin the process of getting pregnant. If you are using fresh semen, the donor should be in the same location you are or nearby. The man should ejaculate his sperm into a clean wide-mouthed jar and close the lid quickly. The sperm should be kept dark and warm but below body temperature. Sperm begins to lose motility (ability to move up the vagina) right after ejaculation, especially after twenty minutes, so you should get it as soon as possible.

Prepare for insemination by lying down and raising your hips on a pillow or towels. Arouse yourself (or have your lover arouse you) to just before orgasm. This opens the cervical os in preparation for the sperm. Then, using a syringe (without a needle), eye dropper, turkey baster or insemination tube (from livestock A.I.), you or your partner should draw the semen up into the syringe, insert the syringe into your vagina and depress the plunger. After the insemination, finish arousing yourself to orgasm if you are able. During orgasm, the floor of your vagina raises, pushing the sperm into the os and into your uterus. Continue lying down with your hips elevated on a pillow or towels for about twenty minutes to give the sperm the best chance for making their trip. There may be some leakage when you get up, so have a sanitary pad handy.

Many women prefer to inseminate on several occasions during the time they think they are ovulating. This requires negotiating with the donor and/or the middle person if someone is transporting the sperm.

Because A.I. can be a lot of work, couples should look for ways to incorporate both women and talk about their feelings during the insemination process. Heterosexual couples using intercourse to get pregnant take an average of six months; alternative insemination (especially if using frozen sperm) is expected to take a little longer. Our best advice is to keep a sense of humor and perspective.

Getting Pregnant the Old-Fashioned Way

Before the late 1970s lesbians had no other option but intercourse if they wanted to get pregnant. There are no reliable estimates of how many women chose this route, but lesbians we know who got pregnant during an ongoing affair or who had sex with a friend to get pregnant speak with much tenderness and appreciation of the men who helped them become mothers. The tone of the nineties, however, is more one of fear: fear of losing custody or of getting AIDS.

But if alternative insemination is unavailable or unacceptable to you, intercourse is an option. If you are partnered, you and your partner need to discuss how you both feel about your having intercourse with a man. If one or both of you are worried or jealous, those feelings need to be worked through.

If you have intercourse to get pregnant, you may unintentionally create future challenges. Consider the following questions carefully, and then plan equally as carefully how to minimize problems later on. If the man knows your intent, do you want him involved in the rearing of the child? If you or he do not want him involved with childrearing, talk together about that decision. Is he willing to forgo custody? If not, there may be problems later if he decides he wants visitation or custody. Do you know the man well enough to know or ask about his family and health history? This information may be vital to your child's health in the future.

If you do not want the man to know about your intention to get pregnant, are you comfortable with the ethics of that decision and do you understand its potential ramifications? It could come back to haunt you when your child begins to ask about her biological father. How much do you want your child to know about her origins?

If the biological father knows about your plans, talk about both of your fantasies of what his role would be. You and he need to write up an agreement with an attorney that articulates your understandings. The worst-case scenario is that the man would decide he wanted sole or shared custody against your wishes and the courts supported him. The best-case scenario, of course, is that everything would work out as originally agreed upon, whether that meant he had no involvement or was an integral part of your child's life. If you know and trust the biological father you increase the chances that you and he can find solutions to the challenges this arrangement presents. Again, we urge you to think about the future as well as the present and plan accordingly for the benefit of everyone.

When You Can't Conceive

If you have not been able to conceive after six months of trying, you or the donor may have a fertility problem that will not resolve or resolve only with help from infertility specialists. You will have to decide whether you want to pursue the lengthy, invasive and expensive infertility procedures. Generally speaking, if you have the financial resources to explore all fertility options, it will take approximately one and a half years to complete the full range of medical procedures. If you are thirty-four or older and have decided to adopt or foster-parent if you cannot conceive, begin exploring adoption and foster options as you start the infertility work. (See Appendix B for details about infertility procedures.) By beginning the legal process you may be able to shorten the waiting time to get a child.

It is painful not to be able to conceive when you want to bear a child. If you decide to pursue infertility procedures, take time to feel the sadness of not being able to get pregnant easily. If you are unable to get pregnant at all, allow yourself to grieve the loss of your biological child.

Sandra and her partner, Laura, had been inseminating for a year when they began an infertility workup at the medical center and discovered that Sandra did not ovulate. Sandra was devastated, as she had always assumed she would have babies; even when she came out she did not give up her dream of having children. Sandra's family was not very comfortable with expressing feelings, and after a month told her it was time for her to move on and let go of her pain. Sandra luckily knew better and decided to have a funeral for her never-to-be child. She invited her closest friends, and she and Laura led a ceremony where they, and anyone else who wanted to, said good-bye to the unconceived child.

Foster-Parenting

Amanda is a fifty-five-year-old lesbian who loves children. She has parented twelve foster children over the years and currently has three living with her. Amanda works part-time as a nurse's aid to supplement the support she receives from the state for being a foster parent. Her social life revolves mostly around the children and her church, which gives her a lot of support for her decision to be a foster mother.

There are many lesbians like Amanda who want to care for children but are unable or unwilling to bear or adopt a child. There are also many children who need parenting while their legal parents and/or the state determine what is best for them in the long term. Lesbians have been foster parents for as long as the foster-care system has existed; however, for most of that time they have had to be closeted.

The earliest public report of children being placed in homes with openly gay foster parents was in Chicago in 1973.[2] The children placed were found by the foster-care agency to have "homosexual tendencies." Thus, the first group of children considered for foster placement with lesbians and gay men are youth that have self-identified as gay or lesbian. Agencies have turned to gays and lesbians usually after a number of unsuccessful placements with heterosexual foster parents.

The children most often considered for placement with lesbian foster parents are the ones agencies call "difficult to place." Typically, hard-to-place children are older (three to seventeen years old) or from a community of color or have one or more disability or a history of neglect or abuse. Many of these children have never had a stable home environment. Increasingly, agencies are also turning to lesbians and gay men as foster and adoption placements for babies born with AIDS.

Lesbians who want to become foster parents must usually do so as unmarried individuals. Some couples have applied as out lesbians and in a few places in the United States have been granted a license to be foster parents,[3] but more often the prevailing attitude is that only married heterosexual couples can provide a truly healthy home for children, regardless of the specific needs of a given child. Any deviation from that norm prompts agencies to investigate more carefully. Thus, even with agencies that will consider using lesbians for foster-care placements, out lesbians need to expect a more rigorous investigation as to their fitness as foster parents. The investigation usually includes at least one home visit, interviews with the prospective parent(s), interviews with others who know the applicant, and numerous forms to fill out. In spite of outstanding qualifications, a lesbian or lesbian couple may still be turned down because of sexual orientation.[4] In places where large, more active lesbian and gay communities exist, foster-care placement administrators often are more familiar with lesbian and gay parents and more likely to make placements with them.

Women who choose to indicate their lesbianism at the beginning of the investigation or who answer affirmatively when questioned directly often do so because they do not want to have to hide their lesbianism for the rest of their tenure as a foster parent. Those who choose not to indicate their sexual orientation often choose that route to give them the best chance of becoming a foster mother. When a lesbian applies as a single woman without disclosing her sexual orientation she may also be scrutinized more carefully. Many agencies will operate from their heterosexist bias and assume she is heterosexual and others may want to avoid a direct question about sexual orientation. One should not count on this form of institutional denial, however!

It is very important never to lie about your sexual orientation if you are asked directly; if your deception is uncovered at a later date you run the risk of losing your foster-care license and any children who have been placed with you.

You can gain clues to how open your state is to lesbian and gay foster-parenting by seeing if your state has anti-sodomy laws. These laws prohibit certain kinds of sexual behavior, including sex between two people of the same gender. When such a law is in a state's statutes, it is it very difficult for an agency to recommend placing a child with an openly lesbian foster parent.[5] Some states have a stated *per se* legal assumption that homosexuality is "in and of itself" proof of unfitness for parenting.[6] It is, therefore, usually easier for a lesbian to become a foster parent in a state that has no anti-sodomy law or *per se* assumption about homosexuality and/or in a state where other lesbians and gay men have already been licensed to be foster parents.

Loving and Letting Go

Sometimes foster-parenting leads to adoption. Usually, however, the foster parent has the challenge of bonding with and letting go of children over and over again. It is the gift of a good foster parent to be able to love and cherish a child and yet let him go when it is time. Foster parents may lose a child because of problems the child has, because the child is adopted by someone else or returned to the legal parent, or because the child has turned eighteen and is no longer part of the foster-care system.

> When Beth discovered she could not bear children, she decided to spend her energy on the age group she liked best, twelve-to-eighteen-year-olds. One of her foster children left after two years to live with her birth mother; two girls left at eighteen and became addicted to drugs. One boy, whom she had cared for from the time he was eleven, ran away, came back, got hooked on alcohol and street drugs and finally asked to go into drug treatment. It had been two years since she had heard from him when a letter arrived asking her to his wedding. He and his fiancée had chosen Beth's last name to be their married name.

Clearly, foster parenting is not predictable in terms of the length or quality of connection. Yet it is crucial that these children receive love and support and the opportunity to have a family. Obviously, that gift of family is not determined by sexual orientation.

We encourage lesbians who want to become foster parents to honor this calling if possible, and we challenge existing legal systems to take advantage of this untapped resource to care for children who need that gift of family.

Adoption

> Kathy and Polly decided to adopt a baby because they strongly believed that there were enough people on the planet already. Kathy's parents, Todd and Jan, who had been very supportive of the two women as a les-

bian couple, had strong reservations when their daughter told them of their plans to adopt. Todd and Jan raised concerns about the health of the birth mother, about the problems some adopted children have when they reach adolescence and about the added discrimination the adopted child of lesbians would face. Polly and Kathy were surprised at Todd and Jan's reactions and realized that they would have to find ways to help the prospective grandparents feel connected to this new grandchild. They were also painfully aware that Kathy's parents had some prejudice against lesbian parents. However, both women hoped that, with time, Kathy's parents would love whatever child they adopted and would support the new family whole-heartedly.

Some lesbians like Kathy and Polly decide to adopt rather than bear or foster-parent a child. Reasons for adopting range from the political to the personal: concern about overpopulation, a desire for an older child, infertility, and so on. Whatever the reason, adoption brings its own set of challenges and rewards.

Women who adopt have waited, sometimes for years, and they are ready to meet their child when she arrives. Many mothers who have adopted a baby or youngster talk about fate's having *given* them this particular child; these are wanted children.

Yet, no matter what part "fate" plays, for a lesbian, adopting a child is usually more difficult than getting pregnant and the adoption process is a different kind of roller coaster ride than pregnancy is. There is no guarantee of when—or if—the ups and downs will be over and a baby will be available, and many women report that it is hard to remember that they are prospective parents because there is no expanding belly or due date.

Crossing Ability, Cultural and Racial Lines

Most adopting lesbians—though certainly not all—have been white, able-bodied and middle- or upper-middle-class. Most children available to single women or out lesbian couples have been, as with foster children, in the difficult-to-place category. These children pose challenges that few of these women have had to live with before.

Most of us take for granted the ease with which we move physically or with which we communicate. When an able-bodied woman adopts a child with a disability, whether mental or physical, she has to change the lens through which she views the world. It may mean remodeling your home, taking sign-language classes or fashioning rejoinders for other people's rudeness. One of the greatest challenges is overcoming our culture's paternalism toward people with disabilities and instead encouraging the child to be and do everything he can. If you are considering adopting a child with a disability, it may be useful to contact relevant advocacy groups such as the Cerebral Palsy Foundation or a speech and hearing center that teaches sign language.

But first, it is important for you to think seriously about whether you want to take on the additional challenge of a child with a disability before you check the box that says you are willing.

If you are white and considering adopting a child of another race or culture, it would be a good idea to talk to lesbians who have adopted children of color or another nationality to find out what has worked for them and to get a realistic appraisal of their situation. We also recommend that you talk to lesbians and parents of color to broaden your awareness of racism in general and parenting issues around race in particular. (See also Chapter 7, "Confronting Racism and Building Rainbows.")

It could be argued that white lesbians are more prepared to deal with children of other races than heterosexual white parents because lesbians know what it is like to live with bigotry. However, racism in this country is a unique issue, and white mothers must equip themselves and their children to confront and survive it. Prospective adoptive mothers must also consider whether they are willing to include elements of the child's birth culture in their child's upbringing.

Sarah and Mary had moved to a small town in Oregon in order to live a slower life; they loved the countryside and most of their neighbors. Three years later they adopted two sisters, Rosita, who was six, and Juanita, who was four, from Guatemala. The women had encouraged the girls to learn about and celebrate their heritage and as a family they delighted in the mix of cultures. As a result, they were unprepared for and stunned by the racism that assaulted them and their daughters. One day when Juanita was playing on the see-saw at school, a student from another class came up to her and told her she couldn't play there because she wasn't white. Juanita was hurt and scared and her mothers were furious. After they had put their daughters to bed that night Mary and Sarah planned how they were going to deal with the school principal to make sure he confronted the racism.

Agency Adoption

Adoption agencies almost universally believe that young, able-bodied, middle- or upper-class, heterosexual couples are the best placement for what they call the most desirable children. Couples of the child's race are usually given first priority. Any other kind of adopting parent—over forty, single, lesbian or gay, or disabled, for example—will get, as we have stated before, the children the agencies refer to as hard to place: older children, children with disabilities and children with traumatic histories such as sexual molestation. White lesbians may also be considered for children of color (whom agencies often include in their hard-to-place category) because there are usually more children of color available for adoption than there are families of color approved to adopt. Lesbians of color may actually have an easier time adopting a child of their own race than their white counterparts.

Most adoption agencies we know of will not do business with a woman they know to be lesbian, and most states will not permit same-gender couples to adopt a child. Thus, adopting as a single woman is the only legal route for most of us, although some lesbian couples have been allowed to adopt: in 1986 lesbian couples adopted children in two northern California counties,[7] and Washington State has also had a lesbian couple adopt a child. Since the laws in each state change, we recommend that you contact your state's Department of Social Services for the current regulations concerning adoption.

A lesbian who adopts as a "single, heterosexual" woman when she is actually part of a couple has the additional issue that only the adoptive mother is the legal parent; her partner has no parental rights by law. Also during the probation period—up to over a year—following the child's arrival, the mother could lose the child if she is found to be a lesbian. As with foster-parenting, do not lie about your sexual orientation at any time during the adoption process. It is far better not to have a child placed in your home, than to have one placed and then taken away later. Lesbians who are out during the adoption process with an enlightened agency are less likely to run into such problems in this regard but they are still vulnerable to losing the child before the final adoption is filed because of the heterosexist legal system.

Though a lesbian couple may not be allowed to adopt a child together initially, they may be able to use the second-parent adoption process to make the other woman a second legal parent. Second-parent adoptions allow the non-legal mother to adopt her partner's child and become the second legal parent. Prospective adoptive parents should explore whether a second-parent adoption option is available in their area. (See Appendix A on second-parent adoption).

As in foster-parenting, prospective adopting lesbians face rigorous evaluations whether they apply as single, heterosexual women or as out lesbians. They may have to work with homophobic case workers and might be held to higher standards than their heterosexual counterparts. Home studies may force the lesbian to rearrange her home to hide evidence of her lesbianism and relationship. As a result the partner may feel disenfranchised as a mate and potential mother. This dynamic does not usually signal problems with the couple, but is, rather, a common response to heterosexism in the adoption process. When the couple can be out in the adoption process, the women can be affirmed as a couple and the richness they bring as a couple be honestly evaluated.

There are both public and private adoption agencies. Public adoptions are handled through county adoption agencies and bring with them two advantages. They are free and often offer stipends to adoptive parents. County agencies predominantly have children in what we have called the hard-to-place category. They may have some newborns and infants on a less frequent basis.

Private agencies charge fees—usually thousands of dollars—to cover their services and are more likely to have newborns and infants in their pool of available children. There may be less red tape if you work with a private agency, but you should evaluate the options available in your area.

Foster-Adopt Programs

Foster-adopt programs are available through both public and private agencies. A child is placed in your home on a foster-care basis with the understanding that he may be available for adoption later on. Usually, foster-adopt placements involve a child who is not free to be adopted yet, but whom the agency expects to be available in the near future. As with all foster-care arrangements, the child could be taken out of your home after you have grown to love him, but the advantage is that you have the opportunity to live with a specific child and determine if the placement is a good match for everyone.

Independent Adoptions

Lesbians may also arrange independent adoptions through friends, acquaintances or a third party. Some states prohibit independent adoptions, so you need to find out what the regulations are in your area. Both independent and agency adoptions allow the adopting parent to become the legal parent of the child, which includes having the child's birth certificate reissued with the adopting mother's name on it.

In independent adoptions you will not face the same challenges you would from an agency, but there is always the possibility of being rejected by the birth parents. However, independent adoptions allow the possibility of the two sets of parents having some contact if you want that. The contact may be only in the selection process or might continue throughout the child's life as the birth parent maintains a caring but non-parental relationship. It is very important to think through any decision about family relationships and to get good legal advice.

Independent adoptions vary in cost, depending on the laws of your state. Usually, you pay the medical and legal fees for the birth mother. In some areas you may also be required to pay living expenses. Be very careful to pay only what your laws allow you to pay to the birth mother; otherwise you run the risk of nullifying the adoption and/or being prosecuted for committing a crime.

International Adoptions

International adoptions can be arranged through an agency, a contact person in this country or directly with the child's country of origin.[8] As with all adoptions, we recommend strongly that you get good legal advice before you begin negotiating to adopt a child from another country.

International adoptions have their own challenges. A child may be available for adoption immediately after birth, but the required paperwork could delay her departure to the United States for months. You may be notified that your child is ready to be picked up and go to the country of origin, only to find that you still have to wait while additional paperwork is completed.

Children from impoverished countries may be undernourished and need particular attention paid to their health. And information about your child's health status and history could be meager, so be sure to press for as much information as possible when you communicate with the agency or government of the child's birth country.

Betty has been approved for adoption as a single mother. She and her partner, Shawna, are waiting for notice that their daughter has left India on a plane for San Francisco. The authorities in India sent Betty a picture of the baby at three months old and told her that the little girl had had bad diarrhea and had not gained much weight. Betty and Shawna have contacted their physician and are a little worried about what this means for their child's health. In spite of this, they have fallen in love with the baby in the picture.

International adoptions usually carry fees similar to those of a domestic, private agency adoption, but there may also be travel costs, lodging fees in the child's birth country if you go there to pick up the child and income loss while you are out of the country.

How Do I Know If I Like Having Children in My Life?

Every Tuesday afternoon Diane spends time with Chris and Sue's daughter, Jennifer. They go for a walk to Diane's home, or go to the zoo or do something together for several hours. "Aunt Diane" is an important member of the family. If she decides to become a parent herself, her child will also become part of this extended family.

As you consider whether to have a child you may need to find out if you like spending time with children. You could become an "aunt" or adult friend to a friend's child, like Diane did. In these cases the adult friend usually agrees to be in the child's life for the foreseeable future. In addition to your getting information about whether you want to become a full-time parent, there is the lovely benefit of the child's mother having time for herself on a regular basis. This is a godsend for single mothers and a gift of couple time for two parents.

There a few possible drawbacks to this type of arrangement: the mother could use the adult friend as a babysitter, potentially "burning out" the friend or devaluing the special relationship, or the adult friend could intrude into the family and take on a parenting role that has not been clearly agreed upon with the parents. It is important to discuss openly everybody's expectations of these extended relationships as they begin and whenever anyone is uncomfortable with any aspect of the relationship. It may also be helpful to discuss how the arrangement could change if you become a parent.

Some women choose to become Big Sisters with a local branch of the national organization. Big Sisters volunteer to spend one-on-one time with a girl and are usually asked for a minimum time commitment, often one year. A caseworker screens you and if you are accepted as a Big Sister you are matched with a child on the agency's waiting list. Some local branches of Big Sisters are willing to take lesbian volunteers, but you should inquire with your local organization to establish what their policy is.

Camp Fire Girls, Girl Scouts and YWCA programs all need women volunteers. With these organizations there are opportunities for one-on-one time with a girl or contact with a group. The YMCA and Boys and Girls Clubs may give you opportunities to work with both boys and girls of a variety of ages.

There may be a program in your area, similar to the Rise 'N Shine program in Seattle, Washington, that works with children whose lives have been affected by AIDS, whether someone in their family or they themselves have contracted the disease. Volunteers may participate in a number of ways, including meeting weekly with one child, serving as a group facilitator or helping out at large group functions.

Volunteer possibilities may also exist with organizations who work with runaway teens or drug rehabilitation. For instance, Seattle has opportunities for adults to work with youth offenders to help them provide restitution to those they have victimized. Many cities and counties have a guardian ad litem program that assigns adults to children who have become involved with the court system because of custody issues. Guardians become advocates for the children and help ensure that their voices are heard by the people making the custody decisions.

Volunteering can give you opportunities to be around the very young or around older children. This may be particularly helpful if you are planning to foster parent. You may find an age that is a great match for what you have to offer a child. Hospitals often want adults to come in and hold infants who have no family or to spend time with children whose parents cannot visit during the day. And most towns and cities need people to coach, manage and administrate youth sports teams and organizations. Usually sports programs are listed in the telephone book or are organized through schools or community centers. Schools want tutors and volunteers to help children who need more attention than their staff can manage, and some universities and colleges have offices that match volunteers with a variety of youth programs.

Jean was wonderful with children but was very clear she did not want to parent. So, she had searched her town for ways to spend time with children. Jean had been a varsity soccer player in college and loved the game. She also really liked teenagers, so she called the high school soccer coach and asked if she needed any help with the girls' team. The coach jumped at the idea, and in two weeks Jean was spending an hour and a half five days a week, plus games, with the team.

You do not have to be a parent to have relationships with children. You can use the opportunities above as your testing ground to discover whether you want to have your own children or as a way to be with children. Your work can be an ongoing gift to your community whether or not you have children. No matter how you use this time with children, it can be one of the highlights of your adult life.

3 Branches on Our Family Tree:
Partners, Fathers, Siblings and Others

When Allison's nine-year-old nephew, Eric, came to visit, she arranged for her godson, Taylor, to come over so the kids could play computer games together. She couldn't help but chuckle when she overheard part of their conversation.

Taylor had apparently mentioned that he had two mothers, and Eric asked, "How can you have two mothers?" Taylor explained matter-of-factly, "Well, there is my birth mom, Linda, and my new mom, Hallie." Eric must have had a puzzled look, because Taylor went on to explain his family in more detail: "And I have three fathers and Allison and my Big Brother, Ray."

Clearly baffled, Eric could only respond, "Oh." And then the boys went back to playing their game.

Although it was difficult for his friend Eric to grasp, Taylor is quite clear about and comfortable with having a family that includes two mothers, three fathers, his godmother and his Big Brother. Lesbian family constellations are often complex, and involved adults may be members of the chosen as well as the biological family.

Of course, we face the reality, and the frustration, that the English language does not have the words to adequately describe our relationships. If people are not related biologically or legally, descriptors are in short supply. For lesbian couples who decide to have an alternatively inseminated child, is the non-biological mother called a co-parent, or a co-mother, an "othermother" or "my Denise"? This tyranny of language applies to men in the child's life as well. Sometimes the name problem may reflect confusion over what role a particular adult is going to be taking in the child's life; for example, does the term "uncle" or "dad" best describe the involvement?

In this chapter we discuss the significant others in a child's life. These people include lesbian partners (whatever their title may be), men (fathers and father figures), siblings and extended family (chosen and biological).

What's in a Name?

Whether your lesbian family is created "from scratch" or formed with children from one or both partners' previous relationships, the same question arises: What is the title, and the role, of the non-biological parent? If a partner is to feel part of the family, she needs to have a sense of who she is and where her place is in the family picture.

In our culture, "mother" is a biological and legal term. You are a mother if you get pregnant and bear a child or if you legally adopt a child. Other kinds of motherhood status can be acquired by marrying a man who already has children or by getting licensed by the state to foster-parent, although the status is limited in that it depends on your relationship with a third party, namely the husband or the state. If you don't have that connection, you lose the title; you become a "former" or an "ex." In any event, to be a mother, even of limited status, you must be female and there can only be one of you. Of course, many children are raised by adults other than their biological or legal mothers. When this is the case, we may hear descriptions such as, "She was *like* a mother to me." The point is that the term "mother" is linked to the biological and legal status, not to parenting behavior and the role the adult takes in a child's life.

For lesbians, as well as for many racial and ethnic groups, heterosexist "nuclear family" concepts and language do not describe the reality of our family connections. That challenges us to be conscious of and creative with our ideas about what family is and with the language we use to describe ourselves. What to call the lesbian partner of the biological mother depends on her role with the child, on how and when she comes into the child's life, and on how the adults involved see her role and feel about the "mother" title.

Between them, Margie and Tre have five children. In their blended family, both woman act as parents to all of the children. The kids describe themselves as each having a mother and an "othermother."

If Bianca's husband knew she was a lesbian, she is sure he would try to take their children away from her. Although her partner, Lee, has taken on a parenting role with the kids, she is Lee—"Mommy's roommate" or "Mommy's friend."

Timmy was only three years old when his mother, Jean, got involved with Pam. Pam always wanted to have children so when Timmy began to call her "Mama," she loved it. Jean very much wanted Pam to be a parent to Timmy, but she wasn't sure at first that she wanted anyone besides herself to be "Mama."

When Jennie and Arlene decided to have a family, they both wanted to be mothers to each other's biological children. Now six and nine, their two girls call Jennie and Arlene some variation of "mother" or, sometimes, by their first names.

Emma's children were in their early teens when she got together with Joy. The children really liked Joy, and their relationship was very positive, partly because she didn't try to become another mother. They already had a mother, a stepmother and an involved father with whom they spent every other weekend. Joy's place in the family was as Emma's partner, and they simply called her "Joy."

Leah had already raised a family when she and Judith met. She was not interested in being a mother again, but she was supportive of Judith's desire to have a child and was willing to have some involvement in raising him or her. They talked about how it could work: Judith would be the primary parent, and Leah's role in child-rearing would be as a support to Judith. Judith would be "Mother," and Leah would be "Leah."

It goes without saying that whatever a couple's initial plans are for roles and names, they may well change. For example, Leah may get more involved in parenting than she initially anticipated, or the child may come to call her a mother regardless of how she would describe herself. A child may be comfortable with using the term mother for a woman who herself is not comfortable with it, even though she is in a parenting role.

Although she had helped raise Adrian since he was a baby, Sharon never wanted to be called any version of mother. For her, "mother" meant primary caretaker, and since that was Gena's role, Sharon didn't feel okay about the title. She was clear that she was Adrian's parent, but she was not his mother. There was "Mama" and "Sharon." However, Adrian had a mind of his own. One day he came home from preschool, where there was another child from a lesbian family who made it clear that he had two mothers. Adrian announced that since Gena and Sharon were both "girls" that meant he had two mommies also and he wanted to call them both "Mommy." So he did, and Sharon adjusted.

If being a parent describes a role and a relationship rather than a biological or legal status, the possibilities are wide open. Children in lesbian families understand this. Even in a world that says it's not possible or not acceptable, it is not strange to have two mothers if you grow up in a lesbian family. In fact, it's *normal*. Children are often more flexible than adults are with their use of these terms. For example, one child we know had four mothers and five fathers at last count.

In addition to the roles and language within the family, there is the question of how lesbian families present themselves to the world. Even when parents are out, they have to decide how to introduce themselves to others. Although they may be consistent within the family, they may still decide to vary the introductions depending on the circumstances. For example, although it may be "Mommy Lynn" and "Teresa" at home, both women may wish to be seen as equal parents by the school. In that case, they need to present themselves as a two-mother lesbian family. Otherwise, Teresa will not get full recognition of her parental status.

◆ ◆ ◆

Beyond Our "Job Descriptions"

What a partner is called can be important in that it describes who this person is in the family. It can help clarify to the children, to the world and especially to the partner herself what her role is. But no matter what her title or job description, it's the actual doing of the job that defines a partner's sense of who she is and where she belongs in the family.

In a family that is a lesbian family from the beginning, the challenge may be for the non-biological or non-legal parent to feel equal. This may be particularly true if she is not a primary caretaker. For this reason, many lesbian couples devise strategies that balance out parenting to encourage bonding between the non-biological parent and the child and to ensure that others view both of them as equal parents. For example, they may introduce the non-biological/non-legal parent first in new situations and take turns going with the child to day care and the doctor.

Beth had just adopted her son, Robert, when Gloria came into her life. Two years later they expanded their family to include a daughter, Penny. Beth was the legal parent of both children and that bothered Gloria some. However, there was no question that Gloria was their parent. When Beth's job changed to include a lot of travel, Gloria took on the role of primary caretaker. Being the at-home mom guaranteed that Gloria felt like an equal parent. In fact, sometimes she felt too equal!

Some lesbian couples start off with parenting responsibilities being other than fifty-fifty; sometimes the percentages shift over time. Parenting relationships do not have to be equal to work well. What is important is that the adults are honest and realistic about their own interest and commitment to parenting and about their expectations of each other.

In a blended family with children from one partner's earlier heterosexual relationship, the new lesbian partner is less likely to be concerned about being an equal parent because she is coming into an already established family. At first a new partner is usually just trying to figure out, and work out, what her role in the family will be. She needs to get clear on what she wants, how involved she wants to be in parenting and what kind of commitment she is willing to make. The family she is entering has to do the same. Sometimes this means almost formal negotiations between the couple; sometimes it all seems to fall into place without much discussion.

Maya was having a hard time figuring out how she fit into the situation with her lover, Barbara, and Barbara's six-year-old-son, Justin. They had been together, although not living together, for just over a year. Sometimes Barbara seemed to want Maya to be like a parent to Justin and sometimes not. And there was the complication of Barbara's "ex," Sandy, who was Justin's co-parent. One day Barbara told Maya that she was not to discipline Justin; the next day Maya got a call from Justin's school asking her to come and get Justin because he was sick and the school couldn't reach Barbara or Sandy. Maya was not aware that Barbara had put her on the school's list. Maya was pretty confused about her role and, at that point, decided that she needed to sit down and talk with Barbara about how this parenting thing was going to work.

A lesbian partner who is in a parenting role but does not have a legal relationship with the child is often painfully aware that she has less power in the situation than her partner, and this may affect her bonding process with the child. She knows that if she and the legal mother part, she faces a potential double loss of both partner and child. Agreements and legal contracts can help allay these fears, but they cannot guarantee parental rights. A non-legal lesbian parent knows that her relationship with the children is ultimately dependent on the wishes of their legal parent or parents, which can affect her attachment to a child and her willingness to make a commitment to parenting. But important decisions are usually calculated risks. And if we are looking for guarantees in relationships, we will miss many opportunities.

Randy had no idea how important her relationship with Danny would become for her. She came into his life when he was four, and she and his mother, Cheryl, raised him together until he was twelve. There was no question in her mind that Danny was her son. After she and Cheryl broke up, Randy continued to support Danny financially and to spend time with him every week, like a regular non-custodial parent.
There were good times and bad times. Bad times were when Cheryl

and Randy fought about money and about Randy's role in making deci-
sions about Danny's life, like where he would go to school, or when Cheryl
got angry and would threaten to refuse to allow Danny to see Randy. She
never followed through on her threats, but it was painful to Randy none-
theless. The good times were when Cheryl and Randy and Danny's father
and stepmother all sat together at Danny's hockey tournaments and
cheered themselves hoarse or when Randy and Danny sat around a camp-
fire on what they called the "Dandy" annual camping trip and hiking ad-
venture.

    Randy would do it all again. She describes being a co-parent to Danny
as being as one of the most challenging and rewarding experiences of her
life.

It is not only the new partner or the non-biological parent who may have concerns and reservations about forming a new lesbian family. Children have their reactions, too. Their reaction is likely to vary depending on their age, their relationship with their mother and their comfort with their mother's lesbianism. The children's experience of gaining and losing adults in their life and the new partner's parenting style will also affect their response. While each situation is unique, we can make some generalizations:

- Younger children tend to adapt more easily to having a new adult in the family.
- Adolescent boys tend to be more accepting of new lesbian partners than are adolescent girls.
- Children who have lost significant adults, through divorce or breakup of the mother's relationship with a lesbian partner, are less inclined to bond readily with her new partner.
- When children have to compete with their mother's new partner for attention, they are not likely to welcome her into the family.
- If the new partner's parenting style and values are consistent with what the children are used to, it is easier for them to relate and for the new partner to fit into the established family life.

All relationships, including those between children and their mother's new lesbian partner, develop over time. Lesbians who follow a serial monogamy pattern in relationships may need to be especially aware, and patient. You may have moved on, but the children may still be grieving the loss of your former partner and not yet be ready to bond with your new one. The feeling of being a family is usually not instant; in fact, it may take years. Clarifying the titles, roles and expectations of parents, co-parents and new partners (who are on their way to becoming part of the family) requires self-awareness, honesty, mutual respect and good communication. Ongoing parenting and involvement in family life with children require these skills and more. Other essential ingredients you need to put in the mix are patience, cooperation, the ability to recognize what is in the best interest of the child and the willingness to put the child's needs first. Raising children requires a big investment, but the potential return is enormous.

Fathers and Other Men in Our Lives

Are men necessary for the well being of the daughters and sons of mothers? This question is often debated among lesbian mothers. Conventional heterosexist wisdom has it that both men and women are necessary for the rearing of healthy girls and boys. Our belief is that in an ideal world our children should have good relationships with other girls and boys and adult men and women as well as with us "moms." Having a variety of adults in their lives, including men, allows children to experience different styles, get feedback about themselves from different perspectives, try on different identities and see themselves, and the world, through different lenses.

> *Although his donor father died of AIDS when Jamaica was ten, he is as alive as ever in Jamaica's mind. His mother, Elena, found this out one day when she asked him how he had come to the decision to take a class she thought would be too hard for him. He told her, "When I have to figure something out, I think about what you would tell me; then I think about what my dad would tell me, and then I decide."*

> *Edie and Shannon wondered if their twelve-year-old daughter, Erin, might have a crush on their friend Luke. Could she be flirting with him? Every time he came over, Erin got a little weird. She would ask him all kinds of questions: Did he like her hair this way? Should she take algebra next year? Would he take her for a ride on his motorcycle?*

Luke had noticed it, too, but he was cool. He reassured her mothers that Erin's behavior was perfectly normal—and would pass. As a junior high teacher he had had lots of experience with adolescent girls getting crushes on an "older man."

Nine-year-old Chad hung on every word his Big Brother Dominic said. He also imitated how Dominic walked and gestured and laughed. Sometimes Chad's mothers got tired of hearing, "Dominic says..." over and over but they were grateful that Dominic's advice about being a good "guy" included good manners.

When a woman is partnered with a man and has children, the father is supposed to maintain contact with the children if the couple divorces. As we know this is not always the case. In addition, if contact is maintained, the quantity and quality can range from indifferent or abusive to involved and wonderful. When an out lesbian chooses to have children, she has a different set of choices about her children's relationships with men. Many lesbian mothers have chosen not to have any men involved with their children except those the children meet in the course of their lives, such as teachers and coaches. Other lesbian mothers have consciously involved men in the rearing of their children. We'll explore the different kinds of relationships children can have with men in their lives and how lesbian mothers can maximize the benefits of them.

Fathers via Marriage

Fathers from heterosexual marriages have varying amounts of contact with their children following a divorce. Although there are obviously many involved fathers, non-custodial fathers are more likely to break off contact with their children.[1] It is also quite common for divorced men to maintain contact but to spend minimal amounts of time with the children. Financial support from fathers also varies. Although many fathers meet their child support responsibilities, many pay less than they have agreed to and some default altogether. One study found that, on average, women with minor children experienced a seventy-three percent decline in their standard of living during the first year after divorce, whereas their husbands experienced a forty-two percent increase in their standard of living.[2] It is clear that a biological or legal tie does not guarantee responsible, continued or engaged parenting.

When fathers disappear or are minimally interested in their children, it causes damage to the youngsters. Even when children are angry with their fathers, they still need them; inevitably when their fathers don't see them the children assume that they did something wrong. If children are not able to work through losing their father, their ability to form long-lasting intimate relationships can be seriously harmed.

When fathers stay involved with their children after a divorce, the children get a positive message. They feel loved and valued by both parents, increasing the chances that they will be able to put the divorce behind them and move on with their lives. Sometimes the mother does not want the father to have an ongoing relationship with his child, perhaps out of anger or hurt or a desire to have little or no contact with men, or just because she cannot muster the energy to keep the kids available to him. Assuming the father-child relationship is not abusive, however, children benefit from contact with their fathers and should not be denied that contact.

Generally speaking, lesbian mothers have a good track record for helping their children stay involved with their fathers. But what if the father is homophobic?

When ten-year-old Brianne came back from spending a weekend with her father, she seemed upset. When Nancy asked her daughter if anything was bothering her, Brianne responded that she was fine. But later, when they were eating dinner, Brianne asked her mother, "Mommy, are you going to get AIDS?" It turned out that Brianne had overheard her father saying that AIDS was God's punishment of homosexuals.

Even when a father undermines a lesbian mother's relationship with her child, the mother may still want to support the father-child connection—for her child's sake. In this instance, Nancy needs to correct any misunderstandings Brianne may have about AIDS and to talk to her child about her father's prejudice. Nancy could also speak to her ex-husband about the incident, pointing out to him that his comments upset Brianne. Children will eventually form their own opinions about their parent, and it is wise to let them make an informed judgment about their father based on contact rather than one based on longing for him in his absence.

The father who is able to embrace his children, provide emotional and financial support and respect his ex-wife's choices gives an immense gift to his children and himself. He increases the chances of healthy adaptation of his children and gives himself the opportunity to be an important part of his children's lives.

Donors: Anonymous or Known?

Biology dictates that lesbians who want to make babies rather than adopt them require the cooperation of a male of the species. The man's involvement may range from donating sperm to being actively involved in parenting. As we discussed in Chapter 2, the decisions you make about his involvement are very important because they have far-reaching consequences—emotional and legal. No one way is best for everyone, but whichever option you choose needs to be carefully thought through.

Even then, life sometimes foils the best laid plans. For example, many lesbians who used anonymous donors contacted by third parties later discovered who their donor was and had to decide whether and how to include the donor in the child's life. And the donor has his own deciding to do.

Their son Austin was six years old when Diana and Lise accidentally discovered the identity of their anonymous donor. After much discussion, they decided that they were willing to have the donor involved in their son's life and conveyed that message to the third-party intermediary. They were disappointed to hear back that the donor preferred to have no contact.

Felix's moms had used sperm from an unknown donor to get his biological mother, Clair, pregnant. The mothers used an intermediary to contact the donor and while they knew his identity, they agreed to keep it a secret from everyone else. Felix grew up simply knowing he had a biological father somewhere in the city and had not much bothered with that until he hit ten. Then he became desparate to know who his "father" was and began to pester his moms about finding him. When he found out they knew who he was, he wanted to meet him. Clair and Zoe struggled with whether to contact the donor. On one hand they were worried that Felix would be disappointed; on the other hand, they were scared he might prefer the donor to them. They finally decided to contact the donor and see if he was interested in meeting Felix. He was interested and they agreed to a meeting. At first the meetings were a little awkward but then Felix began to like spending time with the man he called his dad. They took a couple of camping trips together and Felix began to want to live with his father some of the time. When Felix finally told his moms they were a little tearful, and said they had never expected him to leave until he left for college. Felix was thrilled when they began to talk to his dad about the possibility.

Somewhat different situations may arise with known donors. For example, sometimes donors who have good-faith intentions of remaining uninvolved or having minimal contact as a "friend of the family" change their mind. In addition, if the child has contact with the donor, she may develop her own relationship with him, and her feelings and wishes may result in her calling him "father" regardless of how involved he is in day-to-day parenting. What started out as a lesbian family with a known donor may become a lesbian family that includes a donor "father."

Some lesbian couples use a known donor who is a biological relative of the non-biological mother. Then the non-biological mother has a biological connection to the child, which may be particularly important to interracial couples.

Angela and her partner Dawn decided to ask Angela's gay brother Tomas if he would donate sperm to inseminate Dawn. He agreed and now Dawn and Angela have two children who look very much like both of their mothers. Angela and Tomas had always had a very close relationship, and at first Dawn sometimes felt excluded when they all got together. However, over time the adults were able to discuss their feelings openly and resolve issues when they came up.

Fathers via Chosen Family

Lesbians who want a father in the family unit have a different vision from those who want a donor only: they are choosing the richness, and the complexity, that this kind of co-parenting can provide. When it works well, the co-parents reap the benefits of shared responsibility and mutual support and the children receive lots of love and attention. However, the interpersonal dynamics can be very challenging.

The biological co-parents probably do not know each other as well as married parents do. The desire to be a parent and the ticking of the biological clock may be the main factors that brought them together. There is no sex to ease any tensions and no marriage vow to add some sticking power to the relationship. And if there is a lesbian partner in the family, she may feel less important or less of a parent than her biological counterparts. A lesbian parent who opts for a biological father in the family needs to be comfortable negotiating the differences and disagreements that will inevitably arise. Serious problems can lead to nasty custody battles.

Todd and Carmen agreed to conceive and rear a child together. Eleven years later they found themselves barely speaking because of a disagreement about where their son should go to school. There had been a steady buildup of disagreements over the years, but it was the school choice that blew apart the family. They had never realized how important it was to Todd that his son go to private school. Carmen, on the other hand, was totally committed to public schools. The family had to call in a mediator to help them settle the issue.

Another kind of father is one who is not biologically related to the child but who agrees to enter into a fathering relationship. This parenting role allows the mother to protect her legal custody of the child while providing her youngster with a good, ongoing relationship with a man. The man is legally very vulnerable since few courts recognize this kind of relationship. He does, however, gain a father-child relationship with relatively few responsibilities. In our experience, the child lives virtually full-time with his mother and spends varying amounts of time with his father. It is normal for the child to want to spend more time with the dad as their relationship deepens, and it is highly possible that he might want to live with the man's household for a while. Again, any disagreements between adults need to be worked out so that they minimize distress for the child.

We recommend that parents think through very carefully their expectations of any parenting relationship and put their agreements in writing.

Shortly after their son, Evan, was born, Makela and Kate decided that it would be good for him to have a man in his life. They talked to their friend Roy about being a father-figure to Evan in an "uncle" sort of way. Later on they realized they had not been very clear about what they had in mind. Evan's mothers were thinking "uncle," and Roy was thinking "father." To complicate matters Evan began to call Roy "Dad." When Roy began to concern himself with decisions about day care and health care providers, Kate and Makela felt he was encroaching on their parental territory. The adults had a rather painful talk. Both mothers were committed enough to Roy's relationship with Evan that they found a way to work things out that honored the relationships that had evolved. Evan still called Roy "Dad" but Roy agreed to back off from a role that spelled "parent" rather than "uncle" to Evan's mothers .

While it is helpful for lesbian parents to be clear in advance when they ask other adults to be involved in their child's life, relationships have a very fluid quality and circumstances change. Everyone involved needs to be prepared to renegotiate the agreement to best meet the child's needs.

Father Fantasies

Do alternatively inseminated children reared by lesbian mothers really miss having a father? We haven't found any definitive research about this question for lesbian families, and there doesn't seem to be any way to predict a child's response. If he looks like you, or has father-figures in his life, he may not be concerned about his donor. Yet some children, regardless of an obvious genetic connection with their mother, show an early interest in meeting their donor. Others don't seem to care or become interested when they are older.

If people in your child's world emphasize that a dad is missing, she may pay more attention and ask questions about who he is and if she will ever meet him. However, for many children it is not until later that fathers become an issue. Our clinical and personal experience is that children do not seem too concerned about whether they have a father until they are about eight or nine.

It is very normal for children to ask about and long for a father. It is not necessarily a reflection on your parenting job or the need for a father type in your child's life. It is important to listen to your child and to answer questions. You may want to explore with your child what her fantasy father is like and help her test the reality of that fantasy. Usually the fantasy takes the child away from all of her problems and into a wonderful world of joy. You may need to help her realize that no one's family is like the fantasy.

It is natural to feel defensive when your child longs for a father. We encourage you to hang in there while she works through her grief at never having a father. She needs to do it, and it will be easier for her if you are available to support her as she grieves. Children who are adopted may grieve the loss of birth parents; children of divorce may have to deal with losing contact with a parent; and A.I. children of lesbian parents may grieve never knowing their biological father.

Male Role Models

If having adult men in your child's life is important to you, there are ways you can make that happen. Extended family as well as the broader community can provide wonderful male role models for your children.

Karla and Ben loved their Uncle Ned dearly. Ned lived on a small farm, which the children visited every summer. When they were old enough, they flew by themselves and stayed for two weeks. As city kids, farm chores like feeding the chickens, gathering eggs and stacking wood seemed like great adventures to them.

Most lesbian mothers we know have included friends as part of their extended family. They have straight and gay male friends who participate in holiday celebrations, are part of a religious community, share community housing or spend time with the family. The men may spend time with the children informally or arrange specific times to go on outings with them.

Charlie and Alice lived next door to Ann and her daughter, Sandra. They barbecued together in the summer and shared a vegetable garden. Sandra liked to play with Charlie and Alice's dog and often spent an evening with her neighbors when her mom had a meeting. Every now and again Sandra asked Charlie to come to a Dad's Day at school or at her Girl Scout troop. They became good friends and Ann eventually asked Charlie and Alice to be Sandra's guardians if Ann died before Sandra was ready to be on her own.

Just being in the world brings children into contact with men—school teachers, coaches, counselors, police officers, store clerks, rabbis, ministers, priests and friends' fathers—and some lesbian mothers make a conscious decision to maximize the opportunities to have men in their children's lives by requesting male teachers or coaches when there is a choice. Some ask for Big Brothers for their sons.

One of the important things to remember is that many of these men will come and go. As we discuss in Chapter 6, your children will need support if they have bonded to someone who later moves on. You may be particularly worried about their having to let go of good male friends, but your children will do fine if they are supported in their sadness over the loss.

Changing Relationships

As your children grow, relationships with the men in their lives will change, too. For example, if a man who used to baby-sit your child weekly has become one of the most important people to her, you may have to extend your sense of family to include your child's sense of family.

However, you the parent need to be clear about who is responsible for your child's well-being. If you and a man co-parent, you may have to refine your agreements every few years or so to reflect who does what and where your child is living and when. If you have extended family or a chosen father it needs to be clear to everyone that you are the main parent and that the others are akin to assistant coaches. Your children need to know that as well.

Children stretch us, they demand by their being here that we do things differently than ever before and that we continue to evaluate and modify our family life. For example, as lesbians we may live a life which has little to do with men, but we may want to encourage and support our children to find and develop healthy relationships with men who can communicate to them that they are loved by men as well as women.

◆　◆　◆

Extended Family: From "Goddess-Parents" to Grandparents

Children love to know where they came from. When they are young they often like to hear stories about their parents when they were little. As they mature, children usually want to know more about their ancestors and immediate family. Both boys and girls can benefit from spending time with extended family and hearing family stories. An uncle can enliven his nephew's life by recounting how the boy's mother used to best him at arm-wrestling. A little girl can be charmed by her grandmother's stories of relatives who came across the country in covered wagons.

Extended family gives children a sense of having a broad base upon which they can rely. There is an African saying that it takes a village to raise a child. Chosen and related extended family help do just that.

Sometimes distance can adversely affect relationships with grandparents, aunts, uncles and cousins, and sometimes homophobia gets in the way. If you have broken off contact with your family of origin, it is still useful to let your children know about their relatives, including the reasons contact was broken. But it is our experience that families often reconnect when a lesbian becomes a mother. Children offer a face-saving reason to resume contact. Luckily, lesbian families often include chosen family members as well as biological ones in their extended family network. Chosen family is especially important when biological family is not available or not accepting or supportive.

TJ and Jennie and their two children live on one coast, and the grandparents are on the opposite coast. A creative solution to the lack of grandparent roles in their kids' lives came from friends, an older lesbian couple whose children were grown. These women were ready for grandchildren in their lives, but their own children did not have children yet. So this couple became "goddess-parents" to Jennie and TJ's kids. The kids got "grandparents" who lived close by; Jennie and TJ got emotional and childcare support as well as sage advice when they wanted it.

The Significance of Siblings

Some lesbian parents decide to have more than one child, in part so that the children will have siblings with whom to share the benefits, and the stresses, of being from a different kind of family. This may be of particular concern to parents whose child is of a different race or culture from their own.

A child in a lesbian family may, or may not, have the same mothers, or fathers, as his siblings. Which parent and which siblings he lives with may also change over time. All of these circumstances can have a bearing on how he is treated by the adults in his life, how he sees himself and how he treats, and is treated by, his siblings.

MaryAnn's oldest son, John, lived with his father and stepmother for three years while MaryAnn dealt with her own coming out and getting her life together. He came back to live with her when she moved into a house with her partner, Dee, and Dee's two children. John never did develop a very close relationship with Dee's kids. MaryAnn figured it was because there was such a big age difference between him and the other kids, or maybe because John had another family, his dad's, whereas Dee's kids had only the one.

It was difficult for Bobby when his brother, Paul, "found" his biological father. Both boys had been conceived with sperm from unknown, and different, men. Then, by accident, the identity of Paul's father was discovered, and he came into their family's life.

Although they never talked much about it to each other while they were growing up, Tom and Elizabeth later acknowledged that they appreciated having each other. They didn't really know any other kids whose mothers were lesbians so having a sibling helped them feel less isolated and alone.

We need to be sensitive to how being in a lesbian family might impact our children's relationships with each other, as well as with the adults in their lives. Then we can more easily help them talk about their feelings and provide them with the support they need.

New Visions

Our children are not the only ones who may find themselves in uncharted territory. The adults in lesbian families often have this experience as well. Whether we are a new partner searching for our spot in an established lesbian family, or a lesbian couple deciding about the role of men in our children's lives, we are challenging old beliefs and traditions about who and what family is.

Many of our visions are still new, even for us. And they are evolving. It can be exhilarating—and sometimes scary—to be painting a new and different lesbian family tree on the canvas. Perhaps your tree is tall and slender with a few willowy branches, or compact and complex like the "bramble bush" described by Ethan in Chapter 1. Whatever its size and shape, stand back and admire your handiwork every now and then. Take pleasure in your creation! And appreciate the loving work required to translate your vision of lesbian family into reality.

4 Coming Out to Our Children and Families

Imagine this scenario: You and your partner are playing with your son in the neighborhood park. Another mother smiles and says, "Oh, he's adorable! Which one of you is his mother?" How do you respond?

As an individual, you often have the luxury of coming out only when it is comfortable. You can make coming-out decisions based on your personal desires for privacy or for closeness, on your sense of safety and on your political values about visibility. But being a parent changes the situation. Children attract people's attention, and it is quite socially acceptable for people to make comments and ask questions about children. Day care, school, playgrounds, health care provider offices and stores are all places where well-meaning people may ask questions that put lesbian parents on the spot. To come out or not to come out? And then, how out to be?

Another difference with being a parent is that the consequences of coming out are not limited to you. Your coming out affects your children as well. Not only do you have to balance your own personal factors of privacy, safety, comfort and political ideals but you also have to weigh the fact that your children are listening. What you say gives them a message about honesty, about how you feel about yourself, your family and about lesbians and gays in general.

We believe it is ideal for lesbian parents to come out to their children and be out with them for a number of reasons that we explore in this chapter. However, we know this is a calculated risk. Because of homophobia there is always a cost involved in coming out, or in not coming out, and this cost must be weighed by each lesbian parent in making her decision. We support strongly each parent's need to consider her situation carefully and assess the consequences of remaining closeted or coming out.

Defining Our Terms: Coming Out, Heterosexism and Homophobia

When we speak of coming out we are referring to the different degrees of recognizing, accepting and declaring a lesbian identity. A useful way to think about this process is Joan Sophie's three-stage model of identity development.[1] The first step is recognizing and accepting lesbian feelings. When a woman becomes aware of her attraction to another woman or women in general, she may be beginning a process of coming out to herself as a lesbian or bisexual woman. Some women stop there. They never act on their attractions or discuss them with anyone else, nor do they accept a lesbian identity. The next step is coming out to oneself, which usually involves some social support and the development of a positive philosophy about lesbianism that makes it acceptable. The last step is coming out to others.

Coming out typically refers to a public announcement, like marching in a Pride parade, or a private announcement, such as a letter, phone call or face-to-face discussion, about being a lesbian. Being out refers to the approach that you take toward your visibility in the world. Do you tend to be out everywhere or are you carefully closeted except to friends and family? In this chapter we focus on coming out to your children and to your family of origin, which, as we have learned, often results in being out in the world.

In coming out you run smack into heterosexism and homophobia. Heterosexism refers to the assumption that the world is and must be heterosexual. This puts the burden on a lesbian either to contradict the assumption that she is heterosexual or to live with it until such time as she decides to come out. Either way, she has to come out to be seen as who she is. When a lesbian woman is pregnant or has children in tow, the assumption of heterosexuality is particularly likely. Lesbians and motherhood are not assumed to go together. According to Suzanne Pharr, heterosexism and homophobia work together to enforce "compulsory heterosexuality and that bastion of patriarchal power, the nuclear family."[2]

We live in a society in which we may be disliked, feared and even hated simply because we are lesbian. These negative attitudes—which can range from silly to deadly—are called homophobia. Homophobia exists in both lesbians and heterosexuals because everyone is raised in the same heterosexually dominant atmosphere. All of us, including "future lesbians," were likely exposed to warnings about what we wore, how we looked and behaved so that we would avoid being accused of being lesbian. "Don't wear green on Thursdays or yellow on Fridays [or whatever], because that means you're queer." Or "Try to look more feminine." Or "Stay away from those people." Or "Show more interest in boys." Most of us heard, and perhaps used, derogatory terms such as "lezzie," "bulldyke," "pervert," "queer," and "man-hater" to describe lesbians. In addition, societal myths portray lesbians as sex-crazed monsters preying on innocent women and children or as pitiful types so unattractive they can't find a man. We are portrayed as not only inferior, but also perverted, sick, abnormal and even evil.

When we ourselves have negative attitudes about lesbians, the homophobia is described as being internalized. The effect of the homophobia of others is the sometimes subtle, sometimes not-so-subtle oppression that we face in our daily lives. The effect of internalized oppression ranges from self-hatred to lowered self-esteem. Whether from the outside or the inside, homophobia imposes damaging limitations. From the outside we may be restricted from legally marrying or adopting children. From the inside, we may limit ourselves. It is probably not accidental that the lesbian baby boom came after, not before, the Gay Pride movement. If we thought of ourselves as inferior, not to mention abnormal, choosing to be a mother would likely not even enter our minds. Being lesbian would not be compatible with being a mother, unless a woman had children before she came out.

The Advantages of Coming Out to Our Children

We advocate that lesbian mothers come out to their children and the sooner the better.

Lesbian parents of alternatively inseminated children are usually out before the child comes into the family. The child is born into a lesbian family so the task is interpreting the situation to the child rather than making an announcement. Under these circumstances, parents can provide explanations over time in ways that are appropriate to the child's age.

For mothers whose children came from heterosexual unions, coming out has more of an announcement quality. It also means taking calculated risks. The risks—such as temporary or even longer term rejection by the children, custody problems, overt hostility toward the mother's partner by the children, or protecting the children from stigma—need to be taken seriously. However, there are some clear advantages for lesbians in coming out and being out with their children, especially as they get older and the mother's sexual orientation is more difficult to hide.

Intimacy vs. Secrecy

Secrets interfere with intimacy—between adult partners, between the children and adults, and among the children themselves—and puts a strain on the entire family, particularly when the lesbian mother lives with a partner or spends time away from home to be with a lover.

If the women feel restricted and unable to be affectionate and close in their own home, their relationship suffers and they may even come to resent the children.

> *Lynn was terrified that her two young daughters would hate her if they knew she was a lesbian. Although she and her partner, Devonne, shared a room, Lynn was convinced the children had no idea what was going on, and she wanted to keep it that way. Her fears placed severe restrictions on how she and Devonne interacted: they were never affectionate with each other when the children were around, and even when they were alone in the apartment, Lynn was often worried that the children might come home. Her worry almost put a complete stop to their sex life. Any attempts to discuss coming out to the children ended in a fight. Devonne found herself thoroughly frustrated, resentful of the children and ready to end the relationship. Finally, Lynn agreed to go with Devonne to see a lesbian-affirmative therapist to talk about their situation.*

◆　◆　◆

Being out rather than closeted allows lesbian mothers to be themselves and to acknowledge and nurture their relationships with partners or lovers, and the children have an opportunity to see what a healthy intimate relationship between adults looks like. When there are no secrets, everyone in the family can work on defining and clarifying a definition of family which suits their particular wants and needs.

Open Communication

Choosing to be closeted with your children may foster communication problems, especially with older children. How could they not notice that their home life is different from that of their friends? Not discussing these differences gives the message that these topics are off-limits and confirms the negative impression that the children get about lesbianism from the outside world. In addition, the child may get the message that any discussion of sexuality, including her own, is not acceptable. She may stop asking questions or sharing her thoughts and feelings about a variety of topics based on the "we don't talk about these things" message. In contrast, being honest with your children will foster open communication with them and strengthen your relationships.

Self-Esteem

Finally, when lesbian mothers do not come out to their children, they run the risk that the children will find out about their lesbianism from others. The information will likely be presented to the child in a negative light, and the child may be too shocked, upset or afraid to bring it up. Telling children up front means they do not learn homophobia from their parent; instead, they see their lesbian mother modeling self-esteem. In fact, children are proud of parents who stand up for what they believe. If they have the opportunity to discuss and work through their concerns and feelings with a supportive parent, youngsters are also in a better position to recognize and deal with homophobia in other people.

The Risks of Coming Out to Our Children

Having discussed the benefits of coming out to children, let's look at the risks. The ones most often cited are custody problems, the child's being stigmatized by peers, the child's hostility toward the mother's lesbian lover or partner and most important, the child's rejection of the mother. With all of these risks the challenge is identifying which situations require caution and which do not, and learning the difference between realistic caution and unrealistic anxiety. Because homophobia is real, a lesbian mother's parental rights regarding custody or visitation can be at risk, depending on the laws and who is interpreting them. However, it is still important to assess realistically what the risks are rather than automatically assume the worst.

Some of the questions lesbian mothers can ask themselves in deciding whether or not to come out to their child (or anyone else) are:

- What is the worst thing that could happen if I came out to my child?
- What are the other possible negative consequences and can I accept them?
- How can I reduce or minimize the negative consequences?
- Can I turn the consequences into positives?
- What is the best thing that could happen?

These questions can help you to be more realistic, to anticipate difficulties and to problem-solve where necessary. The following examples illustrate how two lesbian mothers evaluated their particular situations and worked through their decision to come out.

May, divorced and in her forties, had been living life as a single parent with her three children when she fell in love with Bernice and came out to herself as a lesbian. She was not worried about custody because her ex-husband had never been very involved with the children and because she lived in a city where the legal system took a relatively supportive approach to a lesbian mother's parental rights.

May was more concerned for her children. How would others treat them if they discovered their mother was a lesbian? She tried to focus on how to minimize the negative consequences and how to turn that situation, if it happened, into an opportunity.

As she reviewed the possible scenarios, May came to appreciate how much she trusted her children's judgment about who they would tell and who they wouldn't. As African-American children, they had developed skills for dealing directly with discrimination and prejudice. Coming out to them would draw on their family history of discussing and dealing with oppression. May felt badly, on the one hand, about adding another burden to their shoulders, but on the other hand, she was proud of her children's skills and the family's solid foundation.

Long after their relationship was effectively over, Denise and her husband stayed together in their suburban home in a small city. They were both unhappy, but they told themselves they were staying together "for the children's sake." The children were seventeen and thirteen when changes in Denise's life started happening fast and furious. While out of town at a training session for her job she met Maureen, a very out lesbian, and fell instantly in love. Her husband heard about it from a mutual friend who also had attended the training. He got furious, threatened to tell the children their mother was a lesbian and to go to court to get a divorce and custody. The battle between them raged off and on for a few months. Denise was overwhelmed and very torn about what to do. She imagined the worst: her husband would get sole custody of the children, and she wouldn't even be able to have visitation. Then again it wouldn't matter because her children would hate her and wouldn't want to see her anyway. The only consolation she had was her relationship with Maureen, but she wasn't clear about that either. Mostly she was confused and scared.

Finally, she concluded that her husband was serious about his threats; it was just a matter of time. She felt compelled to take some action, which to her meant talking with her children about what was going on. It would be worse for them to hear it from her husband. She could only hope that her relationship with her children was strong enough to weather whatever storms they faced. Denise decided to focus her energy on when to talk to her kids and what to say. The other concerns would have to be worked out as she went along.

Even parents who identify as lesbians prior to creating their families face coming-out situations with their children.

Ever since their daughter, Kim, was a baby, Jane and Latisha had made sure there was lots of diversity in their extended family and community. Because Kim's family was multiracial, her parents wanted her to be around people and families who looked like them. They had talked with Kim about people being of different colors, about racism and about different kinds of families, but they hadn't used the "L" word yet. Then one day when Jane picked her up from day care, Kim asked her, "Mommy, what's a lesbian?" Although Jane had rehearsed what she would say, she still took a very deep breath before she answered her daughter's question.

Each lesbian mother and family are unique. Because one person's decision would not be right for another, the best advice we have is for each woman to get the support and assistance she needs to make the right decision for her. Resources for information and assistance may include a gay/lesbian-affirmative counselor, supportive friends and family, and organizations such as the Lavender Families Resource Network. (See Resources.)

How to Come Out to Children

Regardless of the uniquenesses of individual situations, all lesbian parents have to deal with if, when and what to tell their children about their sexual orientation.

What do we know about how children react to having a lesbian parent? In the research for her book *Gay Parenting,* Joy Schulenburg had contact with more than five hundred gay and lesbian parents. She reported that most of the parents interviewed said their children responded positively when they came out to them.[3] Children are usually more concerned about their relationship with their parent than their parent's sexual orientation: "Just so she's still my mom, I don't care about that other stuff" is a common reaction.

However, the child's age has a significant influence on his or her reaction. In general, negative social conditioning about homosexuality is pretty well established by the preteen years and boys seem to be more susceptible to this conditioning than girls. Also, children's feelings about their mother's lesbianism may change over time. Just because a child is accepting, or uncomfortable, at one point, does not mean that he will remain that way. Continuing to talk with your child about his feelings is important.

How a child responds also depends on the relationship between the parent and child, and on the mother's timing and approach. As we mentioned previously, when a child is born or adopted into a family that is lesbian-identified, coming out does not have the same unsettling quality that an announcement made to children from a previously heterosexual family may have. For example, if children have two mommies from the beginning, then that is just how their family is. Or if parents in a family include Mommy and Wendy or Aunt Sue or Papa Ron, or all of them, then that is who makes up the family. To the child, and to the parents, this is perfectly normal and natural and right.

The following are some general guidelines for coming out to children, particularly when coming out is an announcement:

- *Sort out your own feelings about being a lesbian first.*
  If you are confused, or ashamed or panicked, your children are less likely to react with calm and acceptance. The most positive coming-out experiences are reported by parents who were comfortable with themselves. When parents accept and affirm their own sexuality and identity, their children are more able to do so as well.

- *Plan ahead.*
  It is best to plan ahead not only about the time and place and tone you want to establish, but also about possible reactions and how to handle them. Choose a time when you will be unhurried and a place that is private and free from interruptions. Keep the tone conversational and matter-of-fact. You are informing, not confessing. You may wish to rehearse with someone beforehand. By practicing problem-solving "what-ifs" in advance, and getting feedback from others, you may be more at ease and better prepared to deal with your children's questions. You may also want to line up supportive people to "debrief" with afterwards.

- *Reassure your children that your being a lesbian does not change your relationship with them or your feelings for them.*
  This is particularly important for younger children. Make sure they understand that you are still the same person and that you love them just as much as ever.

- *Be prepared to answer questions.*
  Young children may have little curiosity and no questions—yet, but older children may want to know, for example, why you can't

just find a man to fall in love with and marry, or why people don't like lesbians.

- *Be prepared for your child to withdraw for a while.*
Withdrawal is more common with preadolescents, adolescents and even adult offspring. They may not want any additional information and may resist talking about their feelings. Give them time and check in periodically. You need to recognize that adolescents' main concern is likely to be for themselves—how this will affect them. The assurance that you will be sensitive to their feelings and will not embarrass them in front of their friends may be helpful.

Another typical concern of adolescents is their own sexuality: are they going to be gay or lesbian because their mother is? Although they may not ask this question directly, parents are wise to address it. Being a child of a lesbian parent does not mean you are or will be homosexual.

- *Stay calm.*
Even children who have a negative initial reaction often come around. Just as it often takes time for a parent to accept having a lesbian daughter or gay son, so it can take time for a child to accept having a lesbian mother.

- *Use resources.*
In some areas, most often urban ones, support groups and/or activity groups for lesbian families may be available. These allow children to have contact with other children whose families resemble theirs. Books, films and videotapes about lesbian families can also be helpful. (See Resources.)

- *Keep talking with your child.*
We cannot emphasize enough that coming out is ongoing. As a lesbian you have to deal with coming out to new people or in new situations as they come up in your life. Similarly, your children will continue to confront new challenges and situations, some from the outside world—a classmate putting down lesbians or gays, or a teacher asking everyone to draw a picture of their family, for example, and some from the inside as they develop intellectually and emotionally. A two-year-old likely never questions having two mommies. A three-year-old may notice that other families

look different from hers and ask why. Adoptions and racial differences of parents or, of parents and children, add other dimensions of complexity to the coming-out discussions. Conversations about these topics need to be ongoing.

"But What's a Lesbian?"—Coming Out to Young Children

In coming out to your children, your comfort level, tone and body language are at least as important as the words you use. This is particularly the case with young children, as they may not understand all of what you are telling them anyway. Make sure you use age-appropriate language in both your explanations and responses to your children's questions. Don't overload young children with information: discuss topics at their level of comprehension, and give them whatever information they need at the moment. If a child seems satisfied with an explanation, you can leave it there as long as you make sure she knows the door is open for more discussion. This is a process for your children as well as for you. Other questions and concerns will come up later as they think of them and as they get older.

Janine kept putting off coming out to her two kids for one reason or another. Immediately after the divorce seemed like a bad time because the children were upset. And besides, she thought they were too young—six and eight—to really understand.

It wasn't until her best friend, Ramona, challenged her that she began to seriously plan coming out. "After all," Ramona said, "Wouldn't you rather they heard it from you than from someone else?"

Janine chose her time carefully: Saturday morning breakfast was a time associated with waffles, good feelings and togetherness. When they all were almost finished with breakfast, she began the conversation by saying, "There's something important I want to talk about. I've been spending time with different people, and at some point I might want to be with a special person like I was with your dad. And if that happens, the special person will be a woman. One of the things I have learned about myself is that I am a lesbian."

The kids looked at her blankly.

She asked, "Do you remember when we talked about how our friend Ramona is with Marta the same way your dad and I were together? It's like they are married."

Her six-year-old piped up, "Yeah, and some people don't like that and are mean to them."

Janine responded, "That's right. Well, I am a lesbian like Ramona is. My special person will be a woman."

Her eight-year-old asked, "Are people going to be mean to you?"

Janine answered, "They might be, and they might say mean things to you, too. So we need to keep talking about this. It's okay to talk to your dad, too, because he knows, and so do your grandma and grandpa."

This coming-out discussion was actually a lot easier than Janine had anticipated. After she breathed a sigh of relief, she reminded herself that this was only the beginning of a process.

"What If She Hates Me?"—Considerations with Adolescents

Lesbian parents are often most concerned about coming out to their adolescent children. Young adolescents are usually insecure about their own sexual identity, concerned about their popularity and what their friends think, and critical of their parents. While these are normal characteristics of early adolescence, they can actually complicate coming out, or a parent may worry that they will.

A mother who is considering coming out to her children often fears rejection. Since adolescents are in the process of separating from their parents, and may be rejecting and pushing their parents away already, many mothers do not want to give them extra ammunition: "What if she hates me for being a lesbian?" or "What if she doesn't want to live with me anymore?" or "What if he never speaks to me again?" are some of the fears. And, of course, potential custody issues can complicate matters further.

After she had been divorced for about two and a half years, Trudy fell in love with a woman. She always prided herself on being honest with her children, but she was having concerns about how honest to be about her newly discovered lesbianism. She waited until she was more sure about the relationship with her lover and about her own sexual orientation. Then she went ahead and told Dylan and Nanci. Dylan was nine at the time, and Nanci was thirteen. Dylan seemed to take it all in stride. His response was, "Who cares who you love?" Nanci, however, freaked out: she *was furious, talked about going to live with her father and kept saying, "How could you do this to me? You've ruined my life!"*

Trudy had to reassure herself that it would take time for the children to get used to the idea. She told herself that she needed to stay calm and keep the lines of communication open with Nanci. Although Nanci's response hurt Trudy's feelings, she was not surprised. At thirteen, Nanci wanted to fit in and be like the other kids. Having a lesbian mom was not part of that picture.

Even though her own feelings were hurt, Trudy made sure she validated Nanci's feelings. Sometimes Nanci refused to listen or talk; but Trudy kept telling her that she understood it was difficult for Nanci to feel different from her friends, that she loved her very much and that she hoped they could work through this.

They were distant for about six months. Then an emotional disaster occurred in Nanci's life. Her best friend was after the boy that Nanci liked, and she was devastated. Nanci initiated one of what she and her mother called their "heart-to-heart" talks. They talked about Nanci's situation and eventually discussed Trudy's lesbianism and how the last six months had been for each of them.

Trudy was enormously relieved. Even though she knew there would be other difficult times, for now she felt reconnected with her daughter.

Nanci and Trudy began to work through their estrangement relatively quickly, but not all coming-out discussions will resolve quickly, or positively. Some lesbian mothers experience the pain of rejection from their adolescents over a longer period; some may never reestablish their relationship.

Coming Out to Adult Children

In his book *The Final Closet*, Rip Corley notes that many lesbian parents of adult children have a very difficult time coming out to them.[4] For a parent to acknowledge that she is a lesbian to her grown children is to acknowledge her sexuality. This is a topic that many parents, and many grown children, feel uncomfortable discussing. In addition, a lesbian who is coming out to her adult children may be concerned about her relationship with her grandchildren, if she has any.

Most of the guidelines we discussed for coming out to children apply to coming out to adult children as well.

Toni was widowed when she was fifty-four. At sixty-five she fell madly in love with a woman she met at a meditation retreat. The more they got to know each other, the better their relationship got. Toni was amazed that she felt so comfortable with Peg and with loving a woman.

As time went on and the relationship deepened, the two women started talking about living together. Toni was faced with the challenge of how to describe Peg to her four grown children and their families. She was very fond of each of her six grandchildren and wanted her family to delight in Peg and share in the happiness Toni had found with her. For the most part, Toni was confident that her children would be supportive even if they were slightly shocked at first. She called a meeting of the clan, and asked that the grandchildren be left at home. She wanted to take this one step at a time, and to allow her children to make the decisions about how and when they would share the information with their children.

When everyone was gathered at the house, she thanked them for coming and introduced the topic with the old cliché, "Perhaps you wonder why I've called you all together?" Although they had no idea, her children laughed at that line and the laughter helped lighten things up for Toni. She simply told them that she had fallen in love with someone and that they planned to live together and that the someone was Peg. She was very honest with them about her happiness and about how she hoped they would respond to her and to Peg. She emphasized that she was telling them because they were a family who had always valued honesty and openness.

There was a silence after her announcement. Then the questions began. Mostly her children were concerned that she truly was happy. From some of his questions, she deduced her middle son was concerned she might be showing signs of senility, but her answers seemed to reassure him. Her oldest daughter asked her if this meant she was a lesbian. Toni's response was that she was definitely in a lesbian relationship and she was still sorting out how she defined herself. All in all Toni was satisfied with how the announcement went. She knew there would be more questions and more discussions, but she was heartened by her children's initial response.

If a woman who has grown children from a heterosexual relationship decides to have a child with her new lesbian partner, her adult children may get the news about their mother's lesbianism and a potential new brother or sister at the same time, as in the following story.

Laura married at eighteen and had two children by the time she was twenty-one. After their divorce, she and her "ex" worked things out pretty reasonably. Since they both lived in the same town, sometimes the kids lived with her and sometimes with him. Both children went out on their own after high school: her daughter, Noreen, went into the Navy and her son, Jake, started working construction for his uncle.

When the kids were gone, Laura started taking classes at a community college in a nearby city. There she met Joyce and life changed radically. They became best friends and then lovers. At the age of thirty-nine, Laura came out to herself as a lesbian. Eventually, Laura moved to the city to live with Joyce and be nearer their lesbian friends. When Joyce started talking about wanting to have children together, Laura was hesitant at first, but she came around and soon was as excited about the prospect of being a parent again as Joyce was about being a parent for the first time.

When they began inseminating Joyce, Laura decided that she had better talk to her kids about what was going on. Jake took it all in stride. He told her he had already figured out her relationship with Joyce, even though they had never discussed it. Although he was surprised at the news they were planning on having children together, he started immediately trying on the idea of being like an "uncle" to the new baby.

Noreen, on the other hand, thought it was all very weird. With all the publicity about gays in the military, Noreen really didn't want to have to deal with "the gay issue" in her personal life too. Her attitude seemed to be that her mother's business was just that—her own. She didn't want her life to be affected by it and had no interest in being involved with the new baby. While it was not the reaction she had hoped for, Laura could live with it—at least for now.

As is the case in coming out to anyone, the risks of coming out to adult children need to be weighed, realistically, against the price of being closeted. If your children's initial response is less than enthusiastic or even if they are very accepting, give them time to adjust and the opportunity to ask questions. It may take a while for your adult daughter to get used to the idea that her mother and father are getting a divorce, or that she needs to explain to her children that her mother has a woman lover or that she may now run into her mother at the local lesbian bar.

Full Circle: Coming Out to Our Family of Origin

Coming out to your own parents when you plan to have children or when children are involved can be as stressful as coming out to your children. While you might hope that what makes you happy will make your parents happy, unfortunately this may not be the case. In coming out *full circle*—as a lesbian parent—to your family of origin, you must be prepared to face resistance and muster your patience.

Because the lesbian who decides to have a child via alternative insemination or adoption is in a different situation than a lesbian mother who has children from a heterosexual relationship, we address the issue of coming out to one's family of origin from both of these perspectives.

When Lesbian Becomes Parent

Some lesbians are greeted with heartfelt congratulations and offers of assistance when they tell their parents that they are planning a family. The news that you are planning to have a child, and that your parents will have a grandchild, ought to be greeted with excitement and joy and it probably would be if you were part of a heterosexual couple. However, parents may have mixed reactions to the news that their lesbian daughter is planning to be a parent. If your news about parenthood plans is scheduled at the same time as your coming-out announcement, you may be worried that it will really be homophobia time!

When Susan and Jerri began their relationship, it was always with the intention of having children. Susan came from a close family who was generally accepting of her lesbianism and of her couple relationship. Her parents lived nearby and had included Jerri in family gatherings from the beginning of their relationship. Jerri's family, on the other hand, lived half-way across the country and she had never come out to them.

When Susan and Jerri decided to go ahead with getting pregnant, Jerri decided she had better come out to her parents. She was taken aback when they called the same day they received her letter and were all excited about the prospect of becoming grandparents. It was one of those, "they were pretty sure all along that she was a lesbian but were waiting for her to say something," conversations. The extent of Midwestern reserve never ceased to amaze her!

The next surprise was Susan's parents. Rather than being thrilled with the idea of becoming grandparents, they seemed shocked by the plans and challenged the women's decision—had they thought about how the child would feel having lesbian parents and did they really think they could provide financially? Susan and Jerri were very disappointed. They had anticipated some reservations, but not this. It felt as if all their dreams for a happy family with loving grandparents close by had gone up in smoke. They had to reassure themselves that, in time, Susan's parents would likely come around. In the meantime, the positive response from Jerri's parents helped temper the disappointment about Susan's parents' reaction.

As you can see in the case of Susan and Jerri, even for parents who have come to accept their daughter's homosexuality, the idea of a lesbian family may bring up homophobic attitudes and beliefs once again. Your coming out may have been painful to them. It may have taken some time to accept the reality of your identity and your life. Now you are asking them to change even more—to accept your children and your lesbian family. Old concerns may resurface, and new ones emerge. They may worry about the child—the social stigma and effect of having lesbian parents—and about what they will tell their friends. And if you and your partner are of different races? Now your parents will have to confront their attitudes about biracial families. If you plan to adopt, either domestically or internationally, the new family may also challenge grandparents' attitudes about adoption, different racial or ethnic groups or physically challenged children.

If you are a lesbian parent-to-be, planning children and raising them may increase the wish and the need for connection with your own parents. You want your children to have grandparents as other kids do. And you want support for and acceptance of your new parental status. You can certainly survive without their acceptance, but it would be nice to have it. To maximize the chances for immediate or eventual success, you need to anticipate your parents' reactions, be clear about what you want from them and follow through with whatever steps will best support your own family.

Remember this is a process for your parents. Even when you have not officially come out to them, your parents may be working on their homophobia. For example, Jerri's parents had "known" about her lesbianism for years and her coming out as a lesbian and as a lesbian parent-to-be became an opportunity for her own parents to feel closer and more included in her life. On the other hand, Susan's parents were very accepting of her being a lesbian but becoming a lesbian parent was another matter. Susan and Jerri had been talking about having children for years, but only to each other and to their friends. They hadn't mentioned it to Susan's parents before the "announcement." So it was easy for them to forget that her parents were not very well prepared for the news. In fact, it came as a total shock. Which was then a shock to Susan and Jerri. They expected, based on their being accepted and included as a couple, that adding grandchildren would be fully welcomed.

Just as it often takes time for your parents to get used to your lesbianism, it may also take time for them to get used to the idea of your creating a family. In her *Lesbian and Gay Parenting Handbook,* April Martin identifies three factors that influence how fast and how far parents will go toward accepting their daughters and their lesbian families: the parents' individual psychologies, their environment and your help.[5]

By their individual psychologies, Martin means who your parents are as people, based on their abilities and experiences, their strengths and limitations. By the time you are an adult, you have some idea of who your parents are: for example, it is unrealistic to expect your parents to be warm and loving toward you now if they never have been before and aren't that way with anyone else. You can reasonably expect they will do the best they can for you, but they can't give what they haven't got (and probably never got themselves).

How accepting your parents or other family members are of you and how fast they move along in the acceptance process is also affected by their environment: the people and the institutions surrounding them. If your parents have prejudiced and narrow-minded relatives and friends or belong to conservative political or religious groups, they won't get much support from those around them. Consequently, acceptance may take longer and be less complete than it would be if their environment were more supportive of you.

You can help by communicating with and educating your family of origin and by clearly stating your expectations. Try to understand and appreciate their concerns and struggles. You can also let them know where they can get information and support: for example, organizations such as Parents, Families and Friends of Lesbians and Gays (P-FLAG) and books such as *Now That You Know, Loving Someone Gay* and *Beyond Acceptance* which address parents' needs. (See Bibliographies and Resources.)

As you listen and work to understand your parents, you need to be consistent and firm about your expectations of them. They need to know that you understand the difficulties you may present for them, but that the members of your family deserve and expect to be treated with the same respect shown to the families of your siblings. That is, children in your family, whether adopted or born to you or your partner are *your* children and you expect your parents to treat them as their grandchildren.

This may mean confronting your parents if they treat your children differently than they treat your sibling's children, or treat biological children differently from adopted children.

Lee Ann decided to speak to her mother after observing that her mother seemed to favor Lee Ann's biological child over her partner Caryl's biological child. As far as Lee Ann and Caryl were concerned both children belonged to both of them and needed to be treated equally.

Annette felt uncomfortable because her parents seemed to be doing less for her children than for their other grandchildren. At Christmas time, for example, her children seemed to get fewer presents than her nieces and nephews did. She didn't understand what was going on. Did it have anything to do with the fact that she was a lesbian? She decided she needed to ask them about it.

When Parent Becomes Lesbian

If you are already a mother when you come out as a lesbian, you have to decide whether and when to share this news with your own parents and other family members. You may have very real concerns about how your parents will treat you and your children after hearing this information. Although we usually associate custody battles with ex-husbands, there are horror stories of grandparents' petitioning the court for custody. An example is the 1994 Virginia court case in which Sharon Bottoms' mother was awarded custody of Sharon's two-year-old son Tyler because Sharon was in a lesbian relationship. This ruling was overturned on appeal and Sharon was awarded custody of her son, only to have the Virginia Supreme Court reverse the state appeal court's decision. Sharon's fight for justice and parental rights, like many other custody battles fought by lesbian mothers, goes on and on. Although grandparents rarely go so far as to demand or sue for custody, they may react with hostility or even withdraw from their daughter and her children.

In contrast, if you anticipate that your parents will be supportive, you may wish to come out to your parents before you come out to your children so that the grandparents and relatives can be a support and a sounding board for the kids. If you come out to your children but not to your parents, the children are in the awkward position of having secrets from their grandparents. With young children particularly, there is no certainty that they will keep that secret.

How parents respond depends on the same factors we mentioned in the previous section, namely the parents' individual psychologies, their environment and your help. Their concerns for the children are likely to be the same as those raised by parents of the lesbian parent-to-be. However, they are having to deal with two issues at once, namely their daughter's lesbianism and their concerns for their grandchildren. In many cases they may also be faced with news of a divorce.

Maria's life was changing faster than she ever believed was possible. Within a month of meeting Tracy, she had come out to herself as a lesbian and told her husband she wanted a divorce.

She came from a very close and large family. Her children were very attached to their grandparents and to their many aunts and uncles and cousins, so she decided she needed to tell her family what was going on. She didn't want her children to lose their family connections, and she wanted her family's support for herself as well. She started with the siblings she felt closest to and whom she thought would be the most understanding. Mostly it went well. She had one sister-in-law who was quite homophobic, but her brother's acceptance helped balance that situation.

Once she went through the process with her siblings, she felt more ready to approach her parents. What surprised her was that her parents were more upset with the idea of her getting a divorce than they were with her being a lesbian. Since she made good money, financial security wasn't a concern. She wondered if perhaps her parents were focused on the divorce part because they couldn't deal with the other news, but she wasn't about to challenge it. She needed all the positive responses she could get, especially as she prepared to talk to her children.

As with all coming-out stories, the endings vary: some parents are fully accepting from the beginning; others take time to come around and some never do. Remember Susan and Jerri?

Susan's parents never did accept their grandchildren. Eventually Susan stopped taking the children when she visited her parents and ultimately she herself stopped having much contact with them. Extended family consists of Jerri's family and their friends. Susan was sad about the loss for her, for her children and for her parents. But she was unwilling to expose her children to rejection; and she and her family were a package deal. The love and closeness she feels with Jerri's family have helped heal the pain of her own parents' response.

But for every story like Susan and Jerri's, there will, we hope, be more stories like Maria's. Her parents got over their concern about her divorce pretty quickly. The family came together in support of Maria and had that all-too-rare ability to support "whatever made her happy."

Whether you are coming out to your parents or to your children, the decision to come out *is* a decision. Even though it sometimes just seems to happen, you have usually given some thought to it in advance. However difficult it may be to make the decision, coming out provides the possibility for developing closeness and support that are especially treasured by lesbian parents who likely face negative responses from the broader world. Being loved and accepted for who you really are is always a pleasure, but it is particularly sweet for lesbian families.

5 Engaged Parenting: Communication and Conflict Resolution

"Engaged parenting" is a term we've coined to convey the sense of conscious attention, active involvement and commitment we believe is fundamental to parenting. Although the task of parenting is a demanding one, we don't believe it has to be approached with fear and trepidation. At the outset all parents, including lesbian parents and parents-to-be, must realize that any attempt to be "perfect parents" is doomed. In the first place, it is not possible to be perfect, and, second, trying to be perfect detracts from the joys of parenting and the joys of childhood.

However, we do want our children to experience love and joy, to be happy and successful, to have a sense of self-worth, to believe in themselves, and to feel lovable and capable. And we want to feel good about ourselves as parents in the process. So how do we accomplish all this and enjoy ourselves while we do it?

The conditions in which children are most likely to thrive and grow and to learn to love themselves and others have been described in a variety of ways. Some experts talk about providing both nurture and structure; others emphasize communication skills and the language of acceptance, and still others talk about democratic parenting and positive discipline. Whatever the words, the essence of the message is that parents need to convey love and acceptance to their child. The more unconditional this is, the better.

As lesbians, we have firsthand experience with self-acceptance, having had to work through some degree of homophobia—internal as well as external—in order to accept ourselves. What we learn on our own journey of self-acceptance can be translated directly into raising our children.

However, love and acceptance are not enough. Even if we were able to provide unconditional love and acceptance all the time, which no human is capable of, more is required. Children also need to learn limits, skills and standards. The challenge for parents is to combine love and acceptance with structure. Without love and acceptance, the rules and limits of structure are harsh and make no sense to children. With them, children are likely to experience the structure of rules, standards and consequences as believable, acceptable and supportive.

Caring Communication

We cannot avoid communicating to our children. We communicate by not speaking as well as by speaking, by our actions and our words, and particularly by *how* we say what we say. Our non-verbal communication—voice tone, body posture, gestures and touch—may convey as much or more than our words.

As parents we need to talk in ways that engage our children in listening to us and to listen in ways that encourage our children to talk. Why is communication so important? Because it is how our children learn about the world, about themselves, about values, about life. With positive communication skills, we contribute to the development of caring, responsible and self-confident children and avoid making "scratches on their souls." [1]

Listening So Children Will Talk

Are you only half-listening when your child is talking to you—for example, are you reading the paper or doing the dishes? Do you give your child your full attention and show that by your words *and* your body language? Your non-verbal messages, as well as your verbal ones, should invite your child to talk.

Sometimes the best way to listen is to pay attention but to say nothing, conveying acceptance with silence. Or you may intersperse silent attention with brief encouragements to talk, such as "Oh" or "Really" or "Is that so?" If you want to explicitly invite a child to say more, try something like "Tell me more" or "This seems really important to you" or "I'd like to hear about it."

Active listening is a skill that can *keep* the door open to vital communication, rather than merely opening the door. This skill involves listening carefully to the child to understand what he is feeling or what his communication means. Then you translate your child's message into your own words and feed it back to verify that you understood his communication correctly. The key element here is that, as the listener, you feed back only your understanding of your child's message. Nothing more, nothing less. You do not send any message of your own—like an opinion or suggestion. You stick to what the child's thoughts and feelings are. This skill takes practice, but once mastered, it is very effective at helping the child say more, go deeper and develop his thoughts and ideas.

In the following example, Trina uses active listening with her five-year-old son, Brian. Trina and Brian have just gotten back from the neighborhood park. Brian is grumpy and whiny as he has been for the past few days.

Brian: "I hate that stupid park."
Trina: "You really don't like that park!"
Brian: "Yeah, it's no fun anymore."
Trina: "It used to be fun, and now it isn't."
Brian: "Yeah. I liked when Jesse pushed me way up high."
Trina: "The park was way more fun when Jesse pushed you on the swings."
Brian: (looking sad) "Yeah. Jesse doesn't push me on the swings anymore."
Trina: "You miss Jesse a lot."
Brian: (nodding his head) "I never get to see her anymore. I want her to come to our house and play with me."
Trina: "It's hard when you only get to see her on Fridays. "
Brian: "Yeah. And I have to go to her house. She doesn't come to our house."
Trina: "You'd like her to come to our house."
Brian: "I want her to come back and live with us again."

Trina: "It's hard for you that she's left; that you don't get to see her every day; and she doesn't do the things with you that she used to."
Brian: (with tears in his eyes) "I want it to be like it was before."
Trina: "You're really sad that she's moved away and we aren't one family anymore."

Trina's active listening allowed Brian to move from complaining about the park to what was really going on—he missed Jesse. At this point Trina might just hold Brian and comfort him, or continue to talk with him. This is clearly a topic they will need to continue to discuss, perhaps even problem-solving about Brian's contact with Jesse. Now that he has talked about his feelings, Trina can check in with Brian periodically about his missing Jesse.

In the next example, Nerissa is trying to talk with her seventeen-year-old daughter, Yvonne, who has just come home from a date with her boyfriend Ron.

Nerissa: "Hi honey. Did you have a good time?"
Yvonne: "What would you possibly know about my life? You don't understand anything."
Nerissa: "You sound really upset!"
Yvonne: "I *am*. It's all because you are a lesbian!"
Nerissa: "So my being a lesbian is a problem for you."
Yvonne: "If you weren't a lesbian, you would know about things."
Nerissa: "You feel that because I'm a lesbian there are things about your life that I don't understand."
Yvonne: "Yeah, you can't understand about me and Ron. I don't know what to do. How can I talk to you about sex?"
Nerissa: "So you really want to talk to somebody about being sexual with Ron, and you think I won't understand because I'm a lesbian."
Yvonne: "I guess it's not really because you're a lesbian. It's hard to talk about it. You'll probably get mad at me."
Nerissa: "You want to talk, but you're afraid I'll be mad."
Yvonne: "Yeah. You remember when you told me that you'd help me get birth control?"
Nerissa: "Un huh."
Yvonne: "Well, I think we need to talk about that soon."

Obviously this conversation could go in many directions. Mother and daughter could talk about sex, Yvonne's relationship with Ron, birth control or Yvonne and Nerissa's relationship. By active listening, Nerissa can avoid steering the conversation in a particular direction and just allow and encourage Yvonne to keep talking about what is going on for her. Eventually, in this example, the issue of Nerissa's being a lesbian evaporated and the real issue unfolded.

Active listening is one skill in the engaged parenting repertoire that you can use to encourage kids to talk. This does not mean that you have to wait for your child to initiate the conversation. For example, whatever the outcome of Nerissa's conversation with Yvonne on this occasion, she can check in with her daughter at another time about any or all of the topics that came up.

Talking So Children Will Listen

Why do you want your child to listen to you? Sometimes it is because you have information you want them to have and other times because you want them to do something, or to stop doing something. The first involves providing information; the second, setting limits and solving problems.

Becoming an "Askable" Parent

Children are naturally curious about everything. If you want to be their main source of information, you need to talk to them openly, honestly and matter-of-factly about what's important to them, and to you. Children are most receptive to parental guidance up to about twelve years of age. During these formative years the foundation is laid for skills, values and attitudes, so parents need to start early to establish open communication with their children. Being an "askable" parent means encouraging questions and discussion, and not dismissing, punishing, judging or teasing a youngster for asking questions. When your children ask questions, let them know you are glad they asked; otherwise they will stop asking you and seek answers elsewhere.

Correct information and loving support from parents are critical in providing reassurance to children and helping them understand the world so they can deal more effectively with real-life situations. The following are general guidelines for providing information to your child.

- *Be knowledgeable.*

  If you are giving advice, you may need to read up on the topics that you don't know much about so that you can be a more effective source for your child. Sharing your values, beliefs and opinions with your child is important, but you may have more credibility with her if you offer supporting evidence where appropriate.

- *Be trustworthy.*

  Be direct and clear about what you know, and honest about what you don't. There is no shame in not knowing. Your children are asking you because they don't know and aren't sure how to find out. If you don't know the answer either, you can demonstrate to them that it is okay not to know and then show them how to find out the answer. This may involve asking someone else or looking the answer up, or, if the question is about values, just thinking and talking more about it together.

- *Be brief.*

  Don't use a paragraph when a sentence will do. Get to the point, and avoid giving a long, involved explanation or lecture.

- *Be clear.*

  Use simple language that is appropriate to your child's age and comprehension level. Also make sure you are clear about exactly what they want to know. Remember the old joke about the child who asked where she came from? Her mother sat her down for a long talk about "the birds and the bees." Afterwards the child looked confused and said, "My friend Brenda said she was from Chicago; where am I from?" It's easy to misunderstand what your child is asking when you yourself are anxious about a topic.

- *Be respectful.*

  Ask your child what he thinks about the topic rather than telling him what he should think or should do. When you respect your child's opinion, you are sending the message that you are interested in and value his perspective. You are talking with him, not at him.

- *Be willing to revisit the topic.*

  Come back to the topic at a later time if you have more thoughts about it or wonder if your child does. Topics of importance tend to recycle. A child may ask the same question more than once and want the reassurance of hearing the same answer again. Or you may want to revisit a topic to follow up on an outcome, for example, "How did the teacher respond to your request for more help?" Or you may wonder whether your child has had other thoughts about the subject since you first talked.

Some topics, like adoption, divorce or homophobia, for example, require short conversations on an ongoing basis.

Robin was watching the news on television one night with her six-year-old son, Mark, when a feature came on about violence against lesbians and gays. Mark had two reactions. First he asked Robin why people didn't like lesbians. Then he said he didn't want to march in the Pride parade the following week. He was worried they might get beaten up. Marching in the parade was something they had done for years, ever since Mark was a baby. He always loved it and every year they talked about which group they would march with. Would it be the Queer Quakers, the Lesbian Mothers or the People of Color Against Aids Network?

How does Robin handle this situation? Because she and Mark have talked before about prejudice and about how some people don't like homosexuals, she was prepared for that part. Once again she explained that there are some people in the world who just don't like anyone who is different from them. She knew they would need to talk about that over and over again. The part about being afraid to march in the parade was more troubling to her. First of all she wanted to go herself, and she wanted to share the experience with her son.

Robin decided to take the opportunity to talk honestly with Mark about violence against gays and lesbians but also reassure him at the same time. She told him it was true that people who did not like lesbians and gays sometimes beat them up just because they were gay and lesbian. Yet she pointed out that this was not likely to happen at the march because so many lesbians and gays and their friends would be there. Robin reminded Mark of the marches they had been in and even got out the picture albums to remember those good times. Then she asked Mark what they could do if they were in the march and somebody said they were going to beat them up. He responded with lots of ideas. The ones he liked best were telling the person it was not okay to hit people, running away really fast, and getting help from adults. When they finished talking, he was excited again about going to the march.

Instead of getting angry and defensive, Robin demonstrated engaged parenting skills. She provided information in response to Mark's question about people not liking lesbians and she showed respect for his fears and concerns by asking him how to handle different situations. With younger children like Mark parents can use the "what if" game: "What would you do if someone you didn't know asked you to get into their car?" "What would you do if other children called you names because you have two mothers?" With younger children this is primarily a teaching tool, although they may have ideas of their own, too. With older children and adolescents, this "rehearsal" may need to be woven into the conversation more. Parents can still use the "what if" scenario, but in a discussion that includes the reasons for and possible consequences of different alternatives, using the child's input as well as the parents' ideas.

Who's Got the Problem?

Although parents may feel that the number of child-rearing problems they confront is infinite, it's reassuring to know that almost all of them fit into two categories of problems: the problems the child "owns" and those we as parents "own." In the situation involving Mark and his mother, Robin, the child "owns" the problem. Mark is afraid to go to the parade. Robin could have jumped in and made it her problem— because she wanted to go. But she resisted this temptation and kept the focus on resolving the problem Mark had.

When the child's behavior negatively affects you, the parent, in some tangible or direct way, you "own" the problem. In this situation the focus becomes how you can help yourself, rather than how you can help your child. As a parent, you do not want your car damaged, your conversation with your partner constantly interrupted, the bathroom floor covered with wet towels, assigned chores not done and so on. When you own the problem, you have three choices: you can try to modify yourself, you can try to change the environment or you can try to change your child.

For example, let's say the issue is wet towels left on the bathroom floor. Since this bothers you, and not your child, *you* own the problem. You could try changing your attitude by telling yourself that your child will learn to pick up after herself in time and you will just hang in there until then. You could try changing the environment by putting more hooks in the bathroom or you could try confronting the child about the behavior, hoping she will change. Each of these approaches could be successful.

Most of us have a lot of experience with both practicing and receiving the many ineffective ways of trying to change behavior. In fact there seem to be many more ineffective than effective strategies. Most of the ineffective strategies involve telling the child what he should or has to do. "You shouldn't leave the towels on the floor," or "You have to pick up after yourself." In this process we may also disparage the child—"I can't believe how inconsiderate you are," or "Shame on you," or " You are a spoiled brat,"—which can have devastating effects on his developing sense of self-worth. What you will likely get in response from the child is resistance, defensiveness and hostility. In contrast, by avoiding put-downs and including children as much as possible in the problem-solving process, you help your child learn to be responsible.

The Importance of "I" Messages

Instead of "should" messages and "put-downs," parents can use "I" messages. In an "I" message, parents simply tell the child what they see, what they want, what they will or will not do or how they feel when the child behaves in a way that is unacceptable to them. For example, a parent might say, "When you leave wet towels on the bathroom floor, I feel angry because I have to pick them up before I can have my shower." Sometimes that is all it takes. Making children aware that your angry feelings are a consequence of their behavior is sometimes enough, in and of itself, to solve the problem.

The child may respond with, "I didn't know that it bugged you so much. I'll try to remember," or even "I'm sorry. I wish you had told me before," and the behavior changes.

At other times, parents need to use a more involved series of steps to solve problems. A key feature of an effective approach—whether you call it "win-win" or "collaborative problem-solving" or something else—is that the solution to the problem must be acceptable to both parties. The parent *and* the child approach the situation as a problem to be solved. Suggestions from each person involved are offered and considered. Then one idea, which is agreeable to both, is selected. As examples in the next sections will illustrate, there is no need to sell a solution and there is no power struggle.

Setting Limits

Limit-setting is the practice of consistently, and lovingly, establishing rules, guidelines and directions for appropriate behavior and explaining the consequences of misbehavior. Setting limits for children not only teaches values and standards for behavior, but also increases the children's sense of predictability and security. If the boundaries are clear and predictable, and if the consequences of overstepping the boundaries are natural and logical, your child will find it easier to make decisions about what to do and what not to do. Including the child in the rule-making process helps ensure that she is motivated to uphold the rules and that the rules and consequences are clear, workable and understood. Often problems can be anticipated and prevented by discussing situations in advance and rehearsing how to handle them.

In lesbian families, women have to take on both the nurturing and the limit-setting roles. If setting limits and holding the line about rules were part of the man's role in our family of origin, we may have to stretch to take on that part of parenting. If there are two parents in the family, sharing the limit-setting role can prevent a couple becoming polarized, with one being the "disciplinarian," the other the "nurturer."

During the years she was a single parent, Janice had to be the gentle and supportive parent as well as the assertive limit-setter. Although she knew she should set clear limits and hold to them, she sometimes had difficulty being consistent and following through.

One of the qualities she had initially appreciated about her new partner, April, was how clear she was about what was acceptable to her and what was not. Clarity, consistency and limit-setting were definitely April's strengths in the parenting-skills department. Janice and April ran into trouble when their roles got too separated and became extreme. Over time, April took on more and more responsibility for "discipline" and Janice ended up in the middle. She realized she was spending most of her time either intervening with April to advocate for the kids or trying to justify April's behavior to the children. Janice found herself in a very familiar situation—April was the "bad guy" just as her ex-husband and her own father had been.

Lesbian parents who become aware of polarizing around roles have an opportunity to change this pattern. Each partner needs to take responsibility for her individual part in the dynamic and for making constructive changes. For example, Janice and April could re-negotiate their roles. To create a better balance, Janice could take a more active role in setting limits and April could reduce her involvement in "discipline" and increase her involvement in nurturing and fun activities with the children. As they discuss and negotiate these changes, April and Janice need to clarify their expectations—of each other and of the children—to ensure these expectations are clear, realistic and agreed-upon.

Although the approach to conflict resolution discussed in the following section focuses on parent-child relationships, these same skills can be utilized when the conflict is between the parents.

Resolving Conflicts Constructively

When limits are set, children often test them, and the result is conflict, whether the situation involves two children who want the same toy at the same time or a teenager with a midnight curfew who wants to go to an all-night party after the prom. However, conflict can take either a constructive or a destructive course. In constructive conflict resolution, the conflicts are seen as mutual problems to be solved. Destructive conflict, on the other hand, resembles a win-lose competitive struggle. The values, attitudes, knowledge and skills involved in constructive conflict resolution can be modeled and taught to children from an early age. School programs have successfully demonstrated that children in the early elementary grades can learn skills that allow them to resolve conflicts themselves and also to help mediate conflicts between other children.[2]

Since conflict is a reality in any relationship, the key is not to avoid it, but to recognize it and manage it skillfully to get the best outcome for all concerned. Our focus then, as parents, becomes to help our children resolve conflicts positively and successfully.

Parents as Models

When things don't go your way, do you storm off and sulk or have an adult version of a temper tantrum—yelling and screaming and throwing things? Or do you avoid conflict at all cost, giving in to everyone about everything just to keep peace?

As parents, we need to ask ourselves what kind of example we are setting and what we are teaching our children by our own behavior in conflict situations, whether with them or with others in our life. It's important to keep in mind that the values we help instill in our children will be shaped by our actual *behavior*. When our professed values and our behavior don't match up, we may confuse our children. We also risk having them follow our example rather than our advice. This does not mean that we have to be perfect, but we do need to be aware of the models we are providing for our children. Do we engage in win-lose power struggles with our child, or with our partner, or with the world? Or are we able to turn conflicts into constructive problem-solving situations?

When approaching conflicts constructively, you and your child use learned skills to arrive at a mutually agreeable solution. Although this process may take longer than simply "putting your foot down," saying no or meting out a punishment, there is more to be gained by involving the child in the problem-solving process and by practicing respectful and positive communication. The next sections provide examples of how to use this constructive approach.

Resolving Conflicts with Young Children

Angie was at her wits' end. Her four-year-old daughter, Marta, periodically scribbled on the wallpaper in her room with crayons. Angie had tried forcefully saying no, reasoning with Marta and actually taking away her crayons. Still Marta kept doing it. Then one day Angie found lipstick scrawled all over the walls in the bathroom.

If you were in Angie's shoes, what would you do? You might "blow up" at Marta—which might relieve your frustration for the moment but wouldn't solve your problem—or you could try to approach the conflict calmly and constructively, using the following steps:

Step 1: *Prepare.*
You can't problem-solve when you are furious, so the first step involves calming down. You also need to identify what specifically is upsetting to you and what your feelings are.

Step 2: *Set the time.*
Check with your child whether "this is a good time to talk." Sooner is better than later, especially with younger children, but privacy, mutual agreement and uninterrupted time are also important.

Step 3: *Establish the ground rules for communication.*
The communication guidelines of respect and openness apply, but the primary responsibility for modeling these rests with the parent. It is unrealistic to expect a four-year-old or even a seven-year-old to have the skills of an adult. Nonetheless, parents can help younger children learn how to communicate effectively. One way to do this is to insist that the focus be on solving the problem for the future, not on blame about the past.

Step 4: *Reach mutual understanding.*
Make sure you talk about the child's feelings first, and then yours. You might start off with something like "I imagine you must be feeling..." because small children may not have the words to express themselves or they may be unsure that it is okay if they are angry with or scared of you. Be interested and accepting of your child's feelings. Your child will be much better able to listen to your thoughts and feelings when she has had a chance to express hers.

Keep the description of the problem and your feelings about it short and to the point. For example, Angie might say, "We have talked about drawing on paper and not drawing on the walls. When you keep doing it, I feel angry," or "I am sad because the lipstick may never come off the wall."

Step 5: *Brainstorm possible solutions.*
Encourage your child to contribute ideas for solving the problem. Remember this is a brainstorm—all ideas are welcome, and noth-

ing is evaluated or discussed yet. Writing down all the ideas shows your child you respect his input.

Step 6: *Pick a solution and reach resolution.*

At this point, you and your child can talk about which ideas you each like and which you don't. You might say, "I wouldn't feel good about that solution because..." or "That sounds like something I could do," or "That one is okay with me." Identify the solutions you both agree would work, and choose one.

Step 7: *Write down the solution.*

In addition to the agreed-upon solution, you may need to specify other details, for example, what steps, if any, need to be taken and who is responsible for what. And, if necessary, specify a date by which the agreed-upon steps must be completed.

Step 8: *Review and reevaluate.*

Pay attention to how well the solution is working, and revisit the problem with your child if the solution isn't working.

Let's look at how Angie could use these resolution steps with Marta: she would first make sure she was calm enough to talk with Marta and then determine an appropriate time to discuss the problem. She might begin by saying, "I bet it was fun to draw with Mommy's lipstick. And now you may be scared that I am mad with you." Angie can let Marta confirm whether or not she is correct about how Marta is feeling. At that point Marta may also feel bad and be sorry. Once Marta's feelings are clarified, it is Angie's turn to express her own feelings. She might say, "I get very upset when the walls are written on. I have to work very hard to clean them off."

At that point Marta may offer to clean up the scribbles. Angie explains that Marta's solution applies only to the past and that they also need to find a solution for the future. Together Angie and Marta decide that in addition to Marta's cleaning up the bathroom scribbles, Marta will color only on a big sheet of butcher paper that Angie tapes to her bedroom wall, not on the wall itself. After Angie shows Marta how to clean up the scribbles, she can thank her daughter for cleaning up the mess and go to her room with her to tape up the butcher paper. If the lipstick can't be completely removed, Angie might also sit down with Marta and point out how sometimes things just can't be fixed and that it is sad that the wall will never be the same or that the wall will have to be repainted.

The review and reevaluate step may be very critical in this situation. If Marta's behavior persists, Angie needs to consider the possibility that her daughter's behavior may be a reaction to something else. For example, Marta may be angry about the arrival of her new baby brother.

Sometimes conflict may arise between your child and someone outside the family.

Amanda came home from school very distressed. Her class was making Mother's Day cards, and she had wanted to make two instead of one. She had two mothers; she needed two cards. Early in the year, Ann and Phyllis had met with Amanda's teacher to clarify that Amanda's family was a lesbian family. At the time the teacher had seemed open and supportive. Now, however, the teacher had told Amanda that the other children were making only one card, so she had to make only one card as well.

The whole family was upset. Amanda insisted she was never going back to her school, Ann was furious and threatening to call the principal, the school superintendent and the governor, and Phyllis was frantically trying to think how to turn the situation into a family problem-solving session.

After Ann had calmed down, she and Phyllis talked the matter over. It was clear this was not a situation that Amanda could be expected to solve on her own. They discussed a general plan of action and then sat down with Amanda to talk about her feelings, their feelings and possible solutions to the problem. As a family they came up with the following plan: over the weekend the whole family would go out to get materials for Amanda to make Mother's Day cards at home; then on Monday, Phyllis and Ann would meet with Amanda's teacher.

Following the steps in this problem-solving approach is not always easy. It involves taking the time to practice good communication and effective problem-solving skills. Active listening, using "I" messages to describe wants and feelings, and a willingness to work cooperatively with our children to solve problems are basic requirements of constructive conflict resolution. As engaged parents, we have to let go of the urge to solve the problem either by pushing our solution onto our child, which doesn't respect her, or by allowing the child to push her solution onto us, which doesn't respect us.

Sibling Rivalry

No matter what the size of our family is, the phrase "one big happy family" often describes our fantasy of family life. "Sibling rivalry" may describe the reality. When the oldest child tells you to send her new baby brother "back to Honduras," or your six- and eleven-year-olds never seem to stop fighting, many of you may wonder where you have gone wrong.

Children seem to go through four stages on their way to a truce.[3] The first is the "might makes right" stage, in which everything is "mine!" This characteristic two-and-a-half-year-old approach is followed by the uneasy truce of the "you scratch my back, and I'll scratch yours" stage. While this trading-favors approach does not get at the root cause of sibling rivalry, the squabbling may be less intense. Next comes the "it's not fair, you're cheating" stage, in which siblings can often make, and even follow, fairly firm rules, for example, about using each other's things. The final stage, "as brothers and sisters go, you're not so bad" may take until high school, or even college, to arrive. As they say, better late then never!

Here are some specific suggestions to help reduce conflicts between siblings:

- Acknowledge your children's feelings. For example, to an older child who has a new sibling, you might say, "I know you are really mad and sad that I have a new baby."
- Be realistic in your expectations. Keep in mind that most children squabble...a lot.
- Avoid acting as referee, encouraging tattling or comparing your children to each other.
- Separate children from each other if they are fighting. Or if they are not really doing any harm, separate yourself from them.
- Find or plan activities for your children. Children with nothing to do tend to quarrel.
- Plan daily schedules so that children who tend to fight with each other are not together for long periods, especially if they

are unsupervised:

- Use simple and specific rules for behavior, such as "You are not to hit your sister."
- Make each child feel special.

In their heart of hearts, each child in a family wishes the others were gone so he or she could have one hundred percent of the parents' love and attention. Because this wish is at the base of much of the bickering and squabbling between siblings, you can moderate the fighting but likely not eliminate it entirely.

Resolving Conflicts with Adolescents

Communication problems between adolescents and parents can break down if, as parents, we do not treat our teenagers with respect and if we treat them as if they were younger than they are. A good rule of thumb is to speak to your adolescent only in the way you would speak to another adult. This means no put-downs, no ordering around, no superficial reassurances—"Don't worry about it" or "You'll see it differently when you're older"—that don't take their concerns seriously.

Though a collaborative approach to resolving conflicts is usually ideal, there are situations in which other approaches are appropriate; for example, you and your child may find yourselves in a conflict in which it would make sense for you to:

- *Assert your authority.*
  Use this approach only in emergencies, when quick and decisive action on your part is essential or when an issue—such as drinking and driving—is non-negotiable. However, remember that pulling rank typically builds resentment and that if the adolescent is not included in the decision-making she is probably not going to be motivated to make the solution work.

- *Give in.*
  When you are wrong and your teenager is right, be willing to acknowledge your mistake and learn from it. Accommodation, or giving in, is also an appropriate strategy when the issue is not important to you but is important to your teen. For example, you may not particularly want your teen to paint her room fire-engine

red, but if it is not all that important to you, you may decide you can live with whatever color she wants.

- *Avoid the problem.*
  When the issue is truly trivial—such as whether your son wears the blue or the green shirt to your mother's birthday party—let it go. Of course, what one person thinks is trivial may be very important to another. Try to keep your perspective by asking yourself whether the issue will matter to you in five minutes, five hours, five days or five years. Avoidance may also be the best approach when one or both parties are too angry or stressed to deal constructively with each other. However, avoidance does not solve a real problem; if the issue recurs, you need to address and resolve it.

- *Compromise.*
  Compromise may be the most useful approach when the issue is not worth spending a lot of time on or when a decision has to be made quickly. In these situations, "splitting the difference" may work. For example, if your daughter wants a ride to her girlfriend's at seven o'clock and you would prefer to relax and read the paper for a half-hour, the two of you could agree to split the difference and leave at seven-fifteen. The problem with compromise is that no one gets what they really want; all parties settle for less.

For important differences, however, none of these methods really provides a "win-win" solution. Somebody loses, or both parties lose.

The goal of the discussions and negotiations in a collaborative approach is to arrive at solutions that everyone in the family can live with. Another goal is to model and to teach adolescents responsibility for their own behavior and consideration for others. Most conflicts around household responsibilities and personal behavior are not life and death matters. They can be negotiated.

Mary and Rosie live with Mary's biological son, Daniel, who is thirteen. Mary and Rosie have been together for six years. The relationship between Daniel and Rosie was rocky at first. Daniel had lived alone with Mary after his parents divorced when he was four. He didn't want to have to share Mary's time, and he didn't want Rosie "bossing him around." They worked through these issues, however, and it was pretty smooth sailing for a while. Then came adolescence.

The current conflicts involve household responsibilities: Rosie likes things neat and tidy, Daniel is quite uninterested in "neat and tidy" and Mary is caught in the middle. Although none of the specifics—dishes left unwashed, bed unmade, clothes strewn around the living room, toilet seat left up—are really worth starting World War III over, this family is poised on the brink.

Mary, Rosie and Daniel decide to negotiate the issue of household cleanliness rather than have Mary and Rosie engage in a power struggle with Daniel. Notice that the steps they use are the same as those for conflict resolution between parents and young children but that the details are different:

Step 1: *Prepare.*

This first step involves Rosie and Mary, because it is they who have the problem. Daniel is fine with the way things are—at least as far as we know at the moment. The parents need to determine, individually and as a couple, what they want Daniel to do and not do. How strongly do they feel about his behavior? How important is the problem to each of them and why? In some cases the conflict is between the parents; the child's behavior is just the occasion, or perhaps the excuse, for the conflict. Parents may also need to choose a specific instance or problem behavior, rather than several, to focus on in their negotiations. Once they get these specifics sorted out, they are ready for the next step.

Rosie and Mary decide to focus on the dirty dishes because this is the issue on which they most closely agree. From their discussions, they realize they each have a different standard for Daniel and that they will have to sort that out between themselves. However, they are both bothered by the dishes so they decide to start there.

Step 2: *Set the time.*

Rosie and Mary need to speak with Daniel about setting a time and place for discussion to resolve the conflict, and to get his agreement to try and work out a solution. It is best to limit the meeting length (they can always schedule another discussion if necessary) and to pick a time and place where they will not be distracted or interrupted.

Mary asks Daniel when he can meet to talk about the issue of dirty dishes and try to work out a solution to what has clearly become a source of friction and resentment for all concerned. He agrees to meet from seven to seven-thirty the following night.

Step 3: *Set the ground rules.*

The communication ground rules must be clear and agreed-upon. Examples of ground rules include: no put-downs or sarcasm, listening and treating each other with respect, no interruptions, and whatever other guidelines are necessary to establish and maintain a positive atmosphere for problem-solving.

Step 4: *Reach mutual understanding.*

This step requires all parties to express themselves clearly and to listen to each other, to hear what each other thinks and feels. Taking turns works best. Typically, the person who has the "problem" describes what the problem is, sticking to the facts and not using loaded and judgmental words. "I" messages can be used to describe feelings about the situation.

At their meeting, Mary tells Daniel that she feels irritated when she goes to cook or eat something and a utensil or dish that she needs is dirty because Daniel has used it and not washed it afterwards. Rosie says that she knows she is a bit of a "nut" about things being cleaned up and she does not expect Daniel to agree with her or to have the same values himself; however they were both living in the same house and she really wants to work something out that they can all live with.

Then Rosie and Mary listen to Daniel. Mostly he feels picked on. He thinks they are unreasonable in expecting him to clean up the minute he dirties a dish; and besides, don't they appreciate that he is taking care of himself by fixing his own food?

Step 5: *Brainstorm possible solutions.*

All parties generate and record as many solutions as possible to the problem. Quantity, not quality, is the goal. No criticism of ideas is allowed at this point because even crazy ideas can release tension and get the creative juices flowing.

When they brainstorm, Mary, Rosie and Daniel come up with these possible solutions:

- *Use paper plates.*
- *Get a dishwasher.*
- *Set a limit on how long dirty dishes can be left.*
- *Buy duplicates of the most-used items.*
- *Eat out all the time.*
- *Take turns doing the dishes for everyone on a weekly basis.*
- *Set a limit on how many dirty dishes Daniel can accumulate before he does his dishes.*
- *Keep dirty dishes in one place instead of all over the kitchen.*

Step 6: *Pick a solution and reach resolution.*
After each party has contributed every idea she or he can think of, everyone can negotiate which solution or combination of solutions is acceptable to all.

Daniel, Rosie and Mary decide that a solution acceptable to all of them is that Daniel will put his dirty dishes in a dishpan set aside for that purpose. When it is full, he does his dishes. They also decide to purchase duplicates of the most-used items. This solution was agreeable to Daniel because doing the dishes is a consequence of filling the dishpan, not of someone telling him to do them. It satisfies Rosie because Daniel's dirty dishes are confined to one area and the rest of the kitchen is "neat." And it satisfies Mary because there are duplicates of the things she previously had to wash when she wanted them.

If a resolution can't be reached in the amount of time allotted, another meeting should be scheduled to continue the discussion. No one should agree to something that is unacceptable to him or her: the goal is to find a solution that everyone can all live with or is at least willing to try. Consequences for failure to follow-through may or may not be addressed at this step. Sometimes it is helpful and even necessary to specify these consequences in advance; other times it may detract from the negotiation process.

Step 7: *Write down the agreed-upon solution.*

This step may, at first, seem unnecessary; however, writing out the solution and details of the agreement may reveal potential problems or areas that need clarification. In addition, memories are short. Having something written to refer back to will prevent misunderstandings and arguments about what the agreement really was.

Step 8: *Review and reevaluate.*

It is a good idea to set a time in the future to evaluate how the agreement is working. Consequences for failure to follow-through may need to be discussed, or perhaps the agreement just isn't working and needs to be revised. Or the agreement may be essentially solid but need some fine-tuning.

Rosie, Mary and Daniel decide to try the dishes arrangement for two weeks and then meet again to see how it is going. At review time, they agree their solution is working for the most part, but they needed to tweak it a little. Daniel has become very skilled at piling the dishes in the dishpan, so they decided on a height limit of six inches above the dishpan. Because the tension has been relieved around the dishes issue, Rosie, Mary and Daniel can laugh about both Daniel's ingenuity and the family's response. It isn't long before Daniel's height limit becomes a family joke.

At first it may feel awkward to work through these steps, but it gets easier. And now, Daniel, Rosie and Mary have a successful experience to refer to when they work through the other identified sources of conflict, such as Daniel's clothes strewn in the living room.

In the previous example, Mary and Rosie were united in their efforts to negotiate a solution with Daniel. However, a trickier situation is one in which a lesbian mother feels torn between her children and her lover:

After her long-term relationship with Donna broke up, Helen vowed to finish raising her children before she got involved with anyone again. John and Randy were ten and thirteen at the time of the breakup. They were very attached to Donna, and both continued to have contact with her for a few years until she moved across the country. The boys also spent less time with their father as he got involved with starting a new family. Yet, Helen managed well as a single parent, and she and her children became a pretty tight unit.

Three years after the breakup with Donna, Helen met Louise. Her resolve to wait until the boys were grown and out of the house before she got involved rapidly evaporated. She started spending a lot of time with Louise, which led to trouble at home. One night Helen found the boys waiting up for her when she got home from a date with Louise. Both boys were angry with her, especially John. They reminded her of her "promise" to stick together, just the three of them, and told her in no uncertain terms that they wanted her to quit seeing Louise. Helen felt immediately on the defensive.

Helen could have told John and Randy that she would do what she wanted to do and if they didn't like it that was too bad. Or she could have given in and never seen Louise again. With either of these options, someone would have "lost." Instead, Helen took the problem-solving approach.

Since it was late and they were all tired, they agreed to have a family meeting the next day. At that meeting they each talked about their feelings. Then they discussed possible solutions and eventually figured out what would work for everyone.

At the family meeting, Helen's first goal was to listen as openly as she could to her sons' feelings. She had always encouraged them to express their feelings, but she had to work at being non-defensive when the feelings were anger directed at her. So she listened while her sons vented their feelings. She breathed deeply when they used words like "betrayal" and "selfish." When they had moved past blaming her to revisiting their hurt over Donna's leaving and their fears about the future of their family, it was easier to listen. Then they were ready to listen to her. She talked about how much she loved them and how important the family was to her as well. She also talked about Louise—how she had not been looking to get involved with someone, but that sometimes these things just happened. She wanted to have her family as well as her relationship with Louise.

When all the feelings had been expressed, they were able, as a family, to move to listing the possible solutions. Helen insisted that "never seeing Louise again" be on the list, because it was a possible solution, even if she hated the idea. The boys responded by adding "Louise moves in with us," because that was one they hated. It was good to get the extremes out there; it made it easier to evaluate the more acceptable solutions. The solution they finally agreed to outlined a number of details:

- *They would set aside special time to spend together as a family each week.*
- *Helen agreed to invite Louise over to the house so the boys could get to know her a little.*
- *Date nights out with Louise would be once during the week and once on the weekend. (Helen felt a little like a teenager about this one, but she could live with it for a while.)*
- *Helen would keep her sons posted about how serious the relationship with Louise was getting. They were particularly concerned about Louise moving in.*

Helen, John and Randy set a family meeting date for a month from then to evaluate how the new agreement was working. They decided it would take that amount of time to determine if the plan would work as written or would need changes.

When a lesbian mother gets involved with a new lover, it often indicates a new direction in her life. For example, she may be moving in a more conservative direction—from the commune to the suburbs—or the other way around. In any event, her new lover likely exemplifies this new development. It is important that this opportunity to grow and change is recognized and managed. For example, changes in parenting style may accompany the new direction. These changes need to be introduced gently so that the children have some adjustment time. If the new partner represents a shift in direction, the mother needs to make sure that any "new style" of parenting is shared. For example, if Louise represents a new direction in Helen's life—complete with a shift in parenting style—Helen needs to make sure that she, as well as Louise, demonstrate the new style.

• • •

The Tradition of Family Meetings

In the previous situation, Helen and her sons scheduled a family meeting to evaluate how their agreement was working. We encourage you to institute family meetings as a regular tradition, not just when conflicts arise. Family meetings are an ongoing way to not only address problems but also build individual self-worth and a democratic team spirit. They also help teach values and skills such as how to be a good listener as well as a good talker.

Whether you call it a family meeting, family conference or family council, the family meets at a scheduled time—preferably weekly—and with a structured format to discuss issues, plan activities, air grievances, share appreciations and solve problems in an atmosphere of cooperation and mutual respect.

The following are some guidelines for conducting family meetings:

- *Make the meeting a priority.*
  Don't schedule other activities for that time period or allow interruptions like the telephone or other distractions. The meeting length may vary, but usually a half-hour is long enough (perhaps even too long for very small children).

- *Have a chairperson and a secretary to record decisions.*
  Rotate these jobs once children understand the procedures.

- *Agree in advance about guidelines for operating the meeting.*
  Guidelines may include prohibitions on yelling, blaming others, criticizing and interrupting. Family members should take turns speaking until everyone is heard. If necessary, set a time limit for each turn. Two minutes is quite long enough.

- *Begin each meeting with appreciations.*
  Follow that with business from previous meetings and then new business. New items may be spontaneous or complied from an "agenda board" or an "agenda jar" in a handy place where family members can note items they want addressed.

- *Create an atmosphere of safety where the rights and ideas of each family member are respected.*
  Brainstorming, for example, is a wonderful way to come up with creative ideas and solutions, but only if all contributions are en-

couraged and accepted without being evaluated or dismissed.

- *Work for decisions by consensus and refrain from voting.*
  Voting creates winners and losers, and resentment. If you cannot reach a consensus, you can table the issue until the next meeting, or you can take turns trying different suggestions and then evaluate at the next meeting what seemed to work best.

- *End the meeting with plans for a family activity the coming week, or with a game, a family hug or a favorite dessert.*

In addition to their other benefits, family meetings are guaranteed to keep you in touch with each other and to help solve problems. But what if there are problems that are not getting better despite your best efforts?

When to Get Help

There are two times to get help: one is before you need it; the other is when a problem is spinning out of control and is beyond your family's ability to resolve on their own. Sometimes our fear or embarrassment or shame about being seen as a "bad" parent can get in the way of our seeking assistance. Remember that asking for help is a sign of strength.

Getting help before problems occur is a sound approach. This help may come in the form of reading books and articles, attending parenting classes and developing extended family who can give advice and feedback about your parenting when needed, as well as provide child-care relief. Other avenues include:

- talking to a parent who has or did have a child of the same age.
- joining a study group working with a specific parenting system.
- taking a break for an hour, a day or a weekend to renew yourself and regain your perspective.

Sometimes the problems that are identified as belonging to a child or children may, in fact, be difficulties the parent or parents need to "own." As a result, family counseling may turn into couples or individual counseling. Since we each bring our own family-of-origin idiosyncrasies to our new families, it is certain that we will have to sort them out as we grow as a family. Often it is these "ghosts" from our family of origin that are causing the current difficulties. A therapist can be a tremendous help in sorting this out. Or the problems may be rooted in differences between ourselves and our partners. If partners are of different class backgrounds, races, ages, or have different parenting styles, incorporating these differences into family life may need clarification and sorting out as well. Getting help can free us to enjoy our family life more and support us in communicating the values and sense of self-worth we want our children to take with them into adulthood.

How do you know when a problem is beyond your ability to solve? You may not be sure. You may underestimate, or overestimate, your ability and/or your child's needs. But if you have questions, get a second opinion. In general, we encourage you to seek professional help if your child's problems do not improve, if her behavior substantially worsens or if you feel overwhelmed or troubled by the situation. Resources for professional advice and counseling include school counselors, members of the clergy and therapists. (See Resources for advice and assistance in locating professional help.)

6 Helping Our Children Through Loss and Divorce

It may seem strange to think of loss when you are creating a family, but children in many lesbian families have to cope with more than the usual amount of loss. Our children are likely to have close relationships with gay men, either as donors or as part of the extended family, and sadly, they will face the reality of death at a young age if they see one of their beloved uncles or father-figures die of AIDS. In addition, many lesbian families are formed as the result of a heterosexual divorce; before they can be expected to embrace a new parent and family arrangement, children of heterosexual divorce need to cope with their loss. And, of course, lesbian relationships, like heterosexual relationships, are not always "forever,"; you may yourself in the sad and difficult position of having to tell your child that she will no longer live with her two moms together. This chapter offers guidelines for helping your child face and grieve a loss.

The Stages of Grief

When people suffer a major loss, such as the death of a loved one, they usually go through five stages of grieving, which were first described by Dr. Elisabeth Kübler-Ross.[1] Not everyone goes through the stages in a linear fashion, but there is some predictability.

The first stage in grieving is denial and shock. It is difficult to believe that someone will die or has died; and young children, who do not quite have reality and fantasy separated, are particularly prone to not understanding that they have lost a loved person.

In cultures that revere and rely on an ongoing sense of connection with their ancestors, dead family members may be discussed as if they are still present but in another, spirit, form. In other cultures the parent's job is to remind the child gently that the person is gone forever from this world. This may include using openings to remember the loved one in fond ways. Older children are not as prone to such forgetting, but denial can buffer them for a while as their systems absorb the hard reality of loss.

Parents may need to take the initiative in reminding children that a loss has occurred. It is not kind or helpful to pretend that the deceased is just sleeping or away on a trip. Nor is it helpful in the long run to interpret your child's silence as acceptance.

Nola's stepfather had just died after an unexpected heart attack. Her six-year-old daughter, Bryce, did not understand that she would never see her grandfather again. Several times, as Nola was packing their suitcases and making travel arrangements to go out West for the funeral, Bryce asked if Grandpa was going to meet them at the airport as he always did. Nola sat down with Bryce and gently told her again that Grandpa had died and that Uncle Joe would be at the airport. Nola packed Bryce's favorite photograph of two-year-old Bryce on her Grandpa's shoulders. Nola thought this might comfort Bryce when she realized that Grandpa was dead.

The second stage, anger, may be a particularly difficult time. It is normal for human beings to get angry when we lose something we cherish. Usually the more support we get for our anger, the more directly we will show it. Younger and less verbal children may act out their anger physically, throwing things, hitting themselves, hitting others, breaking things or running around. More verbal children and adults may use words as well to express their frustration and anger over the loss.

After Tom's father died from cancer, Tom moved from shock to anger. Tom saw his father only during the summers, but they talked weekly on the phone. His parents had divorced when Tom was ten, and now at thirteen he lived with his mother and her partner. As Tom moved into his anger, he took it out on his mother. He railed at her for leaving his dad and becoming a lesbian. He was sure if she had not left, his father would not have died.

Tom's anger is understandable. Luckily his mother knew that. She listened to his pain, and when he yelled at her, she quietly told him she supported his anger but not his attack on her. It was a hard time, but after a while he eased into the next stage of grief.

Bargaining is the third stage of the grieving process. Someone who is anticipating the death of a loved one is likely to enter a plea bargain with God or the universe. He will promise anything to keep the person alive. A twelve-year-old boy, for instance, may make a bargain to work harder in school if God will let his father live. Whether or not the man dies, that child will need support and help in understanding that he really does not have any control over whether his father lives or dies. A child needs clear and direct information that he cannot cause an illness or cure it with bargaining, and it is your responsibility to initiate these conversations with your children because they are unlikely to bring it up themselves.

Depression often follows bargaining. Your child may feel deflated and lifeless—as if all the air has gone out of the balloon—and it can be scary to watch, especially if she usually has lots of energy and enthusiasm. However, it is important to support your child through this phase as well and not push her to snap out of it because you are uncomfortable.

After moving through the depressed stage, most people begin to accept their loss. The grieving person reaches an awareness that she can live happily even without the lost loved one; that she can feel pain yet recover. It is at this time that the child or adult is ready to invest emotional energy and time in other relationships.

Fourteen-year-old Myra's friend had died two months earlier. She still missed her terribly, but she was beginning to be able to do regular activities without crying or getting massively frustrated. Myra's moms had supported her a lot. They let her alone sometimes and at other times pushed her to join them for walks, dinner or going to movies. Myra decided to make a collage of pictures about her friend as a memorial and display it during the last week of school. That helped her say good-bye and to have her friend be part of the end of the school year.

Sometimes grieving does not ease at all, and then it may be useful to get professional help in assessing what is interfering with the natural process.

Supporting Your Child Through the Grieving Process

When children suffer a loss—regardless of how serious that loss seems to the parent—what they need, above all, is holding. Emotional holding is being present with someone when he hurts. It is listening so that he gets to express how his loss affects him. It is looking at him and giving him your full attention. It is not telling him to "get over it" or "act your age" or "I'll get you another one."

Physical holding is best when it helps a child feel secure while he is hurting. Physical holding should not be used to stop someone from hurting or crying: he will stop crying when he does not need to do it anymore. Physical touch can be very reassuring to a child when he is grieving and may help him feel safe enough to express or even just feel his pain.

In some situations, particularly when a child experiences a loss over which they have some control, it may be useful to do some brainstorming after the listening and holding (this may be quite a while later). If your child, for example, has fought with his father, your ex-husband, and has decided not to see him for a while, the brainstorming can help your son think about how he can feel better and possibly provide remedies for the situation or prevent it from happening again.

Claudette stood looking at her thirteen-year-old son, Marcus. He was so hurt and angry he could barely keep from crying. She listened to him tell about his visit to his father's house, during which he had gotten into a fight with his new stepmother. They had argued about whether he could wear his "in" clothes out to dinner. She had said he had to change or not go to dinner. His father had not intervened and had made it clear that if Marcus did not stop fighting with his stepmother, he could not visit as much at his dad's house. Marcus clearly felt a strong sense of loss because his father had not backed him up.

He was on his third retelling, saying he hated his father and was not going over there again. Claudette remembered when Marcus was five and his grandfather had died. He had crawled up into Claudette's lap and cried while she held him. She wished she could hold him now, but his body language told her "no way." Claudette opted instead to hold him with her eyes. She looked at him with care and listened carefully. When she thought he was done talking, she told him she heard and understood his hurt and anger and his sense of loss. Then she suggested not giving up on his dad. She asked if there was a way he could tell his father how much it had hurt to have him side so strongly with his stepmother. Marcus decided to wait a few days and then to talk to his father. Claudette suggested that she and Marcus talk before then about different ways to approach his father. He said he would think about it.

Claudette wisely decided against trying to hold Marcus physically even though he needed the support. If she had tried to hold him they might have gotten side-tracked from his feelings and onto a discussion about her wanting to hold him and his not wanting to be held. She gave him emotional holding instead. Sometimes, however, Marcus does want a hug or to snuggle up when he is sad. Sometimes Claudette reads that correctly, and sometimes she misses. But she gets it right often enough that Marcus feels loved and supported as he deals with his losses.

Helping Your Child Face Death

The hardest loss a child faces is the death of a parent or other close family member. Regrettably, children of lesbians are likely to have to deal with the death of someone they love from AIDS, and it may be a father or extended family member. Because you will be facing the loss of a loved one as well, it is important that you get support for yourself while helping your child.

Talk to your child about the loved one's illness and impending death: explain what is happening to the person—tailoring the details according to your child's age—and encourage the child to interact with him. Preparing food, stroking the person, talking or reading to him, fluffing up a pillow and walking the dog are all activities that let the child feel useful. When the person is in the hospital, have your child visit and make as much contact as possible. This can include sitting on the bed, examining medical equipment such as stethoscopes, walking around the hospital to check where the person is staying and so on.

Besides the concrete contact it is important for you to talk to your child about death. If you have spiritual or religious beliefs, it is helpful to communicate those. The more you can place death as a part of life, the less scared your child will be. The younger the child, the fewer preconceptions she has about death and the more likely it is that you can shape her view of this transition.

In Mary Kate Jordan's book *Losing Uncle Tim*, a young boy's uncle dies from AIDS.[2] During his illness he spends time almost as usual with his nephew. The uncle, who is an antique dealer, notices that his nephew likes certain articles in his store, and when the man dies, he leaves these items to him. It is clear that the items will be reminders of this favorite uncle and that already they are soothing connections with him. Children do well with concrete symbols and reminders of people they love. When there is advance warning of a death, the dying person himself can give something to the child.

If a death is sudden and unexpected, your child's and your grieving process may be more complicated. An unanticipated death precludes preparation and closure, and you may find yourself making funeral plans and attending to children's questions and shock—all while doing your own grieving. It may be very important to ask for help in handling the immediate demands of running a household in these situations.

Returning to day-to-day life after the death of a family member may be more difficult than the time immediately after the loss. As shock and the acute sense of loss wear off, you and your child are faced with the reality of how the person who died used to participate in your family's life and no longer does. If your partner used to make coffee and bring it up to you in bed every Sunday morning, you may find yourself dreading Sundays for a long time. If your child's biological father used to hide Easter eggs for your family to find, that holiday may bring much pain for years. It is important to talk about your grief at these times, to cry when you feel like it and perhaps to raise the issue with your child if she does not do it on her own.

As we said earlier, before and/or after the person dies, your child will need your support as she moves through the stages of grief. Hope

Edelman quotes Nan Birnbaum in her book *Motherless Daughters* as saying that children grieve differently from adults: while adults often plunge into the stages of grieving, children usually delay the grieving process for six to nine months, partly because they are waiting for the surviving caretaker or parent to recover enough to provide a stable environment in which to risk the pain of grieving. Edelman reminds us that children will grieve to the best of their ability at any given developmental stage and will grieve again as they develop the capacities to understand and absorb the death in new ways.[3] You need to honor the recycling of grief as your child continues the process of integrating her loss.

> *Toby was ten when her mother's ex-partner, Nancy, died. Toby and Nancy had gone to the zoo, played house and gone trick-or-treating together. Toby was sad, but it got really hard for her when she did the things that she and Nancy had done together. Luckily, Toby knew her mother understood when she cried in front of the lions' den.*

Death of a Child

The hardest ordeal a parent can face is the death of her child. We cannot begin to touch the searing pain of this loss in a brief discussion here. If you lose your child, we hope you will reach out for support from friends, family and others who have lived through what you are facing.

We think among the most difficult questions parents face are whether and how to tell a child she is dying, if you have this knowledge beforehand. We encourage you to tell your child for several reasons. First, your child may know a lot more than you think, and not telling her leaves her guessing about what she does not know. Second, depending on her age, a child may have many fears you can allay—she may worry about losing you or getting cold in the grave or about not ever being able to go to college. The last reason is to give everyone the opportunity to say good-bye. Everyone benefits from being able to express closure. Parents feel more complete when the child dies, and the child can let go knowing her parents are there with her.

How you tell your child he is dying depends on your child's age and his individual temperament. Parents need to give each child the amount of information he is comfortable with and to quit when each one signals, in his own way, that he needs to change the subject for now.

Most children respond well to accurate information that is presented in age-appropriate ways. Talking about death and reading books alone or together may be helpful. Allow your child to grieve: this may mean acting out with dolls, getting angry, crying, writing letters to friends and family members or being alone for long periods of time.

Divorce

For children of mothers who come out during or after a heterosexual relationship, the experience of their parents' divorce is often more traumatic than finding out their mom is a lesbian. And children of lesbian-first moms are no less traumatized if their mothers' partnership ends.

Divorce when children are involved means letting go and holding on at the same time. You have to separate from someone you have loved and may still love. At the same time you need to hold on to what your ex-partner gave to your (and his or her) children, *even* if one of the reasons you divorced was differences over parenting. You have to let go of the fantasy that you can erase your children's pain during what may be the hardest time in their lives. And you have to support and care for these children while they experience a wide range of feelings, which may include hating you. You do all of this while rebuilding your own life.

In this section, we discuss divorce both for lesbian mothers breaking out of a heterosexual union and for lesbian mothers whose lesbian-first partnership breaks up. Although divorce is not a word usually associated with lesbian breakups, these relationship endings are in every sense of the word a divorce, especially when a couple has children. Thus, we use divorce to describe the ending of committed relationships regardless of the gender of the partners.

Navigating Divorce: The Challenges for Parents

Judith Wallerstein and Sandra Blakeslee's book *Second Chances* summarizes the results of a ten-year follow-up study on the impact of divorce on men, women and children.[4] Although their book reports on research about heterosexual men and women, we think the issues they raise are applicable to lesbian parents as well. The authors outline the following challenges parents and children face as they navigate divorce and its aftermath:

1: *Ending the marriage.*
Parents need to try to be as fair and understanding as possible and separate their needs from their children's.

2: *Mourning the loss.*
Parents need to feel the sadness, grief and anger that come from losing a beloved or even just the familiar.

3: *Reclaiming oneself.*
Parents need to discover who they are as individuals. This may include getting rid of the parts of their self-image that have been defined by their ex-partner's criticism, demands or nagging.

4: *Resolving or containing passions.*
Parents need to come to terms with their anger or other intense feelings that have erupted as a result of divorce. Strong feelings may arise sporadically as life events trigger pain. Parents must find ways to deal with their pain and not act out in unhealthy ways.

5: *Venturing forth again.*
Parents need to move on to new roles, new relationships and new ways of doing things in order to build good self-esteem.

6: *Rebuilding socially and psychologically.*
This is the opportunity to build a new life with new and old friends and a new intimate relationship with another adult.

7: *Helping the children.*
Parents need to support their children as they navigate the dissolution of the family. Parents must make long-range commitments to provide emotional and financial resources for their children.

What Divorce Does to Kids

Children whose parents divorce are in a peculiar situation: rarely does a child want her parents to separate, so the youngster is forced into a life-altering change she does not want by the people she loves most in the world. Sometimes the degree of damage is not obvious for years, and other times the damage is intense and relatively short-lived. Wallerstein and Blakeslee report that in the follow-up of the children in their study, the child's age affected how she reacted to the divorce and continued to be influenced by it.[5]

Preschool children are most scared of being abandoned. If one parent moves out, these children assume the other one can go away, too. As a result, these children may have difficulty separating from their parents, during the day and at bedtime at night. Young children may return to previous behaviors, such as thumb-sucking or waking at night. Sometimes youngsters imagine that their bad behavior caused the divorce, and they may get sad or depressed. The authors reported that young children who do not have strong memories of the intact marriage may adjust well in the long-term, in spite of their having strong reactions immediately following the divorce.

Kindergartners through third graders are more aware of the losses and may feel rejected and guilty. Sometimes they are torn between their loyalities to each parent. If one parent moves out, the child may worry about being replaced in that parent's affections by a new baby or partner. Many of these children in Wallerstein and Blakeslee's study suffered downhill slides in their school work. They may cry a lot, feel empty and have difficulty concentrating.

Children in the nine-to-twelve-year-old age range tend to get more anxious when their parents divorce. They grieve strongly and feel lonely. This age group may have somatic complaints, especially stomachaches and headaches, according to Wallerstein and Blakeslee. Their peer relationships may deteriorate, but they may be particularly adept at comforting and caring for a grieving parent.

Adolescents often have very strong reactions to their parents' divorce. They become frightened that the structure they need to navigate adolescence may evaporate along with the original family. They often get very angry with their parents, especially the one the teenager perceives as causing the divorce. Teenagers may get quite uncomfortable if they see their parents as having sexual impulses, just as they are trying to make sense of their own sexuality. Children in their teens are concerned about the future and they worry about whether they will be able to have enduring relationships.

Foremost, for children, divorce means loss and grieving. If you are excited and completely absorbed by a new relationship while your son is grieving the loss of your old family, you may be impatient with his mourning. It is a constant reminder of your loss, which you may not be grieving right at the moment, and of your guilt—what you, the parents, have done to this young person you love so much.

According to Wallerstein and Blakeslee a number of factors weighed heavily on the outcome of a child's adjustment in the heterosexual divorces in their study: the lack of open conflict between parents; a child's having good relationships with both parents; a close relationship with a mother who was emotionally available to take care of the children; an organized, non-chaotic life; good relationships with stepparents; and active, caring grandparents.[6]

Children suffer if verbal or physical violence is present in the parents' relationship before, during or after a divorce. Using the children to engage in a power struggle is the most subtle form of parental abuse, but children are damaged by all types of violence and it can hurt their ability to trust themselves, their parents and others for years or forever.

A parent's not continuing his or her relationship with a child can also be devastating to a youngster. The crucial issue is the quality and reliability of the on-going relationship between a non-custodial parent and her or his children, not the amount of time they spend together.[7] A child's adjustment to a divorce does not seem to be dependent on any specific custody arrangement, but more on how much his parents cooperate or fight, the quality of parenting each parent brings to the relationship and what the child has to cope with in the rest of his world.[8]

As do their parents, children also face psychological challenges as they heal from the effects of divorce.[9] They include:

1: *Understanding the divorce.*
The first part of understanding is separating fantasy from reality and learning about the concrete changes that come with the divorce. The second part comes later when the child has enough distance and maturity to understand what her parents did and why.

2: *Strategic withdrawal.*
Children need to get on with being children, which means they need support to go back to normal childhood and adolescent activities. The divorce should not be the center of their attention.

3: *Dealing with loss.*

The principal loss is the intact family and the dreams of the future as a family. If there is only one custodial parent, the child may feel he has lost the other parent. Children often blame themselves for these losses and try to get their parents back together again. When custody is shared and/or parents and children have good relationships it is easier for the child to feel supported enough to integrate the losses and move on with his life.

4: *Dealing with anger.*

Children are understandably angry with parents who have disrupted their lives so much. The task here is to experience their anger and begin to see their parents as fallible human beings who made hard decisions. Along with this comes forgiveness, of themselves for getting so angry, and of their parents.

5: *Working-out guilt.*

There are two kinds of guilt. The first is that of worrying about being the cause of the divorce. The second is the guilt that ties a child to one parent or the other out of loyalty or concern. Children need to work through and past both, and parents need to help by reassuring the child he is not to blame and is not responsible for a parent's well-being.

6: *Acceptance of the permanence of the divorce.*

Denial can last for years. Parents need to be clear about the finality of their decision so that their children can be clear as well.

7: *Taking a chance on love.*

This is the gateway to the "second chances" Wallerstein and Blakeslee write about. Children of divorce need to risk letting themselves fall in love in the face of the memory of parental divorce and the risk of future divorce. The authors maintain this is the central task for adolescents and young adults whose parents divorced.

Telling Your Child About Divorce

Parents should have three goals when they tell their children about an impending divorce:[10]

1: Assuring the children of both parents' continued love.

2: Relieving the children of blame.

3: Easing the trauma of the life changes that will follow.

To facilitate these goals, both parents should tell their children at the same time. This reassures the children of both parents' involvement and also ensures that they get one story. Children need to get straightforward information, but they do not need details of relationship strife. Tell your children at home when you have time to listen and be with them. If you have more than one child, tell them together so that they have each other for support. Remember, as with all major losses, their first response may well be denial; you may have to tell them a number of times as the reality sets in.

Children usually are most concerned about how the divorce will affect them. They may ask where they will live, who will move out, if they will lose a parent, possessions, a pet and so on. Be ready for lots of questions or maybe none for a while. Their feelings will fluctuate, and younger children in particular will not be able to stay with their sadness for very long.

> *Julie and her partner had just told their son and daughter that they were getting a divorce. The two children had gone downstairs to watch TV as an escape. The seven-year-old came up the steps and announced, "I'm done with being sad." Julie said she understood that and gently told him that sadness about divorce had a way of coming back again. He sighed and said he knew, but he was done with it anyway.*

It is important to give the children some advance warning about when the physical separation will happen. Do not wait until one of you is on the way out the door. Younger children need about a week and not much longer, as they can get confused and stay in denial. Older children and adolescents can tolerate a little longer. We think one to three weeks is about as long as the family can tolerate waiting for the changes in living arrangements to happen.

Remember that children process and react to this information in different ways both in the beginning and as they adjust to their parents' divorce. Individual temperament and age will also affect their response.

◆　◆　◆

Catherine and Molly had just told their sons they were going to separate and get a divorce. That night as Molly was saying good-night to the eleven-year-old, Steve, he cried and talked and talked. His seven-year-old brother, Mark, had asked to sleep in Steve's room and had fallen asleep quickly as usual. Steve asked why Mark wasn't as affected as he was. Why wasn't he lying awake in pain like his older brother? Molly held Steve and eventually he fell asleep, too.

At two o'clock Molly heard the younger boy crying in his sleep. She went in and heard him say that the walls were caving in. She tried to comfort him, but he kept crying and worrying that the planet was going to spin out of its orbit. Molly did not want to wake Steve, so she took Mark in her room and held him. He talked again about the walls falling down and the planet flying off into space. Molly told him to look around and see if the walls were different. He did, and then she told him that what he was worried about was from feelings inside himself and that he was making them be outside him. She promised him the walls would not fall down and the earth would not fly away. He said, "Really?" and she said, "Really." Mark sighed, rolled over and fell asleep.

Adolescents are more likely to react immediately to the news of divorce, and younger children are more likely to move in and out of their feelings. There is no correct way for a child to respond to his parents' divorce. It is, however, the parents' job to figure out how to take care of themselves *and* their children. Over time and with attention and support, this transition will be incorporated into your and your children's new lives.

Lesbian Divorce

An unfortunate, but inevitable, side effect of the lesbian baby boom is an increase in lesbian divorces that involve children. Children whose mothers are lesbian have to deal with the same losses as any child in a divorce, but certain issues are unique to lesbian couples.

One main difference between heterosexual and lesbian divorce is the very high percentage of joint-custody arrangements in lesbian divorce. Just as many non-parent lesbians continue to be very connected after their divorces, lesbian mothers may also stay connected to each other,[11] which can strengthen the co-parenting arrangement.

◆　◆　◆

Stella and Yvonne decided to separate after sixteen years of being part-ners. They agreed to leave their two daughters in the shared house for the first year and to have the mothers move in and out alternating weeks. After that they thought that they would get separate homes and have the girls move back and forth. Sharing the house for that year was difficult because it meant an enormous amount of mutual cooperation at the time they needed to develop separate lives. But they thought leaving the youngsters in the house would ease the transition to a two-family lifestyle.

There are times when the mothers do not want any contact and house-sharing is unthinkable. The challenge is to put the lover rela-tionship behind and concentrate on finding a co-parenting relation-ship that takes care of the children.

Cassie and Lynn ended their ten-year relationship with a lot of bitterness. Cassie was so angry with Lynn she couldn't and wouldn't talk to her ex-cept when absolutely necessary. To make matters worse, Lynn kept want-ing to talk and work out parenting plans for their daughter. They agreed that Mae had a right to both mothers and so would live with each one half-time, but that was the extent of the agreement. Cassie would not let Mae call or see Lynn for any reason when Mae was at Cassie's house un-less it was a special event like a birthday. Both women were in agony but could not find a way to do more than the minimum communication as co-parents.

Cassie and Lynn are working through an initial period in which Cassie cannot tolerate contact. Their relationship may stay like this forever or evolve into a relationship that is more focused on their daugh-ter.

If both women agree that their child has a right to both parents, the women do need to work out a parenting plan, and then stick to it or negotiate a change. If you are in Lynn's position, you need to be pa-tient but firm in taking care of your child and yourself. Ask for media-tion between you and your ex-partner, which includes provisions that spell out each woman's rights if the other one does not follow through with her agreements. In extreme cases where you are not being al-lowed access to your child or she is in danger, you may be able to use attorneys and the court system to get an agreement in place. However, we urge you to use all other methods of negotiation first, because courts are not predictable in their dealings with lesbian parents, and you could find yourself with less control, not more.

If you are in Cassie's position, and you absolutely refuse to have any more contact with your child's other mother, you are better off negotiating a more complete parenting plan that includes more provisions than simply "half-time custody." The more guidelines you and your child's other mother have agreed to, the fewer chances for misunderstandings and therefore fewer reasons for contact with your ex-partner. We also encourage you to get counseling that helps you work through your disappointment and anger.

When you let your anger and pain interfere with your child's access to her other mother, you are hurting your child. You may be prohibiting contact to protect yourself from pain, to hurt your ex-partner or it may be to have some sense of control in an out-of-control situation. Whatever the reason, you compromise your child's ability to work through the divorce and may be setting up a situation where she will push you away later. It is in your child's best interests for you and your ex-partner to make the transition from life partner to parenting partner.

Especially during the first year after a divorce people do and say many things that will not be as true for them later on. Just as with any relationship, we need to leave room for each other to change and grow. In *The Good Divorce* the author, Constance Ahrons, says the secret to a good divorce is to love your children more than you hate your ex.[12]

In particular, children of lesbian mothers may wonder if the children will stay together or if each woman will take her biological children and live separately, even if both women have legally adopted the other's biological children. Lesbian mothers need to determine and tell the children what the living arrangements will be for the near future after the divorce.

Yours, Mine and Ours

When the children in a divorcing lesbian couple's family came from one or both women's previous relationships, the non-legal parent may not be invested in keeping a relationship with her ex-partner's children and the children may not want to spend time with her either. This is particularly true when the women have not been partnered for very long.

Or the children and their mother's ex-lover may be close and want to continue a relationship. As in other divorces, it is important to support ongoing relationships when possible. Assuming that these children have other, primary parents, the loss of their mother's partner may not be traumatic. Or the loss could be very hurtful. You need to evaluate each situation and relationship, but we encourage you to err in the direction of supporting your children's ongoing relationship with the woman they have come to know as family.

Legal Issues in Lesbian Divorce

When only one of the mothers in a lesbian family is the legal parent, there is the risk she will try to and succeed at keeping the other mother away from their child. Obviously, when there is abuse by the other parent, keeping that parent and child apart may be called for, but in most cases we think this is a grave injustice to the child and parents. We encourage everyone to use whatever therapy or mediation is available to work out an arrangement that allows the child to keep both parents.

Eight years after their son was born, Pat and Sal split up. They had gone from being passionate lovers to indifferent partners to enraged ex-partners. Pat, the biological mother, was tempted to take Marshall and move to San Francisco from their home in Boston. Sal was frantic, as she adored her son and could not bear the thought of his being so far away. She begged Pat to go into counseling to figure out how to make co-parenting work. Once it was clear that the counseling was about parenting, and not about couples, Pat relaxed a bit. She knew she did not want to be in a relationship with Sal, but she did want to take care of Marshall. In counseling, Pat and Sal came up with a parenting plan that gave each woman half-time custody and clear guidelines about when they needed to consult each other; for example, school, medical decisions and holidays. Pat agreed not to move for at least three years; if she still wanted to move somewhere else after three years had passed, they would engage Marshall in some of the discussions at that point. They agreed to evaluate their plan with the counselor in six months.

◆　◆　◆

If the "legal mother" in a lesbian family falls in love with a man and leaves the lesbian relationship to live in a heterosexual relationship or marriage she may be able to use the mainstream culture's heterosexism to legally prevent the other mother from seeing the children. This degrades her history as well as creating a huge loss for the children and their other mother.

Since most lesbian mothers have not been able to carry out a second-parent adoption, the non-legal parent is in a precarious situation. There is no law that forces child support or protects the child's relationship with both mothers. However, it is possible that a court will find that a legal mother must allow visitation or custody to the other mother, and it is possible that it might award child support to the custodial parent.

Although it may cast a pall over your relationship, we encourage you to think about what you intend to do to care for your child in the event of divorce or parental death. Some people write out their intentions about separations and sign them, and others have formal parenting agreements that include provisions in case of a divorce. Suggestions for items to be included in such a parenting agreement are listed in Appendix C.

We recommend thinking through the issues that are important in your parenting relationship and also getting advice from an attorney as to what you should include. There is no guarantee that your wishes will be honored in the heat of a divorce, but most people do want the best for their children. If you have already talked this over, you stand a better chance of reason winning out over emotion.

Divorce can also bring out the good in people. We know of women who have used a divorce to learn about themselves and their relationship with their children. They have created empowering relationships with their ex-partners that serve to nurture and care for their children.

As with all loss, divorce and death represent endings, but they are also beginnings. As we move through our losses, it is hard to remember that we are building the start of what comes next and that the terrible pain may in the long run bring us joy. We can, however, do our best to take care of ourselves and our children so that we have the best chance of taking advantage of the opportunities each new beginning offers us.

7 Confronting Racism and Building Rainbows

Parents of every generation want to prepare their children for the future. For today's parents that means preparing children to live in a racial and cultural climate never before experienced in the United States. Racial demographics in this country are changing at a breathtaking rate. For example, by the end of this decade, less than half the students in California will be of European origin and by the year 2050, the U.S. Department of Labor has predicted that seventy-five percent of the country's work force will be people of color.[1] Cities, of course, are seeing the widest range of diversity, but less populated areas are changing, too. Although some neighborhoods are still racially homogeneous, statistics indicate that, unless there is an astonishing reversal, children of today will truly be part of a "rainbow" generation in the twenty-first century. So, from a purely practical as well as an ethical perspective, we need to teach our children how to respect, appreciate and live in harmony with people who are different from themselves.

We are well aware that factors such as culture, class, ethnicity, age, gender, physical and mental ability, sexual orientation and religious traditions are major contributors not only to who we are but to how we are treated by others. However, race merits particular attention because of the systematic oppression that racism in this country has caused and perpetuated. If we, as parents, can help build bridges— and rainbows—among different races, we will have made a major contribution toward a better world for ourselves and for our children.

How Racist Are We?

In talking with our children about race, we are not able to start from a neutral place. For many reasons, including the history of slavery, limited contact between racial groups, rapidly changing demographics and the perceived threat of economic and social change, racial stereotypes, negative attitudes, and tension and conflict between races exist already. Because we are all products of our environment, many of us, perhaps most of us, grew up with stereotypes that invited us to fear or make fun of people different from ourselves. Even though we may now reject bias on principle, we are still biased to some degree. So before we can talk with our children, we must first look at ourselves. One way to do this is to ask ourselves how we would complete the following sentence: "When I talk to my child about race, I feel..."[2] Perhaps we might feel sad, nervous, guilty or angry. If we identify our own feelings and come to a truce with them, we can talk with our children more effectively.

When prejudice and discrimination are allowed to exist in any form, that toleration gives tacit approval to all other forms. So, as lesbians, it can be encouraging to remember that to confront racism is also to stand up against homophobia, sexism and other discrimination and oppression based on membership in a particular group. Building rainbows requires us to confront racism wherever we find it—in ourselves, our schools and our communities. And we need to help our children do the same.

Defining Our Terms

Prejudice refers to preconceived ideas and attitudes about a particular race, ethnic background, religion, occupation or group membership. We demonstrate prejudice when we make judgments about others in a generalized way without sufficient reason or information. Most of us learn our prejudices as we grow up and accept the opinions and values of our own group. We may act out our prejudices—that is discrimination—or we may keep them to ourselves. Discrimination, action based on prejudice, is mistreatment. It diminishes both the giver and receiver.

Racism involves prejudice toward and discrimination against people of a different race combined with the power to impose and societally reinforce the discrimination. Racism is prejudice with power and can be expressed—openly or covertly—individually, culturally and institutionally. When a Native-American female senior attorney at a large firm is passed over in favor of a less experienced white male attorney by a white client, we have an example of individual racism (and sexism). Cultural racism is operating when the only recognized experts on Inuit customs are white. And when a workplace has no people of color, or no people of color in management positions, and that practice is never questioned, institutional racism is at work.

By systematic oppression, we mean that the mistreatment of a group of people is embedded in the values, beliefs, laws, code of ethics, social norms, traditions, institutions and/or organizational structures of a society; in other words, the mistreatment is socially sanctioned and maintains an imbalance of power between the group targeted for discrimination and the perpetrators of the oppression. For example, in the United States, lesbians and gays are systematically oppressed based on sexual orientation and people of color are systematically oppressed based on race. And although people of color may show prejudice toward white people or people of races other than their own, they lack the societal power to systematically oppress those groups.

How Racism Affects Individuals

Which groups of people are affected by racism and how drastic those effects are depend on the social and economic power structure of the society. Typically, and unfortunately, the dominant culture creates a hierarchy based on race. The lower a group is in the hierarchy, the more severe the discrimination and the more negative the stereotypes about that group are likely to be. This contributes to competition within and between racial groups for scarce resources such as jobs and educational opportunities. Historically, in European-dominated cultures, the lighter your skin color, the better. If a woman of color has internalized this belief, she may put herself down for being dark, may discriminate against those darker-skinned than herself and prefer to associate with lighter-skinned individuals. Internalized racism is in some ways like internalized homophobia: the oppressed individual believes the myths of the dominant culture.

There are additional pressures for people of color in a racist society. They may be regarded by others as tokens, to be utilized when needed for racial representation. They may be seen as the vessels of some special knowledge and experience that is wanted, but not always respected, by others. And many people of color also feel great pressure to be accepted, since they are seen as representatives of their group rather than as individuals. Many experience having to perform much better than European Americans, just to be seen as equally competent. Even then, they may not get recognition for their accomplishments. As people of color experience racism over time and witness its effects on those around them, a phenomenon called "armoring" occurs.[3]

A woman of color builds a shell, or armor, around herself as protection from the onslaughts of racism. She learns to watch every new situation and person for potential racist comments or dangers and to pace her responses to them. A white woman, on the other hand, has not had to build up this armor. In fact, she may not even notice the racism in a comment or in someone's behavior. Or, if she does, she may not know how to deal with the situation. These differences can lead to difficulties in interracial relationships.

How Racism Affects Families

In our book *Lesbian Couples,* we explored the impact of racism on interracial couples, including the effects of stereotypes and expectations based on race, economic power differences based on racism, and pressures and expectations from the couple's respective communities.[4] These same hurdles exist in multiracial lesbian families.

In multiracial lesbian families, the parents may be of different races, and the child the same race as one of the parents. Or the parents might be one race and the child a different one, which is often the case with families formed by intercountry adoption.

Linda and Eileen describe their family as multiracial. Linda identifies as biracial; her heritage is Puerto Rican and Irish. Eileen is originally from Denmark and describes herself as a Danish American. They have two sons, both of whom were carried by Eileen using a Puerto Rican donor.

Diana and Ruth are both of Eastern European heritage. Ruth is Jewish; Diana is not. Theirs is a multiracial/multicultural family via adoption. Their two daughters were born in Peru.

Jean describes her family as multiracial and multicultural. She herself is African American. Her daughter by adoption is African American; one of her foster daughters is also African American and the other is Vietnamese American.

Some of the issues in these families are different; many are the same. First we look at families formed through adoption.

Thinking About Adoption and Race

It takes extra sensitivity and understanding to parent a child of a different race in our race-conscious society. When you take on raising a child from another culture and/or of another race, you are permanently taking on the responsibility of including that other culture in your life, which has many practical implications; for example, you may select where you live and what school your child attends based on the racial mix of the neighborhood or school.

If the adoption is intercountry as well as transracial, there may also be political implications to be considered regarding how children come to be available for adoption. As a potential adoptive parent, you need to examine and feel comfortable about the system or situation in the country where you want to adopt.

In considering transracial adoption, there are a number of questions that you, as a lesbian parent-to-be, need to ask yourself. Since families are forever, parents in a multiracial family by adoption get to explore these questions in an ongoing way, not just prior to adoption. These questions include:

- *What racist attitudes, or other prejudices in myself do I need to confront and change?*

When Ellen began to talk with people at work about her plans to adopt a child from South America, one reaction she got was how brave and noble she was to rescue a child from a life of poverty in a third-world country. Something about that response bothered her, yet she did feel really good about providing a loving home for a child who might otherwise not have one. It took a conversation with her friend Terry to make Ellen examine her attitude more closely. Terry had strong reservations about transracial/transcultural adoptions and got particularly angered by the idea that white people were doing something heroic by adopting children of color from other countries. As she put it, "It's just another form of exploitation."

Ellen then understood what it was about the conversation with her co-workers that had bothered her. She had basked in the glow of their putting her on a pedestal, and that pedestal was built on the belief that her own middle-class, white culture was preferable because it was more affluent. She started to question how much she had really dealt with her own racist and classist attitudes.

Lesbians who have dealt with their own internalized homophobia are in some ways in a good position to help a child of color develop healthy self-esteem. We know the challenge of developing a sense of pride in who we are in a world that does not validate us, and have had to learn to deal with the subtle and blatant prejudice of others. We understand internalized oppression, and know how important it is to have role models and to be with people who are like ourselves as well as with those who are different. All of this knowledge and experience can be applied in raising children to have a strong sense of who they are and can be.

Yet, we also must acknowledge that understanding one kind of oppression does not automatically transfer into understanding another. A white lesbian will never live as a person of color: unlike most lesbians, who can conceal their sexual orientation if necessary, people of color usually cannot hide. Because of this visibility, transracially adopted children will have a different experience of discrimination than their white lesbian parents do.

- *What racist attitudes, or other prejudices will I have to confront in my extended family?*

Lesbians thinking about forming a multiracial family need to anticipate reactions from their own parents and extended family because family members are an important part of the parents' support system.

Grandparents and other relatives often provide financial as well as moral support, not to mention baby-sitting! If that support is not going to be available because of your relatives' racist attitudes, you need to evaluate the impact that will have on you and your child.

Mary Beth and Delsey were devastated when they talked with Mary Beth's parents about their plans for adopting a child from China. Because they had felt such acceptance of their lesbian relationship, they had not anticipated the negative reaction to the adoption. It took a while to sort it out, but finally it became clear that Mary Beth's mother wasn't sure that she could connect with a grandchild of a different race. What a relief it was when Jenny arrived, and Mary Beth's mother fell in love at first sight.

But what if Mary Beth's mother hadn't fallen in love at first sight with her new grandchild? That possibility is one Mary Beth and Delsey needed to assess, in advance. How serious would that problem have been for them and for their child? Delsey's family was very supportive and also close by; their friends who had children were already planning a baby-sitting exchange, and both women had good jobs, so finances were not a concern. Because of this extra cushion of support, they had decided to go ahead with their adoption plans.

- *Am I willing to acknowledge and maintain ties to the child's ethnic heritage?*

All parents want their children to have a sense of positive identity, including pride in their cultural and racial heritage. Children need access to their cultures of origin and—for biracial/ bicultural children— attention to what it means to have a dual heritage. To provide this access requires effort. Giving your children information about their heritage might simply mean trips to the local library and various cultural centers, but giving them experiences and relationships with people of their race or cultural background will likely be more of a challenge— particularly if you do not share your child's race or ethnicity.

As a white parent, you may be resented by some members of the very community with which you are seeking connection. Your child may be viewed by some as "lost" to their group. You need to be prepared for—and remain undaunted by—these possibilities. Particularly if the cultural or racial community is not welcoming, you may find that your commitment wavers and that your interest declines over time. It is important to find the stamina to keep at it. Your child and your family will be the richer for it.

Over a period of six years, Lynn and Diane adopted three children from India. In an attempt to provide their children with connections to their ethnic heritage, they explored establishing ties with the local Indian community. They discovered that going to public events was fine, but really belonging to that community required a knowledge of the language and the culture that they did not possess. Also, they had concerns about being out as a lesbian couple. Eventually Lynn and Diane concluded that they could and needed to expose the children to the Indian culture and community but that they could not give the children a culture that they themselves did not possess. So they settled into a combination of attending as many Indian community events as they could, celebrating holidays from a variety of other cultures both as a family and with friends, and being more actively involved as a family in their Unitarian Church community.

Living in an Interracial Adoptive Family

Interracial families confront questions and situations based on their race—from the more benign to the very painful—every single day. When a parent is with her children and they are a different color than she is, she may be asked—by total strangers—"Are you a day-care teacher?" or "Are these children yours?" or "Does she look like her father?" Parents may greet these questions with responses ranging from irritation to resignation. Most tend to respond with some version of "These are my children." It's probably best not to take such questions too personally. In our society, people seem to need to categorize others in terms of race. It's as if once they figure out what category a person is in, they can relax.

Martha is a very fair-skinned redhead and her adopted sons are the color of dark coffee. Once when they were on a plane trip, the woman in the seat next to them asked Martha, "Do the children look like their father?" Distracted with getting the children settled and without thinking much about it, Martha responded, "I have no idea." Although this was quite true, it wasn't exactly what the woman expected, and it nipped the potentially irritating conversation in the bud!

Topics of ongoing conversation in biracial lesbian families need to be racism and homophobia. Even though your children may live in a racially diverse community where it is also okay to be gay or lesbian, it is important to talk with them about how people of color may be treated in the larger world. Although lesbian parents may do their best to provide their children with an atmosphere that is neither racist nor homophobic, it is essential for children to be prepared to deal with the reality that not everyone celebrates differences. Lesbian parents also need to advocate for their children in the schools. Teachers, principals and school counselors often need to be educated around matters of race as well as about lesbian families.

"You Picked Me Out!": How Children Perceive Race and Adoption

Until they are about three years of age, children notice racial differences, like skin color, but do not understand the concept of race. Adopted children can repeat what their parents have told them about adoption, but don't really comprehend what adoption means until they have some idea of conception.

> *Jeremy first heard the word "adopted" in improvised lullabies that his mother, Joan, sang. His "othermother," Sheila, loved to tell him his adoption story using the baby book they made with pictures of his foster family in Honduras, his arrival at their house in San Francisco and special events since then. When he was three, Jeremy was proud to translate "adopted" as "you picked me out!"*

Between four and six years of age a child can identify her own racial or ethnic group and notices the racial differences between her and her parents. She may notice that most of her peers are the same race or color of at least one parent, and she may express the desire to be the same as those she loves. In addition to helping her appreciate and value the ways she is different from them, parents can satisfy the craving of every child to be told that she bears some resemblance to her parents by pointing out shared physical similarities, "Mommy Donna has light hair, and you have dark hair like me," or interests, "You and I both love to sing," or characteristics, "You have a great sense of humor like your Mama Laura." Because a child at this age has a beginning concept of conception and pregnancy, she begins to understand what adoption means, that is, that—unlike most of her peers—she wasn't born to her parents. She may get questions about her family membership from her peers, as well as adults, that she needs to be prepared to handle. Explain that she may tell as much or as little as she chooses about her adoption story. Help her realize that she can be proud to tell anyone that she and her parents are more than satisfied with every detail of her history.

When a child is clear about how babies are born, the inevitable question will come up: "Who was the mother that carried me in her tummy, and why didn't she keep me?" She may also experience sadness and anger over the loss of her birth parents.

Between the ages of seven and eleven, a child needs answers to some of the toughest adoption questions. He develops a firmer understanding of his identity and explores what it means to be a member of his racial group. This is a crucial time for multicultural education and experiences because he needs help in understanding his heritage and background. Then he can understand and feel comfortable answering the question "What are you?" from other kids. School is fertile ground for curiosity. Adopted children who are visibly different from their parents need strategies for preserving their privacy and dealing with nosy questions. These questions bother us—and trouble our children—because we know that people ask personal questions only in situations that they perceive to be abnormal.[5] It would never occur to people to ask a white mother with a white baby, "Did you give birth to that child?" Later in this chapter we outline some suggestions to help children field intrusive questions and restore a sense of self-esteem and power.

In adolescence, the quest for identity includes racial and cultural identity. The adolescent is trying to figure out "who am I?" At this age the child understands what adoption means, personally and legally. Her curiosity about her birth parents and background may become stronger. Questions about dating may arise. Neighbors who were happy to have their son play with your biracial daughter when they were younger may not want him to date her when they are older. Normal teenage embarrassment about parents may be exacerbated by multiracial family status, not to mention having lesbian parents.

Transracial adoption has been a very controversial topic, particularly in the African-American community. Many question whether children of color can develop positive racial identities in families in which the parents are white. The results of a recent survey are encouraging. The researchers studied seven hundred families who have teenagers who were adopted as infants. Twenty-nine percent of the youth in the study were transracially adopted. The great majority of them (eighty percent) report being glad they are the race they are. Seventy-eight percent describe themselves as getting along equally well with people of their own racial background and with people of other ethnic backgrounds.[6]

Whatever questions your child has and whatever she is going through, you need to be realistic and prepared so you can help her. Once you have faced and quieted your own concerns and fears about adoption, about racial differences and about being a lesbian parent, you are in the best position to help your children do the same.

Interracial Couples with Children

Lesbian partners of different races who decide to have children together often opt to have a sperm donor of the same race as the non-biological parent. The child's racial heritage then reflects both parents. This can be a very important issue for a parent of color, particularly if she is not the birth mother. Many women of color feel internalized pressure to continue their group by having children, especially if that group suffers from genocide, high infant-mortality rates and racism. She may feel strong family or community pressure to have a child who reflects her color and culture.

When Carey and Donna started talking about having a family, Donna agonized over which one of them would be the birth mother. There were all kinds of reasons that it should be Carey: she was younger, her insurance policy had good maternity benefits, she wasn't as involved in her career as Donna was and, the big one, she actually wanted the physical experience of having a child. Donna had absolutely no interest in being pregnant. She looked forward to being a parent but wasn't interested in being pregnant. However, as an African American, she felt some pressure to be the birth mother. She was concerned that, even if they found an Afri-

can-American donor, she somehow might not feel connected enough with the child.

Talking with other women of color helped her sort out her feelings and her fears. Part of her quandary involved concerns about her family's accepting their grandchild if her partner was the birth mother. Part of it had to do with the expectations, when she was growing up, that she would have children. Some of it felt like internalized racism—because Carey was white, Donna feared she would have more power in the family, particularly if she was the birth mother.

For Donna, and for many other women of color, it is very important to spend time with her own racial or ethnic group. This provides a respite, a relief from being in the watchful eye of the majority culture. With others like herself, she can relax and, assuming some common base of understanding, leave certain things unsaid. On the one hand Carey understands this. For her, attending lesbian events, going to the local lesbian bar and getting together with lesbian friends provide this kind of comfort and rejuvenation. But it is still hard for Carey to feel excluded from a part of Donna's life, and she harbors worries that having a biracial child might exclude her even more.

One of Carey's main concerns was how her own parents, as well as Donna's parents, would respond to a biracial grandchild. Particularly she was worried about her parents. They had already given her the speech about it "being hard enough for a child to have lesbian parents without having to deal with being of mixed race." If her parents were not accepting, how would this affect their child's feelings about his or her dual heritage? If the child identified as a person of color, would that mean that she would somehow be rejected?

One racist legacy in this country assumes and requires that a biracial or multiracial person who is partly of European heritage will identify as a person of color. This form of racism, called "hypodescent," is the assignment of an individual of racially mixed heritage to the social racial group of the parent with the lowest racial status, even among communities of color; multiracial people of European heritage would of course *want* to identify with that heritage but would *have* to identify as a person of color.[7] Of course, in a racist society, a biracial person may lose out if she or he identifies exclusively with *either* heritage.

Donna and Carey's child might want to identify as biracial, as white or as a person of color. Many parents of biracial children notice that about the age of five, the child may divide herself in half to try to make sense of the race issue.[8] For example, "This half is like Mommy Donna, and this half is like Mommy Carey." This is a perfect opportunity for parents to use concrete examples of what happens when you mix two "colors." Donna and Carey could use the example of Neapolitan ice cream that gets mixed together and becomes one color. Or they could use two colors of clay and knead them together to show that once you do this, "You can't get the original colors back. You have something new." Biracial children need to know they have the right to "not to keep the races separate within me."[9]

As celebration of cultural diversity increases, many white parents may feel at a loss because they lack a sense of connection with their own cultural origins or feel their heritage is "bland" or "boring." In a multiracial family where the parent of color can convey a history of ancestors and ethnic origins with pride, and the white parent cannot, a multiracial child may come to identify as a person of color. These children do not necessarily reject their white ancestry, but it is eclipsed by the ethnic heritage of the parent of color. These are all topics that couples like Carey and Donna need to communicate about before, and during, their parenting career.

Raising Bias-Free Children

How do we raise children who are as free as possible from bias? How do we talk to our children about race and about racism?

Children are not born with prejudices. They learn them over time from the society they live in. But children can learn to appreciate rather than condemn or merely tolerate differences if parents encourage them. In *How to Talk to Your Kids About Really Important Things* Charles E. Schaefer and Theresa Foy DiGeronimo suggest that children are particularly open to this teaching around the age of three, the age at which they begin to notice racial differences.[10] However, children of all ages can learn these lessons in a home environment of open communication, support and trust.

◆　◆　◆

Building Self-Esteem and Positive Racial Identity

Self-image describes how we imagine ourselves to be; self-esteem is the feeling we have about our self-image. If children feel good about themselves, they have high self-esteem. In her book *Black and White Racial Identity*, Janet Helms notes that "while Black identification seems related to positive self feelings, there is no research about the relationship between white identification and self-esteem."[11] Low self-esteem among whites is associated with anti-black attitudes, but the whole area of white identity remains largely unexplored.

An illustration of racism is that the research is almost inevitably from the white perspective: how whites see members of other racial groups and how the members of those racial groups see themselves rather than how whites are seen by other racial groups or how whites see themselves. As the dominant group, the role of white people has been to examine, label and critique other groups. It is as if white people don't have to address their own color, don't have to develop a positive racial identity. Confusing ethnic identity with racial identity, whites may identify as Italian, or German or Jewish, not as white, but they need to be sure they include themselves when talking about and conveying positive racial identity. This is especially important for white parents of children of color.

Parents can reinforce their children's self-esteem and increase their resilience to hurtful words by:

- Acknowledging and validating the ways they are different from as well as the ways they are the same as others, including others in the family (in physical appearance, cultural background, religious beliefs, and so on).
- Recognizing, honoring and celebrating their uniqueness and individuality.
- Helping them develop confidence, independence and a sense of humor.
- Teaching them skills to be competent.
- Encouraging them to socialize and participate in group activities.

We also can't expect our children to be unbiased if we don't model that for them, so we need to work on our own biases and our own racism. Being honest with ourselves about how our background and experiences have influenced us is a good place to start. What experiences have we had with members of different racial groups? What conclusions did we draw from those experiences? About ourselves? About members of that group? Our answers to these questions may clarify where we need to look at our attitudes and, possibly, change them.

Being a positive role model for our children means paying attention to how we ourselves talk about and behave toward members of other groups. The obvious things to avoid are ethnic jokes and stereotypes, but there are more subtle messages as well. For example, if we are white, do we identify people of races other than our own by their race—"The Japanese girl who was in your class last year" or "the Asian principal" or "the black family down the street"? If we don't generally describe people as "white" or "European," what message are we conveying when we consistently describe others in terms of their race?

Being a positive role model also requires confronting racism in others. Our children are watching, and learning, from us. If a friend or relative or casual acquaintance makes an offensive remark about another group, we need to be ready, willing and able to respond.

Confronting Racist Comments

If our goal is to educate and create allies, we need to be non-judgmental and compassionate yet firm when we confront racist comments. It helps if we assume the person is speaking out of ignorance not maliciousness. Then we can listen, ask questions and provide more or new information rather than argue with them or make them feel humiliated or ashamed.

The following ideas and suggestions of what to say when someone makes a racist comment can, of course, also be used when someone makes a homophobic comment:[12]

—"I'm sure you didn't mean to offend me, but you did. Let me tell you why..."
—"Did you know that [members of the group] find that hurtful?"
—"What do you mean when you say [for example, the Asians are getting all the good jobs]?"
—"I don't think you meant that the way it sounded but this is how I felt when you said it..."

—"What you just said could be heard as racially biased."
—"Do you really believe that?"
—"I am going to interrupt you because you have just offended me."
—"I can't believe you said that!"
—"OUCH!" [to get their attention]
—"I don't like that."
—"What did you mean by that?" [followed with] "Why do you feel that way?"

But what if the person who makes the comment is a loved one, such as a parent? Darlene and Derek Hopson, in their book *Raising the Rainbow Generation,* suggest three possible approaches.[13] One is to challenge the remark immediately, in which case you could use one of the suggestions mentioned previously; the last one might be particularly appropriate. Another approach is to prepare your child for the attitudes your parent might express. This approach requires preparation before a visit, and a debrief after a visit if biased remarks were made. The third approach is to set clear limits for the person who is expressing biased views. Make it clear that these comments are not acceptable. If they occur, intervene by saying that you object to such remarks being made, especially in front of your children. Having made your point, change the subject and move on.

When Your Child Practices Racism

If you hear your child make a racist comment, you can try to create a teachable moment. First be clear about whether you are dealing with prejudice or with limited experience and immaturity. For example, when a four-year-old points to a Korean adult and says, "Look at his squinty eyes," the child is illustrating a common behavior for his age. At this point in their development, children are noticing and, in their immaturity, commenting on the differences between themselves and others. An appropriate response would be to try to offer facts with an attitude of appreciating differences. You might say, "Yes, his eyes are a different shape than yours. Do you remember the picture of the little girl in the book we read last night? Her eyes are shaped like that, too."

It would be a very different situation if you overheard your ten-year-old son saying, "Don't let 'squinty eyes' play." Ten-year-olds are old enough to understand and demonstrate prejudice. In this instance, you would be well advised to stay calm when you confront your child. If you get angry, he will get defensive and the learning opportunity will be lost. If you ignore the comment, you imply that you accept prejudice. Instead, ask your child why he feels that a child of a different race would not make a good playmate. Listen to his response. Then ask him, "Does the shape of his eyes or his being of a different race make you not want to play with him?" Again, encourage your son to talk about his feelings. Acknowledge that there may be children that he doesn't like to play with, but that the reason should have nothing to do with the way they look or the color of their skin.

Children at this age are usually able to put themselves in another person's position. You could ask your son how he would feel if someone refused to play with him because of something that he could not change—like having a birthmark on his neck or having curly hair.

When Your Child Experiences Racism

Being the target of prejudice, racism or discrimination is very painful for anyone, and children are no exception. Sometimes you may need to intervene for your child, for example, if you believe your daughter is being discriminated against by an institution or organization. Other times, you can teach her ways to deal with the racism herself. Children gain strength by solving their own problems so we must give them the tools they need to resolve difficult encounters on their own. Yet we need to talk to our children about racism *before* they experience it firsthand.

Whether warning your child of the possibilities of racism or discussing something that has actually happened, emphasize that such things do happen and that they hurt, that your child does not deserve such treatment and is a good person just as she is, and that people who act this way don't really know your child and therefore have no right to comment on what type of person she is.[14] When a child has been victimized by racism, she needs our understanding, empathy and strength:

- Acknowledge that the child is upset for good reason. Affirm the child's feelings, which may include pain, rage and fear.
- Rehearse with the child what she could say and do in that kind of situation. Give the child ideas, and try to elicit ideas from her.

- Work with your child to find an approach that works for him. For example, a shy child may need more rehearsal or more creative ways to take control of the situation. Having him whisper a response so that the other person has to lean forward and be quiet to hear is one possibility.
- Talk about racism in language appropriate to the child's age.
- Work with the child's school or other organizations to increase multicultural understanding and combat racism.

Six-year-old Lana comes home from school in tears. At recess a group of children teased her, telling her she couldn't play with them because her skin was "dirty." Then they chased her off the swings.

Lana needs comforting and an explanation that there are mean people in the world who don't like anyone who is not just like them. Giving Lana a "script" of what to say may help her feel less vulnerable. For example, she could rehearse saying, "What you're saying isn't true, so stop it, " or "My mama says that people who say that are ignorant." This communicates that what was said was not acceptable and that her statement is backed up by parental authority. In addition, Lana has taken control of the situation. She can then walk away and find other children to play with. Lana's parents can also talk with the school staff about ways to bring multicultural and multiracial understanding into the classroom curriculum.

Eight-year-old Jamal wasn't invited to a birthday party for Larry, a child he played with a lot. None of Larry's African-American playmates were invited. Jamal was very hurt.

Jamal's parents may need to support him through a series of feelings, from hurt to anger, and validate how hard it is not to be invited to the party. They may even want to talk about an experience of theirs in which they were excluded. They could acknowledge that some people are prejudiced but that their family believes that differences are wonderful. In addition, Jamal's parents may decide to confront Larry's parents and Larry about the situation, letting them know that Jamal's feelings had been hurt. They could point out that the exclusion appeared racially biased since none of Larry's African-American playmates had been invited. If Jamal's parents can approach this confrontation with compassion and without pre-judging, the chance of educating and building bridges increases.

> *Twelve-year-old Ernesto was walking home from school with a group of his friends when they were stopped by a policeman. According to Ernesto, the policeman assumed they were the ones who had shoplifted some cigarettes from the nearby convenience store. "They never would have stopped us if we had been white," he kept saying over and over again.*

Ernesto is old enough to have a more in-depth talk about the realities of racism. His parents might want to say, "If it is true that the policeman was racist, you have every reason to be upset." Of course, even if the officer was not racist, it is upsetting to be falsely accused. This situation presents an opportunity to encourage Ernesto to judge each situation in terms of the individuals involved, and not by a group's race or cultural heritage. It is also an opportunity to acknowledge that racism exists in the criminal justice system in this country.

Walking Our Talk

What we do speaks louder to our children than anything we say: we teach our values by our actions. Confronting racist comments is one way we can walk our talk, but we can also broaden and enrich our family experiences by including more diversity.

Possibilities include making friends with people of other races and cultures, taking our children to celebrations, festivals and arts performances organized by people of other races and cultures, and getting involved in groups and organizations that are multicultural and multiracial. We can also advocate multicultural programs and curricula in our children's schools.

On the home front, we can make sure our children have books and toys that reflect multicultural themes and use illustrations of children of different races. If necessary, hand-color the faces to add diversity! Television and radio programs as well as audiotapes and videotapes can also expose our children to other cultures and races. Watching or listening to a program together about a child from a different culture and then talking about the differences between that culture and our own is one possibility. With older children, situation comedies and dramas that reflect different racial and ethnic points of view can be the jumping-off place for discussions. If you are part of the majority culture, try adopting the perspective of "How am I different from the people in the program?" rather than "How are they different from me?"

When we celebrate racial and cultural differences we offer our children a broader perspective and an acceptance and enjoyment of differences that is stimulating and growth-enhancing. Life is far richer for us all when we can understand and share ourselves with others.

8 Celebrating Our Lives:
New Family Traditions

It is often hard to find enough time to spend together as a family. We may be juggling a job and school and have a teenager applying for college and rebuilding cars in the driveway and a ten-year-old taking drum lessons and playing in a soccer league; whatever the details, most families are very busy. In addition, we may be separated geographically from those we consider part of our family. Whether we are across town or across the country, the result is the same: we don't share a daily life.

Although all families face these challenges of time and distance, lesbian families face a few more. As lesbians, many of the cultural trappings and privileges that define couplehood and family life are not available to us. Some of the restrictions are legal, such as those regarding marriage, adoption, joint tax returns and insurance coverage for partners and dependents. Other obstacles are social, such as lack of acceptance of our couple relationships and families by institutions such as schools, churches and workplaces. This does not mean that we have not found love, acceptance and inclusion. Sometimes we can get them from our family of origin, from our church or spiritual life or from our chosen family and community. However, we do face a general lack of acceptance from the broader culture for our relationships and in particular for our families.

In the face of this lack of acceptance, lesbians have become quite creative in designing ways to affirm our relationships. Many of us have developed anniversary traditions for celebrating important events in our lives as a couple, such as the day we met, or the first time we were sexual with each other or when we made a commitment to the relationship. In the absence of legal marriage, many couples design and celebrate commitment ceremonies such as those described by Becky Butler in her book, *Ceremonies of the Heart.*[1]

We believe it is important for lesbians to apply this same creativity to our families. Traditions and rituals can serve to acknowledge, celebrate and anchor us. When we develop our own rituals and celebrate our special traditions, we enrich our family life, increase our sense of family unity and have fun, all at the same time.

Reclaiming Rituals and Building Traditions

To even begin thinking about the possibility of developing new traditions and rituals, we have to revamp our ideas about what these words mean. Our ideas about tradition often come from our experiences growing up. Some of us may miss those times, remembering with nostalgia the smell of our mother's homemade pasta sauce on Saturday night, or the lighting of Shabbas candles on Friday night or piñatas at birthday parties. Others of us may lament that we grew up without the warmth and connection that family traditions provide. Still others reject anything that reminds them or connects them to their past.

Tradition is defined by Merriam-Webster's dictionary as "an inherited, established or customary pattern of thought, action or behavior." Whatever our situation, traditions handed down over the generations often do not fit the realities of our lives today. In her book *Family Traditions*, Elizabeth Berg suggests that a tradition is "something you do once and it feels right; and so you do it again and again."[2] Rituals are ceremonies that may become part of a tradition. So we can reclaim and redesign traditions and rituals from the families we grew up in, borrow some from other families or just make up our own. They don't have to be complicated, laden with meaning, or ancient. We can approach developing new rituals and traditions with an attitude that is playful as well as serious, heartfelt as well as thoughtful, and experimental as well as time-honored.

Some traditions may continue forever, or at least as long as a family continues to live together. Other traditions will die out as new ones take their place. Singing favorite songs and reading stories at bedtime, for example, is a tradition that is very important in a child's early years but will stop at some point. Yet we want to emphasize that even if a tradition lasts for only a few years, or happens only a few times, it can still be meaningful and fondly remembered.

The examples and suggestions in this chapter have been gathered from lesbian families as well as other sources. All of them are ways for people to add love, comfort, order and meaning to their lives and to the lives of those they love. We encourage you to adapt these ideas in whatever way suits your family. What holds a family together is its sense of caring, commitment and responsibility to each other. Traditions and rituals serve to reinforce and remind us of that. In her book *New Traditions*, Susan Abel Lieberman describes traditions and rituals as "family insurance against outside pressures that threaten to overwhelm our days and weaken our ties to one another."[3] And they can also be a lot of fun.

Everyday Rituals

As we said earlier, all of us seem to be have become busier and busier. Our often hectic schedules eat into the quality time we spend with our children and fray our connections to one another. Single mothers in particular feel pulled in many different directions. If you are a single mother, you might be thinking, "Forget 'ritual' or 'tradition,' I'm lucky if my daughter and I can share dinner together each night!" But rituals don't have to be time-consuming affairs. If you really stop to think about it, you would probably be surprised to realize how many everyday rituals you have created—from leaving colorful notes for your child on the refrigerator to tucking her into bed at night.

Lots of everyday events are worth celebrating, and you can build traditions around ongoing activities in ways that add zest to your daily life. Here are some that we've heard about:

On their phone message, every member of Winnie and Fran's family is always represented, including Bob, the cat. And they change the message often. For holidays they go "all out" with special effects such as jingle bells for Christmas, creaking doors for Halloween and laughter for April Fool's day.

Alice and Jenny both describe themselves as recovering Catholics, so they have developed their own way to express their spiritual beliefs with their three boys. Before eating dinner they all join hands and observe a few moments of silence to be grateful for what they have, including being together as a family.

Once a week Jan, Ilse and their children have a two-to-three-hour family activity time. They keep a jar in the kitchen where family members put suggestions about what they want to do together. Activities are chosen on a rotating basis, a different person's suggestion each week. Not everyone enjoys what other family members like to do, but part of the lesson is to appreciate each other's point of view.

Every morning, three-year-old Alexis crawls into bed with her moms, and they each tell what their wish is for that day. Then before they go to bed, they check in about whether their wishes came true.

Betty keeps a picture album for each of her children. She updates it regularly and periodically sits down with that child to look through the album and reminisce.

Marnie and her sons, Cory and Cody, all take their lunches to work and school each weekday. For the past year they have made them together, assembly-line style. It makes the task more fun and has become a time to find out what's happening with each other.

Particularly when their friends with children have been visiting, Lee and Linda provide a sendoff by jumping up and down while waving good-bye as their friends' car pulls away. This was a tradition in Linda's family when she was growing up, and it always gets a great response from kids. In fact, their two-and-a-half-year-old godchild likes it so much, that now she insists that her mommies jump and wave with her when people leave their house.

Wednesday night is family dinner for a large household that includes Brina and her six-year-old daughter, Stacey; Pat and Lorraine and their two teenage boys, Dan and Jordy; and Roseanne and Grant, who are the single members of the clan. Two adults and one child are assigned to cook din-

ner together that night, and the one requirement is that there be a special dessert. The other family dinner tradition is that during the meal each person shares his or her answer to the question, "What was the best thing that happened to you this week?"

Earthly Delights

Certain traditions suggest themselves at certain seasons. For example, winter beckons us indoors to play board games or gather around the fire to tell stories about the day's adventures in the chill outdoors. Summer's sultry days call for trips to the beach, running through the sprinkler or catching fireflies.

Often these seasonal activities allow us to celebrate the earth and to notice the drama unfolding around us. And we can plan activities that provide an opportunity to teach our children how to care for the environment and to make a commitment, as a family, to contribute to making the world a better place to live.

Geri has taken her children hiking with her since they were very young. Over the years they have developed their favorite hikes and their own traditions about which hike they do first in the spring, and which one last in the fall. They also volunteer together as a family to do maintenance work on local trails.

Gardening is a family activity for Donna, Denise and their two children, and the first planting in the spring is a big event. The Farmer's Almanac is consulted for the best planting day, and that day is set aside well in advance. Donna's job is to make sure the beds are turned over and ready. Denise is in charge of purchasing the seeds. On planting day, everyone gets into their gardening clothes and heads out to the garden after a hearty breakfast. While they plant, they reminisce about past gardens, prize pumpkins and when they can start eating the vegetables they are planting.

Each month, the Barnes-Ross family focuses on one thing they can do to contribute to a better community and environment. They collect ideas from books, school, the radio or their own imagination and record them in a notebook. On the first day of the month they decide as a family on the suggestion for the month. Sometimes it is a resource-conservation idea, such as taking shorter showers and estimating how much water they've saved. One month they collected warm clothing from their neighbors and friends to give to a homeless shelter.

Margaret remembers fondly her father's making an ice skating rink in their yard each winter. The first year her children were old enough to stand up on skates, she made the first of many rinks in their backyard.

Every summer, Angela and Cyd organize a huge barbecue and picnic for all their friends after the Pride March. There are games and races and lots of visiting. A special tradition is the sharing of food that reflects each family's ethnic, cultural or geographical roots.

Holiday Celebrations

Holidays are typically times of family focus and may bring with them joyous anticipation and expectations, or lots of anxiety and even dread. Families are supposed to get together and have wonderful, fairy-tale holidays, but that is often not the case. The traditions that many of us grew up with assumed that people lived relatively near each other and that someone, almost inevitably female, had time to plan and prepare and cook on a grand scale. Reality is often very different!

As lesbian parents, we face unique challenges as well as those familiar to most parents at holidays. If your family of origin is homophobic, you and your partner—not to mention the children—may not be invited to family gatherings or may not feel comfortable if you do attend. Even when families are fully accepting, the decisions and logistics regarding who spends holidays with whom can be daunting. You may feel pulled in competing directions by invitations to Thanksgiving dinner from your parents and your partner's parents. Or your divorced parents who live on opposite sides of the country may each want your family to spend Christmas with them. Holiday plans may also be governed by the parenting agreement between you and your ex. And you may have to coordinate around not only your agreement with your ex, but also your partner's agreement with hers!

Religious holidays present their own challenges. The religious meaning of a holiday may no longer be relevant to you, or you and your partner may have different religious backgrounds. Observe and preserve conventional religious traditions if they fit your family, and design new ones if the old ones don't work for you.

New traditions can often be fashioned from a blend of past and present, or they may need to be cut from a whole new cloth. Ask yourself: What is this holiday all about? What parts of it are most meaningful to me? What is the message I hope my children will absorb? Who are the people I want to share this holiday with? The answers to these questions can help design family traditions that will fit you and your family.

As a biracial family, it was important to Gwen and Pam that they celebrate Kwanzaa, both because it is a tradition with African roots and because it integrates their values for their family. A uniquely African-American tradition, Kwanzaa, which means "first fruits" in Swahili, recalls the customs and values of African harvests.

For seven days, beginning on December 26, Gwen and Pam light a candle at dinner and talk about the Kwanzaa principle of progress for that day. When their twin sons were younger, Gwen and Pam did most of the talking and even read stories. Now that the boys are older, each person talks about how the principles relate to her or his life.

The boys attend a small, alternative school and one year their teacher did a unit on Kwanzaa. Partly because theirs was the only family that celebrated the tradition, Pam and Gwen agreed to do a ritual with the whole school, which turned out to be a very affirming experience for them all.

As a Jew, Barbara has strong feelings about Christmas. For example, even though her partner, Teresa, delights in outdoor Christmas lights, they are simply out of the question for Barbara. Teresa and Barbara decided that Christmas and Hanukkah each deserved to have its own traditions observed in their family. They wanted their three children to have the opportunity to understand and experience both. So whatever else they include in their December holiday festivities, they always light the Hanukkah candles and decorate a Christmas tree.

In fact, they have developed their own family traditions around each holiday. For instance, at Hanukkah, the Festival of Lights, each family member has his or her own menorah. Now, when all the candles are lit, there is quite a glow to celebrate the values of religious freedom.

Molly and Karen adopted three children from India. Their approach to holidays is to acknowledge and celebrate traditions from various cultures, sometimes adapting traditions in a respectful way. At first they celebrated so many—one year they had five different New Year's celebrations—that it became overwhelming. Now they celebrate some holidays every year and others from time to time. Because of their children's cultural heritage, they celebrate Divali, the Hindu festival of abundance, each fall. One feature of this festival is attracting the goddess of prosperity by putting lights outside. The children particularly enjoy stringing Christmas lights along the path from the front gate to the house and the ritual of turning them on in the evening.

At last count, six-year-old Robert listed himself as having four mothers and three fathers. The cast of characters includes his biological and adoptive mothers, each of their subsequent partners, a gay male couple who agreed prior to his birth to take on a parental role with him, and the brother of his biological mother's partner. An important family tradition for Robert is Thanksgiving dinner, because that is the one time in the year that he can count on all of these adults being together with him.

Miriam and Emily identified Passover as a way to acknowledge their cultural and religious heritage as well as the message about the importance of freedom. Miriam was raised in a religious Jewish family, and Emily describes her family as secular Jews. However, their cultural Jewish heritage is important to them both and to their children. Theirs is a blended family, both parents had children from heterosexual marriages, and the celebration has evolved to include ex-husbands and their families as well as friends of many different backgrounds. The focus of their Seder is a play that the children put on depicting the flight of the Jews from Egypt. This play has become an important event not only for their own children but for the children in their extended family as well.

Spur-of-the-Moment Gatherings

Whereas holidays give us events to anticipate and plan for, some of us are more likely to subscribe to the adage, "Life is uncertain; eat dessert first." Spur-of-the-moment celebrations have a special sweetness, and if we enjoy them enough, they have a way of becoming next year's traditions.

Kim, a Kentuckian by birth, is part of a group of transplanted Midwestern-ers living in Seattle who bonded because of homesickness and misery over the seemingly interminable grayness of the Northwest winter. During her first year in Seattle, watching her beloved Kentucky Derby with only her daughter for company seemed too depressing. In a fit of inspiration, Kim invited all her Midwestern friends over for a Kentucky Derby party. Now every year on Derby day, this group of gay, lesbian, heterosexual, single, coupled and familied Midwesterners gathers to watch the race on TV and enjoy an afternoon of barbecuing.

At Dee's house, a card game has become the focus of spontaneous gath-erings. A very simple but loud and energizing game, PIT, is based on the commodities trading market—instead of diamonds and spades, cards represent grains such as corn and oats. When Dee's children, who are now grown and living in another state, come back into town, their presence is a great excuse to play PIT and have a big dinner that includes extended family members and friends.

Becky is a genius at concocting special occasions on short notice. She and her kids once invited another family over for a "Beach Blanket" picnic in December. They turned the heat on high enough to wear shorts and bath-ing suits and set up a whole picnic scene in the living room—beach blan-ket, picnic basket and a big paper sun on the wall. They even put on sun-tan lotion!

What started as a spontaneous art activity blossomed into a tradition that encourages family unity in Holly and Fran's large blended family. One day their children designed their own sibling flags and hung them on a bam-boo pole outside the house. Now four times a year they celebrate National Brothers and Sisters Day. On those days they focus on talking about spe-cial times together, examples of considerate behavior and what they ap-preciate about each other.

◆ ◆ ◆

Birthdays and Rites of Passage

Birthdays give us a day that is especially our own. We have a chance to take an ordinary day and make it more meaningful and celebratory. Like birthdays, milestones such as confirmation, bar or bat mitzvahs, getting a new job, graduation and registering to vote acknowledge the passage of time as well as responsibilities that may come with our new status.

Melanie and Shareen celebrate two "birthdays" with their daughter, Lee Ann. One is the day Lee was actually born, and the other is the day she arrived in the United States from China. The familiar cake, candles and ice cream mark the actual day of her birth. Watching the video of friends and family at the airport to greet the new baby is always a feature of her arrival-day celebration.

Dana believes it is important for her son, Chris, to have a rite of passage to mark his transition from boyhood to adulthood. She asked the men in his life to plan a ceremony or ritual or even a group camping trip to celebrate the transition. They were taken aback at first, never having participated in such an event before. However, they are now busily researching other cultures and traditions for ideas to incorporate into their ritual for Chris's thirteenth birthday.

Bette, Sunny and their blended family of six children have a hallway in their home they call the Family Hall of Fame. During the first year they were together, they talked with the children about the talents, accomplishments and successes of people in their immediate and extended family. This included all of them, of course! They used snapshots, drew pictures and used words to identify the people and note their skills and accomplishments. They add information about successes as time goes on, and the children take friends and guests on a "guided tour." Last year they had a ceremony to induct two new members of their extended family, Uncle Jack and Otis (the dog), into their Hall of Fame.

When each of their children turned thirteen, Kate and Darlissa continued to teach them money management by giving each child a clothing allowance and the responsibility for buying their own clothes. The mothers have only had to exercise veto power once, when their youngest daugh-

ter came home with a dress that would have been appropriate for a night-club act in Las Vegas!

Education is a very important value for Jeanette and Kip, so graduation parties are a big deal in their family. They invite adults and friends who have been important to their child, and after the eating and mingling are over, the graduate says a few words, often rehearsed, to the guests and each guest, in turn, says something to the child—it may be a wish for the future, a memory of a past incident, a poem or a gem of wisdom from their own experience.

While We're Apart

Family members can't always be together: some parents have a job that requires them to travel, or they may not live with their children on a daily basis. Children go off to camp or to college; eventually they leave home entirely. Once again we are challenged to create new traditions to maintain connections over distances.

Every night, Joyce makes up another installment in the adventures of a rabbit named Hortensia to tell her daughter, Melanie, as a bed time story. If she is traveling because of work, Joyce calls Melissa from wherever she is and tells her that night's episode over the phone.

When he was only four years old, Jamie was in the hospital for months for a series of surgeries. For the times that neither of his mothers could be with him, they made a "love pillow" out of red velvet. It was shaped like a heart and had a pocket on one side that contained a picture of his whole family.

Rob knows that when he returns to college each semester, a care package will be waiting for him. His mothers take great pleasure in assembling the mix of practical items, home-baked goodies and what they now all call the "special surprise" item. The "special surprise" title originated when an embarrassed Rob opened the first care package in front of his new roommate. It contained a package of condoms.

Every day when she came home from school, Terry was welcomed home by her favorite teddy bear, which her mother would place in the window.

Now a mother herself, whenever any member of her family goes away, Terry welcomes them home with that same teddy bear in the window. Sometimes she adds others of her old and careworn stuffed animal collection to the welcoming party as well.

Cass and Stephanie raised Stephanie's two daughters from the time they were toddlers until they were grown. Now Cass and Stephanie have retired to Florida; the daughters, both married, still live in Michigan. They love the climate, but miss their children—and grandchildren. Since both daughters are raising families and money is tight, Cass and Stephanie decided one year that they would provide airplane tickets for everyone to come visit them in Florida. They all agreed that spring break would be the best time, and the visit was such a spectacular success that they have done it for three years running.

With six grown children between them and family scattered all over the country as well as overseas, Mary and Rita started a family letter. They write to the oldest, and she adds a letter and pictures and sends them on to the next oldest and so on until everything makes its way back to Mary and Rita. Then they replace their letter in the packet with a new one, and the circle begins again. Each person is supposed to send the family letter on within ten days. This means a turn at letter writing only about once every three months. The news is a bit stale sometimes, but the pictures are great and everyone gets a feel for what is going on with each other without incurring high phone bills.

Death

Volumes have been written on our culture's inadequacy in dealing with death and dying. We have few traditions, for example, that acknowledge a person's death after the memorial service is over. Our culture's approach seems to be to get the grieving over as quickly as possible. All of us have or will have people who are close to us die; many of us have lost or will lose loved ones to AIDS. Death is a part of life, and traditions that acknowledge that can help ease the pain and nourish the places in our heart where we keep our loved ones forever.

Although she is not Jewish, Lana lights a twenty-four hour Yahrzeit candle on the anniversary of her son's death. It makes her feel good to have a

defined amount of time to remember the good times and to feel the grief
and loss of her firstborn child and only son.

Jesse knew and had a close relationship with her biological father before
he died of AIDS. On his birthday, Lynn and Deborah bring out pictures of
him. As a family they talk about what he was like and the things they did
together. Lynn also makes connections for Jesse with present-day events.
For example, after Jesse's ballet concert, Lynn reminded her of how Jim
enjoyed dance and how proud he would have been of her performance.

Creating Your Family Traditions

Many families already have a number of rituals and traditions. We
encourage you to recognize and appreciate the ones you have already
established. And perhaps you may want to add new ones or be more
deliberate or consistent about existing ones.

Some traditions may start out big and have to be whittled down to
manageable size; others start small and fill out as they go. Building
family tradition feels most inclusive if the whole family is involved,
but whoever is most enthusiastic may carry the ball until the tradition
is more firmly established.

The goal of celebrating traditions is to foster a sense of family connection and continuity. Whatever nourishes that intention and moves
toward that goal can be woven into the tapestry of traditions in your
family.

II

PARENTING OUR CHILDREN AS THEY GROW

9 At the Very Beginning:
Pregnancy and Childbirth

Great Expectations

Congratulations! You are pregnant, or your partner is! Being pregnant or being partnered with someone who is pregnant brings up a host of specific issues—from preparing for the baby to dealing with health care providers to simply coping with the myriad changes pregnancy brings. If you are waiting to adopt a baby you will face both similar and different demands. In this chapter we discuss what to expect during pregnancy and childbirth, as well as information for adoptive parents-to-be. We have also listed books in the Selected Bibliography on these topics for further reading.

A Pregnancy Preview

When you are pregnant, your first priority is to give your baby the healthiest possible start in life. You need to get good nutrition, adequate rest and exercise, and good prenatal health care.

A nutritious diet is one that includes a wide variety of fresh vegetables and fruits, cereals and grains, and foods that are protein-rich and high in iron, calcium and other minerals. Some women increase their intake of meat and dairy products, others decide to maintain a balanced vegetarian diet. No matter what your nutritional values, it is important to find out from a health care provider what diet you should follow to best support you and your developing baby. It is common for pregnant women to get cravings for specific foods or drinks. If you have cravings for something nutritious—grapefruit, for instance—feel free to indulge. But if you find yourself craving a pint of double-fudge ice cream try to limit your consumption, or find a substitute food or activity—have your girlfriend give you a massage instead.

Certain substances such as alcohol, cigarettes and other drugs can severely inhibit, distort or terminate the health of the developing fetus. These substances need to be avoided by pregnant women. Each year thousands of babies are born addicted to drugs due to their mother's addiction. These babies go through painful withdrawal within hours of their birth and suffer life-long consequences, including neurological and other physical damage. Drinking excessive amounts of alcohol during pregnancy, especially in the early months, can cause a child to be born with the condition known as Fetal Alcohol Syndrome (FAS). Many women want to know if there is a "safe" level of drinking alcohol during pregnancy. While one glass of wine is unlikely to do harm, alcohol consumption does appear to have adverse effects on the fetus, and physicians do not know how much alcohol is needed to do damage. For this reason, we recommend complete avoidance of all alcoholic beverages during pregnancy. Cigarette smoking during pregnancy also can cause a host of serious problems, from increased chance of miscarriage to a low birth-weight baby. If you cannot avoid these substances and want to get pregnant, or if you are already pregnant, get professional help now.

Resting and exercising are two other ways to take care of yourself when you are pregnant. Some authorities go further and recommend more contemplative time and less stress. Many women cannot help but rest more, especially during the first three months (first trimester)—they are exhausted! Some report falling asleep early in the evening...or any other time they sit still for more than five minutes. Others say they get a surge of energy in the second trimester and need more rest again during the final months. Getting exercise is generally beneficial to expectant mothers and their babies, and many women develop a daily routine. While you may find an exercise regimen difficult to stick to, it is a good idea to find some kind of regular, moderate exercise that strengthens your cardiovascular system as well as your muscles. (Relaxation techniques and pelvic toning—or Kegel exercises—are also helpful.) By the end of your pregnancy you will probably be carrying an extra fifteen to forty pounds, so it helps to be fit.

No matter what you do on your own to nurture your body and safeguard your health, you will need to get good prenatal care throughout your pregnancy. The earlier you begin, the better. Most pregnant women seek prenatal care between the sixth and eighth week of pregnancy (counting from the last menstrual period). A variety of options for prenatal care are available. M.D.s (Medical Doctors) and D.O.s (Doctors of Osteopathy) in family and obstetrical practices provide the majority of prenatal care in the United States. In states where they are available, midwives, naturopathic physicians and other health care providers offer additional options. Ask other lesbian mothers or lesbian-affirmative health care providers for recommendations of lesbian-affirmative prenatal care providers.

You may decide that you want to undergo prenatal testing to find out the gender of your baby or if your fetus has a detectable abnormality such as Down syndrome or spina bifida. (Down syndrome incorporates a cluster of characteristics including a distinct facial shape and mental retardation; spina bifida is a deformity of the spinal column, a condition that can vary from very mild and surgically correctable to severe and life-threatening.) The procedures used in prenatal diagnosis are usually performed in the first and second trimesters and include ultrasound, amniocentesis, chorionic villi sampling (CVS) and alpha-fetoprotein (AFP) screening.

An ultrasound involves the use of sound waves (rather than an X-ray) to see the outline of the fetus. It does not give specific genetic information but can be useful for determining certain conditions of the fetus. Amniocentesis is a procedure in which a small amount of amniotic fluid is extracted and studied for genetic abnormalities. This is done by a physician who locates the fetus and placenta with an ultrasound, then uses a long needle to penetrate the abdomen and uterine wall, drawing out the amniotic fluid. Amniocentesis is usually performed between sixteen and eighteen weeks of pregnancy, and there is some risk of inducing an abortion. Chorionic villi sampling is a relatively new procedure which, like amniocentesis, is used to screen for genetic abnormalities. Its main advantage is that it can be performed earlier in the pregnancy, usually between the eighth and twelfth week, but it has a slightly higher risk of miscarriage than amniocentesis. The procedure involves the extraction of fetal membrane through a thin catheter inserted through the vagina and cervix into the uterus (again, an ultrasound is used to locate the placenta and fetus).

Screening for AFP is a simple blood test, generally done between sixteen and eighteen weeks. It is mainly used to screen for neural tube defects (like spina bifida) and does not provide genetic information like CVS or amniocentesis.

If you are interested in prenatal diagnosis, you should discuss this with your prenatal care provider so that you understand clearly the specifics of each procedure and the risks involved for you and your baby.

Getting Support

The second trimester of pregnancy is a time when the physical changes of pregnancy begin to be more obvious. If you are the partner of a pregnant woman, you can now put your hands on your partner's belly and feel the movement of the fetus—something your partner has already been feeling for weeks. If you are pregnant, this is the time when you will need new clothes! You may feel energetic and ready to take on new projects that seemed too tiring during the first trimester. Many expecting parents prepare the baby's room or begin to gather clothes and accessories for the baby during this time. (Some cultures view preparing the baby's room as tempting fate, and preparation begins only when the baby is born and comes home.)

As a pregnant woman moves into the second trimester, she becomes more relaxed because the probability of miscarriage is greatly reduced after the first trimester. During this period, both parents can begin to more fully imagine what the baby will be like—they are more aware of the baby's activity level and patterns of movement, and if there has been prenatal testing and the baby's gender is known, they may begin to relate to the baby as a girl or boy. The exhaustion and newness of the first trimester gives way to appreciation of the changes and anticipation of the baby's arrival.

The final trimester of pregnancy can be relaxed and fun; or it can be tiring and stressful. If you are pregnant you will probably have more difficulty moving, especially bending, and you'll feel more fatigued. Depending on how large you get, you may be reduced to wearing only a few comfortable pieces of clothing. Many women report being very ready to have their baby after eight or more months of pregnancy! The last month or so, however, has its special dimensions. Lesbian communities often love being able to celebrate the ritual of childbirth that once was reserved for heterosexual women only. Baby showers are usually held in the last month of a women's pregnancy, and you can have fun assembling the furniture, clothing and general paraphernalia you need to care for a baby.

> *Carly's friends from Act Up threw her a baby shower and it was in fine style! The men and women gave her outrageous baby clothes and thoroughly loved finding nonsexist toys, such as the rainbow-colored mobile to be hung over the crib.*

Being pregnant and anticipating the arrival of a child are life-changing events that demand attention—and support. We encourage couples to develop and use a network of family and friends to take care of *both* parents-to-be. The pregnant woman needs people who will listen to her descriptions of the physical and emotional changes she is experiencing—which to her are endlessly fascinating! The partner of a pregnant woman also needs attention, especially if she feels excluded by her partner's preoccupation with her pregnancy or baffled (even frustrated) by her partner's hormonal mood swings.

If you are the partner of a pregnant woman, the early months of the pregnancy may be especially difficult. There are few outward signs of the pregnancy, yet your pregnant partner may be obsessed with the bodily changes she is experiencing. You may feel superfluous and left out at times. Ideally, every non-pregnant partner should have a friend who has been in the same position, someone who understands and can give a listening ear and reassurance.

If you are a single expectant mother, you will need to make an extra effort to get the support you need. You can turn to friends, chosen and/or biological family, or hook up with a single mother's support group. Fortunately it is not uncommon for a lesbian to have developed extensive support networks by the time she becomes pregnant. Some women, however, may find themselves isolated for any number of reasons. It can sometimes be difficult to ask for help, especially if you have prided yourself in being independent, but reaching out to others can bring surprising rewards.

Because dealing with pregnancy is a relatively new phenomenon in lesbian communities, sometimes other lesbians don't know how to support the expectant lesbian parents. If this is your situation, tell your friends directly what you want from them—whether that is interest in how you are feeling or what the fetus is doing, or acts of assistance such as finding items you still need to get ready for the baby's arrival.

Your lesbian friends can also help *after* the birth. This can range from having a friend live in and control the flow of phone calls and visitors, to having them come over once in awhile to help out wherever needed—cooking a meal, doing a load of laundry, weeding the garden. The best time to set up these arrangements is during the pregnancy, to avoid having to worry about them after the baby arrives.

A deeply important aspect of pregnancy is to get the emotional support that affirms your choice to have a child. It is lovely to have other people with whom to share this powerful experience as well as to lean on when you need to be taken care of. For all parents this is important, but it has particular salience for the lesbian parent-to-be. At a time when you are experiencing great joy and anticipation, you may find that you must deal with other people's reactions to the pregnancy that are not supportive. For example, if your family of origin has been critical of your lesbianism, they may be more so when they find out about your pregnancy. Co-workers who learned to tolerate you because you are a reliable worker may regress to their former level of discomfort when they find out you are expecting a baby.

Sally and Yvette told their families that Sally was pregnant and due in November. Their families had very different responses. Yvette's parents told her they were happy for her but did not quite understand what their relationship to this child would be. It wasn't like their son's child, their grandchild. Sally's parents asked her not to tell people, especially any of their extended family. Sally and Yvette were both disappointed, so they called Yvette's sister who whooped and hollered on the phone and asked when she could buy presents.

Sometimes, however, you may find support from family members when you least expect it. Parents of lesbians who have distanced themselves from their daughters out of disapproval or discomfort may now push themselves to reconcile because of the impending arrival of a grandchild. Support from one's family can be wonderful and add untold richness to your pregnancy; it communicates both love and a continuity with history that is sometimes missing for lesbians and gay men. Many of us have learned to do without our families because they have pulled away, or because we have chosen to disengage due to their homophobia. Yet the presence of familial support and the sense of connection with one's history is a blessing.

A Word for Adoptive Parents-To-Be

Adoptive parents experience the same excitement and anticipation as pregnant parents-to-be. You get the baby showers, the gifts, and hopefully, the same support and affirmation. However, instead of a relatively simple nine-month period of waiting for the baby's arrival, there is no predictable timeline for adoptive parents. Even after you have been approved for adoption, the wait is indeterminate—months may pass without any word, or you may get the phone call telling you a baby is available sooner than you expected. Once notified, you may only have a few days to prepare for the baby's arrival in your home. If you are doing an international adoption, you may arrive in the other country and then have to wait some more, often several weeks, until all the paperwork is finalized. It's a good idea to prepare yourself for such eventualities and to line up your support network to be in place.

> *Leela had been approved for adoption ten months ago and had still not gotten word that "her" baby had arrived. She had been told once that she was one of the three adoptive homes a birth mother was considering. After she had gotten her hopes up, the baby had been given to a young heterosexual couple. Leela is absolutely sure that she will eventually become a mother, but she is disappointed and frustrated at the moment.*

If you are adopting through an agency, they often have support groups for parents-to-be. Resolve and Adoptive Families of America, Inc. have information and support for adoptive and preadoptive parents (see Resources). Local newspapers and parenting magazines are also good places to look for announcements of support groups.

◆　◆　◆

Days in the Lives of Pregnant Lesbians

Rest assured that nearly every aspect of your life will be affected by pregnancy—from your job to your relationship with your partner to the way you fit into your jeans.

Linda is eight months pregnant and very much slowed down in her every day life. She loves to sit in her rocking chair and look out the window at the bird feeder and the clouds in the sky. She thinks of her sitting times as the most spiritual part of her day. Linda has read a little bit about Zen Buddhism and thinks that her sitting, watching and enjoying just being are Zen-like. Her whole being calms as she rocks and watches.

If there are other children in your home you are not as likely to have long, uninterrupted times for reflection, but make time for sitting if you can. Your relationship with the other children, in fact, may undergo changes. Young children may be excited or anxious, teenagers may swing from enthusiastic interest to complete indifference. You may not be able to do as much of the physical caretaking of young children—such as carrying and lifting them—that they were accustomed to. It's important to find ways to stay connected with your children, even when your day-to-day physical contact is reduced. One pregnant woman we know has a ritual of sitting on the couch with her three-year-old every afternoon, reading to him and letting him sit on her lap or lay his head on her belly. He loves being able to feel the baby move and have his special snuggle time with his mother.

If you work outside the home, you will also be encountering reactions at your workplace. If you cannot come out as a lesbian at work, you are likely to be viewed as a single, heterosexual woman. It is ideal if you work in an environment which supports and is excited by the impending birth. If you are out as a lesbian and comfortable with your co-workers, your workplace can be a wonderful source of support as workmates tease, listen and wonder at the miracle of pregnancy.

The experience at the workplace for the nonbiological parent-to-be is another story. With no pregnancy to explain her role, she has to come out as a lesbian (if she is not out already) to be counted as a mother. If she comes out she may face prejudice or get support, much like her pregnant partner. Or she may be made painfully aware that her parenting role is discounted by her co-workers. If she does not come out she has to keep one more secret, and her sense of self and her work may suffer as a result. These are issues that both partners must work on in order to find ways to support the non-biological parent.

And on the home front: pregnancy affects one's romantic relationship in numerous ways! Some pregnant women feel *very* sexual, while others lose interest completely. Some women need a lot of reassurance, others feel more self-assured than ever. Some want their partner to stay very close, others need more space. We know two women who became a couple while one of them was pregnant. They compressed getting to know each other into a few months—in addition to dealing with the changes due to pregnancy. They talked a lot! There is no "right way" to handle the changes a pregnancy brings; each couple needs to talk about them and find ways to meet both women's needs.

Tess is three months pregnant. She got the surprise of her life when she realized how much she now craved sex! Before she was pregnant, Tess had wanted sex about once a week; once pregnant she had been warned by her friends that she and her partner, Jan, would probably have sex less frequently because Tess wouldn't want it very much. So it was a shock to both women when Tess wanted sex almost every day. Whenever she lay down for her daily nap, Tess felt turned on within minutes and could not go to sleep until she had had an orgasm. The other surprise was that what she wanted most was vaginal penetration. Tess would masturbate with their dildo when she was alone or ask Jan to penetrate her when they were together. At first Tess was embarrassed, but when she realized Jan loved it, Tess relaxed and enjoyed herself. They would never have guessed that pregnancy would spice up their sex life so much!

Childbirth

Getting Quality Prenatal Care

Many prospective mothers do not have access to lesbian-affirmative prenatal care, an unfortunate fact. However, when possible, we encourage you to talk to your caregiver about the kinds of support and services you want during your pregnancy and birthing process. When a caregiver is not supportive, you face the decision of either staying closeted or changing providers. We believe all caregivers have the responsibility to provide quality care to all their patients and being lesbian-affirming is one part of that care.

When choosing a prenatal care provider, consider these questions:

- Have you heard good comments about this care provider from previous patients?

- Do you feel comfortable with the provider? Does she or he encourage questions, involve you in decisions and allow flexibility in health care plans?

- Does her style of care match your values? For instance, do you want painkillers during your labor, and a certain provider does not believe in medication? Or do you want as natural a birth as possible, but your provider is dismissive of such ideas? Not a good fit, in either case.

- If the provider is part of a group practice, how is the practice organized? Will you get a chance to get to know each provider, and are you comfortable with the providers who might attend your birth if your primary care provider is off-call?

- Is the provider inclusive of both you, the pregnant woman, and your partner or labor support person?

- Has this provider had any experience working with lesbian mothers before?

- Will your partner be welcome at the hospital during labor as the other parent? Or if you are closeted, will she be welcome as a close friend and primary support person?

If you find a lesbian-affirmative provider or group practice, take the time to ask them about other issues that might come up for lesbian mothers at the hospital, during or after labor, and how they can help minimize any potential problems.

Ann's second son needed emergency care after birth and was taken to a hospital. Her midwife called the pediatrician and asked him to tell the hospital staff that the baby's family included two mothers and to respect and include both of them as full parents; in this way she was able to buffer Ann and her partner from the hospital's inexperience with lesbian mothers.

◆　◆　◆

Birthing Issues for the Pregnant Mother

What kind of birthing experience do you want? Do you want to deliver at home with your friends around and the Indigo Girls blasting on the CD player? Do you want to be in the hands of a midwife at a birthing center, or will you feel more reassured to have a hospital birth? If you have a complication—you are bearing twins, for instance, or have a health problem such as diabetes—you are more likely to require a hospital birth with doctors and/or specialists on hand. However, most women have uncomplicated pregnancies and births and can choose more freely the kind of birthing environment they want.

Yet unless you have been to a birth, you may not know exactly what it is you want, because you don't know what to expect. A birthing preparation class and your prenatal care provider should be able to give you some information. There are also many helpful books on childbirth—some are listed in our Selected Bibliography—so make a trip to the library or bookstore. The best source of information is, of course, other women who have done it before: talk to mothers who have had different kinds of births. Ask them about their experiences—what changes they would make if they could do it again and what they would keep the same.

Although many pregnant women are excited about giving birth, some are quite scared. If you are feeling fearful, talk to your caregiver. Fear can drain you, and it is not a helpful emotion as you prepare for your birth. You may want to get specific support in anticipation of labor, such as hypnosis or relaxation exercises.

... and Her Partner

You, the partner of the pregnant mom, are crucial to the birthing process. Talk to your partner and then to your prenatal care provider, very specifically, about what your role will be and how you will be incorporated into the decisions made during childbirth.

Your primary job will be to support your partner during labor and birth. This can take the form of helping her to relax and breathe the way you learned in a childbirth preparation class, or bringing her ice chips to suck on, or talking to her between contractions. Labor is a time when the two of you work together intensely in birthing your child. You may end up rarely leaving your partner's head as you reassure her throughout a long labor. You may be prepared to rub her back but find that she wants you to hold her hand instead. Make sure you have support for yourself, too, and if it is a long labor, plan in a few breaks so that you can eat, use the bathroom or take a walk. Be flexible. There really is no way of knowing ahead of time what your partner will need from you. Plan as best as you can and trust yourself to do what is needed.

Labor Preparation: From Birthing Classes to Popsicle Supplies

Many prospective parents attend birth preparation classes, whether they plan on having a hospital, birth center or home birth. (See the next section for descriptions of these birthing sites.) Depending on where you plan on having your baby, the emphasis of the class may be somewhat different. Classes that are preparing mothers for hospital births may spend more time on the high-tech instruments that might be used than would classes which are geared for home births. All of them are likely to show you a video of a birth in the setting in which you are most interested. The goal is to give you confidence and knowledge so that you can have the most positive labor and birth experience possible.

Such classes are usually held in the last two or three months of your pregnancy. A class can be small—three or four mothers and their partners—or they can be much larger. If size is an issue for you, check around and find out your options.

Birth preparation classes can be a lot of fun if the other parents and the instructor especially are enthusiastic about your pregnancy. The more these folks are uncomfortable with a pregnant lesbian the more outside support you will need from friends and family.

> *When Carol and her partner, Beth, were taking a labor class, it was common for the instructor to bring in a parent from her previous class who had given birth recently. The instructor chose a lesbian couple to return and give their story to the class. Carol and Beth felt incredibly supported and affirmed.*

Tour the hospital you will use. This is a good idea even if you are not planning a hospital birth, in the event of complications requiring hospital care. Get to know the layout of the floors; find the nursery and the mothers' rooms. Some hospitals have birthing rooms which are a combination of bedroom and delivery room; others have just delivery rooms. Take a look at them so that you know where you might end up. And be sure to ask the staff questions if you have any.

Whether you are single or partnered it is often useful to have other support people present at the labor and birth. These supporters need to be prepared for what happens at a birth and given some clear ideas of how they can help. Some women hire a professional labor support person as part of their support team. Penny Simkin's *The Birth Partner* and P. Perez's *Special Woman: The Role of the Professional Labor Assistant* are good resources as you consider who you might want at your baby's birth (see Selected Bibliography).

Regardless of how much you anticipate, be prepared to be flexible. One woman we know laid in a supply of twenty popcicles to get her through what she expected to be a long labor. She ended up hating the taste of popcicles after four bites and had a five-hour labor! Other women get tapes or CDs ready to listen to, then discover they want total silence to focus during contractions. Once you are in labor your body will tell you what you want, so don't worry that you guessed wrong or that the careful plans are thrown to the wind. Trust your body.

Giving Birth at a Hospital

Most women have their babies in hospitals. Depending on the hospital there can be some choice in the setting. A number of hospitals are beginning to provide birthing rooms for women who have uncomplicated pregnancies. Such rooms are an attempt to move away from the sterile atmosphere of the delivery or operating room. They vary widely in how comfortable and home-like they are; usually they are furnished with informal furniture in addition to standard hospital equipment. You will be able to see for yourself if you visit ahead of time.

Most hospitals, as a matter of policy, routinely use technological aides such as fetal and maternal monitors; others refrain until the medical staff feels their use is necessary. Some hospitals allow midwives as well as physicians to assist with the delivery. Depending on hospital policy, you may be able to have as many support people as you want in a birthing room, provided they do not interfere with the staff's ability to work.

One important advantage of a hospital birth is that equipment and medications are close at hand if the mother needs or wants medication, or if she or the baby have medical difficulties. Some women feel safer in a hospital and this allows them to relax more during labor.

A disadvantage to a hospital birth is that it is a relatively impersonal, sterile environment which some women find unpleasant. And even though most birthing mothers do not require emergency care, hospital staff are likely to use high-tech instruments or monitors during labor and delivery, whether or not they are truly necessary. You may have more interventions at the birth than you really need or want. Another disadvantage is that you have to leave home to get there, and you have to leave the hospital to go home.

Hospitals also tend to be slow-moving in their acceptance of lesbian couples as legitimate families. As a result, the non-pregnant partner may have more difficulty in gaining full acceptance as the other parent; she may also be challenged, for example, if she tries to sign the legal and financial paperwork for the delivery. If you decide to use a hospital for your child's birth, we recommend talking with their financial department *in advance* so you do not have to deal with their heterosexism at the same time you are welcoming your baby into the world.

Ginger and Gayle decided to have a hospital birth. The hospital they picked had a birthing room with a wonderful chair that allowed the birthing mother to sit, lie or adjust to whatever position felt good. There was even a cut-out area of the seat that allowed the physician to assist with the delivery easily. Two long-time friends were with Ginger and Gayle for support, one of whom was a nurse with years of hospital experience and the other a friend who had worked with Ginger using hypnosis to help prepare her for the birth. About eight hours into labor, Ginger asked for pain medication, which helped ease her through to the pushing stage. The hospital staff was wonderful and their physician proved to be relaxed and suppportive. Gayle and Ginger were euphoric after their son was born and agreed that the hospital had been a perfect choice for the birth.

At a Birthing Center

A birthing center is a well-equipped facility specifically geared to pregnant and birthing women, operated indepedently of a hospital. It is usually directed by a physician or midwife, sometimes near their home or workplace. Women who prefer a home birth but are too far away from emergency care may opt to come to a birthing center. The setting is very informal and "the baby catcher"—either a physician or midwife—usually has emergency equipment such as oxygen or suction set up but not the full array of hospital high-tech devices, as the focus is on a non-interventionist style of care.

An advantage to a birthing center is that it provides a comfortable, home-like environment for low-risk pregnant women who prefer such a setting rather than a hospital, but do not want to use their own home.

As with all health care options, it is important for you to assess whether any particular birthing center has a good reputation for thoroughness and competency. Just because a center advertises itself as an alternative to the heterosexist hospital system does not mean that it is a good one.

Marcia and Ruth lived in rural western Washington. They wanted a home birth but were worried that if there were complications they were too far away from a hospital. After interviewing midwives, they chose one who operated a birthing center in Seattle. At the first signs of labor they drove the four hours to Seattle and took up residence at the center. During the sixteen-hour labor their two support people came and left a few times. The midwife remained with Ruth until she was fully dilated and effaced. Then she and her birth assistant and the two mothers and their friends welcomed the baby into the world. The two proud mothers and baby drove home several hours later.

A Home Birth

There has been an increase in home births since the late 1960s. Some states prohibit home births and some do not license midwives as providers in any setting. Other states provide for both. Both physicians and midwives can attend home births.

Home births allow women to stay in their own homes for labor, delivery and the getting-to-know-you period after the baby is born. Women who choose a home birth are also choosing a natural childbirth delivery, as well. A good midwife is very careful to screen out high-risk pregnant women and to refer them to physicians for prenatal care and hospital births. Most midwives also have physican and hospital back-up for emergencies.

The most obvious advantage to a home birth is the comfort and familiarity of the setting. Women can arrange their home to fit exactly what they anticipate wanting during labor and delivery. If you have a young child you would like to be present at the birth, a home birth may best facilitate that. An advantage for lesbians is that at a home birth they can choose who to have at the birth and can maintain a lesbian-affirming environment.

The biggest disadvantage is that it may take longer to get emergency care, in the rare instance that it is required, than in a hospital.

Kit, a thirty-five-year old single lesbian, was about to become a mother for the first time. Kit had always wanted to have a baby, but when she had come out she had abandoned the idea because everyone said that lesbians did not have babies! After she realized that she really could have a child, she made plans to go ahead even though she did not have a partner to do it with. She was a journeywoman carpenter and made good money; she had a huge friendship network who were very supportive of her being a mother, and she had several sisters and friends who had agreed to help with childcare and baby-breaks. Kit decided to have her baby at home where her friends and family could be around her and help celebrate after the baby arrived. She laid in her favorite foods, asked one sister to video the birth, had her mother make receiving blankets and got her dad to rub her feet during labor. All in all it was a very large welcome home party for the newest member of Kit's family.

There are women who have given birth in every one of the above settings and who swear it was the most perfect place to have their baby. One midwife we know says that the most important variable is the quality of your care provider, not the location. A good care provider should honor your choices and respect you and your family. Of course, skill is important, but there are many skilled physicians, nurses and midwives. The important issue is what and who you want for your delivery. Ask women about their experiences and then choose what you think will work best for you.

•   •   •

Miscarriage and Stillbirth

When a woman miscarries, she suffers an invisible loss. This loss may be particularly painful for a mother who has carefully planned and worked on getting pregnant, as a lesbian mother usually does.

Women who have learned they are pregnant and then miscarry usually have bonded with the fetus, dreamed about the future child and shifted internally to the expectation of being a mother. Both the biological and non-biological mothers need the recognition of their pain and loss and the support to grieve for as long as they need to.

Women who have very late miscarriages or stillborn children have the added complication of going through labor and delivery. Thus the hard work of delivering a child has at its end the sorrow of loss instead of the joy of a new life. If there are other children in the home they, too, have been expecting a new family member and will need help with grieving the loss.

As with any loss, miscarriage and stillbirth can be opportunities for love and relationship-building. When your family has lost an expected child, you may be able to find ways to support each other and grieve together. Tell your other children how much you love them. Plant a flower together in honor of the lost baby; this gives a young child something concrete to see as she grieves. Take a trip together as an acknowledgment that your family needs time away from the daily routine. Ask your partner, if you have one, for extra touch and expressions of love, and give her the same. Tell your friends when you want company and when you want time alone. Whenever you can ask for, and receive, support from friends and family, you will feel loved; and so will they.

Diane Cole's book, *After Great Pain: A New Life Emerges,* is a moving account of living with loss, including miscarriage; we recommend it highly (see the Selected Bibliography).

10 Your New Baby:
The First Eighteen Months

Sarah and Pat adopted Mallory from Guatemala when she was four and a half months old. After returning home, not only did they feel jet-lagged, but Mallory's feeding schedule was all mixed up. She was completely unpredictable and sometimes cried for her bottle every hour. The two women were exhausted. They had anticipated some of this, and Pat had taken two weeks off from work in addition to the three-month leave Sarah had taken. Their answering machine had recorded twenty messages since they had returned, but they had only managed to return three of them. Both women were normally very efficient, and they were stunned at how confused everything had become. They were also surprised at how utterly happy they were.

The first few weeks after giving birth or bringing home an adopted baby are amazingly disorienting. Most mothers make comments something to the effect of, "All I did today was feed the baby and change him, where did the day go?" Your regular home routine will be in flux as you concentrate on the needs of your new family member—feeding him, bathing him, putting him down to sleep. As you settle into a pattern, you can go about adding the extras, such as getting dressed, going out or writing thank-you cards for baby presents. Your new baby is in your life to stay, so get ready for the big changes your tiny child will bring to your home.

Development Guideposts

Infancy has several subcategories. We have chosen to look at two broad stages: newborn to six months, and six months to eighteen months. Remember that children differ and that developmental guidelines do not adhere to a rigid timetable. Any guideline needs to be adjusted for a particular child. If you are interested in a more complete description of infant development, we recommend some books in our Selected Bibliography.

Newborn to Six Months: Pee, Poop, Tears ... and Smiles

The infant's primary physical task is to use her body to eat, pee, poop and cry. It may seem to you that she does nothing else! But she is also undergoing enormous physical changes and is slowly learning how to control her body.

Babies are born with almost no voluntary control over their bodies, although they do have reflexes which mimic later abilities. Many of these reflexes reflect an infant's instinct for survival. One is the sucking reflex: touch a young infant near its mouth and he will turn his mouth toward that side and suck. Another is the grasp reflex: stroke the palm of your baby's hand and he will wrap his fingers tightly around yours. Babies develop physical control from the head down. First they become adept at using their mouths and focusing their eyes, then they develop some control over their arms, hands and fingers. Finally, babies learn to control their legs and feet.

By six months most babies have learned to sit up. With their improved control they can also maneuver their bodies by twisting, bending and rolling over. This gives them new perspectives on their world and encourages them to explore more.

Infants begin immediately to learn about their environment. They learn to discriminate voices, colors, shapes and people. Research has shown that young infants are more attracted to patterns that resemble faces than to other patterns. Studies have also demonstrated that a young baby can pick out its biological mother's voice from others.[1] Young infants need enough cognitive stimulation to engage them, but not so much that they shut down because they are overwhelmed. They thrive on play and engagement with the adults around them.

One of the most delightful developments is your baby's smiling, which usually begins during the second month. Some say that babies begin to smile just as their parents are beginning to run out of energy! Those heartstopping smiles give you renewed encouragement to keep on getting up for two a.m. feedings and changing endless diapers.

As an infant begins to develop emotionally, she learns to trust first her parents, then herself and then the broader world.[2] Since the baby cannot take care of herself yet, it is up to the parents to provide the environment which makes trust possible. You need to nurture and protect your child, and develop a loving relationship with her so she can bond with you. You must interpret your baby's signals, then provide what she needs. When your two-month-old cries it is up to you to find out why she is crying and to correct the problem if possible—such as feeding her if she is hungry or offering comfort if no immediate solution is possible. Sometimes no cause of distress is obvious; even though this can be frustrating, your job is still to comfort your child.

Six to Eighteen Months: Learning Through Movement

A baby who is six to eighteen months old is beginning his *doing* on this planet—learning through movement and physical play. He learns to trust that he can do things independently of his parents; he begins to get his own needs met. This ranges from learning to hold a cup and spoon so he can feed himself to learning to use words to ask for something. A result of his increased independence is the baby's growing awareness of being a separate person from his primary caregiver.

One common developmental marker is stranger anxiety: fear of anyone the baby does not know. This generally happens between six and twelve months, the same time your baby demonstrates a particularly strong attachment to his mother or primary caregiver. He is also quite fearful of being separated from her. Strangers are not tolerable substitutes for mom and may even intensify the baby's fear that he will be taken from his mother. Some children never evidence this and others are terrified by a new person. This behavior passes in time and is believed to be part of a child's developing sense of a separate self.

Among the biggest developmental milestones between six and eighteen months are the advances in how your baby gets around. At seven months some babies begin to crawl; at nine months many are accomplished at this task and are beginning to stand and "cruise" around the room, holding onto furniture.

Many babies begin walking at about one year and by eighteen months most walk well. This single change, from horizontal to vertical, dramatically affects your child's view of the world and motivates him to explore it further. The increased independence that comes with being able to walk seems to be a little unnerving to children. You may observe your child walk away from you while looking back over his shoulder every few steps to make sure you are still there.

During this time children move from babbling and vocalizing sounds to using about ten or more words and people's names. They like physical play with "safe" playmates (like a parent) and by eighteen months may enjoy rough and tumble play. This is a time of rapid physical, social and cognitive development. As your child explores her expanding world, she needs a safe environment. This means moving things out of her reach that you do not want touched or broken, covering electrical outlets, blocking stairways and generally altering your entire house temporarily.

One night ten-month-old Brendan was crawling around the main floor of the house while his moms and older brother were finishing dinner. Dorsey asked Margaret, "Did we lock the baby gate leading upstairs?" Just as Margaret was about to answer they heard the tinkling of the toy piano upstairs in the older boy's room. They were all silent and then laughed with relief. Their very active Brendan had discovered the steps and "up."

Parenting Issues

When a baby becomes the center of your life, learning how to take care of him and adjust to his demands requires an enormous amount of energy! If you gave birth, your body is recovering from the end of pregnancy and the physical stress of labor, while also undergoing new changes—the onset of milk in your breasts, the boost of hormones that keeps you going even with little or no sleep. If you are the partner of a woman who gave birth you, too, are adjusting to a whole new focus, too little sleep (but without the hormones to help), and the expansion of your family by one more—vocal—member.

What happens to your partner relationship when you have a baby? The only certainty is: it changes. Some women find that having a baby adds a wonderful new dimension to their relationship. Others report that having a baby stresses the relationship to the breaking point. Usually a couple has less time and energy for sexual intimacy. This may be replaced by more time together focused on the child, but quality time with one another is hard to come by.

When you lose sexual and physical intimacy with your partner it can feel like you are living with a sibling instead of a lover. Often it is the non-biological mother who misses sex first, because she is not as physically occupied with the new baby. Even if both of you feel too exhausted to be interested in sex, we encourage you to find small ways to be together as a couple without the baby. Have a friend care for your baby for one or several hours. Strengthening your couple relationship is not only important for each of you, it will also help energize you for the shared work of caring for your child.

Who Does What?

One of the first issues that a couple has to deal with is who does what with the baby. Some couples share everything, even the nursing. (The non-biological mother can use a supplemental nursing system with breastmilk or formula.) Most, however, leave the nursing to the birth mother. We encourage you to breastfeed your baby as this is, with a few exceptions, the healthiest option for a child.

When your infant does not nurse well, it can be very unnerving. Mothers who worry that they are breastfeeding incorrectly should talk to their health care provider for tips, or contact someone from La Leche League, an organization which advocates breastfeeding and provides support and information for nursing mothers. (Books are also helpful—see our Selected Bibliography.) Babies vary in how they approach nursing. Some suck very hard and are finished quickly; others suck intermittently and take an hour per meal. If you are breastfeeding your baby, you may feel overwhelmed by the enormous amount of time it takes, not to mention your sore nipples. Remember that nursing your child is a learned skill—make sure you get lots of support, then relax and enjoy this special period of your child's life.

Sometimes breastfeeding does not work for either the baby or for the mother. Some mothers decide not to breastfeed before the birth because of personal preference or work schedules; others try to breastfeed but switch to bottlefeeding. If you had a fantasy of breastfeeding but have decided it is better to bottlefeed, don't berate or criticize yourself, even if you feel disappointed. Your baby will be fine with bottlefeedings. You can still hold and nurture him and tell him how much you love him while you feed him.

If you are a non-biological mother you can share in the feeding times with your baby by bottlefeeding formula or milk expressed by your partner. Of course there are many other ways to bond with your baby. You can hold him close and caress him; you can engage him with your voice and eyes. You can carry him in a front carrier and dance with him to music in your living room. Develop your own ways of communicating your love and attention.

The amount of time each of you spends bonding with and caring for your infant also depends on your work commitments and schedules. When one parent is working outside the home and the other is a full-time parent and housekeeper, the job sharing reflects this division. The at-home parent often does most of the daytime routine such as infant care, shopping and cooking. It is crucial, however, that you develop a system which ensures each of you adequate time to develop a strong, nurturing relationship with your baby.

Susan and Terry had their first child three years ago; now their second daughter had arrived. Terry, the biological mother this time, took four months off from work to take care of both children. Susan continued her job after a two-week break. Terry loves nursing but feels tied down because of having to be with the baby for every feeding. Susan, remembering the closeness of nursing their first daughter, is anxious to find ways to connect with the new little one. The mothers agree that Terry will express milk for at least five feedings a week so Susan can feed the baby and Terry can take breaks. Susan offers to come home an hour early two days a week so Terry can have some free time when it is still light outside. When Susan feeds the baby for the first time, Terry looks back through the window as she walks outside. Susan is nestled on the living room couch, smiling beatifically at her tiny daughter.

Your schedules are not the only thing you will need to work out in the early months. You and your partner may not see eye to eye about the baby's schedule. One issue where differences in opinion can emerge is whether the baby should be fed on demand or whether the parents should establish a set schedule.

Paula and Sharon had decided that Paula would nurse their daughter, Carrie, for about six months while Paula was on leave from her job. Paula had grown up in a family where strict schedules had been kept, especially for meals. Sharon's parents had believed in letting the kids eat whenever they were hungry, as long as they also ate at mealtimes. When Paula wanted to put Carrie on a four-hour nursing schedule so she could do some work at home, Sharon reluctantly went along until Carrie started crying three hours after her last feeding. The two women got into a terrific fight that scared them both. The situation was further complicated by the fact that each of them wanted to prove to her own family that lesbians could be good mothers. After they calmed down they called their family physician for advice. She told them to keep track of Carrie's natural feedings for a week and then come up with an appropriate schedule, based on what they found out. Paula and Sharon realized that they needed to evaluate their daughter's needs rather than automatically using one of their family's systems.

Equally controversial is the question of when to put the baby down for the night. Women who get up early may be content to have the baby go to sleep after a seven or eight o'clock feeding and wake at five a.m. Others may prefer to stay up and feed the baby again at ten or eleven p.m. so the baby will sleep later in the morning. It is important to respect each other's preferences as you balance everyone's needs and sort out what works best for the whole family.

Doreen and Randa are in the throes of putting their five-month-old daughter down for the night. Doreen nurses Iris at nine-thirty p.m., then Randa rocks and holds Iris until she falls asleep. Up until recently this had been a great way for both of them to feel connected to Iris at the end of the day. But now they've noticed that it's taking longer and longer to get Iris to fall asleep. Both women are starting to feel exhausted. Finally, they call their pediatrician for advice. She recommends that they stop rocking Iris to sleep and let her cry for a while, then go in after five minutes and reassure Iris verbally, then let her cry for ten more minutes before going in again. The doctor adds that the mothers should not pick up the baby to help her get to sleep. Doreen and Randa are horrified! They can't imag-

ine letting their baby cry herself to sleep. So they ask a friend who has a thirteen-year-old son about her experiences. The friend tells them that she rocked her son to sleep and had years of trouble getting him to fall asleep on his own. She suggests following the doctor's advice.

Should you go out for a date while the baby is still under a year old? A simple question such as this can lead to some fairly large disagreements. One mother defends the couple's right to a life of their own, the other defends the child's right to what he wants (all of the parents' attention, all of the time!). In these cases it is useful to get good common-sense advice from other mothers and from your health care provider. There is no one "right" way to parent an infant and it is important that both partners discuss areas of disagreement as they come up.

As your baby becomes more mobile and active, other parenting differences may emerge. Very often the parenting style of a mother may resemble the style of her family of origin—or a rejection of that style. For example, some families believe that babies should adapt to the adult environment and don't bother to move any breakables, while others strip the place clean. Neither approach is ideal. We suggest instead that you move enough things so that the child is free to explore and touch without danger or constant reprimand. One practical way of doing such "baby-proofing" is to crawl around the house at your baby's height and remove all potential dangers. As your baby's reach increases, you can repeat the process at higher levels. Your house may look like herds of grazing animals are living there, but these precautions create a safe space for your intrepid young explorer and minimize the stress of having to supervise his every move.

Family and Friends: Help or Hindrance?

Especially in the first months of parenting, you will need outside help. For starters, parents of newborn children are sleep-deprived. Between grabbing naps when they can, they don't have enough time in the day to get everything done. Any strategy which helps you get more sleep is of primary importance. Try to nap when your baby sleeps, or have a friend or family member watch him for a few hours each day.

•   •   •

Sabrina's mother-in-law offered help when her son was born. She came over every afternoon and did house jobs like laundry and walking the dog, which helped keep the household running. This gave Sabrina and her partner some extra time to sleep and had the added benefit of freeing up the mothers to do baby care with more energy.

Friends and family members who already have children are usually good at figuring out how to help, but even they may need specific suggestions, as may those with little child care experience. Don't be afraid to give them guidance or specific directions for what to do, and make sure you express your appreciation for their efforts.

Family and friends can be a much-needed source of support—but they can also drain you, depending on how they approach you and your child. Clearly, affirmation for lesbian mothers is positive support. Heterosexism is a drain.

Tina's mother, Gert, is visiting her new grandbaby for the first time. Gert is a take-charge kind of woman and gets right to work organizing Tina and her partner Flora's household. Most of the organizing is fine with the new mothers, but today Gert began screening who could come visit the baby and mothers and who could not. She seemed particularly uncomfortable with some of Tina and Flora's more 'dykey' friends. This is too much for Tina. She has a talk with her mother and says that she and Flora will decide who can come and when.

If you have a family member who is draining your energy rather than giving you more, you may need to create ways for them to be helpful or find ways to keep them away. For example, you could tell your mother you'd like her to wait until the baby is a month old before she visits. Ask the brother who is good at fixing things but awkward around people to build a cradle for the baby. Gently explain to your father that he can only visit the baby if he promises to smoke *outside* the house (you can even get him a chair and an ashtray for the porch). Sometimes you just have to tell a friend that you do not need the type of help they are offering. Thank them anyway and, if you want to, try brainstorming other ways they could help out.

As your child begins to sleep through the night and develops a routine, you will probably think about spending more time away from the baby. Here again is a natural place for friends and family to pitch in—they can take the baby for a few hours during the day or at night to give you a rest or time to go out. If you work outside the home during the day and your baby is in day care, you may feel some ambivalence about getting additional "child breaks" so you can enjoy yourself. But even mothers who work outside the home need time with adults for relaxing and rejuvenating.

Even with good support, parenting an infant can sometimes be daunting. If you want help with specific issues there are many great books on caring for and parenting infants. Your library and local bookstores are good places to browse until you find one or more resources that fit your style and situation. (See both Bibliographies at the end of the book.) Consider joining a parent support group. You may be able to find them listed in children's stores, in parenting newsletters and magazines, at local colleges and in newspapers. Above all, keep your sense of humor—it will help you get through the days when exhaustion and the demands of caring for an infant wear you to a frazzle.

Karen had just begun to see friends again, four months after her daughter was born. She was feeling almost like her old self. At least she thought so, until she heard her response to her friend Sarah's question. Sarah had asked simply, "How are you doing?" And Karen said, "Oh, she's fine."

Out in the World

When a child comes into the world, it is an event of celebration, not only for the happy mother or couple, but for the community—at your church or synogogue, for instance, or at your workplace. Yet as we said earlier in this book, being out with a child creates certain dilemmas for lesbian parents. There is the constant threat of homophobia as well as the subtle and overt assumptions of heterosexism. Here, and in subsequent chapters, we discuss "out in the world" issues typical of each stage of your child's development. For instance, if you belong to a religious faith, will your religious community welcome your baby into the world as a child of a lesbian or lesbian couple?

Kathleen and Erin attended a Catholic church in their neighborhood. When their child was born they had her baptized by their priest, as they knew him to be supportive of lesbian-headed families. Although he never disagreed publicly with the Church's official stand on homosexuality, personally he was supportive and inclusive of gay and lesbian families, including Kathleen and Erin's.

Miriam wanted her son to have a bris just as her father and brothers had had. She was proud of being Jewish and wanted Joshua to begin his life the way Jewish boys had begun theirs for thousands of years. Her rabbi encouraged lesbians and gay men to be active members of the congregation. Miriam felt pleased to ask him to officiate at the ceremony for her son.

Depending on the particular congregation, a lesbian family may feel affirmed or rejected by their religious community. We urge you to find an affirming congregation which will welcome and support your whole family's participation in worship.

Another arena of life that is affected by the arrival of a child is the workplace. There are an unlimited number of ways to introduce your child into your work life—from putting baby pictures on your desk to swapping diapering tips on the factory line. How one comes out as a parent depends in part on your work situation. Obviously, the more lesbian-affirming the workplace, the easier it is to tell about your child.

Sadly, it is not always safe for a lesbian to come out or to announce her motherhood. For non-biological mothers it may be easier to stay closeted, but it is painful to do so. Find support if you cannot come out or if you are out in a hostile work place.

Most lesbian parents we know prefer to show pride in their parenthood and be open about who they are. Such honesty can enhance your life—and make it easier when you have to call in sick because your child has the chicken pox. But whether you are able to be out or have to stay closeted, life with an infant is demanding, and it requires constant juggling.

Ann worked for the city as an unskilled laborer during the day; at night she was taking gardeners' classes. She planned to start a gardening business—and try to get pregnant—as soon as she was finished with the class work. She was terrified of how the men on the job would treat her if they found out she and her partner were lesbians, let alone lesbian parents.

Within a year she had quit working for the city, started up her business, and gotten pregnant. She stopped gardening when she was six months pregnant, then resumed when the baby was two months old. She loved working with the baby in a front carrier or asleep nearby in the truck. She couldn't understand why she hadn't done it all sooner.

Ann, of course, is lucky. She is able to take her baby to work with her. Her situation is rare.

It can be painful when you leave your baby at home to return to work. You may be sad at losing your time with him or you may be worried about whether day care is good for him. Talk to other women who have put their young children in day care settings; their stories may give you reassurance and ease any worries you have about leaving your baby with someone else.

When choosing a day care situation for your baby ask friends for referrals. Talk to the prospective day care staff members about your family situation. You will discover a variety of child care options to choose from. If you plan to use a day care facility, here are some questions to consider as you visit each site:

- What is the teacher-child ratio? Generally speaking, the younger the children being cared for, the smaller the ratio needs to be.
- What are the credentials of the staff, how are they trained, and is there any provision for ongoing training?
- Is there a quiet room for children who are sleeping?
- Are there adequate play areas and toys which allow for a variety of play themes, such as dress-up, toy kitchen and utensils, dolls, blocks and cars and trucks?
- Are there clean bathroom and changing facilities with adequate attention to sanitation?
- Is the facility licensed by the state? (Check to see that the licensing is current.)
- Is the staff affirming of lesbian and gay families?
- Is the staff anti-racist and affirming of different religions?
- Does the setting feel welcoming and friendly—in short, would you feel comfortable leaving your child there?

◆　◆　◆

Cindy took her daughter to the day care center for her first day. She sat there for fifteen minutes, as the staff had suggested, while her sixteen-month-old explored the room and met the teacher. Cindy found herself feeling irritated with every little thing the teacher said or did. As she walked out, Cindy wondered if she had done the right thing by bringing her daughter here and not postponing working for another few months. When she got to the car, she burst into tears. Her heart ached for her baby and their time alone together. When she picked up her happy, giggling daughter at the end of the day, she felt a wave of relief and realized the separation might be harder on her than on her daughter.

You might decide to hire a nanny to come work in your home instead of using a day care facility. If you are considering this option for your child, consider a few additional questions as you interview prospective caregivers.

- What references does this person have? Talk to one or more families that this nanny has worked for. Ask about her work with the child in that family and other questions, such as whether she was on time and organized.
- If this person has never been a caretaker for an infant, find out why they are interested in doing it now and what experience they have with very young children.
- What plans does this caregiver have for interacting with your child? How does he play, put a baby down for a nap or feed an infant?
- Ask about her philosophy of limit-setting and discipline.
- Are this person's beliefs about childrearing and his behavior with children a good match with yours?
- Are you comfortable with this person as a caregiver and as someone who will spend many hours in your house?
- Has this person had any experience with lesbians and how does she feel about lesbian parents?

Tia's baby, Max, is nine months old. He is happy and very interested in the world around him. Tia had worried about having to send him to day care when she went back to work, so she had been ecstatic when she met a young lesbian woman who was exploring having a child. The young

woman agreed to take care of Max at Tia's house. Tia can't imagine a
better set-up.

•   •   •

We have covered a lot of territory in this chapter—from sleepless nights comforting a newborn to days spent running after an eighteen-month-old. Your home, your family, your lover relationship, and your heart and soul have been forever changed. Your life will never be the same again, yet the parenting journey is really just beginning. You will probably never be so challenged or so rewarded by any other job. Get all the support you can, and go for it!

11

Parenting the Toddler:
Eighteen Months to
Thirty-Six Months

Two-year-old Shane was having a hard day. First his mother, Perry, gave him the "wrong" cereal for breakfast, which infuriated him. (It didn't matter that he had loved it yesterday.) When he arrived at day care, he clung to Perry as she got ready to leave, then screamed for a full three minutes before letting the child care worker hold him. When Perry picked him up at five-thirty, he was balky and stubborn and made her wait while he struggled with his coat—no help, thank you. At dinner he insisted on eating his potato "his way" and then threw it on the floor in frustration. When Perry put him to bed that night he wanted to cuddle with her and read book after book, "all night."

The period of a child's life we call toddlerhood, roughly eighteen months to thirty-six months, is one of the most challenging times for parents. It is the age when children begin testing parental authority, from throwing things inappropriately to refusing to eat their breakfast. As a result, parents are engaged—seemingly constantly—with the task of setting and enforcing clear limits. This period also marks the beginning of a child's awareness of himself as an individual: he begins thinking for himself and having opinions which are different from his mother's. As in the story of Shane and Perry, a parent may have some very trying days as her toddler changes from a pleasant, compliant member of the household to a demanding, churlish one.

Yet the thrill of watching of your small child learn to talk, solve problems and become more physically adept is one of the peak rewards of parenting. Many parents look back at this period of their child's life with great fondness—sometimes only after a number of years have passed! Toddlers are endearingly affectionate; they love being read and sung to by their "mommies" and like to accompany them on day-to-day errands. Going grocery shopping with an inquisitive two-year-old can change an ordinary event into an adventure. It is an amazing source of pride to watch your child begin the process of becoming an independent person.

Development Guideposts

The eighteen-to-thirty-six-month period is characterized by a steady continuation of physical development rather than by any great quantitative leaps in ability. It is in the cognitive and psychological/social realms of development that the toddler shows the most growth.

Physical Skills[1]

An eighteen-month-old usually has mastered several gross motor skills—she has learned to walk and can run awkwardly. She may be beginning to crawl backwards down the steps—as if she has realized her body can work in reverse, too. She likes to practice climbing and may try to climb out of her crib. Children at this age enjoy playing with balls but usually have not mastered the idea or act of kicking one. Some children are beginning to show interest in using the toilet but do not have sufficient control to do so.

Fine motor control is rudimentary. Your son may like to turn pages of a book, but two or three pages at a time; he may tear paper books because of his lack of coordination. Most children can build a tower of three to four blocks and turn knobs on the TV or radio.

At two years, toddlers have become more stable as they walk. They do not bump into things in the house as much as they did at eighteen months, but their running is still awkward. They climb up steps well but have difficulty coming down (unless they crawl down backwards). Two-year-olds love to throw and throw again. They have enormous amounts of energy and love to play actively on outdoor swings, slides and climbing structures. Their fine motor skills continue to improve—they can hold a crayon with an adult-like grip and they can build a tower of five blocks.

By the time your toddler is thirty-six months old, she can run well, even if she has difficulty stopping and starting quickly. A thirty-six-month-old can usually walk down stairs, both feet on every step. She can ride a tricycle or other three-wheeled vehicle. Most three-year-olds have begun working on bowel control, although many do not get full control for months to come.

Your three-year-old's fine motor control is better, too. He can build a tower of eight blocks and has good hand and finger coordination. He can draw beyond a scribble and enjoys the process of making marks and experimenting with colors.

Cognitive Advances

Eighteen-month-olds have a vocabulary of about twenty words, most two-year-olds have mastered around two hundred, and three-year-olds can jump to over nine hundred! Children understand far more words than they can express at this age. You can stimulate their verbal progress by helping them learn to label objects in their world. As you walk in the park, say the word "tree" when your child touches a tree. Say "cat" when she pats the family cat. Labeling is the true beginning of learning language. Encourage your child to listen, mimic sounds accurately (like meow for the sounds cats make) and to use the right word for a familiar object—"cookie!"

Sometime between eighteen and twenty-four months, most children begin to combine two words to make simple phrases, which often mean much more than the two words alone: "Me up" translates into "Mommy, pick me up right now." At age three, children begin to use complete sentences and ask more varied questions. You cannot speed up your child's ability to make complex sentences, but you can encourage him by listening attentively when he talks and by using clear, complete sentences when you respond to him.

As toddlers explore the world around them, they start thinking about their discoveries: *problem-solving* begins. The eighteen-month-old does this through physical trial and error. A favorite game at this age is putting differently shaped blocks into a shape sorting box. The toddler learns which shapes match by putting a square block into a round hole to check if it fits. By age three the same toddler is able to solve similar puzzles by thinking it through, instead of trying it out physically. But even though the thirty-six-month-old is far more advanced intellectually than his younger counterparts, he needs to be watched by parents carefully as he explores. In his exuberance and curiosity he is quite unpredictable in his judgment.

Psychological/Social Development

One of the hallmarks of the toddler years is the blossoming development of the child's separate identity: becoming independent. Independence and assertion of self, for the toddler, usually begin by defining herself as different or separate from others—her parents. Her physical and cognitive advances make it easier for her to act and express herself independently. One way your child asserts her new sense of self and proclaims "I'm me" is to dress herself; yet another way is to feed herself. Unfortunately, children at this age are not quite coordinated enough to be adept at these tasks without assistance. They also get frustrated easily. But ask to help and you will hear, "No!"

"No" seems to be, universally, the word of choice for children in this age range. (Unfortunately, no sometimes means yes and can cause much confusion for the family until the context and true meaning is figured out.) Parents, as well as children, can overuse the word no during these years. While the child says "no!" as a means of self-discovery, the parent says "no" to try to keep her child's expression of self and increased exploration under control.

This age of negativity has prompted many parents to refer to it as the "Terrible Twos." Friends and family may begin hinting that you are doing something wrong to have a child so negative or with such a temper. Actually, you are likely doing something *right* if you respect and support your child's saying no while continuing to ensure her safety. When your child says no, she will not wear those blue tights, you can tell her you understand, but that she needs to wear something warm on her legs because the weather is cold. It helps to give a two-year-old choices when she says no; offer a choice between the blue tights and the red leggings. That makes it possible for both of you to be winners. Avoid open-ended choices, which can be too overwhelming for toddlers and end in tears.

The toddler demands attention; he wavers between dependent baby and independent child, he clings to you then struggles to be free. He is testing his ability to venture out on his own, but needs you there when he comes back. Fortunately, for everyone, a positive side of the toddler's need to be the center of the universe is that they are worth paying attention to! They are fun and stimulating to be with, and it is a delight to explore the world with them—even if it can also be exhausting.

Parenting Issues

Becoming Independent

As your toddler cycles back and forth between dependence and independence, you may feel like you are caught on a roller coaster ride with no end in sight. Buckle your seat belt, and stay calm. Try to be consistent yet flexible in the face of toddler whims. Don't take your child's mood swings personally or worry that you have done something wrong. This is not about you, this is healthy development!

If you have adopted a toddler, you may have to cope with exaggerated mood swings—or your child may withdraw if he does not feel safe enough yet to test your limits. He may need extra time to learn to trust that you are not going to abandon him or punish him excessively when he acts out, depending on your child's history. With patience on your part, he will flourish and become as assertive as any other toddler. We recommend that you talk to parents who have adopted toddlers and read books which discuss how adoption affects early child development.

The roller coaster of toddlerhood is an extremely important phase of a child's development. These years lay the foundation for a child's ability to become a healthy, *interdependent* person, capable of connecting and cooperating with others while maintaining a separate identity. The skills of interdependence are only beginning to form, however, at the toddler age. Cooperation with others, in fact, is in scant evidence. In play groups, for example, most toddlers are apt to say, "mine, mine!" rather than share their toys politely with other children. Parents need not worry about this, and you should not push your toddlers too early to "share." Up until the age of thirty months or so, toddlers are still establishing their egos and thus a certain amount of selfishness is both needed and normal.[2]

"I Go Potty!"

One developmental skill that highlights the up-and-down process of a toddler's striving for independence is toilet learning. Children usually begin expressing interest in using the toilet between the ages of eighteen months and thirty-six months or so—but each child is different and has her own timetable. And don't get your hopes up too fast, because interest and skill are not the same thing! It may take your child a year or more to learn this skill well.

There are many ways for parents to ease the process of toilet learning. Some read books to their children about it or talk to them matter-of-factly when they, the parents, are using the toilet. It is a good idea to have a child-sized potty in the bathroom or a seat that attaches to the toilet. (Most children are scared of sitting on a regular-sized toilet because they can fall in so easily.) There are lots of books and resources on how to go about this task. Your patience and praise will be the keys. Follow your child's cues when she indicates an interest and readiness in trying the potty. Then encourage her with praise and support.

As with other developmental changes in toddlers, avoid getting into power struggles with your child about using the potty. Children *do* want to become independent of their diapers and will do so eventually. Toilet learning is not necessarily a linear process, however. Some toddlers progress in fits and starts; their resistence may be due to their discomfort with a new behavior, or it may be their ambivalence about becoming independent.

Yet, "avoiding power struggles" is often easier said than done! Some toddlers become so angry at age two about having their diapers changed that it takes one person to hold them down and another to put the diapers on. One would think that such a child would be delighted to use a potty at this point—but that transition may still be months away. Or a child may vacillate back and forth between eagerly demanding to use the potty and refusing to sit on "that thing." Although this sort of "one step forward, two steps back" can be frustrating for both you and your child, it is absolutely essential that you not shame or humiliate your child if he does not perform according to your timetable. Use praise, not punishment.

After weeks of wrestling on the changing table, Georgia told her three-year-old, Mallory, that she wasn't going to fight with her about changing her diapers. If Mallory wanted to wear diapers, she would have to let her mother change her without a fight, otherwise she had to learn to use the potty. Mallory stopped yelling so much and within a short time began to show interest in using the potty, which had been waiting in the bathroom for a year.

Connor, a particularly verbal boy of two-and-a-half, was visiting friends of his mothers'—a family with a four-year-old. The two boys disappeared into the bathroom. Twenty minutes later they reappeared with Connor announcing to his mothers that he now knew how to use a potty and wouldn't need diapers anymore. And he didn't.

It is a bumpy, ungraceful process for a child to learn how to separate and still maintain dependence. And it can be a bumpy, ungraceful process for a parent, too, as you wonder whether your child's anger and stubborn self-assertion is normal. It is. Imagine what your child would be like without the ability to say no. A child who has difficulty saying no may, later in life, not know how to say no to pressure to have sex when she does not want it, or how to say no to drinking and driving.

The Gentle Art of Discipline

A parent's central task with a toddler is to set limits while allowing her to think for herself and problem-solve. Allow natural consequences to happen, provided that they do not jeopardize your child's safety.

Karen, a two-year-old, wants to pour her own milk on her cereal. The first time she tries it the milk spills everywhere. Karen's mom gives her the sponge and lets Karen "clean up" the mess. Afterwards they talk about what would help the next time. Karen says, "Too big." The next morning, Karen's mother puts some milk in a small pitcher and lets Karen try again. Only a small amount spills. Karen is thrilled with her new accomplishment. "More!" she yells.

Successful parenting of toddlers requires that you learn the art of gentle discipline. People often think of discipline as punishment, but *Webster's Seventh New Collegiate Dictionary* lists another definition of discipline before punishment, which is worth bearing in mind: *instruc-*

tion. In disciplining our children, we are instructing them about living cooperatively in a world with other people; we are helping them establish good habits. When we use the punishment-only version of discipline, we may in fact instill bad habits and set the stage for a lifelong power struggle with anyone in authority. Virtually all parents at some point punish their children. Yet, as we discussed in Chapter Five, the more we can incorporate a win-win approach to discipline, the more likely it is that our children will develop a respect for limits and a habit of setting their own.

> *Two-and-a-half-year-old Sean refuses to put his toys back in the toy box after his mother tells him to do so. Sean's mother then tells Sean that the blocks on the floor are a problem for her. Sean insists that he does not want to put them away and that instead he wants to play with his friend, next door. Mom tells Sean that he can either pick up the blocks himself, or they can pick them up together. She adds that when the blocks are all picked up, he can go ask his friend to play.*

To some children, "clean up your mess" means put things in a neat pile by the wall, to others it can mean throw away your art pictures. Be specific: "Put your blocks back in the toy box." Accentuate the positive instead of the negative. Rather than telling your daughter, "Stop yelling!" try asking for the positive behavior you want. Tell her to speak in a soft, "inside" or quiet voice, instead.

There are two kinds of rules and limits: negotiable and non-negotiable. It is important that you figure out which is which and be able to communicate that to your child. For instance, in Anna's home it is negotiable whether her two-and-half-year-old, Sophie, wears a bib at meals. Sophie frequently rebels against wearing a bib, and Anna decided it wasn't worth a fight unless Sophie is wearing her best clothes. In contrast, Anna makes clear that it is not acceptable for Sophie to hit her, her younger brother or *anyone*. She explains to Sophie that it is OK for her to hit the couch if she feels angry.

Consistency is the key. Most children have excellent memories for your lapses in limit-setting, and they will remind you. It is important to be consistent and clear with children so they can trust the limits you have put in place.

◆ ◆ ◆

Roberta's twenty-month-old daughter, Maggie, wanted to go to the store with Roberta's girlfriend to get the ice cream for dessert. Since she had a cold, Roberta told her no. Maggie had a full-blown tantrum—she lay on the floor, kicking and crying. When Maggie threw her doll at her mother, Roberta told her that throwing things was unacceptable behavior. "If you throw it again," Roberta told her, "you'll have a five-minute time-out in the dining room." Maggie threw the doll anyway and Roberta immediately picked her up and took her to the dining room. She sat Maggie on a chair and set the timer for five minutes. She repeated that it was not okay to throw things. "Time-outs" were part of the discipline structure in the family. Maggie knew she had crossed the line her mother had set. She sat crying for about one more minute, then sucked her thumb until the timer dinged. Then she got up and joined her mother in the kitchen.

She Said . . . She Said: Being Consistent as a Couple

If you are in a couple, toddlerhood is a likely time for differences of opinion to arise, especially about discipline. It is common for two women to have similar ideas about the kind of parenting environment they want in their home, yet have quite different approaches for creating that environment. One mother may give their child one warning, then impose consequences. The other mother may explain the problem and negotiate with their child every time. Such inconsistency can undermine each mother's style, as well as make the limits confusing to the child.

The issue of *who* disciplines can come up even before the struggles about *how* to discipline. Some coupled parents choose one mother to be responsible for the bulk of discipline decisions. A drawback to this arrangement is that the parent who doesn't do much discipline becomes more "fun," while the day-to-day limit-setter becomes the heavy. This dynamic quickly becomes hard on the whole family. The child may resist the fun parent's attempt to do work-related activities; the disciplinarian may have trouble finding relaxed play time with the child. It is important for both parents to have chore-related *and* fun time with the child.

We encourage you to talk to each other about what values and approaches are important to you. This can include a discussion of the ways in which your families of origin set limits—and your perspectives on those methods now. Read parenting books, take classes together on parenting, and stay engaged with each other as you work out effective ways to set limits for your toddler.

If you are the new partner of a mother of a toddler, this time can be a difficult one. It is typical for a new partner or girlfriend to dislike some of the mother-child interactions but be unsure of how or whether to object. You may believe that the child should not be allowed to speak back to her mother, or you may think that your girlfriend is too strict. Either way you should talk to your partner and tell her about your discomfort. If you are only dating, you do not really have the right to dictate how your partner should raise her child. If you start making strenuous objections to her parenting decisions, you are likely to find yourself looking for a new girlfriend! On the other hand, if you are developing a committed relationship, the two of you need to find ways to meld as family.

If you are the family newcomer, keep in mind that almost everyone would like to change something in her girlfriend's parenting style—be patient. Remember that she has been parenting for a couple of years and that there may be reasons for her actions of which you are not aware—be respectful.

You may also discover that your partner's child is critical of you. He may reject your invitations to play and escalate his "no"-saying and attention-getting behavior if he is angry about having to "share" his mother. Work together with your partner to find ways to smooth the transition of adding a new family member. Eventually, he is likely to warm up to you, but respect his limits until he does.

Bill always seemed to have a tantrum when his mom's girlfriend, Kate, came over to dinner. He refused to eat and threw his spoon on the floor. Kate kept picking up the spoon and offering it to him, but he would just throw it down again. Kate switched tactics and started praising Bill when he did something well, such as when he drank from his cup. One night, weeks later, Bill asked Kate to give him more milk. Kate realized that was the start of their friendship.

If you are a single mother, you also need to think about and develop your own particular style of parenting. The advantage of being single is that you don't have to coordinate your parenting with someone else. The disadvantage is you don't have someone else at home to nudge you if you get too lenient or strict, or back you up when your toddler is rebelling. Hang in there: with time comes confidence.

Support Groups and Play Groups

Parenting a toddler requires resilience and energy. Get enough rest, and make sure that you spend time alone as well as with friends, your partner, and other children in the family. As with many other phases of parenting, dealing with your child's behavior may unleash feelings about unresolved issues from your own childhood. You may want to read helpful material or see a counselor for help.

Ann had had it with her daughter, Caryl, who refused to do anything Ann told her to do. Ann came close to yelling at Caryl that she needed to "do better" or she would have no dinner and would have to stay in her room until she apologized. Then Ann had remembered how often her mother had done that to her and how often she had cried herself to sleep. Ann decided she needed help in finding new ways to respond to her daughter's behavior.

In many areas of the country there are organizations and support groups for parents as well as a version of informal play groups for your child. Support networks of parents with similarly aged children can be enormously helpful. One group of lesbian moms in Seattle has been meeting for more than ten years. There have been additional children born, divorces and new partnerings but a core group continues to meet regularly, offering friendship and sometimes child care. The children of the mothers have become friends and sometimes act as an unofficial support group for each other.

Some women also form child care groups. You can rotate who has the kids on any given morning or you can designate a weekend night where one household takes all the children for the evening or overnight, giving the other parents a night off. There are all-lesbian groups, gay and lesbian groups, and mixed/heterosexual groups. The point is to find a group of like-minded parents in your community and create ways of getting support.

If you are a single mother you may need to make extra efforts to guarantee yourself time alone or with friends. Sometimes parent support groups can provide that, but you may also need to make an arrangement with a specific friend or relative to share the load. It is not uncommon for lesbian mothers to have selected lesbian or gay friends spend time on a regular basis with their child. Some mothers specifically ask male friends to become involved (see Chapter Three). Usually these special friends take the child to their house or on an outing for a regularly scheduled time. This arrangement seems much more common in lesbian/gay communities than in heterosexual ones.

Mitzi and Sue asked Carl to be an "uncle" to their son Josh. Carl baby-sat Josh during the first six months, and after Mitzi had finished nursing, Josh spent every Thursday afternoon and night at Carl's house. When Sue, Mitzi and Josh went on a week-long church retreat, one of the childcare workers came up to the moms after a few days and told them that Josh was the only child out of ten in the under-two crowd who did not obviously prefer a woman to change his diapers—he liked both genders. The two women smiled and realized that their goal of having Josh be comfortable with women and men was off to a good start.

Out in the World

Toddler "Outings"

One day Kelly and May went to the post office with their three-year-old son, Henry. They waited in line behind a very tall man. Henry leaned back against Kelly's leg, looked way up and announced to the stranger, "These are my moms."

Once your child becomes verbal, you begin to lose control over whom you come out to. Your child now has the capacity to do it for you—and will! Being single offers a little cover if you wish it, but if you have been open and comfortable about your lesbianism, your children will pick that up and reflect it in their dealings with other people.

We think it is wonderful for the world at large to learn that lesbians are real, regular people with every-day parenting responsibilities and concerns. This does not mean that our children have to carry a political agenda to their day care centers. What they *will* carry everywhere, however, are the values and attitudes you model for them at home.

By the time their child is a toddler, most parents will have had to interact with a variety of institutions involved with their child: day care centers, physicians' offices, hospitals, churches, synagogues, cultural and community centers. The list goes on and on. All of these interactions provide the opportunity to come out as a lesbian mother, with the potential for either support or pain, or both.

Patsy and Toni are the parents of thiry-two-month-old Keith. They are attending a picnic at a church they have recently started attending. They know few people there but they like whom they've met. At the picnic, a man they don't know comes up to them and asks Toni if she is Keith's mother. Toni and Keith both have dark brown skin and Patsy has olive-complexioned white skin. When she says "yes," he asks where Keith's father is, he'd like to meet him. Toni doesn't know what to say, as she and Patsy had not decided how out they wanted to be at this church.

If you do not want to be out, you need to develop strategies that will protect you from your child's accidently outing you. It may work best to have your toddler call you by your first names instead of "mom"—it's difficult if not impossible for a two-year-old to remember you as mom at home and "Dorcas" at the grocery store. It is, however, often the case that wherever you and your child go, people respond to the child rather than you.

One time when Evelyn was in the grocery store with her daughter, Beverly, she noticed a middle-aged man scowling at her. She guessed it was her political button protesting an anti-gay measure on the upcoming ballot. Just as she took a deep breath and prepared to walk past the man, Beverly toddled up to him and flashed a grin. He smiled back and the tension eased.

Parents who live in large urban areas have more options in finding lesbian-affirmative institutions. Women living in more rural or suburban areas may not have such optimal choices. Yet many lesbian mothers from rural areas report that they are treated well if they do not force the issue of their lesbianism. These women may come out if asked, but they put their identities as neighbor, teacher, churchgoer, secretary or doctor first, and their identity as lesbian farther down the list, sometimes not on the list at all. While this may not be your first choice of how to be in the world, it is one way of surviving in the place you want or have to live.

Out at Work

Since it is very common for lesbians to work outside the home, staying home from the job to care for a sick toddler can pose difficulties, particularly if you are a "non-out," non-biological mother.

Carla and Kim shared the resposibilities of housework and parenting their two-and-a-half-year-old daughter equally. But when Abby kept picking up colds at day care, they faced a problem. Kim, a manager at the fish packing plant, could not risk coming out and so could not say she was staying home with her sick child. Carla, the biological mother, was allowed by her job to take the time off. As a result, it was Carla who stayed at home with Abby. She was worried she would use up all of her sick leave, and she wanted Kim to come out—or at least to tell her boss that she had a daughter. Kim was certain she would be fired or demoted if she did.

This scenario is not uncommon when one mother is out as a parent and the other is not. In this case Kim and Carla sat down and talked about what might *really* happen if Kim came out at work. Kim's boss had fired a man the previous month because he had AIDS and he had made it clear to everyone at the office that he hated queers. They both agreed that Kim should not come out. They also agreed that to take the pressure off Carla, Kim would begin looking for a job that paid equally well as the fish packing job, but where she could be comfortable being out. Even though this plan might take a long time, they both felt relieved.

When you are out at your workplace, you automatically begin the process of educating workmates about lesbians and motherhood. Tell them about the millions of children with lesbian mothers. Show them pictures of your child. Talk about your parenting issues. Lesbians are so used to hiding that we sometimes forget the very real, humanizing effect we have when we complain about our two-year-old's temper tantrum. Virtually all parents respond to that experience—by sharing it you may make friends and lay the groundwork for support when you need to stay home with a sick child or when you bring your son to work.

Given the current political climate and the attempts to enforce anti-gay legislation, it is important to do what we can do to ensure equal rights for all lesbians and gay men. This may mean coming out at your church or it may mean writing your representative in the state or national legislature. As a lesbian mother, you may end up confronting heterosexist institutions or policies which have nothing to do directly with your child in order to provide a healthy and positive environment for all children.

Couple Time

Time alone together is crucial for couples with a toddler. Sometimes you will need to spend this time resolving childrearing conflicts before you can simply relax together. It is easy to get irritated with each other when you are coping with a willful, irrepressible two-year-old. Take the time to commiserate about how hard it can be to parent with a cool head! Try to find time to work together on adult projects like remodelling a room, doing your taxes or putting all your photos of your child in the album—finally. Play time—for parents—is perhaps most important. This can include going to a bed and breakfast for a night of great (uninterrupted) sex, listening to lesbian-affirming love songs (instead of the Sesame Street tape), going out with other lesbians for the evening or just having a quiet hour in bed to talk and touch.

If you are single and dating, make the time with your girlfriend feel like a *real* date, not just a quick break from mothering—for her sake and yours. Time with your lover will feed your heart and mind. It is always important to nurture the non-parent sides of yourself.

Yvonne and her girlfriend, Jackie, bought season tickets to the local college's football games when Yvonne's son turned two. Her best friend came over and spent four hours with the boy while mom and girlfriend went out and cheered happily.

Maria and Gloria took the night off and went out to dinner and then home for an overnight alone while their daughter stayed with friends every Monday evening. It took some time for the mothers to relax and get used to not having their daughter with them, but by the time the morning rolled around they always remembered how much they loved to cuddle together—in the days before their daughter woke them up at 6:00 a.m.

Consider doing things that help you feel like an alive, happy adult. Don't rule out the activities that you used to take for granted, which now seem like luxuries: sleeping in, going to sporting events, having an intellectual conversation over tea or a meal, watching TV late at night, concentrating on a good book or reading the entire Sunday paper, taking a long bath or going for a solitary walk at sunset.

One of the best ways you can parent your toddler is to model interdependence. Nurture and support your child, attend to her many needs—but do the same for yourself. Being a healthy, happy parent is the most solid foundation for raising a healthy, happy toddler.

12 The Emerging Child:
Three to Six Years

Four-year-old Patrick and his three-year-old friend Steve were playing Superman in Patrick's backyard when Patrick decided he wanted to "fly" from the garage roof. He was sure his super powers would protect him. Steve wasn't as sure, but there was no way he was going to be left behind. The two boys were climbing up the ladder to the roof when Patrick's mom saw them from the kitchen window.

Welcome to the exciting world of three- and four-year-olds!

As your child moves through the three-to-six age range, he will swing back and forth between being focused inward and being more expansive; between being insecure and feeling powerful and wonderful. These changes will challenge you to find ways to be nurturing and responsive when your youngster needs holding and to be consistent and firm when he needs limit-setting. The peaks and valleys of guiding your child through these years are smoothed over by the immense satisfaction of engaging with a youngster who is excited about learning and who thinks you are the most wonderful being on earth because you know so much!

During the ages three to six, a child's primary job is to find out who he is and how he fits into the world. He needs to integrate his expanding capacities—including language skills that express complex thoughts and feelings—into that emerging sense of self. His development is an interplay between his physical, emotional and cognitive selves, and is further influenced by social interactions and the events that happen in his family's life.

This is the age when a child begins to discover how powerful she is and that adults are not all-powerful; she begins to learn the difference between fantasy and reality. To do this learning she needs accurate information about herself, her body and the world. She needs to be taught that both genders are to be valued, that being female is wonderful and so is being male. She must be guided to practice socially appropriate behavior and to experience both the positive and negative consequences of her behavior.

The world of this child also begins to expand beyond his immediate family to include more children (peers) and more adults. By the time he has reached the end of this age range, he will probably be in some sort of school setting, perhaps for the first time, marking an important physical and psychological shift. The three-to-six-year-old stage is a stepping stone between home and the world; it is full of whirlwinds and wonder.

Development Guideposts

Spirals of Change

"I don't know what's happened," a distraught mother said to her friend. "Casey was so confident and coordinated when he turned three, six months ago. Now he's insecure, whiny and clingy—he even seems clumsier!"

Casey's mom need not worry, and neither should you if you notice your child swing back and forth from competence to insecurity within the space of six months. According to a current theory of child development, he has simply moved from "equilibrium" to "disequilibrium."[1]

This theory describes early childhood development as six-month swings between equilibrium—a state of confidence and balance, and disequilibrium—a state of being "out of sorts." These spirals of change tend to happen in all areas of development. A physically well-coordinated five-year-old may start stumbling at five-and-a-half; a four-and-a-half-year-old might start stuttering even though he was speaking clearly at four; an outgoing three-year-old ready to meet the world with open arms may pull back and be shy at three-and-a-half. This is not "backsliding" but rather a swing into a disequilibrium phase that unsettles your child; he will move through it in a few months.

Sketched out, the spiral of equilibrium and disequilibrium looks like this:[2]

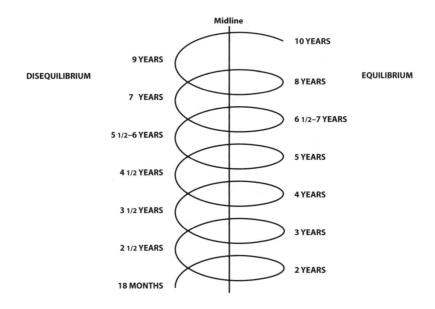

Some children have good equilibrium no matter what age; others seem to be in a state of disequilibrium most of the time. Usually, however, there are some shifts as a child ages, even if only for a few weeks before the child's basic temperament reasserts itself.

It's important to remember that each child moves through developmental stages at *her own pace*, whatever her temperament. Some children are particularly quick in one or more areas, some are slower, and some seem like they have read the books and do everything according to the charts' timetable. A small percentage of all children are truly gifted in one or more areas; some are developmentally delayed. If you have particular questions or concerns about how your child is progressing, we recommend that you onsult your pediatrician or your family health care provider.

♦   ♦   ♦

Physical Skills[3]

A child's gross motor skills improve rapidly in the first year of the three-to-six period. Most four-year-olds can run, climb, hop, jump down from a two-foot height and walk up and down stairs unassisted, one step at a time. They can ride a tricycle and steer it well. By the time children reach six they can run easily with stops, starts and zig-zags in between—sometimes outmaneuvering adults. Some six-year-olds can even ride two-wheelers.

Children in this age range also make big strides in their fine motor development. By age four, they are not reliably right- or left-handed yet, but they may show hand preferences for particular tasks. They can draw rudimentary pictures of human beings, and the *product* of their drawing is now the focus, in contrast to the three-year-old who is more concerned with the *process*. Four-year-olds can thread small beads on a string but cannot yet thread a needle. Five-year-olds can copy some letters but they frequently reverse them. As a child nears six, he can hold a crayon or pencil much like an adult does between thumb and forefinger. He can draw a house, copy some capital letters and is usually well established as right- or left-handed. His fine motor control is quite good—he can thread a large needle—and his hand-eye coordination is almost as fine as an adult's.

With the mastery of physical skills comes a sense of pride and often a willingness to try other, non-physical challenges. Improvement in one developmental area interacts with and facilitates the development of other areas; thus success in physical development helps a child's confidence and spurs progress in his cognitive and emotional development.

Cognitive Advances

Cognitive development includes a wide range of abilities within which we include language, memory, manipulation of concepts, and imagination. Some researchers have demonstrated that children's cognitive development advances in stages.[4] Because every child is unique, their readiness to move from stage to stage varies.

Most children develop their capacity to understand symbols by the time they are in the middle of this age range. They begin to understand the relationship between a symbol, or word, and the thing itself.

The figures your four-year-old can now draw are the beginning of symbolic representation, the use of one thing—a picture—to represent something else—her mother. However, a child this age cannot yet organize these symbols into concepts. For instance, your daughter may see six black cats on a walk to the park and not know whether she is seeing the same cat over and over again or a series of individual black cats. She understands what "cat" means but she does not yet understand the concept of cats as a group of animals and that they come in a variety of colors and sizes. As she moves through the three-to-six stage she will develop the ability to think about a single cat as part of the class of cats.

Thus, a three-year-old may see the parents of four families as just individual sets of parents. But a five-year-old with a lesbian mother may recognize that his family is part of a class called "families" and that his family is less common than the heterosexual families of most of his friends. As a result, he may question the whys and hows of different kinds of families.

> Toby's five-year-old, Nan, comes home from kindergarten and asks her mother, "Where is my dad?" She is trying to make sense of the difference between her family and the families of the rest of her classmates. Nan "knows" that her biological father was a donor that her mom never met; now she is trying to make this knowledge fit with her new ability to recognize classes of families.

Part of this shift in perceptual ability is due to an increase in children's memory capacity. Four-to-six-year-olds are very good at the card game "Concentration" and can beat many distractable adults.

Language skills also increase. Three-year-olds have an average vocabulary of about nine hundred to a thousand words; they can use them in three-to-four-word sentences. They reorganize what they hear to fit their ability to structure language. You might say, "Don't pat the kitty until she knows you." Your three-year-old may hear, "Don't pat kitty," only. Language at this age is mostly used for self-expression as opposed to conversation, although three-year-olds can communicate well enough to be understood at home most of the time. Six-year-olds have an average vocabulary of 2,500 words and can make full sentences. They love to talk to other people and will engage in remarkably long conversations.

Your child may be beginning to ask questions—lots of them! When a child is between four and five, she usually reaches the peak of question-asking. She may ask *why* a hundred times in a day as she attempts to gather information to feed her expanding data base. A six-year-old begins asking more focused questions, which give her specific information about something she is interested in. Language skills help a child experiment with personal boundaries and provide a way of expressing them. Language acquisition at age three paves the way for the increased independence of the four-year-old. The four-year-old learns to say "Mama and me have our own rooms," recognizing that he and mama are two quite separate individuals. This in turn sets the stage for the five-year-old to feel more comfortable with his family connectedness; he might say, "We live in the apartment together." He is prepared to move with assurance into the broader world.

Children in this age group are also tremendously interested in information that is geared to their level. Their expanding ability to understand and manipulate data drives them to learn as much as they can about whatever sparks their interest. For instance, a three-year-old may want to know what a lesbian is, and a six-year-old may want to know if any other of her friends have lesbian mothers.

Imaginary play is one of the hallmarks of this age group. As a child's capacity to draw on his memory and use symbols increases, so does his ability for imaginary play. And as his world enlarges, so does the scope of his play-acting. For many children, age four is the zenith of imaginary playmates and pretend play. They ask to wear capes so they can be super heroes; they play house or spend hours creating scenarios for their dolls or stuffed animals. Experts say that imagination and pretend play can increase a child's range of feelings. As your child moves through this developmental stage, his imagination can take him places his physical and language abilities cannot take him in real life. He gets to try out different endings to imagined and actual situations. In the words of a colleague, "Play is their lab for understanding their everyday experiences." As he matures, your child will begin to separate fantasy from reality. Although he may leave behind a boundless imaginary world, he will take with him the experiences his mind created and be ready to engage with the world beyond his family.

• • •

Emotional/Social Development

At Three: A Calm in the Storm

The age of three can often seem like a calm in the storm of childhood. Three-year-olds are typically self-confident and generally pleased with themselves, their family, and their world. They are quite focused on their family and show a growing attachment to their parents and to other consistent adults in their lives. Three-year-olds are becoming less self-absorbed and more social. They are interested in playing with others, at least some of the time. Along with this development comes an understanding of and an ability to follow more rules.

At Four: Feelings and Fears

Four-year-olds are expressively expansive and outgoing; they are also opinionated, sometimes intensely so, and headstrong. Some pediatricians say that this age is the peak of self-esteem. They have sharp mood swings and distinct likes and dislikes; they are not neutral in their feelings. In this regard they are not unlike two-year-olds, but four-year-olds can articulate themselves verbally, often in surprising ways. For instance, a four-year-old may start using potty language—calling someone a "poophead"—as she experiments with her sense of independence and new command of language. While this is healthy psychological development, it can be upsetting to parents. Don't worry, fascination with potty language will diminish in time and, like most developmental shifts, it is a temporary phase that can change seemingly overnight. Your child needs both support and limits as she flexes her new skills.

Along with the new intensity of feelings comes increased fears. Your child may now be afraid of the dark or of monsters in the closet. The objects of her fear are usually symbols of her inability to contain strong feelings: she projects them outside of her into the dark or the closet as a way of managing them. Your four-year-old may push you away one minute as she struggles to assert her opinions, then the next minute need you to reassure her that monsters do not exist.

At Five: One Step Forward, Two Steps Back

Five-year-olds are self-confident in a contained sort of way, and they are usually careful to start only activities which they can accomplish, as opposed to the less cautious four-year-old, who blithely tries anything. A five-year-old is beginning to focus less on her family and more on her playmates; she is usually well-adjusted and content. While they are not as easily frightened as four-year-olds, five-year-olds may worry about concepts such as death and want to talk about it. In spite of their mature exterior, five-year-olds are still markedly different from older children and adults. Their sense of right and wrong has not solidified and they may lie or take things and hide them. They are usually amenable to correction, especially when it is done without anger and is explained at their level. Their views of the world are still very fluid and they need accurate information and limits from you as they begin the process of developing a more solid belief system.

At five-and-a-half, however, your child may seem to become unsettled. This shift to a state of disequilibrium may last a full year instead of the usual six-month swing and marks the slow-down from the rapid growth cycles of the early years of childhood. Five-and-a-half-year-olds are more willing to disobey you and can swing from one opinion to the opposite on any given issue. Your child's increasing cognitive abilities allow her to recognize inconsistencies in her world. Perhaps because of this, five-and-a-half-year-olds can be tense, in contrast to the five-year-old's relative calm. Even their bodies reflect this disorganization. In spite of improved physical coordination, many five-and-a-half-year-olds lose some of the body control they had six months earlier. Even their baby teeth begin to fall out! This disorganization precedes the next stage's reorganization. By the time your child is six she will have made tremendous strides in all areas of development and the turbulence of these years will settle down to a calmer phase of childhood.

Gender and Sexuality

As your child begins to ask questions, you will notice that many center on sexuality and gender identity. Children in this age range are very concrete; they try to make sense of their world by understanding gender differences. Three-year-olds begin to notice and act on sex role differences; four-year-olds tend to ask lots of questions about sex and the difference between women and men, girls and boys. Five-year-olds are not as concerned with sex-related issues, but most have a tendency to engage in very gender-stereotyped play and wear gender-identified clothing. Girls, however, are more likely to wear androgynous clothing and play games that are identified with both boys and girls, as opposed to boys, who tend to follow strict gender stereotyped behavior. This can frustrate lesbian mothers who hold an androgynous ideal for themselves and their children! Your job is to to listen to your child without ridicule, correct any misinformation and expose him to alternatives when you can.

As your child works to develop his gender identity he may be particularly interested in older boys and men. Since your child probably has more contact with women at this age, boys and men can provide your child (whether a son or a daughter) with additional information about what it is like to be male. Your child can learn by watching and interacting with new people; many children this age love having male babysitters and child care providers.

Parenting Issues

A parent's job is to support her child as she navigates the ups and downs of these years. You are both the mirror, reflecting back to your child the image of who she is, and the limit-setter, making it safe for her to explore her feelings, thoughts and actions. How you communicate your support and limits to your child will dramatically affect how successful you are.

Moms as Mirrors

Reflecting back, or mirroring, is communicating in words and/or actions what you see and hear your child do and say. This teaches him the words that match his feelings and thoughts, and gives him an alternative to simply acting out what he feels. It also lets your child know that you can see him when he is behaving well and when he is behaving badly. In doing this, you communicate that you are not afraid of whatever he is saying, feeling or thinking; this gives him the support to experiment. You are also telling your child that nothing is so bad that you cannot continue to see and love him. It is an unfortunate fact that many adults report not feeling seen or known by their parents, and that because of this, they are unable to believe that their parents really loved them.

An important part of mirroring is emphasizing your recognition of appropriate behavior. A common parental error in communicating about behavior is to say what you don't like ("Stop pulling the kitty's tail!") instead of noticing and commenting about what you *do* like ("The kitty likes it when you pet her!"). Too many negatives and no specific positives leave a child wondering what really *is* expected.

Another specific that a parent can reflect back is positive support of the child's gender. You need to tell your son that it is good he is male, or your daughter that it is wonderful that she is female, and that people of the other gender are special also.

Race is an especially important specific. Reflect back the beauty you see in your child's skin color and hair texture as well as the shape of her eyes and nose. If you are a different race from your child you need to pay particular attention to this communication so that your child knows that you value her just as she is. Since the importance of white skin is mirrored all over this country, a child with dark brown skin needs especially to hear that you see the richness of her skin and how beautiful you think it is and she is. Start this early in your child's life so that she carries those messages and can draw upon them when confronted with hostility.

> *Frances adopted a baby when the child was two days old. Now her daughter was three years old. She has grown into a beautiful girl with short black hair, nut-brown skin and big brown eyes that tug at Frances' heart. Frances makes a point of telling her daughter how beautiful she thinks she is. One day when Cicely had been running her fingers through Frances' long straight hair, Frances put her daughter on her lap and said, "I love your curly hair. I love your beautiful brown skin and eyes; I love you exactly the way you are. I like that we are the same in some ways, like girls, and I like that we are different in others, like in our colors." Cicely snuggled in and exulted in the glow of her mother's love.*

The "Why" Years

With your child's developing ability to articulate her feelings and thoughts with words comes the inevitable barrage of questions. Welcome to the "why" years. Children will struggle to understand differences and anything else that does not make immediate sense to them.

An important dimension of good parental communication is giving your child accurate information and correcting inaccurate information. Do not tease, name-call or try to distract a child when she is trying to sort out fantasy and reality. For example, a child this age might try to figure out where her dad went and make up a fantastic story that solves that question. Do not make a joke about it or belittle the child. Teasing can shut a child down. It is also a good idea not to withhold information from a child about what is going on in her environment. If Uncle Rick has AIDS and his illness is obvious in the way he looks and how tired he gets, you need to tell your child about her uncle's illness. How you explain this depends on your child's age. You might tell a three-year-old, simply, that Uncle Rick is very sick. But be prepared to answer many more questions from a six-year-old, who may want to know what disease Uncle Rick has and whether she can catch it.

Your family structure is likely to become a frequent topic for your child's questions. You can take advantage of this developmental stage to expand your child's knowledge about lesbians, adoption, different races, sexuality and any other issues that may be related to how your family came to be together. Take, for instance, the question Martha faced as she was cooking dinner one night.

Martha's four-year-old son, Sam, looked up from his drawing and asked, "How come you divorced my father?" Martha was momentarily speechless, as she had never been married, much less divorced. But since Sam's friend Jody lived alone with his mom, who was divorced, Sam had reasoned that his mom was divorced, too—even though he had been told several times that Martha had gotten sperm, through a third person, from a man she did not know. Obviously, all the ramifications had not sunk in. Martha decided to take the opportunity to talk more thoroughly about how she got pregnant. First she told him she had never been married to a man because she wanted to be partnered with a woman instead. She then explained briefly about sperm in a man's body and eggs in a woman's body. She said that a woman could get pregnant by having her husband put his penis in her vagina and getting the sperm into the woman's uterus that way. Sam began to squirm. Martha went on to say that, in her case, her friend Molly had asked a man she knew if he would give his sperm so that Martha could have a baby. She described how the sperm had been put in a jar and how she had taken it out and put it in her vagina. But by this point, Sam had put his hands over his ears and was making a face. He was on information-overload!

Martha should respect Sam's clear message. He has heard as much—probably more—as he can handle. The lesson here is that you must balance your child's need for accurate information with his ability to absorb and make sense of that information; this four-year-old obviously is not ready to hear about all the intricacies of reproduction and alternative insemination.

You can also offer information in a way that affirms your child's growing sense of identity and counters negative feedback she may have received. For example, the following mother became concerned when her five-and-a-half-year-old began to say that she wanted white skin and blond hair. She used her daughter's questions to open up the topic of adoption.

Juanita had been adopted by Carol when she was two months old. Juanita was from Honduras and had light brown skin, brown eyes, and silky black hair. Carol, a Minnesotan with Scandiavian roots, had pale white skin, freckles and straw-colored hair. Juanita asked Carol, "Does my Daddy have brown skin like mine?" and "Why don't I have white skin like you?" Carol explained again that she had gone to Honduras when she had heard that Juanita needed a new family. She said that Juanita's mom had not been able keep a baby and wanted Juanita to have a family who could take care of her. She added that Juanita's mother had not had enough food to feed her daughter and had wanted Juanita to be able to have enough to eat. Juanita interrupted to say, "Yeah, we have food and money." Carol said that she did not know anything about Juanita's father but that probably both her mother and father had beautiful brown skin because most of the people in Honduras were brown. She ended by saying that even though Carol had white skin she loved Juanita's brown skin and did not want her any other way.

Topics like reproduction or adoption are complex issues. Parents of young children need to decide which part of a question they want to deal with. As children age, the complexities of an issue will unfold, allowing parent and child to explore them more deeply.

◆　◆　◆

Out in the World

Structured Environments: Preschool and Kindergarten

This period of childhood ushers you into contact with one of the most onmipresent institutions in your child's life—school. Unless you do home schooling there is no way around long-term involvement with schools. This institution can be supportive and wonderful, and it can be homophobic and frustrating.

Preschool and kindergarten usually introduce a more structured learning environment than your child has experienced before. Going to school may add some stress or trigger a return of separation anxiety, especially if your child has not been in day care. Thus you may see your child regressing slightly so that she can return to a more comfortable developmental stage while she adjusts to the new situation.

As your child enters school you will also come into contact with other adults whom you have not chosen to be in your life. This can mean more coming out or more people from whom to keep your lesbianism a secret. There will be plenty of opportunities to explain prejudice to your child. And as your child gains more acquaintances, she will begin noticing how her family life differs from theirs.

It is very useful to interview prospective schools and teachers to see if they are a good fit for your child. This includes evaluating the academic fit, but for the lesbian mother it also means assessing the degree to which heterosexism and homophobia are present. Larger urban areas may have more preschool, kindergarten and first grade options, some of which may even include out lesbian or gay teachers. But no matter where you live you can ask teachers and administrators what their views are about lesbian families. Ask what experiences they have with families like yours and watch and listen for their comfort level. If you cannot afford to be out as a lesbian mother you can gain valuable information by asking about the school's experience with diversity of all kinds, including sexual orientation of parents. Ask about how they celebrate diversity as well as how they combat prejudice. Just because you are not out does not mean you should not be concerned about the appropriate and informed care of your children. Many heterosexual parents are concerned about the same issues. You could even ask a heterosexual parent to ask the questions for you if you cannot risk anyone's guessing about your lesbianism.

Once your child enters school you will have to cope with paperwork which identifies who the parents are, who the emergency contacts are, who can sign what papers, and so on. If you and your partner are a couple who parent equally, you'll need to alert the school that both of you should be considered full parents. If you are functioning as a parent to your partner's children and are out, you might want to check with the school about their policy regarding stepparents or other significant adults. If you are a single mother with several friends who are very involved with your son, you might want to discuss your particular extended family structure and find out what you can and cannot do legally. You might also have a legal father involved with your child; his role should be clarified. Consider obtaining powers of attorney to protect your partner's right to act as a legal guardian for your child in the eyes of the school district. Some lesbian mothers have spent years crossing out mother and father on school forms and writing parent and parent or mother and mother.

Pat had lived in rural Hill County her whole life, as had her dozens of relatives. When she invited her girlfriend, Barbara, to move in with her two daughters, Pat came out only to a select group of her extended family. One of Barbara's daughters, Sally, was a six-year-old kindergartener when she started the school year at the elementary school down the road from Pat's farm. The second week of school the teacher asked everyone to say what she or he wanted to be when they grew up. Ten or so children said teacher, mommy, farmer, astronaut, doctor and so on. Then the teacher called on Sally. She stood up and said, "I want to be a lesbian."

Religious Groups

Kevin was three-and-a-half when he and his mothers moved into their house near the Greek Orthodox church. Whenever they drove by the church Kevin would say, "So tell me about this Jesus guy." He never seemed to tire of hearing new stories about Jesus's life and what churches were for.

Children become more curious about death, God, and other spiritual issues as they mature. Some mothers want their children to have a religious base from which to explore these questions, and decide to get involved in a church, synagogue, sangha or other spiritual group. Other parents simply try to answer the questions as they arise.

Organized religion does not have a good track record with lesbians and gay men, yet many lesbian mothers get some of their primary support through their religion. A nurturing religious home can be an invaluable base of support and information in a cross-generational setting. If you are looking to get involved in such a setting, get recommendations from friends and shop around until you find a spiritual home which welcomes your lesbian-headed family. Lesbians and their families can offer invaluable gifts to a religious group who is genuinely interested in expanding its definition of the family of God. There is much to be gained by everybody.

Some lesbians become involved on their own with Wicca (woman-focused religion) groups or circles which combine a variety of spiritual practices. Sometimes these groups include family members in some way and sometimes they are support for the woman only. In either case the whole family benefits when a parent is able to find support for her spiritual self.

International and Interracial Adoptions

Women who have adopted children from other countries or of different races may find that their three-to-six-year-old children have an increased desire for more information about their birth parents and culture. It is particularly important that these children be mirrored by people who look like them and are proud of themselves. Attending appropriate cultural events, reading books and magazines, learning games and watching selected television and movies are some ways of providing this information and exposure to their birth culture.

Ann and Kim are Teri's adoptive parents. Teri was born in India and came to the United States when she was four months old. Ann's family is of northern European descent and has been in this country for two generations. Kim's family is Korean-American and has been here for three generations. The two women believe they have the understanding and strengths to provide a good home to a child of color. Now Teri is three and the family is going to spend the day at a festival celebrating aspects of Indian culture. Even though she has been shown many books about In-

dia, Teri is fascinated by the bright colors of the saris and bindis, or red dots, on the foreheads of the women. When they get home Teri dresses up in pieces of bright cloth and paints a red spot on her forehead with her mom's nail polish.

Time Out for Relationships

You and Your Partner

A mother's romantic relationship will always be affected by the presence of a child. In the case of the three-to-six age range, the adults' relationship with each other may be affected by the child's developmental changes—especially new congnitive abilities—and the particulars of the child's relationship with both his mother and her partner or girlfriend.

If you are a mother who has newly partnered, your child's three-to-six stage may be a period of testing. For example, you might find yourself being asked endless questions about how a woman could be dating another woman or hear your child assert that two women cannot get married. These challenges are often an attempt to gather information about something that is different from the cultural norm. It is easy to feel defensive, especially if you have divorced your child's father and this is your first female romantic partnership. It is important, however, to be responsive to your child's curiosity and to answer questions as openly and clearly as possible, no matter how adamantly she is expressing her perhaps opposing views on your choices. You also need to gently but firmly assert your right to date whom you want.

It is important for couples to talk and agree on what role a new partner will take with a child. The mother needs to decide whether she will remain the only parent or whether she wants her partner to function as an additional parent. The new partner needs to decide what role she wants and is willing to do. And it may be that the adults' timetable will have to be adjusted to match the child's emotional readiness. A child may resent the attention her mother gives a new adult and may not want to spend any time with the new partner.

Kate moved into Barbara's home after ten months of dating. Barbara was not ready to share parenting of her six-year-old daughter, Mary, just yet, but she did want Kate and Mary to have a relationship. Kate, who had originally wanted to become a full parent, agreed to live together with the family for a year and then reevaluate the parenting arrangement. The three of them sat down to talk about what this meant in day-to-day life. Mary liked Kate and was glad to have her move in full-time, but she was full of questions. She was in first grade at the local elementary school and wanted to know if Kate would attend parent teacher-conferences. Kate had already been to a school concert and Mary thought that was okay, but she didn't think she wanted Kate at parent conferences. They agreed that Barbara would attend these conferences alone. Mary also asked if she could have a "play date" each week with Kate—without her mother. They agreed that Kate would pick Mary up from after-school care on Tuesdays to spend a couple of hours with her.

Educating Your Extended Family

If you have family members who have had an ongoing relationship with your child, now may be a good time to encourage them to spend more time together, since three-to-six-year-olds become interested in relationships beyond their immediate family. Or it may be time to involve family members who have been on the periphery until now. Depending on your family's comfort with your lesbianism, you may decide to discuss with your family ways to respond to your child's questions about differences in sexual orientation, race, culture and so on. At the same time, you may also want to explain to your child that different people have different perspectives about your unique kind of family, so that she will not take any thoughtless comments too personally.

Mallory had just turned six and was flying to her grandparents' farm in California all by herself. She was very excited about being without her mom for a week. She loved being on the farm and she loved her grandparents. Yet her mother, Stacey, was more anxious than excited. She was worried about her mother's homophobia and wondered if she could trust her mother to be supportive of her lifestyle when Stacey was not around. She decided to call her mother and tell her that ever since she had started first grade, Mallory had been asking a lot of questions about lesbians and men and women. She asked her mother to be supportive of the different kinds of families if Mallory asked, and said that she didn't want Mallory to feel bad about herself. Her mom agreed, but not without chiding Stacey for not trusting her.

Your three-to-six-year-old's development will take you and her into new territories. Encourage her to explore her world with gusto and support her as she tests new limits. Your steady guidance will help her as she moves into the next stage of childhood.

13 Logic and Rules; Fairness and Morals:
Six to Ten Years

Sigmund Freud called it "latency," parents call it "the calm before the storm," child development specialists refer to it, simply, as "middle childhood." Whatever the term, this seemingly quiet period in children's lives—roughly when they are six to ten years of age—is the least written about in the literature of child development. In reality there are enormous changes taking place inside your child, which greatly shape how she sees herself and thinks about her expanding world.

Development Guideposts

Middle childhood is marked more by cognitive and social changes than by physical development. Children are consolidating and fine-tuning the tremendous physical changes that have already happened in their bodies, while their intellectual and social explorations surge forward.

The Logical Child

Jean Piaget referred to the period between seven and eleven as the time of "concrete logical operations." (We have chosen to divide developmental stages in a somewhat different way than many other writers. We view age six as the beginning of middle childhood and age ten as the end of middle childhood.) The following is an overview of some of the accomplishments that you can expect your child to make in this time period.[1] Remember—and it cannot be said often enough—that children do not develop at the same rate and a child who seems to be behind the development guideposts will often "catch up" at a later date.

- She realizes that operations are reversible, such as the understanding that subtraction is the inverse of addition. (This contributes to an awareness that a mother's words are not cast in concrete.)

- He is able to understand symbols, such as words, and plays with them by making up jokes and puns. (This means he may understand homophobic slang that is used.)

- She understands that another person may have a feeling or perspective different from her own, even about a shared experience.

- He begins to copy or imitate others beyond his immediate family.

- She develops her own moral conscience instead of relying on external guidelines.

- He is able to organize objects into certain orders or categories, such as increasing or decreasing size, and can form mental representations of the objects' relationships to each other. (An example of this is noticing that Catherine is taller than Bill but shorter than Tyrone. It is during this period that children are most likely to start using put-downs based on perceived difference, e.g., "queer," "fag.")

As children develop these cognitive capacities, they learn to think on their own and to collaborate with others. In order to think and concentrate, children need to develop a logical thought process that involves an understanding of cause and effect. Parents who give their children clear limits and who show them the consequences of their behavior will help their children develop logical thinking. In order to collaborate with others, a child needs to separate her own goals and ideas from those of other people. Parents who encourage their children to form their own opinions and model both cooperation and healthy disagreement will support their children's budding collaborative skills.

♦ ♦ ♦

Rules and Moral Reasoning[2]

- "You can run and play games on the school playground but not on the street at home because there are too many cars."

- "It's okay to swear at home but not at school."

- "You can play in the parents' bedroom at Joey's house but not in our bedroom at home."

During these years children are learning about the rules within the environment of their family as well as in the outside world, and figuring out how the rules differ. They also experience the consequences of breaking them. For example, your child might discover it is acceptable to swear at home, but she will be sent to the principal's office for using the same language in her classroom. The reality of the world demands we be flexible enough to follow different rules at different times—a lesson that begins in childhood.

Along with awareness of rules comes the development of conscience and moral standards. Children begin to think about the values held by people and institutions outside of their own family. Your daughter may recognize that your family deals with prejudice by talking about it, but her friend's family ignores it or even stops her from talking about it at their house. She may hear—or be the target of—derogatory slang on the school yard. She then begins the process of deciding whether to ignore hurtful comments or to respond in some way. You can help her in this journey by listening and talking with her, but you cannot force her to think your way.

Your son may come home and ask why his friend's family doesn't say grace before a meal and yours does. He may be challenging your belief or sorting out differences in families—or both. As your child matures and begins forming his own judgments, he will begin to disagree with you and others in a more serious way. It's important to respect your child's beginning attempts to develop his own values and rules. As he establishes a moral standard that is uniquely his, he will be able to get along with others and retain what he believes is right.

Tanya's nine-year-old son came home one day from school and, over cookies and milk, started a conversation with his mom about whether it really was okay to be gay. Tanya almost fell off her chair. This was the child who begged every year to march in the Gay Pride march! Her first impulse was to tell him not to be ridiculous, but she held her breath for a few minutes and listened while he explored the ideas he had heard at his school from a teacher who said it was sinful to be gay. Tanya eventually steered the conversation to what Tony himself thought about this. He popped the last cookie in his mouth and headed out the door saying, "Well, I don't agree with the guy, you're okay by me, Mom."

It can be very hard to sit still while your children tinker with your most cherished beliefs. If Tanya had jumped in with her opinions, Tony would likely not have gotten to that point on his own. Later on she may choose to talk with Tony about whether he wants to say anything to the teacher, or Tanya may say she wants to respond to the teacher herself.

One of the most difficult challenges for parents is witnessing their child's movement away from them as the only trustworthy authority. This shift often occurs in tandem with a child's ability to recognize that mental operations are reversible. Reversibility opens up the possibility that not everything is fixed just because "mom says so." Children start quoting teachers, who become the first in an ongoing series of authorities which challenge the belief of parental infallibility.

Peers are also influential in the development of moral reasoning. Psychologist Ann Cale Kruger did an interesting experiment to explore moral development in a group of eight-year-old girls.[3] She had the girls come to an interview with their mother and a friend their age. The interviewer presented one of four stories and asked the girl to discuss it with the interviewer. Then the girls were paired with either their mother or their friend and given two stories to discuss together. Finally, the interviewer met with the girl alone again and presented the last story. The girls who had discussed stories with a friend showed more improvement in moral reasoning than the ones who had interacted with their mothers. The girls who showed the most improvement in the mother discussion group had mothers who interacted in a more peer-like fashion as opposed to the mothers who tried to lead their daughters in the discussion.

Our children move into the world of their peers during these years whether we like it or not. It is good to know, however, that this movement away from us is good for them in many ways.

Emotional/Social Development

Children develop at their own speed. Yet research does indicate that during the six-to-ten age range girls tend to develop emotionally faster than boys. Girls in this age group also tend to be especially physically active and adventurous. This time can be a haven for girls because it precedes the shift to adolescence, a period in which limits of sexism settle in and romantic interest in boys often becomes a mandatory part of "girl culture." Between the ages six and ten they are still free to be tomboys, to excel in sports, to speak up in class, to compete against boys without worrying about their "popularity." Some girls are able to carry this well-honed self-confidence into pre-adolescence and adolescence; others, very unfortunately, are not.

Both girls and boys in this age group are relatively stable emotionally, due in part to there being fewer demands for change in the child's environment.[4] Most children are in elementary school during these years and have already adapted to the transition from the home environment to a school setting. (If, as in some cultures, your child leaves home for the first time at six or seven, middle childhood can be very stressful. You may need to use the guidelines from the three-to-six age range for ideas of how to support your child through this transition.)

The Importance of Peers

As children in middle childhood solidify their gender identity, peers of the same gender become very important to them. They copy each other and want to do what their friends are doing. Bonding with peers seems especially central to the lives of boys in this age group, perhaps because it is more difficult for them to get a solid sense of gender identity. They often do not have enough day-to-day time with men to internalize what men are like and do. (Ironically, gender roles for boys get more restrictive during these years, in contrast to the relative freedom for girls' roles.) Girls, on the other hand, have women in their lives most of every day. Many lesbian-first mothers have gone out of their way to have male teachers, coaches and friends for their sons and daughters.

Our society has assumed that the presence of a live-in father is necessary for the healthy development of boys. Unfortunately, the amount and quality of time fathers spend with their children varies widely.

We really don't know what specific combination of parental involve-ment is optimal for a child's healthy gender development. It will be interesting to see over time whether lesbian's sons have an easier or harder time developing their gender identity than do boys with live-in fathers.

Many lesbian mothers have spent the previous developmental stages of their child's growth encouraging a mix of boy and girl cultures. You should certainly continue doing this if you value it, but don't be sur-prised if you begin to get resistance from your child.

Fear of Failure

Erik Erikson, the psychiatrist and developmental theorist, used the terms "industry vs. inferiority" to describe the developmental chal-lenges of middle childhood.[5] He believed it was crucial that children develop a sense of accomplishment; if they did not, they risked feeling like failures. Between the ages six to ten children begin to recognize "good, better, best." They start evaluating their own performances and can be very hard on themselves. Fear of failure, in fact, becomes a prominent feature of these years. It is important to support your child's attempts at success, so she can enjoy the learning process and risk ex-ploring new areas. If a child does not discover she is competent, she may hate learning anything new.

Children who have learning disabilities or different learning styles from their peers are particularly vulnerable at this stage. It is common for these children to discover for the first time that they cannot do some-thing that most of the children around them seem to be doing fairly easily. Learning differences that are not caught and helped can cause extreme frustration and, in some cases, lifelong resistance to formal learning environments. A disproportionate number of students who do poorly in elementary school are children who have difficulty learn-ing with traditional teaching methods.

Jerry came home from second grade and threw his backpack on the floor. His mother asked him what was wrong. "I hate school, it's dumb and I'm never going back," he said angrily. After he finished his snack she gently asked what had happened. It turned out that Jerry's reading was the most noticeably slow in the "whole class." Jerry had always loved school until this year. His second-grade teacher strongly emphasized reading skills and

Jerry was now miserable. Jerry's mom remembered that her brother had had trouble with reading and had been diagnosed with a learning disability, dyslexia. She wondered if it was time to get Jerry tested before he burned out on school like her brother had.

Physical Skills

Although children's physical growth diminishes somewhat during middle childhood, you will still notice some strides in this area. Children continue to develop their physical strength and endurance and become well-coordinated. By age eight, for example, children can do such things as maneuver a bike, use hammers, saws, rakes and shovels and run longer distances without tiring.

Fine motor skills also greatly improve. Six- and seven-year-olds can learn to cut food with a knife and fork, they can wash themselves and tie their shoes. At nine they may draw well (depending on encouragement and native talent) and most have learned cursive writing.[6]

Children of this age love to be active as they fine-tune their ability to control their movements. Perhaps this is one of the reasons so many become involved in team sports. Most children thoroughly enjoy learning new physical skills with groups of peers during these years.

Children with disabilities should also be encouraged to expand their physical abilities whether it means participating in the Special Olympics or learning how to use their wheelchair more efficiently.

Jeremy was nine and loved baseball, but he had cerebral palsy which kept him from playing the game with his friends. He felt so discouraged that he decided to give up ever trying to play anything. Jeremy's mom had talked to him a lot about her being different as a lesbian and his being different with his C.P. Now she decided to have a talk about baseball. She reminded him, "Being different has its drawbacks, but it has advantages as well. For instance, you are much better with computers at school than your friends." Then she added, "I want you to do something physical to build up your strength, even though it is hard for you." Jeremy got angry at her and yelled, "What's the point, I can't do anything fun!" She responded gently, "If you were stronger you would be able to walk a little more easily and that would help you your whole life. But more immediately, you might be able to be manager of the baseball team—if you can carry the equipment bag and walk out on the field to get the bats." She smiled. "I bet you could get the job. Besides, you could keep all the player and team statistics on the computer better than anyone else." Jeremy was cautiously excited. He did love baseball! He agreed to walk a little more and do some exercises each day. His mom agreed to call the coach.

The Playing's the Thing

Cognitive researcher Jerome Bruner said, "Play is the principal business of childhood."[7] You will see your child engaged in several types of play. Two typical types of play are constructive play, when children manipulate objects to create something like a puzzle or Lego sculpture, and imaginary play, when children use their imagination to create a scenario. The latter is often used to practice different ways of feeling and behaving. Six-to-eight-year-olds use imaginary play to try on other people's perspectives by acting out the scenes. Eight-to-ten-year-olds become more skilled at putting themselves in another's place and judging that person's intentions as well. As children get older, they spend less time engaging in imaginary play as structured games gain in popularity; however, some creative children continue to use imaginary play well into adolescence.

Structured games, which are governed by rules, cover the spectrum from Candyland to soccer. When children play structured games, they get to experiment with the life skills of rules, relationships, winning and losing.

Many six-to-ten-year-olds develop a readiness and interest in team sports. Boys in particular like to play in large groups at games which are governed by rules. One of the ways they display their recognition of difference and appreciation for rules is in their penchant for arguing about whether someone has broken a rule. A group of boys playing baseball may argue intensely over a play and then call for a replay.

Girls tend to prefer games with fewer rules and fewer participants, perhaps just two or three girls. It is not uncommon to see girls break off a game and start another one rather than risk fighting about some rule. Relationships are generally more important than any particular game or its rules.

Obviously, girls also like team sports; witness the popularity of girls' soccer leagues and other team sports in many parts of the country. And, of course, some girls will join the boys' informal soccer games (and often be standouts because of their faster physical development), just as some boys will prefer to play in small groups. But in general, a minority of children "cross over" to play with the other gender. This may be very frustrating to the mother who wants her daughter to play sports with both boys and girls, or to the mother who wants her son to feel free to avoid the competitive games that seem to dominate school recess. You may need to talk to teachers or coaches if you think your child is being unduly pressured to participate in gender-restricted games or sports. However, it is equally important for parents not to push their children's involvement in particular games. Let your *child* tell you what games or sports she wants to try. There are some marked differences in boys' and girls' cultures; parents need to be sensitive to these differences and respect their children's choices.

Historically, our society has rewarded boys for competiveness and girls for cooperative behavior. Lesbian mothers who have taken great pains to encourage their children in non-stereotypical behavior may be dismayed to see their daughters and sons move into girls' or boys' culture with little appreciation for the other gender's world.

> *Paula had been a tomboy in her childhood and had shunned dolls, dresses, and anything pink. So she was horrified when her daughter asked for a Barbie for Christmas at age five, wanted a frilly party dress for her first school play at six, and wanted her room painted pink at age nine. Paula kept reminding herself that she had vowed not to push her children towards her own preferences the way her parents had pushed her toward femininity. But it was hard!*

Whatever form it takes, game-playing allows children the opportunity to test rules, strive for success, and develop relationships. Piaget stressed that games also offer spontaneity and activity, two qualities he believed are important to moral development. Play is the crucible in which your children try on and manipulate the cognitive, physical and social changes they are experiencing.

Parenting Issues

As your child moves through her developmental challenges your job is to remain engaged in your parenting. You need to impart values and set limits through your opinions and rules, while at the same time providing loving support as your child tests the water and dives in. Providing both nurturance and structure means giving your child space to think and form opinions on her own, and it also means setting non-negotiable limits. Engaged parenting requires parents to work continuously to find the right balance for each individual child.

Playing by the Rules

You can help your child explore the rules which exist both inside and outside your family by helping to interpret them and make them understandable. The way you and your child do this depends on many variables, such as the ethnic culture to which you belong, the dynamics in your own family of origin, and your generational values.

In some ethnic cultures, for instance, it is not an option for children to test their parents' rules. These families are hierarchical in nature, with children expected to obey their elders. A child's testing of rules will then likely happen outside the home environment.

Family therapists and researchers have noted that many parents of the "baby boom" generation have raised their children with more permission to challenge parental authority than did their own parents. This has resulted in more children who feel emboldened—especially by age eight or nine—to challenge family rules, and more parents who feel somewhat overwhelmed and want to "get that child under control!" But suddenly shifting gears and imposing the strict disciplinarian approaches of the previous generation isn't wise, especially if you have not reared your children to be frightened or submissive. Instead, you must continue to find new ways to engage with your child and come up with win-win solutions to disagreements.

Be clear which rules in your family are negotiable and which are not. For instance, let's say you have a rule about how many hours your child must spend on her homework. If there is no leeway on those hours, make sure your daughter knows that. If you are willing to negotiate if special circumstances arise, be clear about that as well. If your son is supposed to clean the bathroom, be specific as to what that chore entails and how often it is to be done. But don't be surprised if your child decides to test both your negotiable and non-negotiable rules no matter how clear you have been. Your job is to provide both consistency and flexibility—and to stay patient.

It is very common for children in this age range to become fixated on "fairness" and to vocally counter your rules or someone else's with, "It isn't fair!" Fairness is often confused with "sameness." A child may demand to have the exact same privileges as her mother or siblings in her quest for fairness. Sometimes you may need to listen to and act on your child's complaint; other times it is enough to just acknowledge it and move on. It is important to teach children that fairness does not necessarily equal sameness, and that with fairness come privileges *and* responsibilities. These concepts are not always immediately obvious to children and you may need to reinforce the message over the years.

Another important aspect of rule-setting is to let your child experience the consequences of her actions, so long as they are not dangerous. If your daughter is responsible for starting her homework at four o'clock and working for two hours, but one day she puts it off until five, one consequence may be that she does not get to watch TV that night. It is very helpful to explain the consequences clearly to your child; when possible you should negotiate them in advance so that both you and she have agreed on them.

Jean Ilsley Clarke, author of *Self-Esteem: A Family Affair,* suggests one way parents can help their children learn the consequences of their actions. She calls it "healthy hassling."[8] Healthy hassling is when you use fun teasing to challenge your child's actions, ideas or beliefs. If your son decides he will not wear a coat to school on a day you think is too cold for just a sweatshirt, you can hassle him healthily by asking in a fun way if he is trying for an Iron Man award. Unless you think he will really get sick, let him experience the consequences of not wearing enough clothes.

Engaging with your child over your rules can also provide you with a chance to reexamine them yourself. Take advantage of this time and reflect on your way of doing things. A willingness to reevaluate rules will increase your flexibility to respond to your child and give you more empathy for his developmental work.

Joan grew up in a strict household in the Midwest. Mostly she had gotten rid of the rules her parents had used, but just recently she realized there was one she had kept: "Always finish what you start." Joan noticed that when her seven-year-old daughter and her friends stopped in the middle of a game and moved on to something else, she had to bite her tongue not to interfere! Watching the girls' happy spontaneity helped Joan realize it was time to reevaluate this rule, too.

Values—Yours, Mine and Ours

Another task is to let your child develop his own set of values. When you have a difference of opinion with your son or when he seems unclear about what he believes, you can use healthy hassling to help him evaluate his values. Keep in mind that if your child is sensitive to teasing, even in fun, you should find other ways to challenge him. Notice and praise him when he thinks logically and creatively. Engaged parenting is particularly important in this stage of a child's life, as he learns what values exist in and outside his family and decides which values he wants to make his own.

Tom is ten years old and in the fourth grade. He started at a new school at the beginning of the year, so there were a lot of kids he didn't know and who didn't know that Tom's mother was a lesbian. One day he comes home and begins talking to his mother about whether he should tell these kids about her being a lesbian. Tom's mother, Randi, strongly believes that people should come out of the closet, but she also knows that Tom needs to make his own choices. She listens to him, asks questions about why the issue has come up—he has to make a family tree for class—and helps him brainstorm some ways to deal with the problem. He decides not to tell anyone until he feels they would not tease or be mean about his mother's lesbianism. He doesn't put anything on the family tree that explicitly shows Randi is a lesbian, but he decides not to lie right out either if someone asks, because being honest is important to him. Randi wishes the world were different and praises Tom for figuring out a way to take care of himself.

Part of helping your child learn about values includes exposing your son or daughter to new environments and experiences. As your family visits new places or tries new experiences, you can use the opportunity to talk about the differences you each notice and what they might mean. For instance, one family we know took their son to Chile so that he would be exposed to his parents' birth culture and extended family. They spent a lot of time talking about the differences in manners between the United States and Chile, including why people behaved more politely in Chile. When you expose your family to different environments it highlights your own values and enables your child to notice what she has always before taken for granted.

Out in the World

Sports

As we noted earlier, middle childhood often marks an increased involvement in organized sports. Depending on how large your community is, you may be standing on the sidelines with old friends or with people you've never seen before. Our experience is that the parents, children and coaches involved in organized sports are not particularly interested in your sexual orientation. If you live in a very conservative area, of course, you are more likely to experience censure and maybe open hostility. But usually the focus is on the children. You might decide to tell some of the other parents to get a sense of their reactions to your sexual orientation.

If you're the partner of a lesbian mother, you may find that other parents don't know what to do with you—you don't fit any known niche. Some people may be welcoming and others flat out rude. Talk to your partner and plan a strategy of how to introduce and include yourself at sports events.

Claudia has been actively parenting her partner's daughter for several years. Marty is going out for baseball this year. She ends up as one of five girls on a co-ed team where the boys are respectful of girls playing on the team. Claudia, on the other hand, feels awkward. She wants to volunteer to help coach but no other women are coaching in this league. There's also the problem of the head coach, who doesn't realize that Claudia is Marty's other mother. After practice one afternoon, Claudia takes a deep breath and tells the coach she wants to help. To her amazement he says only two things, "Have you played before?" and, when Claudia tells him about her four years of varsity softball in high school, "The pay's low, take first base."

◆ ◆ ◆

Sports bring your child into contact with a broader world. And you may find yourself an onlooker as *he* deals with other people's questions.

Donna and her son Eli were filling out a form to enter his first post-season soccer tournament. Donna, her partner Alicia, and Bob, the man who functioned as Eli's dad, all went to Eli's soccer games and were well known to the team parents. But the woman collecting the forms was a league official and she was clearly confused by the different last names and addresses. Eli's last name was a combination of his two mothers and Bob's was completely different. The woman started off by asking who Eli lived with, and he answered, "My moms, except on Mondays, then I'm with my dad." She missed the "s" on moms and asked if his parents were divorced. He said no. The official looked at Donna, who decided to stay quiet and let Eli handle this unless he got into trouble. The woman then asked Eli who was taking him to the tournament. He said, "My dad." By this time Eli thought the woman was very dense. Finally she asked why his name was different and he replied that it was the last name of his two mothers. As the light dawned on her at last, she giggled and got on with the business of collecting the form.

School

School is where your child will do most of her socializing with her peer group. As her peers become more important to her, she may become more cautious about risking their censure. You may have to spend time helping her make her own choices about coming out as the child of a lesbian mom. Children whose mothers came out after having the children tend to be more cautious about telling their friends about their mother. Children of lesbian-first families are usually more comfortable in being "out" in the world.

Thatcher had an innovative way of counting his parents. He certainly counted his two mothers. They each had different partners now, so he figured he now had four moms. He knew he had a biological father (though he'd never met him) and that, added to the two men he called "Dad," meant that he had three fathers. One day Thatcher's mother, Sandra, picked him up at school. While she was waiting for him, a seven-year-old buddy of Thatcher's ran up to her and said, " Is it true that Thatcher really has four moms and three dads?" Luckily, Sandra was familiar with Thatcher's current method for counting parents. She laughed and said that Thatcher was right. Even so, she felt a slight twinge at being "lost" in the body count.

Lesbian parents often consciously and actively prepare their children for life in a heterosexist world, including possible confrontations at school. We believe that lesbian (and gay) parents, parents of color, and parents of special needs children are more likely to talk to their children about prejudice—and ways to confront it—and to celebrate difference than are most white heterosexual parents. For these groups of parents, this preparation is a survival issue, not a luxury. Such discussions are also particularly helpful during the middle childhood years, so that children are encouraged to move beyond the rigid classifications of right/wrong, better/worse that are so characteristic of this age.

Martha's son, Seth, came home from school one day very upset. During recess a boy in his fifth-grade class had told Seth that his mothers were queer and that he, Seth, must be a fag if his moms were. Seth is angry and adamant as he says to his mom, "Come to school and talk to my class about lesbians. You can tell them all about it." Martha lets him vent his pain and anger and asks, "Have you talked to your teacher about what happened?" "No," he says, "and I don't want to, it's too scary." Martha promises to call the teacher. When she gets him on the phone, he says, "I'm really sorry about the incident but we've already covered lesbianism in the sexuality class and I don't think we need to do anymore." Martha is not satisfied with this answer and points out that the incident has larger ramifications. The teaches agrees and promises to take care of the situation. The next day, when the boy who insulted Seth gets off the bus, the teacher takes him to the principal's ofice, where they talk to him about why it's not all right to insult people with stereotypes or put-downs. The boy apologizes to Seth during recess, and later that day, during the sexuality class, the teacher encourages Seth to tell the group what it feels like to be taunted. His classmates are sad that Seth felt so hurt and promise to be careful of what they say. The teacher then encourages them to talk about how each of them is different from the others and how much more interesting the group is because of those differences.

Unfortunately, not all teachers and administrators are as responsive as Seth's. Sometimes you may need to intervene very assertively in order to support your child.

Cally's daughter, Nan, announced at the dinner table that her fourth-grade teacher had not allowed her to talk about Cally and her partner BJ's wedding, which was taking place in a few weeks. The teacher had said flatly, "Women cannot get married." Nan felt embarrassed and was mad at the teacher. "He's wrong," she said, "and he's not being fair." Cally asked her daughter if it was okay to call the teacher and talk to him about it. Nan agreed but told her mom, "Don't make a big deal out of it." Cally met with the teacher and told him she had two concerns. The first was that he had stopped Nan from sharing appropriate information about her family, the second was that the teacher was wrong. Cally didn't tell him she was upset with his homophobia because she thought it would start a fight. Instead, she explained about her wedding and how her church, United Church of Christ, had agreed to marry her and her partner. The teacher was dumbfounded and clearly in disagreement with the idea of letting women get married to each other. But he apologized and agreed to let Nan talk about it in class. Cally then went to the principal and requested some diversity training for the staff that included lesbian and gay awareness and appreciation. It took months of persistent follow-up on Cally's part, but eventually it happened.

Sex Education

Your child may attend a human sexuality class at school as early as the fifth grade. He may also receive secondhand information from older friends or siblings. Whatever the source, your child will begin to consider your sexual orientation from a different perspective. Some children at the older end of this age range are curious about sex as well as a little titillated by it. Deal with curiosity about sex as you would other topics: give accurate, age-appropriate information and help your child sort out what it all means by listening and reflecting back what you hear him saying. Remember that many children won't want to take this all in at once.

Peg's thirteen-year-old sister, Kris, was asking their mother, Dot, what sex was like, now that their mother was dating again. Dot fielded the ques-

tions mostly by asking Kris what she meant and why she was bringing the topic up. She reminded her daughter that infomation about her sex life was private. Peg, at nine, sat frozen at the dining room table, listening in horror. She couldn't stand the idea that her mother kissed someone on the lips. Peg left the table as soon as she could, but later that night she asked Kris if she had kissed anyone.

Your child's curiosity about sex does not mean that he is ready to or interested in having sex. And even though his questions may seem to challenge your sexual orientation or your choice of partners ("Why don't you like men?"), this is more of the information-gathering typical of his age. He is forming his values and sorting out who he is. When the topic is sex, though, it can be easy to get on the defensive and forget that our job is still the same: providing information and loving support.

Moving and Making Friends

Moving at any time is stressful for children. Generally speaking, the older your child is, the more difficult it is for her to change schools and make new friends. If you move to a place where your family does not know anyone, your child has to decide whether to come out as the child of a lesbian or lesbian couple. This is more difficult than coming out in a city where your family is known and has a network of support.

It is crucial that you and your child talk before, during and after the move about what you are leaving behind and what you are moving to. Support him as he grieves the loss of his friends, former home and the familiar life your family is leaving. As he navigates the new environment, ask him what things he is looking forward to or is excited about and brainstorm ways your family can help each other during the transition. Some ideas are:

- Get names (from friends or other resources) of lesbian or gay parents in the new city.
- If you belong to a church or synagogue, get recommendations from your minister or rabbi for a new congregation that is welcoming of lesbian families.
- If your child has a special interest or sport that she plays, get infor-

mation about where she can continue that interest in the new location.

- Allow for phone calls to old friends.
- Plan on doing fun things as a family at least once a weekend for the first month or so.

◆　◆　◆

As your child moves through middle childhood, she learns about herself in a variety of contexts. Your family is still her home base and crucial to her well-being, but she is moving out into the broader world, making new friends and relationships. She is learning about rules and the consequences of testing them, and she is developing her own set of values. Your nurturance and willingness to stay engaged throughout these years of change can give her the support to complete her developmental tasks.

14 The Journey of Adolescence:
Not Necessarily a Nightmare

The idea that adolescence spells trouble has been a part of our folklore for generations, and parents often anticipate the teenage years with dread. Conventional wisdom has it that adolescence is inevitably a time of stress and storm, and that those parents whose teenagers don't get into trouble are just lucky.

Do lesbian parents anticipate their children's adolescence with any less fear and foreboding than other parents? Probably not. Lesbian parents may even have more concerns about parenting adolescents than do their heterosexual counterparts. Or the concerns may have a particular twist. In adolescence, the child is becoming a separate and independent person with her own opinions, values and attitudes; she is learning to be responsible for her own thoughts and feelings and for meeting her own needs. All the work of the previous developmental stages gets revisited with the added dimension of sexuality. Because sex and sexuality are often a major focus in adolescence, lesbian parents may have special concerns during this stage. Questions such as "How do I talk to my son about sex?" or "What do I tell my teenage daughter about my new lover?" or "What do I do if I don't like my daughter's new boyfriend or my son's girlfriend?" take on a particular significance for lesbian parents.

Some of the challenges we discuss regarding parenting adolescents are unique to lesbian parents but most are not. It is not unusual to wonder: "Is this an issue for me and my teenager *because* I am a lesbian, or is this just a typical parent-adolescent struggle?" Our goal is to cover the parenting territory broadly, while maintaining a lesbian-parent perspective and emphasis.

In this chapter we examine some myths about adolescence, give an overview of adolescent development, including differences between girls and boys, and outline general guidelines and approaches for parents. Subsequent chapters address topics related to the different stages of development: Chapter 15 focuses on preteens and young adolescents, Chapter 16 on the middle and late teen years and Chapter 17 on adult children.

Four Myths About Adolescence

In the 1970s psychologists began to study adolescents—how they think, what they think about, how they feel about their lives, why they behave as they do and how they respond to different types of parent behavior. At first research focused on troubled teenagers, but more recent work has looked at regular, everyday adolescents. Much of what passed for conventional wisdom has been exposed as myth.[1]

Myth #1. *Adolescence has to be a very difficult period.*
Adolescence *is* a complicated and confusing time for both parents and children. In *The Turbulent Teens,* James Gardner suggests that we might think of adolescence as a tapestry of complex but not yet completed patterns.[2] This image conveys a sense of the uncertainties and anxieties of this stage of life as well as its possibilities. Part of the complexity is due to the development of new thinking skills and cognitive capacity in adolescence. Particularly between the ages of twelve and fourteen, adolescents are using their increased capacity for abstract reasoning and hypothetical thinking to reexamine the values and beliefs of their parents and themselves. This process is not mysterious, but it can be disconcerting for parents.

So while adolescence is often fast-moving, intense and even bewildering, it need not be catastrophic. In fact, psychological problems, family conflict and problem behavior are no more common in adolescence than in other stages of the life cycle. It is true that some teenagers are troubled and that some get into trouble, but the great majority, almost ninety percent in fact, do not.[3]

Myth #2. *Peer pressure makes good kids turn bad.*
It is true that adolescents are concerned about what their friends think. They want to fit in, and they seek guidance from peers about style and appearance. However, we now know that parental and family influences are what help kids develop the skills necessary to select positive peer relationships and make good decisions about behavior.[4] Maintaining a healthy environment at home and raising children to make healthy choices provide the best insurance that children will not succumb to peer pressure.

Myth #3. *Adolescents rebel against any and all attempts to control them.*
In fact, the majority of adolescents feel that their parents are reasonable and patient with them most of the time. More than half admit that their parents are right when they are strict with them. However, they also note that they get angry when that happens. It is not the assertion of legitimate authority but the arbitrary use of power, with little explanation of the rules and no involvement of the teenager in the decision-making process, that fuels rebellion.

Myth #4. *Parents have no influence with their adolescents in today's world.*
In fact, parents remain a major influence for adolescents. Teenagers care what their parents think and listen to what they say, although they may not admit it or agree with every point. Research indicates that adolescents continue to look to their parents for advice about important issues like the future, values and education. They look to peers for guidance on matters of style and appearance.[5]

Many apprehensions about raising adolescents can be reduced. Like other parents, lesbians can approach parenting their children during this developmental stage knowing that adolescence does not have to spell disaster. However, if significant problems do arise, families can benefit from seeking professional consultation.

Adolescent Development: An Overview

Adolescence is a complicated time, but it is no more of a mystery than infancy and toddlerhood. Like these earlier stages of development, it is a period of rapid growth and change. Each teenager develops according to his or her individual timetable, but the sequence of changes is more or less predictable. It is useful to think of adolescence as having an early and middle phase, followed by young adulthood. Preteens and young adolescents (roughly ages ten to fourteen) have different needs and concerns than those of either middle and older teenagers (ages fourteen to eighteen) or young adults (ages eighteen to twenty).

Yet keep in mind that the boundaries of these phases are fluid. It is also important to remember that there is a wider range of variability between age and level of development in adolescence than in the earlier developmental stages.

Early, Late or on Time

Some teenagers show signs of puberty at age ten or eleven. Others do not begin to develop until fifteen or sixteen. Either pattern is normal. Although maturing very early or late is normal, it can present particular problems, and risks, for an adolescent. For example, if your son is the last boy in his peer group to shoot up in height, have his voice change and develop body hair, he may feel very anxious about his lack of development. Late bloomers often need special reassurance. Similarly, a daughter who is physically mature at twelve may feel lonely and isolated from her peer group. In addition, she may feel pressure to start dating or behaving like a teenager.[6] The parents of a girl who matures early need to emphasize that their daughter is not a teenager yet; for example: "It's nice that people think you are so mature, but it's not so important how old they think you are as how old you really are. I like and respect you as the twelve-year-old you are and I'm happy you are twelve, and not yet eighteen (or however old other people think she is)." The girl's mothers may also need to help her rehearse how to handle specific situations such as being approached by older males who do not realize how young she is.

Skills: Now You See Them, Now You Don't

One of the mysteries of adolescence is that one day—or one moment—your adolescent may seem very adult and then the next may resemble a four-year-old in a large body. A skill, like logical thinking, for example, is present one day and disappears the next, only to return the following week. This variability is very characteristic of adolescents.

Adult skills depend on both maturation and practice. Mature thinking skills include problem-solving, logical thinking and using good judgment; adult feeling skills include being able to identify what emotion one is feeling, connecting the feeling with an event and feeling empathy for others. These are all very complex skills in and of themselves. And the goal is to be able to use them together, to be able to think and feel at the same time.

The development of these skills in adolescents is understandably a bit erratic. In addition, adolescents are torn between wanting to grow up and not wanting to, which influences whether or not they use the skills they have. The quotation in the title of a recent book about teenagers by Anthony Wolf, *"Get out of my life, but first could you drive Cheryl and me to the mall": A Parent's Guide to the New Teenager*, captures this inconsistency.[7]

Raising Boys . . . and Raising Girls

Although the underlying forces in adolescence are similar for adolescents of both sexes, the behaviors they produce can be quite different.

Boys are likely to become very private. According to Wolf, "Once adolescence begins, teenage boys go to their room, close the door, turn on the stereo and don't come out for four years."[8] Boys may also spend a lot of time away from home. They tend to resolve the adolescent challenge of how to separate from their parents by separating physically. They can literally vanish, especially when parents want them to do something. They often respond to requests by agreeing, but then add, "I'll do it later" or "in a minute..." and then they disappear. Parents need to understand and honor the need for privacy and still stay engaged with their sons.

> *Lynn is a single lesbian and a dedicated parent. She and her son, Jerry, had always been very close until he hit adolescence. Then Jerry always seemed to be off with his friends or in his room listening to music. The things they used to do together no longer seemed of interest to him. She*

wasn't sure they had anything in common anymore. Lynn's work sched-ule had changed, and she and Jerry were spending very little time to-gether. When she realized that part of the change in their relationship might be due to her own confusion about how to relate to an adolescent male, she decided to approach the issue directly. She talked to Jerry about wanting to spend some time together and proposed that they have lunch together every other Friday. This arrangement became a tradition for them that they continued for more than two years.

Sometimes the meal was tense because they had not yet resolved a conflict. Sometimes Jerry was talkative and enthusiastic, sometimes he was moody and sometimes he read the sports section of the newspaper for most of the lunch hour. Still they continued to get together, and years later both of them recall the tradition fondly.

A lesbian parent may imagine that her teenage son's withdrawal is because of her lesbianism. It is more likely because she is a woman and that he is deeply attached to her. Not only is he working on be-coming independent from his parents, he is also getting his new and fairly free-floating sexuality under control. In the meantime, strong feelings about his mother may pose a problem. Everything tends to get sexualized for a teenage boy. For that reason, he may want to avoid strong emotional contact with his mother until he becomes more sepa-rate and gets his sexuality better focused. In his quest to avoid emo-tional contact, he may opt for no contact. So the challenge for a mother is to give her son room to establish this necessary independence with-out losing her connection with him.

Sexuality does not usually drive such a wedge between teenage girls and their parents. Rather than leaving, adolescent girls are more likely to resolve their need to separate by fighting. Stories of clashes be-tween preteen and teenage girls and their mothers are legendary. The mother is usually the main target because it is in relationship to her that the daughter needs to establish her independence and separate-ness. Mothers can take heart that as difficult as it may be to deal with a battling teenage daughter, she is definitely still in contact and thus still able to get support from her parents, even as she fights with them. And she can use all the support she can get because teenage girls typi-cally struggle with significant negative feelings about themselves.

Although girls enter adolescence with an edge over boys in terms of academic success, social skills and confidence about the future, they are vulnerable to a slide in self-esteem about the time they enter junior high. A number of research studies have identified this phenomenon. In 1990, for example, a study by the American Association of University Women surveyed boys and girls between the ages of nine and fifteen.[9] Eight-to-nine-year-old girls were described as confident and assertive. Sixty percent of these girls, and sixty-seven percent of boys the same age, were happy the way they were. However, by early adolescence, the percentage of females who said they were happy with the way they were dropped to twenty-nine. Male self-esteem dropped much less dramatically, to fifty percent.

Both white and Hispanic girls showed this pattern, but African-American girls did not, although they certainly reported other problems. The drop in their self-esteem was much less significant than for the other two groups of girls. While the data does not explain why this is so for African-American girls, there has been speculation, which we will return to shortly when we address how mothers can help their teenage daughters.

The Damaging Messages Our Daughters Hear

Girls are subject to different social pressures than boys are. In this culture, male sexuality tends to focus outward, toward the object of desire. Adolescent males, at least heterosexual ones, tend to focus less on how they look and more on how females look. That means that *everyone* is focused on the girls, because adolescent females are also focused on how they themselves look. And, of course, they never look right.

In the United States the cultural message we are exposed to daily is that it is important for a woman to be beautiful. The media also tell us what "beautiful" looks like, and it's not what we see when we look in the mirror. No wonder teenage girls are painfully aware of their looks and how they fall short of the supposed "ideal" in terms of beauty and weight. In her book *Reviving Ophelia: Saving the Selves of Adolescent Girls*, Mary Pipher sounds an alarm.[10] She describes teenage girls as more oppressed today than ever. The culture in which they are coming of age is more dangerous, more sexualized and more media-saturated. With puberty, adolescent girls crash into what Pipher calls "junk culture." Here the gap between girls' true selves and what the culture says is properly female creates enormous problems. The pressures can be too much for them to handle. They may become overwhelmed, confused, even traumatized. Thus the drop in self-esteem.

What's a mother to do? Strengthen and prepare your daughter before puberty, and support and guide her in adolescence. And work to change the broader culture. Create a culture in your family and community which supports teenage girls to value themselves and the women they are becoming. This brings us back to the AAUW study and to speculation about why African-American adolescent girls did not show as significant a drop in self-esteem as white and Hispanic girls did. Perhaps it is because African-American girls often have a powerful role model in their mother.[11] African-American mothers, single or not, have been portrayed as the glue that holds the family together. Although they certainly do not have problem-free lives, African-American daughters may be more likely to get the message that women are strong and in no way inferior to men.

Based on this speculation, lesbian mothers are in a good position to help their daughters be strong and self-reliant. In lesbian families, women do everything. Household chores, financial support, parenting and whatever needs doing are assigned on the basis of ability, interest or availability, not gender. Whether single or partnered, as lesbian parents we are not looking to a man to rescue us or take care of us. Our adolescent daughters are thus at an advantage in having models who do not conform to the culturally limiting roles for women.

There is another potential advantage for daughters in lesbian families. As lesbians we are by definition outside the heterosexist system that defines how women are supposed to look and to be. This does not mean that we have no interest in our appearance, or in our daughter's appearance. However, we are not bound by the usual cultural prescriptions. We can model for our daughters an alternative to the belief that teenage girls have to look and be the way the culture, including the adolescent culture, says they should in order for them to be okay.

When their thirteen-year-old daughter, Tauni, started to act obsessed with her appearance, Pam and Carly got concerned. Here was a child who used to have to be dragged out of bed in the morning. Now she was getting up an hour early to get ready for school. She complained bitterly that she had nothing to wear and she fussed with her hair for what seemed like hours. She had to be literally driven from the bathroom so they could get to work on time. The only thing that seemed to be important to Tauni was how she looked, and she never seemed to be satisfied.

When they compared notes with other parents of adolescent girls, Pam and Carly heard much the same story. That relieved them somewhat. However, it was still hard to see Tauni so caught up with appearances. So they tried to appreciate that this was a stage, and got into discussions with each other about how women are oppressed by rigid cultural definitions of beauty. At the time they weren't sure she heard any of it. Then they overheard Tauni in a conversation with her best friend saying, "I don't care what anybody says, I like my dreads."

Putting Your Own Adolescence in Perspective

Your own past, or at least how you remember it, influences your parenting. You may focus on all the things you did as an adolescent that could have gotten you into trouble, or perhaps did. Then you worry that your children will do those same things—or worse. Or you may focus on the painful times and experiences, and anticipate that the teenage years will also be painful for your children. Or you may remember the happy times and expect that your teenager will have the same idyllic experience you had.

When you understand your own past and how you were affected by it, you can use that knowledge to be a more engaged parent. You do need to remember that your past experiences are *your* experiences. They do not dictate what is in store for your children. Times have changed. Your children are themselves, *not* a clone of you. And they have different parents than you did.

Bonnie's parents immigrated to the United States from Burma with four young children. Her parents were focused on working hard, making a living and trying to establish a secure future for their children. Bonnie remembers her struggle to learn English and keep up with her schoolwork at the same time. Most of all she remembers desperately wanting to fit in, to be an American. And she remembers that her parents weren't able to help her with this.

Bonnie's oldest daughter, Kim, is now eleven. When Kim wants to look the same as her friends—same haircut, same clothes, same everything—

Bonnie understands. She realizes that the situation is different for Kim than it was for her; she can understand wanting to fit in and feels she is in a good position to help Kim cope with it.

Kim recently told her mother that a teacher had asked her to be on the yearbook committee. She wanted to be on it but none of her other friends were interested. Bonnie got Kim to talk about what the yearbook committee was all about and what she might like about it. Then they talked about why her other friends weren't interested and how it might be for her to do something different than her friends did. She wanted her daughter to hear the message that it was okay to follow her own interests even if they were different from those of her friends. Bonnie wasn't sure any of it had sunk in, but later in the week Kim announced that she had signed up for the yearbook committee.

When we have dealt with our own past, we can be of more help to our children in dealing with their present. As our children get older, our memories of our experiences at that point in our own lives get activated. Most of us have clear memories of our own adolescence. If we always wanted to be popular, or athletic, or something else that we weren't, we need to face that and acknowledge the disappointment, grieve the loss and put it behind us. Then we can avoid placing expectations on our children that they will do for us what we were not able to do for ourselves at their age. Our daughters won't have to earn the high school track letter than we never got; our sons won't have to go on lots of dates because we never did; our children won't have to be on the honor roll just because we were. These are good things; we sure wanted them. Our children may not.

Shifting the Parenting Gears

Adolescents need their parents in a different way than they did when they were small. Parents need to adjust to these changes. At one extreme parents can refuse to recognize that their child is growing up. They may try to direct and control their teenager as if he were still an immature child. This over-control may encourage rebellion. At the other extreme are those who conclude that "there is nothing parents can do with teenagers" and give up trying to relate or give up on providing structure and guidance. In this situation, the teenager may get the message that his parents don't care about him and feel abandoned.

There is no magical formula for raising a healthy, well-adjusted teenager. There is not even an agreed-upon definition of well-adjusted. However, there are descriptions of different kinds of parenting styles and their effects, and some strategies are more effective than others.[12] A collaborative style of parenting, which we call engaged parenting, is more effective than the autocratic style of "Do what I say because I said so." The main flaw of autocratic parenting is that it depends, in part, on creating fear. Fear can breed anger and resentment. Autocratic parenting is also intimidating and can cause a child to lose confidence in herself. Another serious drawback to this parenting style is that it sends the message that fear and intimidation are a necessary and acceptable way of getting what you want in everyday life. This is not what parents should be teaching their children.

Engaged Parenting . . . Adolescent-Style

As we said in Chapter 5, engaged parents are loving, they use firmness with dignity and respect, and they have rules and limits—some of which are negotiable, some of which are not.

Parenting—parenting adolescents in particular—is not simple. No technique works all the time with every child. Nor are there techniques that work for every parent. Each parent-child relationship is unique. What you can do is get good information about adolescent development, hone your parenting skills, and trust your own wisdom and common sense as you do what you think and feel is best. After all, you know your adolescent better than anyone else does.

It can help to keep the following points in mind:

1. *None of us is perfect.*
   We all have good days and bad days, and all parents at times lapse into the "Do it because I said so" style of parenting or slip into simply giving up, as in "I'm tired of arguing with you; do whatever you want." Recognize that it is the *pattern*, over time, that matters more than any one incident.

2. *Spending time together is important.*
   When their children get older and the peer group becomes very important, some parents assume their child is no longer interested in the family. In fact, research indicates that most teenagers say

they want to spend more, not less, time with their parents than they actually do spend.[13] What they want to do may have changed from when they were little, but going to a special event, sharing an activity or task that is enjoyable to all, or even just hanging out around the house can all count as time together.

Most teenagers like to talk, and when parents show a sincere interest, the teenager is more likely to open up. Too many parent-teenager conversations are about chores, schedules, grooming and other ho-hum topics. "When do you have to be at the game?" or "Did you take out the garbage?" or "What did you do to your hair?" are not great conversation starters. One study asked teenagers what they wished they could talk about with their parents. They listed eight topics: family matters, controversial issues, emotional issues, the big whys (for example, why do we have wars?), the future, current affairs, personal interests and parents themselves.[14]

3. *Love and trust are the keys.*
If your children know that you love them no matter what, you (and they) can make lots of mistakes and still come out fine. In particular, adolescents need to know that their parents are there for them and that they don't have to stay little and cute to be loved. Maintain positive and caring contact with your adolescent child by talking with her about her interests and concerns and sharing some of your own, treating her with respect and trust and by being supportive. Parents who trust their kids assume the best instead of suspecting the worst. They maintain a belief in their child's good intentions, even when things go wrong.

Although love is basic, love alone is not enough. Parents of adolescents also need judgment, courage, the ability to say "no" and, if necessary, the ability to handle having their children not like them for long periods.

4. *Setting limits is essential.*
Adolescents, especially in the earlier teen years, need consistency and structure from parents. It helps counterbalance the feeling that they are coming "unglued." This means clear, consistent and reasonable rules.

Adolescents are more likely to rebel when parents use their power arbitrarily, don't explain the rules and don't involve the teenager in the decision-making process. "Because I say so" just doesn't work at this stage. If you take this tack, your teen will likely complain and whine or go ahead and do what she wants behind your back. Including your adolescent in the decision-making means you are recognizing that your child is growing up and has the right to participate in decisions that affect her life.

Although most rules can be negotiated, some rules need to be non-negotiable, for example, ones that have to do with your child's physical and emotional safety or with deeply held family values. A "no drinking and driving" rule has to do with safety; a "no name-calling" rule, that is, not using racial, ethnic or sexual-orientation epithets, reflects a deeply held family value.

Particularly because she is a lesbian and gay rights activist, Roz was shocked when she overheard her thirteen-year-old son Nathan and his friends calling each other "stupid faggots." When she asked him about it, he shrugged it off as just talk, saying, "Nobody really means anything by it."

Roz, however, had very strong feelings about it. Using that kind of language in her presence was not negotiable. She spoke up when complete strangers put down gays and lesbians, so she certainly was not going to allow her own son to go unchallenged. She told Nathan how she felt and why.

The challenge for parents of adolescents is to know when to give in, when to put the adolescents' desires first, when to shield them from the consequences of their behavior and when not to. If it is not a matter of their safety or your strong values, how do you know whether you are being too controlling or too lenient? You need to use your best judgment and then be open to the information that time and experience provide.

5. *Privileges are tied to responsibilities.*
One way to approach raising adolescents is to think about what your goals are. You likely want to raise children who are responsible for themselves and considerate of others and who become separate and independent people with identities and values of their own. To accomplish this, you need to grant your children freedom

in stages, tie privileges to responsibility and then stand back. The art of parenting an adolescent is helping him get started and then bowing out as gracefully and unnoticed as possible. For example, the ultimate goal for your son is autonomy, but you would never hand him the keys to the car when he turned sixteen and tell him to "enjoy." First there is driver's education, the examination, the learner's permit and practicing with an adult in the car. And then after he has his license, you see how he does on short drives in the daytime before you agree to his driving at night or a long trip on the freeway. As he follows through on the agreed-upon responsibilities such as washing the car, coming home on time and refilling the gas tank, more privileges are available.

Yet parents also must learn to stand back. Unless health and safety are at stake, you need to resist intervening so that your adolescent can learn from the consequences of making mistakes. For example, if the established consequence of not refilling the gas tank is no car privileges on Saturday night, hold firm to that agreement and allow your son to experience the loss of a privilege.

Since every adolescent breaks the rules at least occasionally, some guidelines can be useful:

- *Don't jump to conclusions and overreact.*
  There may be a reasonable explanation for your child's behavior. Remember the concept of trusting your child and the principle of "innocent until proven guilty."

- *Be consistent, even in the face of being unpopular with your child.*

- *Do not use physical punishment.*
  Study after study shows that violence begets violence. Physical abuse and verbal abuse are both wrong and ineffective. If you or your teenager are too angry to talk, wait until you cool off. Tell your child, "I'm too angry to talk now." And if you do lose control, don't try to justify your behavior. Apologize. "I was wrong to hit you (or call you names). I'm sorry, and I will try to make sure that it never happens again." If you or your adolescent lose control regularly, get professional help for your family.

- *Use logical consequences instead of punishment.*
  Sometimes expressing disappointment is enough. "I am disap-

pointed and don't want this to happen again." Make sure this is not guilt-tripping of the "how could you do this to me" variety. Express your displeasure with the behavior, not with the adolescent as a person.

Consequences need to be related, respectful and reasonable. It is best to have agreements of the "if-then" type in advance so the adolescent knows the consequences of breaking the rule. That way, as one teen put it, "A punishment is something that parents do to you; a consequence is something you do to yourself."

Some examples of "if-then" agreements involving logical consequences are:

—If you damage the car, you are responsible for the insurance deductible.

—If you come home intoxicated, you are grounded for a month.

—If your grade-point average falls below 3.0, you need to quit your after-school job and devote more time to studying.

—If you finish your homework before 8 p.m., you can watch one hour of television programs from the list of acceptable ones.

—If you put your dirty clothes in the hamper before Monday morning, they'll be washed. If you don't get them in the hamper by then, you have to do your own wash.

—If you are late coming home from a date, you won't be able to go out the following weekend.

Having the adolescent help decide the consequences, even after the fact, is another way to avoid power struggles. Often teenagers will impose stiffer penalties on themselves than parents would. It may take a while for your adolescent to understand the connection between his behavior and consequences, but hang in there; "if-then" is a lesson in life that is well worth learning.

• *Take action when safety is an issue.*
If you can't work out an agreement with your child, let her know what the consequences will be for breaking the rule. And save stiff penalties for major violations, such as sneaking out of the house or coming home drunk.

◆ ◆ ◆

Adolescence is a stage. Although it may sometimes seem like it will never end, it does. Parents who survive and even thrive through the teenage years may get all they ever wanted at the end of the process: a caring and responsible adult child who genuinely likes and respects herself and you, and whom you genuinely like and respect. Perhaps you may even get to hear the words: "I know I gave you a hard time sometimes, but I really appreciate all you did for me. You were a good parent."

15 On the Road to Adulthood:

Ten to Fourteen Years

One mother we know recently returned in shock from taking her daughter for a regular visit to the family doctor. "The doctor talked about Shaya's being in puberty! She actually used the word 'puberty.' Can you believe it? For heaven's sake, she's only eight years old! "

The internal physiological changes called puberty begin well before there are any outward signs of sexual maturation. The average child has entered the stage of biological development called puberty by the age of eight or nine. Although it may be several years before there are external signs of the transformation of a child's body into an adult one, children—and their parents—need to be prepared.

Development Guideposts

In addition to the obvious physiological changes of growing up and filling out that accompany puberty, intellectual, emotional and social changes occur during early adolescence as well.

Considering that each youngster is on an individual timetable, what can a parent expect, in general, between the ages of ten and fourteen? There will be rapid and dramatic spurts in physical and intellectual growth as well as sexual development and awakening. Preteens and young adolescents are becoming more independent and responsible, are learning to do things their own way, are internalizing rules and are developing a separate identity. Typically, this age group is concerned about being popular with peers. In this chapter we look at the developmental changes of preteens and young adolescents, and what lesbian parents can do to help steer themselves and their children around the sometimes rocky shoals of these changes.

Physical Changes

Because puberty is different from anything a child has experienced before, parents need to provide information to prepare children for what is and will be happening with their bodies. "Am I normal?" is the essence of many concerns of this age group. At a time when young people want to be like everyone else, they find themselves the least alike. Although their peers are all growing and changing, they are doing so at their own pace. Best girlfriends may start to menstruate at very different ages. Boys who were the same height as most of their classmates one year may find themselves a head shorter, or taller, than most the next year.

In addition, the outcome of all this development is uncertain. Some individuals become muscular, others do not; some young women develop large breasts, and others small; some men have big penises, others have small ones. Adults know that bodies come in all shapes and sizes, that physical appearance is not the only ingredient in attractiveness and that the size of sexual organs is not the key element of being a good sexual partner. However, young adolescents do not know these things. Because they don't know how they will turn out, their anxiety about the what and the when is understandable. At times, all adolescents feel uncomfortable with their changing bodies. Complaints such as, "I hate my body," "I don't want hair on my face," "I'm ugly" or "I don't want to grow up" need to be listened to. Try to find out specifically what your child is concerned about. Then address the issue. If your daughter is upset about developing breasts sooner than her friends, deal with that. Reassurance can be useful. Bras and clothing that doesn't overemphasize her breasts may help, too. If your son is upset over his face breaking out, make sure you have accurate information for him about what to do and what not to do. If he is experiencing severe acne, see a physician.

Generally, the more young people know about physical changes to expect during puberty, the easier time they will have. Parents are more likely to prepare girls for puberty than they are to prepare boys because girls need to be prepared for menstruation and told how to avoid pregnancy and because the topics of male erections and ejaculation bring up potentially embarrassing questions about sex.

Although lesbian parents may find it reassuring to know that heterosexual parents find it easier to talk about puberty with their daughters than with their sons, that does not let us off the hook. After all, the majority of children conceived by lesbians using alternative insemination are male. However the family was created, lots of lesbian parents are raising sons, so we need to be prepared.

When should you talk to your children about puberty? Before it begins. This means you need to start talking to them specifically about menstruation or nocturnal emissions when they are about eight or nine. These two changes happen suddenly and can upset or frighten a youngster who doesn't know what's happening. And since you can't know when they will experience these changes, information is better provided sooner than later. Before about the age of nine, children are likely to ask all kinds of questions. They want to know about the differences between boys and girls, and where babies come from. If you have been talking with them about sex all along, the groundwork has been laid. Now you need to talk more directly about what changes are going to happen to their bodies. And you will likely have to initiate the conversations because they may no longer be asking you questions the way they did when they were younger. Of course you need to have the information yourself before you can share it with your children.

Many of us were not well prepared for puberty by our own parents and may even be unaware of how little we actually know about the developmental changes our children will be going through. Lesbians who have never been involved with men and are now facing educating their sons about puberty may feel particularly at a loss. Thankfully, there are a number of good books available for parents, as well as for adolescents. (See Selected Bibliography.)

In addition to a lack of information, you may have attitudes that get in the way of talking with your child in a matter of fact way. You may be embarrassed or feel inadequate or not want to be too pushy. The best approach is to discuss issues informally, as they arise. Don't make too big a deal of them. For example, if your daughter casually asks you how old you were when you started menstruating, use the opportunity to talk some about yourself—the facts and your feelings about it: "I was eleven and I was so excited. I came home and announced to my mother that now I was a woman." Or "I was fifteen, and all my friends started before I did. I worried a lot that I would never start." Your daughter is likely not just asking an idle question. You may want to ask her about her friends. Have any of them started yet? You can also inquire as to what else she is wondering about and what more does she want to know.

And if your child does not ask questions, it doesn't mean that he is not interested or that you should just wait until he asks you. You need to initiate.

> When her eleven-year-old son, Jeremy, suddenly began expressing interest in doing the laundry, Rachel didn't know what to make of it. Finally she realized that he had likely begun to have wet dreams. The previous year they had talked about nocturnal emissions. She had given him the information she thought he needed, including what was happening physically and that most boys have them and that it was perfectly normal. She also made sure that the family bookshelf had resources so he could read more. What she had not talked about with him was what to do with the damp sheets.

Sexual Awakening

Puberty is also the time of sexual awakening. Sexual development starts in puberty and continues throughout adolescence. Preteens and young teenagers are dealing with their sexual feelings and sensations mostly by *thinking* about sex and relationships. Later in adolescence they will focus more on what to *do* about sex and relationships.

Parents can help their children develop attitudes toward sex and sexuality that are realistic, informed, positive and responsible. To do this successfully, you should be well prepared with clear information and be ready to model the kind of attitudes about sex and sexuality that you want your children to have.

Most heterosexual parents don't think much about the possibility that their son or daughter might turn out to be gay or lesbian. And if they do think about it, it may not be a happy prospect. Lesbian parents, on the other hand, are quite aware of the range of possibilities and can be more affirming.

All parents need to remember that early adolescence is a period of wondering, fantasizing and experimenting. Sexual preferences are often still tentative. Many of us know people who say they were certain of their lesbian or gay sexual orientation at a very early age. You may be one of those people yourself. However, many of us came out later. There is no need to second-guess the outcome of your children's developing sexuality. The important message to convey to them is that whatever their sexual orientation turns out to be, it's okay with you.

As a lesbian parent, you may discover some unexpected reactions at this point in your child's development. You may find yourself hoping your son turns out to be heterosexual, because you are afraid of AIDS and fantasize that he would be safer as a heterosexual. Or you may fantasize that your daughter becomes a lesbian so that you and she will have more in common and be closer somehow. Or you may be afraid that she will be a lesbian to please you or that your son will start being sexual with females at an early age to prove to everyone including himself that he is not gay. You may find yourself concluding that your tomboy daughter will likely be a dyke or that your sensitive, emotional son is probably gay. Your own homophobia and stereotypes may surprise you.

When he was twelve, Marta's son, Jason, told her that he thought he was gay. Marta's reactions surprised her. She was pleased that their relationship and communication were open enough for Jason to talk to her about his feelings. However, her mind was flooded with questions and concerns. Was it true? How was high school going to be for him if he was openly gay? What about AIDS? Was Jason really gay, or was he trying to please her somehow or trying to please his gay dads? Perhaps she hadn't arranged for enough straight men to be in his life so that he had that option.

When she started thinking a version of "Where did I go wrong?" she realized that she sounded very much like her own mother. At seventeen, Marta had come out to her mother, whose response was an emotional combination of "You'll never be happy" and "What did I do wrong that I have a lesbian daughter?"

Marta realized that she needed to slow down. Jason was just begin-

ning to explore his sexuality. Maybe he was gay, maybe not. Whether he was or wasn't, she needed to keep the communication lines open to support him as he explored and sorted out what was right for him. This wasn't about her; it was about him. And she knew from experience that being gay or lesbian and having a rich and full life could go together very nicely.

The point here is don't beat yourself up for having reactions you think you shouldn't have. Because our society is homophobic, we each may reflect society's judgments about homosexuality in some of our attitudes. We may also have some of our own unfinished business about our sexual orientation. Realize that even though your children have grown up in a lesbian household, they also live in a broader society that is not so affirming of lesbians and gays and they may have worries about who they will turn out to be. Preteens and early teens face the challenge of this stage's emphasis on fitting in and being liked by peers. It may be fine with a son that his mother is a lesbian, but not be acceptable to him that he might be homosexual or that his peers would think that he was one of those "faggots." A daughter may always have been very proud and excited to march in the local annual Lesbian, Gay and Bisexual Parade, until she turned twelve. Now she is afraid her friends might see her and think she is lesbian, too.

Lesbian parents have the same informational issues to cover with their children as do heterosexual parents. These include the physical changes in puberty, masturbation, sexual orientation, conception, pregnancy, sexual feelings and relationships, sexually transmitted diseases, AIDS and whatever other information the child wonders about. In addition to actual information, how parents talk with their children about sex conveys their attitudes. If you want them to be positive, responsible, open and realistic, you need to model these qualities as much as possible. Here are some guidelines that should help you and your child communicate effectively about sex:[1]

Guideline 1: *Start early.*
If you have been talking frankly and age-appropriately about sexual issues with your child all along, the foundation is in place. If that is not the case, start now. Remember that children are less likely to ask questions after about age nine. This means that you probably

need to initiate the conversations. Don't wait for them to ask.

Ideally, you should talk with your child before she has become sexually active. Ten-to-twelve-year-olds are less likely to get defensive and more likely to say what is on their minds than a sixteen-year-old who already has a boyfriend. It is much easier and less embarrassing to talk about "what if" situations than about ones that happened last night or may happen next weekend. If you have delayed these discussions, say so. Volunteer that you should have talked with her before this, but that you didn't and want to start now.

Guideline 2: *Spread out the discussions over time.*

It is not possible, or desirable, to cover all the information at once. If you want your child to consider sex a normal part of life, the best approach is the most natural one. Weave discussions of sexual topics into everyday conversation. Television shows and magazine articles, for example, raise opportunities for discussing sexual behavior and values.

This does not mean, of course, that you only have conversations with your child when the topic is sex or that you talk about it all the time. In trying to avoid the One Big Talk approach, don't go overboard into too many little talks. Balance is the key. If your son or daughter asks a question, answer it and ask if there is anything else they would like to know. Your goals are to find out what your child knows, to correct any misinformation and to communicate that it is okay to talk about sex.

Guideline 3: *Respect your child's privacy.*

The desire for privacy increases in adolescence. Preteens and teenagers don't want you going through their things or prying into their thoughts. Using other people, such as people they know or even TV characters, as a starting point for discussions allows for adolescents to keep the conversation more general if they wish. So, if you want to broach the topic of masturbation with your son, you might ask him what teenagers today think about masturbation rather than asking him directly if he masturbates. Then the choice is his about how personal he wants to get.

This privacy rule works both ways. That is, you may or may not feel comfortable talking about your own experiences. If not, say so. You can have useful and informative discussions with your child about sex without going into intimate details—on your part or his. However, adolescents usually do want to know where their parents stand. In addition to factual information, they want to know your values about sex and relationships.

Guideline 4: *Help your child get what he or she needs.*
There may be some occasions or situations where your child has needs you are not able to meet. For example, your twelve-year-old son may be worried about the size of his penis. Reassurance from you may not be enough for him. What are your options? A physician or a trusted male friend or relative may be possible resources. One mother we know spoke to her son's doctor prior to her son's physical examination for camp. The doctor was able to talk with her son and provide the needed reassurance.

Intellectual and Moral Development

Young adolescents not only start to *look* more like adults, they also begin to *think* more like adults. Parents need to know what to expect in this shift from immature to mature thinking; otherwise there can be misunderstandings. Because adolescents are developing the capability of thinking more like adults, the way they see themselves, other people and the world changes. Your child will become not only more interesting but also more challenging because she is thinking for herself.

In the preteen and early teen years, the young person enters the world of abstract ideas, hypothetical situations and logic. The simpler world of childhood, where things were either good or bad, smart or stupid, mean or nice, turns into a more complicated world of uncertainty, ambiguity and debate. And young adolescents often try out their debating skills with parents. They are flexing their intellectual muscles, which may mean they want to debate issues you consider closed or argue for the sake of arguing. This can be unsettling. Now your child has skills that only you had before.

Once again, Sandy's thirteen-year-old daughter, Kathleen, was bringing up the topic of staying by herself when Sandy was out of town for a week. Sandy had always been clear, and firm, that Kathleen would be staying with her grandmother. However, this kid did not give up. They had talked about the issue at least four times the previous week. Every time, Kathleen seemed to have a new argument or a new approach. This time she announced that she had called Louise, Sandy's ex and Kathleen's co-parent, who had told Kathleen that she would be willing to stop by every day and check in on how she was doing and if she needed anything. Sandy wasn't sure who she wanted to murder first, Kathleen—or Louise.

Young adolescents are also able to imagine possibilities such as a world without war, or life with a different set of parents. Since it is only a small step from thinking about what *could be* to thinking about what *should be*, they can turn from visionaries to social critics in the blink of an eye. Again, parents are nearby and often receive the closest scrutiny and the harshest criticism.

Another intellectual development is the ability to use logic and reason. Increased ability to reason and the ability to challenge the reasoning of others, begins to emerge in early adolescence, or even sooner. By eleven or twelve, most young people have some grasp of abstract concepts, possibilities and formal logic. Teenagers can think problems through and see the logical consequences of different positions or actions. They often apply their developing logical reasoning skills to family rules.

Ruby and Jean agreed and were clear with their son, Adrian, about the rule that he could not go out on weeknights because he needed to do his homework. It had never been an issue. Then one Wednesday at dinner he casually mentioned that he was going over to his friend Biko's after dinner to check out Biko's new computer game. His mothers looked at each other, then at him, in disbelief. When they told him that he couldn't go and reminded him of the rule, he countered that he had finished his homework already, so why couldn't he go?

Mary Kay had always been able to have reasonable conversations with her daughter, Jessica—until Jessica turned twelve. Now they seemed to get into arguments all the time. Mary Kay was sure that if she said the sky was blue, Jessica would insist that it was any color but blue.

Their latest confrontation was over the no-alcohol, no-drugs rule. Jessica pointed out that Mary Kay herself drank coffee, smoked cigarettes and even drank alcohol sometimes. So why was she insisting that Jessica do none of these things?

In these examples, Adrian and Jessica have presented their parents with an opportunity to clarify the reasoning and values behind their rules and to help their children improve their reasoning skills. Often the young adolescent's reasoning sounds logical and approaches being logical—but it doesn't quite make it. In his book *The Turbulent Teens*, James Gardner describes the logic of young adolescents as often being "pseudo-logic."[2] He cites an example of this from a television sitcom where the adolescent says to an adult, "I moved out of the house so my mother would have one less mouth to feed." When the adult responds that his mother must miss him, he replies, "No, I see her every day when I go over for dinner." While this pseudo-logic can amuse parents sometimes, it can also be frustrating.

Remember that if you want to raise a curious and independent individual, you need to encourage discussion and debate—not stifle it. This does not mean, of course, that you want to get hooked into daily discussions about such things as chores. But discussions about political, moral, personal and interpersonal problems are good ways to encourage your child to try out her new intellectual wings in a supportive place. If she learns at home how to stand her ground or how to lose an argument without losing face, she will be more prepared to deal with peer pressure and inappropriate demands by other adults.

Because children at this age can think more like adults does not mean they can apply their thinking to everyday life situations. They lack experience. For example, sometimes your daughter may seem to complicate things unnecessarily: she can't decide what to wear or takes forever in a restaurant deciding what to order. This is because she now understands that there are innumerable choices, but she hasn't yet learned how to narrow the choices. She may also appear to be very hypocritical: one minute she is preaching about healthy eating and criticizing you for your weakness for chocolate; the next minute she is eating junk food and gets huffy when you point out the discrepancy between her talk and her actions. Do not take these things personally. Having difficulty making decisions and being hypocritical are just part of the intellectual development process of adolescence—and unfortunately some of us never grow out of it!

Another characteristic of adolescence is egocentrism—young adolescents act as if they are the center of the universe. Because he is now able to think about what others are thinking, your son may imagine that everyone is thinking about him. One way for parents to think about (or remember) what this is like is to imagine that everything you do or say is being noticed and evaluated by an audience. That is how your child may feel. Your daughter is convinced that everyone at school will notice the pimple on her chin. The feeling that one is the center of attention can lead to an exaggerated sense of importance and uniqueness. It can also contribute to the personal fables that adolescents develop. These usually involve their being so unique and special that the usual rules and natural laws that apply to other people do not apply to them. For example, your son may believe that he won't have a problem if he hitchhikes or that bad drug trips won't happen to him. Because these personal fables may be dangerous, parents need to be aware of the young adolescent's tendency to create them and to imagine himself as invincible.

Right, Wrong and Other Moral Questions

Because young adolescents are able to think more like adults, they start to evaluate moral questions differently. These changes follow a predictable course. The young child's morality is based on self-interest. To six-year-olds, getting an equal slice of the pie is what's fair. They don't do certain things because they don't want to get into trouble; when they do something nice, they expect something back. The general rule is tit-for-tat. You do something nice for me, and I'll return the favor. Do something mean, and I'll do something mean back.

Around eight or nine, children start being concerned about how others see them. What's right at this stage means doing what's expected by people who matter. The reason to be good is to get approval from others. Because of their intellectual development, young adolescents can put themselves in another person's place. They understand the concept of the Golden Rule, to do unto others as you would have them do unto you. They realize that getting even has long-term consequences in relationships.

Preteens actually want to be good and want others to think well of them. This stage has been called the "good boy/nice girl" stage of development. Parents are usually thrilled when the child is in this stage of moral development because she seems more caring, more co-operative and generally easier to get along with. Why? Because she is eager to please. However, the strength of this stage of moral reasoning, namely the desire for approval, is also its weakness. In junior high, she shifts to wanting to please her peers rather than her parents. Plaintive whines like, "But, Mom, everybody gets to stay out until eleven," are heard frequently.

Parents can't do anything to stop a young adolescent from caring what her peers think. It is a normal part of her development. But you can help her to develop the inner strength and security to resist peer pressure and make up her own mind when faced with making moral decisions, some of which affect her health and safety such as using drugs and alcohol, being sexual, smoking cigarettes and so on. In his book, *Raising Good Children: From Birth Through the Teenage Years*, Thomas Lickona suggests some guidelines for bringing out the best in young adolescents.[3]

Lickona points out that because adolescents are able to think differently than children do, you need to use different approaches than you did when they were younger. You are better off to appeal to their better self and to their ideals with approaches such as the following:

- "We're trusting you to do what we agreed on while we are away. Can we depend on you?"

- "Try to look at the situation from my point of view. What would you do if you were me?"

- "I am exhausted and have a lot to do. I really need your cooperation right now."

- "This is a favor we are asking. Think of it as a good deed."

To help young adolescents develop a positive image of themselves, which will help them resist peer pressure, Lickona encourages adults to do the following:

- Tell adolescents you love them, and praise their efforts.

- Avoid shaming, intimidation and put-downs.

- Encourage interests and activities in which the adolescent can succeed.

- Give real responsibilities including other-oriented activities such as helping cook for the family or collecting money for a charitable organization.

- Encourage independent thinking by asking what your child thinks. Encourage him to think his own thoughts, especially when he tells you what all the other kids are saying.
- Support friendships, and talk with your child about what being a friend means and how to choose positive relationships.

Emotional Growth

Adolescents are moody. Early adolescence, in particular, is a time of emotional highs and lows—and worry. This stage of development involves an increased sense of vulnerability and great concern about looks, abilities and popularity. Your daughter, who never worried about her school performance and has been an A student, is now fraught with anxiety about every report she has to do. Your son seems obsessed with whether he will be able to get a good job when he grows up. Young adolescents worry about all kinds of things, some of which they can have no control over—which makes them worry more.

Self-esteem tends to decline temporarily in early adolescence. As a rule, the self-consciousness and self-doubt of early adolescence are more intense for girls than for boys perhaps because they begin puberty earlier and are socialized to get along with others and be popular, and perhaps because society sends very mixed signals to girls about sexuality and achievement, among other things.

Recent research by Lyn Brown and Carol Gilligan suggests that girls abandon their own voice and sacrifice their sense of self for the sake of relationships, which the girls think are possible only if they become obedient girls and good women.[4] The authors note that seven- and eight-year-old girls speak up directly and consistently. They show a confidence in their perceptions and a sure sense of entitlement. By the ages of ten or eleven, however, girls have replaced this feisty outspokenness with confusion and "I don't knows." They seem caught in a struggle to maintain their own truth about what they think and feel but at the same time be acceptable to adults in authority who hold up a model of how girls are supposed to be.

By the ninth grade, self-esteem has begun to stabilize, and by middle to late adolescence, the sense of self-worth has usually increased. However, the previously cited research suggests that for females, the price paid for this may be the silencing of their voice. A number of recent books, specifically for parents of girls, speak to how parents can help their daughters develop their full potential. (See Selected Bibliography.)

The self-doubt and worry of this developmental period can be very distressing not only to young adolescents but to their parents. Lesbians who pride themselves on their non-sexist, woman-affirming child-rearing may feel like failures when their daughter's views on what's appropriate behavior for women start sounding as if they were written by Phyllis Schlafly. Early adolescence is one of the most sexist periods of the life span. Because young adolescents are insecure about their sexual identities, they sometimes go to extremes of femininity or masculinity to reassure themselves. Suddenly your tomboy daughter becomes obsessed with clothes and makeup, or your son spends his time lifting weights instead of practicing the cello.

Parents need to appreciate how important popularity and fitting in are to the young adolescent. The last thing this age group wants is to stand out from the crowd. Not until middle and late adolescence do young people have the self confidence to stand alone.

Expect young adolescents to be moody, to sulk, to be irritable and to demand privacy. Remember that vulnerability and moodiness are normal at this stage of transition from childhood to adolescence. Most youngsters work through these upsets on their own and want to do so. You cannot do it for them, although you can be supportive and empathetic. What you do need to do is deal with your reactions to your adolescent's behavior. General guidelines are to avoid overreacting or prying, but to draw the line when need be. You are not required to tolerate rudeness or disrespect. Teenagers can learn not to be rude, even when they are moody or irritable. Respond to your daughter's temper by using "I messages" and letting her know how you feel, rather than lecturing or criticizing her, for example: "When I ask a simple question and you jump on me, I feel hurt. I would prefer that if you don't want to talk about something, you just tell me. I can understand that because sometimes I don't want to talk either." You can also add consequences to these messages. "If you tell me you don't want to talk, I'll respect that, and we can talk another time," is an example of phrasing consequences positively.

Is This Problem Serious?

Sometimes it seems as if there is a fine line between the misbehavior that is to be expected in adolescence and problem behavior. It can be hard for parents to distinguish between normal adolescent concerns (like physical appearance) and behavior that indicates an eating disorder, or between normal adolescent moodiness and a serious depression.

One way to think about this is to imagine that there is a continuum from *normal* problems and misbehavior (that are not a cause for serious concern but which merit a serious talk), to *troubled* behavior (which indicates that the adolescent is distressed, or likely to get into trouble or needs to change) to *serious* emotional problems or behavior (indicating significant disturbance and calling for immediate action, including professional intervention).

Parents need to be able to sort out where their child's behavior falls on the continuum in order to deal with it appropriately. School and community programs, books and pamphlets, local or national hotlines (see Resources) and consultation with others—friends, family, parents of other adolescents, and professionals including school counselors, clergy, and therapists—can provide valuable information and support to parents who are trying to understand and sort out these issues.

Behaviors in each of the following areas can fall anywhere along the continuum from normal to troubled to serious problem:

- Moodiness
- Eating behavior
- Drug and alcohol use
- School achievement and/or attendance
- Sexual behavior
- Defying authority
- Delinquency
- Running away

There are some danger signs that indicate that the problem or behavior may be serious and consultation with a professional is advised. You should seek professional help—a school counselor or a therapist or your physician or clergyman—if any of the following describe your adolescent:[5]

- Is withdrawn for long periods of time and shows no interest in others.

- Has no friends of the same age (within two years of his or her age) and is not integrated into any peer group.
- Is persistently angry and irritable.
- Suddenly changes his or her pattern of after-school and weekend activities and he or she is reluctant for you to meet new friends.
- Goes out of his or her way to avoid you or other adults.
- Is docile, never acts independently and never initiates activity.
- Suddenly changes his or her school attendance and/or performance for the worse.
- Continually runs away from home or school.
- Frequently gets into fights and physically abuses others.
- Engages in indiscriminate sexual activity with a number of partners.
- Is often drunk or under the influence of drugs.
- Is either frequently or persistently anxious or depressed.
- Loses a dangerous amount of weight out of excessive concern for appearance.
- Talks about or threatens suicide.

Serious Problems

Moodiness and heightened feelings of vulnerability are normal responses to the transition from childhood to adolescence. However, serious problems, or the initial signs, can appear in early adolescence. We address depression, suicide and eating disorders in this chapter; drug and alcohol use as well as school and behavior problems in Chapter 16 on middle and late adolescence. Because emotional and behavior problems, just like physical growth and change, happen according to each adolescent's personal timeline, some parents of young adolescents may find the topics addressed in the next chapter applicable to their child now.

Depression

Adolescent depression is often overlooked, partly because adolescent moodiness is common and partly because the symptoms of depression in adolescents may be mistaken for problem behavior. For example, depressed adolescents may use action and activity to ward off feelings of helplessness and hopelessness. Unable to face the feelings of despair, a youngster may run away, experiment with drugs, throw herself into new activities and then lose interest, vandalize a school or eat compulsively. Other possible signs of depression include difficulty concentrating, fatigue and physical complaints and the extremes of dreading to be alone or withdrawing from people.

Although it is important not to overreact to normal adolescent emotional highs and lows, it is critical to be able to recognize when the problem runs deeper. Pay attention to *dramatic* changes in school performance or levels of activity or social behavior, or to sadness that is way out of proportion to the event and that *persists* over time.[6] Remember that depression is a serious emotional disorder. Depressed adolescents cannot "snap out of it." They need professional help.

Suicide

Suicide is a leading cause of death among young people. It is estimated that as many as half a million teenagers attempt suicide each year and that five thousand succeed.

Teenagers who commit suicide tend to fit one of three patterns.[7] Some, especially boys, have a history of problem behavior such as substance abuse or delinquency. Others, especially girls, are depressed. And some teens are rigid, ambitious perfectionists who tend to be isolated from others.

The important things to remember about suicide are:

- Any attempt or threat of suicide is a cry for help.

- Any threat of suicide demands immediate professional attention.

- If someone close to your child (or a celebrity your child identifies with) has committed suicide, it is important that you talk to your child in a realistic and unromantic way. Adolescents need to understand that there are alternatives to suicide to deal with problems.

• • •

Eating Disorders

The eighties and nineties have seen an explosion in the incidence of eating disorders. Although some boys are affected, it is primarily a girls' problem. Mary Pipher states in *Reviving Ophelia*: "Girls developed eating disorders when our culture developed a standard of beauty that they couldn't obtain by being healthy. When unnatural thinness became attractive, girls did unnatural things to be thin." She reports that on any given day in the United States, half of our teenage girls are dieting and one in five has an eating disorder.[8]

Anorexia nervosa, commonly referred to as anorexia, often begins with ordinary dieting, but instead of stopping the diet, perfectionistic adolescents continue. The essential features of this disorder are intense fear of gaining weight, refusal to maintain a minimal normal body weight and a significant disturbance in the perception of the shape or size of one's body.[9] Individuals become progressively obsessed with weight, increasingly rigid in their thinking about food and firmly convinced that nothing is wrong. Although the average age of onset of anorexia is seventeen, data suggest peaks at both fourteen and eighteen.[10] Anorexia is especially serious because at least ten percent of those with the disorder eventually die.

Although it usually appears in late, rather than early adolescence, bulimia nervosa—or simply bulimia—is more common than anorexia. The essential features of this eating disorder are binge eating and inappropriate compensatory methods, such as induced vomiting and laxatives, to prevent weight gain. Life for bulimic adolescents becomes a relentless preoccupation with eating, purging and weight.

Anorexia and bulimia are primarily a problem of the middle and upper classes. Another problem, compulsive eating—using food to "medicate" emotional pain—is an equal opportunity problem; it occurs in adolescents of all socioeconomic classes, primarily among young women.[11]

We hope you will not encounter any of these serious problems with your child. However, if you even suspect that your child is suffering from depression or an eating disorder or is at risk of suicide, get information and professional assistance immediately.

•　•　•

Parenting Issues

Separation and Independence

The adolescent is working on becoming an independent, separate person with his or her own identity. You may ask, "Independence from whom? A separate identity from whom?" The answer is simple— from you. The early development of independence almost always begins in the home. This means that confrontations between you and your child are likely to increase in early adolescence. Because striving for independence is easy to confuse with rebellion, parents need to be able to distinguish between the two.

To become her own person, the young adolescent needs to break away from home and family, at least to some extent. She needs to separate herself from you and from your view of her. She begins to question your values and to challenge your authority and opinions and lets you know in so many ways that you and your opinions don't count for much. At the same time, she acts as if her friends are the final authority on everything. The phrase, "Oh, Mother!" in a disdainful voice and with the possible accompaniment of rolling eyes and a disgusted look, is common. For some mothers this phrase and the tone in which it is delivered are like a knife to the heart.

> Stacey felt as if she was living a nightmare. Her daughter, Nicole, seemed to have turned into a monster. Nothing Stacey did was right. They got into fights over the most absurd things. One day Nicole criticized her mother for "chewing funny," and they had a big argument about it. Another time Nicole just lost it and started screaming at Stacey when Stacey asked her whether she wanted oatmeal or French toast for breakfast.

One of the most difficult parts of parenting an adolescent, particularly an adolescent girl, is learning to cope with the hurt feelings that can result from unreasonable and unfair attacks. Remember that young adolescents tend to be melodramatic. When they say they hate you, it is different than if a mature adult said the same thing. Remember that these youngsters often feel, and are, out of control. It won't help if you are out of control as well. On the other hand, parents do not have to take whatever is thrown in their direction. Tell yourself not to take everything your daughter says too personally, try to stay calm, let her know that what she is saying is hurtful and set firm limits: "What you are saying really hurts my feelings. I feel really bad, and I don't want to talk to you when you are yelling at me like this. When you calm down, we can talk about it."

Adolescent boys do not have the reputation for melodrama that their female counterparts do, but they, too, are involved in separating from their parents at this age. Your son, for example, may act as though he doesn't want you around. He may not want to be seen in public with you and may prefer to do things with friends rather than family. He may also refuse your assistance with anything and want lots of privacy. Getting some young teens to talk about their thoughts and feelings at this juncture is like pulling teeth. In addition to separating from you, your child needs to remove you from the pedestal he had you on when he was a child. Part of the separation process is learning that his parent is a person, not Wonder Woman or whoever else he may have thought you were. Often this means that he is very critical of you and idealizes other adults. His coach really understands him; you do not, and so forth.

The challenge for parents is to let go without losing control and to allow freedom without jeopardizing safety. Some suggestions here are:

- *Don't take your adolescent's strivings toward independence too personally.*

  He is going to challenge you on rules no matter how democratic you have been; she will prefer her friends' advice about style to yours no matter how good yours is; he will want privacy no matter how effective your communication has been.

- *Allow rebellion within limits.*

  Adolescents learn to make choices by having choices to make. Let them make decisions about the things they can safely decide, such as how to decorate their room or what music they listen to. How much freedom you allow depends, of course, on the child. Some young adolescents are able to handle a lot of responsibility; others are not. Be clear about your parameters within the choice zones. For example, your daughter can spend her Saturdays how she likes, but you expect to know where she is going, with whom and what they plan to do. You can retain your authority as a parent without having to be heavy-handed or authoritarian.

- *Expect some mistakes.*

  Adolescents are neither experienced nor mature, so they are bound to make some foolish choices and errors in judgment. Help your preteen or young teen save face by saying something like, "We all make mistakes sometimes," and help her to learn from the experience by planning together ways to avoid the same kind of mistake in the future.

- *Don't be afraid to say no.*

  Although adolescents need freedom to make mistakes and learn from them, they also need guidelines and limits. Setting limits shows you care. Even if your daughter is furious with you about how early she has to be home, the message that you care about her is there. A good rule of thumb for parents of adolescents is to say "yes" when you can and "no" when you have to. Often the way to be able to say yes is to establish the conditions necessary for your response to be in the affirmative.

Gail's eleven-year-old daughter, Laura, wanted to go to the mall on the bus, by herself. Gail said "no" to that plan. However she was agreeable to Laura's going if she went with a friend and if Laura agreed to be back by four o'clock.

But sometimes you just have to say no.

Debra and Rochelle agreed that their thirteen-year-old daughter, Shannon, was not allowed to go to parties unless an adult chaperon was present. Every time this came up, Shannon went through the "Everyone else can go. Why can't I?" routine. Her parents would explain that they didn't believe it was appropriate for young people her age to be at parties without adult supervision; Shannon would storm off to her room in tears and slam the door. While this was never a pleasant interaction, Debra and Rochelle knew it was perfectly normal. Shannon did not understand that "everyone else is doing it" was not a good reason. She was just being an adolescent, and her parents were being responsible parents.

Striving to be independent and the quest for a separate identity go hand in hand. Our identity is made up of the thoughts and feelings we have about ourselves. These feelings come from what we think about ourselves and what we think other people think about us. When our ideas about ourselves become fairly set and stable over time, we have a sense that we know who we are. Forming one's identity begins early in life. It is hammered out in the interaction between the child and his or her environment. The child responds to people and events, and people respond to the child.

By ten or twelve, the child usually has a relatively clear and well-defined sense of self. "We are a multicultural family," "I am good at math," "We don't watch violent television shows," "I am not very good at sports," or "I have two mothers." By this age youngsters have gotten a grip on life and have begun to act with some consistency. Then what happens? They are overwhelmed with massive doses of hormones that sweep away the clarity about who they are and what life is about. In addition, their developing intellectual prowess pushes them out of the earlier world of absolutes into a world of possibilities and ambiguity. They have to reassess everything—family rules, politics, social conventions, religion, themselves and others.

Using these developing reasoning abilities to reexamine familiar ideas and values is a central theme that continues throughout adolescence. Preteens and young teenagers know they are not who they used to be, but they aren't sure who they are going to be. In the meantime, they are sure they are not who *you* think they are. Parents may hear statements like, "You don't understand me" or "You don't even know who I am." Never mind that they may not know either. Lost in the confusion of it all but unwilling to take their parents' word on things, young adolescents turn to their peers. Peers are important at this stage not only because they provide a sense of belonging but also because they help answer the question of identity. Group or clique membership solves the questions of what to wear, how to behave at school, what music to listen to and the like.

School and Social Life: Get Involved or Steer Clear?

A major institution in young adolescents life is school. Not only is school their "job," but it is the center of their social life, and we have already discussed how important social life is to them. Many youngsters are temporarily disoriented during the transition from elementary to middle school or junior high. Your daughter will go from being a "big kid" to being a "little kid" again, from being rewarded for effort to having rewards based on performance only, from having one teacher to having many, from being closely supervised to being on her own more. You can help her in this transition by preparing her to know what to expect, supporting the friendships she will carry over from elementary school and realizing that her grades may drop slightly and not getting upset about it.

Regarding a young adolescent's academic achievement, here are five basic rules for parents:[12]

1. *Base your demands and expectations on a realistic appraisal of your adolescent's abilities.*

2. *Don't impose your goals on him.*
   Respect his ambitions for himself even if they are different from what you would like them to be.

3. *Remain interested in her school career but don't get overinvolved.*
   School is her job not yours.

4. *Examine your own attitudes toward education to make sure you are sending clear messages rather than mixed ones.*
   An example of a mixed message is "Do well...but not too well" or "Do well...but not better than I did."

5. *Make sure he knows you love him for who he is and not for what he achieves.*

Ideally, a parent is involved without being unduly interfering. But there are those times when you do need to "interfere." If your child has special needs, such as being learning-disabled, the school has the legal obligation to help him, but it is up to you to see that this obligation is fulfilled. If your child is gifted, or if you think he is gifted, you may need to get involved to explore options such as enrichment or advanced placement. Your child also needs your assistance if he is bullied or victimized, or bullies or victimizes others.

After their fourteen-year-old daughter, Tuwanna, was mugged on her way home from school, Becky and Sheryl enrolled the whole family in a self-defense class. Although they knew the class didn't guarantee their children's safety, they all learned useful skills. For Tuwanna, especially, it was a confidence-builder after her scary experience.

Eleven-year-old Jeff was having a hard time at school because one kid kept picking on him. It was getting to the point that he didn't even want to go to school. When he finally told his mother, Heidi, what was going on, she wasn't sure how to handle it at first. She got some advice from other parents and friends and then sat down with Jeff to talk about options. He really wanted to try handling it himself first. So they talked about what he could say and what he could do. Because the problems happened at school, they also came up with a fall-back plan to get school staff involved if Jeff needed more help.

When a child begins middle school or junior high, once again lesbian parents have to deal with how much information to share with the new school. Do you come out to each of your adolescent's teachers? Do you get involved with the parents' organization at the school but stay in the closet because your daughter has given you strict instructions that she does not want anyone to know her mother is a lesbian? In her book *The Lesbian and Gay Parenting Handbook*, April Martin shares her approach: although she and her partner continue to fill out all the forms as two mothers and continue to attend school conferences and events, they do not actively educate school staff about their family as they did in elementary school.[13] They feel their daughter has the skills to do her own advocacy work and they are leaving it up to her to decide how much information to share about her family and with whom.

However, some situations may call for active parental involvement.

Within the first month of junior high, Patricia's son, Jermaine, came home very upset. One of his teachers had made some very negative remarks about "queers." Jermaine didn't like what the teacher had done but he was not willing to say anything to him in class because he was afraid of what his friends would think if he defended "homosexuals." He and Patricia had quite a talk about it. She understood his concern about how he was seen by his friends, but she was not willing to ignore the teacher's behavior. And she wanted to model for Jermaine the importance of speaking up for what one thinks is right.

With Jermaine's permission, Patricia decided to talk with a school counselor. She had heard that the counselor was easy to talk to and that he had a reputation for being accepting of "different lifestyles" as her local newspaper put it. She wanted some advice about how to handle the situation.

After strategizing with the counselor, she spoke to other parents whom she knew would be concerned about the situation and supportive. They arranged for a group of them to meet with the teacher. They expressed to him their concern that diversity be respected at the school and that no group of people should be belittled. They clarified that if he was willing to refrain from negative comments about homosexuals, or any other group of people, they would not find it necessary to go to the principal.

After the meeting, Patricia felt satisfied with her approach and with the outcome. She suspected that the teacher's willingness to agree to modify his behavior was because a substantial group of parents expressed concern. By enlisting like-minded parents, she was able to get support for herself and protect Jermaine from being identified as the source of the information.

Afterwards she asked Jermaine how he felt about it and whether there was anything that he wanted to do. There wasn't. But he did say he was glad that his mom had done something.

Extracurricular activities can also play an important role in the life of an adolescent. A young preteen or teenager can feel accepted by a peer group and develop her own identity while she is involved in activities her parents know about and support.

When she was thirteen, Nora's daughter, Ericka, joined the youth group at the Unitarian Church the family attended. Frankly, Nora was surprised because Ericka had never been much interested in church activities. As she did with everything else, Ericka threw herself into the group's activities including the religions of the world study group, fund-raising car washes and, of course, the Friday night dances. It didn't take Nora long to figure out that a main attraction of the church group was a fifteen-year-old boy named Mike. Since Nora was very clear that she did not want her daughter to be dating, Ericka had figured out a way to spend time with Mike without actually dating.

◆　◆　◆

Steve had never been a particularly good student, but he was a fine gymnast. His mothers were very supportive of his dedication to his sport. Until he was able to drive, they drove him to all his practices and got involved in the parents' program to help raise money for traveling to meets. They had never missed seeing a competition. In fact, out-of-town meets had become family vacation events.

Betsy's first experience away from home was attending music camp when she was twelve. The camp was only for a week, but it was halfway across the country so the trip seemed like a major event both to Betsy and to her mother, Carol. Betsy's life outside of school revolved around her music. She was busy after school with practicing and lessons and rehearsal for the Youth Orchestra. Her friends were all musicians, too, and many were going to the camp at the same time. Making plans for this trip made Carol realize that Betsy was growing up. She had a social life separate from her family and an identity of her own, as a musician.

Engaged parents naturally want to know what their young adolescent is doing, and with whom and where. When their youngster is involved in extracurricular activities that are supervised and safe, parents can more easily relax as their child heads off on the journey toward adulthood.

16 Independence and Identity:
Fourteen to Eighteen Years

Something curious happens as children move into their teen years. For example, when you inquire about the school play that your daughter was so excited about trying out for last month, she informs you that it was a boring play and, besides, she has changed her mind about being an actress. Any comment from you about not giving up one's acting aspirations may be greeted with the familiar, "You just don't understand." And she's right—how can anyone understand a chameleon? Your daughter's unique identity is forming, but it is not formed yet. As she experiments, you may feel you have no idea who you're dealing with at any point in time. Psychoanalyst Erik Erikson described the teenage years as being about identity versus confusion,[1] and as a parent you may feel as confused about your teenager as she is about herself.

The development of identity is a gradual and cumulative process that goes on throughout adolescence into young adulthood and beyond. For preteens and young adolescents, the search for identity often leads to overidentification with peers and conformity; being like everyone else is the goal. Then, in the middle teens, adolescents are likely to begin trying to distinguish themselves from the crowd. This search for identity involves exploration and experimentation. Teenagers try on various identities, including different personalities, political attitudes, romantic involvements, career plans and clothing styles.

Sometimes they move quickly through these experiments, although at the time they may have an all-or-nothing, do-or-die quality. Someone or something that was the most important thing in the world last month, or even last week, is now of little interest or consequence.

What can parents expect during middle and late adolescence? Expect that adolescents will test themselves, and others, in the following ways:[2]

- *Changing interests, plans and friends.*
  Commitments made at this stage of life are usually tentative and have no strings attached.

- *Obsessing about appearance.*
  Because adolescents are exploring different personalities and identities, looking the part may become all important. Having the right haircut or clothes or vocabulary takes on great importance.

- *Falling in love.*
  Sex is not the only or even the most important motive for teenage romance. So much of young love is conversation—just talking—because the teenagers are trying to arrive at an identity for themselves in part by seeing themselves reflected through the eyes of someone else.

- *Taking up causes.*
  Being involved in a cause allows teenagers to feel special and important at the same time as they belong to a group. Whereas the young adolescent wanted to fit in, the emphasis in the middle teens is to stand out, but still be in the crowd.

- *Doing nothing.*
  Listening to music, playing with the dog and "spacing out" can be valuable to adolescents because some of the most important experiments in trying on identities happen in fantasy and daydreams.

To help adolescents in their quest for identity, parents can accept the teenager as a separate person, encourage healthy experimentation and provide psychological space while staying connected. The focus needs to be on the teenager and his identity, not on what the parents want him to be.

⋅ ◆ ⋅

Judy always had high hopes that her son, John, would become a doctor. He was bright, did well in math and science and had even expressed interest in getting a part-time job at the hospital where she worked in the accounting office.

Then when he was a senior in high school he announced that he wasn't applying to college—at least not right away—because he planned to work for Greenpeace to protect Alaska from damage by oil exploration. Judy was deeply disappointed and angry. Not that it wasn't a good cause. She just wanted something different for John. She had imagined him as a successful specialist, maybe even practicing at the hospital where she worked. He would never have to worry about money, people would look up to him and his work would really matter—she believed.

When she examined her motives, Judy realized that in her plans for John, she was wanting him to help her with her own unfinished business. She herself had wanted to be a physician, but her family needed her financial help so she went to work instead of college. Working at a hospital was as close as she could get to being a doctor—and it often felt a long ways away.

Judy caught herself in the mistake of overidentification. It is John's life to live, and John's choice of career to make for himself. Once Judy realized what had happened, she was able to back off and help John gather more information about occupations, including working for organizations that focus on protecting the environment.

Another error parents can make regarding their adolescent's developing identity is overcontrol. As a parent, you want to protect your children and letting go is not easy. But the teenager's search for identity requires that her parents let go. Sometimes the temptation to step in and take over is strong, but you really need to evaluate whether taking over is appropriate. If personal health or safety is at risk, you may have to act, but often you need to allow the teenager to make her own mistakes, develop her own resources for dealing with frustration and disappointment, and experience the pain and consequences of making a foolish decision. When parents overidentify with their teenagers or try to control them in terms of their developing identity, adolescents tend to react in one of two ways: they either cave in and accept their parents' definition of who they are and where they are going in life, or they go the other direction and reject everything their parents stand for and hope for them. In either case, the adolescent develops an identity that is a reaction to the parents, not the product of an exploration of who he is and wants to become.

One way parents can guide an adolescent without interfering is by helping their teenager develop a clearer picture of himself. Ways to do this include encouraging the teenager's special interests and extracurricular activities, acknowledging and praising his strengths, and reassuring him that he doesn't have to have everything in his future figured out at this point.

Developmental Guideposts
Intellectual and Moral Development

Young adolescents have not yet fully developed their own sense of what's right and wrong. Because they want to be liked, they are susceptible to peer pressure—at least around style. In the teen years, however, adolescents begin to move toward a higher level of moral development.

At this age, the adolescent can see the bigger picture. She can assess behavior from the perspective of "What if everybody did it?" This ability leads to a different kind of understanding of social rules. Whereas the younger adolescent sees rules as something imposed by adults (and often unfairly), the older adolescent sees rules as coming from society and being necessary. At this level of development, the adolescent can take the perspective of other people, including people she doesn't know, and think through the consequences of a rule being broken. The adolescent feels a moral obligation to something larger than herself, but her morality is conventional in the sense that she goes by the book—whatever that book may be. It may be the Bible or the Constitution or the Red Book of Chairman Mao. Adolescents are willing to stand up to parents, and to peers, but they are not yet willing to stand alone. Standing alone usually emerges later in life.

The idea that an adolescent stands for law and order may strike some adults as ridiculous and way off the mark. Surely teenagers are rebels, not advocates for law and order. How can we make sense of this? For one thing, adolescents are not consistent. Sometimes they show flashes of the "law and order" morality, but most of the time they are operating in the mode of pleasing others. Also, they may seem like rebels because the basis of their law and order approach may be radically opposed to their parents' values and beliefs. For example, very politically liberal parents may find their son espousing ideas from the far right about eliminating social programs. Or he may reject his parents' "materialism" and join a religious group that advocates no private ownership.

When your daughter challenges your position with something like "If you follow this through to its logical conclusion..." she has reached the law and order stage. It is often easier to live with teenagers who are at this point in their moral reasoning as they tend to be more reasonable than they were during the earlier stage of pleasing their peers. However, they can be unbelievably self-righteous. They see the problems of the world, and they have the answers. Usually idealistic and often naive, they are angry with adults for having made such a mess of things, because to them, the solutions are clear. Although we may see the problems and solutions as more complex than our teens do, we can also acknowledge that adults do mess things up.

How can you best encourage your adolescent to become his own authority on what he believes? By giving up some of your authority. Encourage independence by allowing your teen to make his own decisions. A parent can help an adolescent make good decisions by asking questions that will help him think the decision through, questions like, "What do you think will make you happiest in the long run?" or "What are the pros and cons?" or "What options do you have?" or " Is there another way to resolve the problem?" The decision may be whether to quit taking piano lessons or to stay friends with someone who got arrested for breaking into the school or whether to break a date or not. Because these decisions are important, but not life and death ones, it is a wise mother who helps her adolescent consider the possibilities and perhaps tells him what she would do, but who lets the decision be his.

Adolescents need to practice making decisions. How else are they to learn? Plus they need to experience the consequences of their decisions—the positive, the negative and the in-between. Otherwise they don't make the connection. Unless adolescents, and younger children as well, learn that there is a connection between their behavior and later events (that is, the consequences), they are poorly equipped to have their futures turn out the way they want. They can end up with either an irresponsible attitude, "I can do whatever I like," or feeling helpless to affect anything, "It doesn't matter what I do."

Anita was at her wits' end. Her seventeen-year-old son, Matt, continued to bring the car back with little to no gas in it after he used it. Their agreement was that he would replace the gas he used, but when this would happen was less clear. He always seemed to be short of cash or in a hurry when he returned the car. This morning she had almost been late to work because, once again, she had had to stop and get gas because Matt hadn't put in any. When she got home, they had a big argument. This got nowhere and left them both feeling terrible.

Using the conflict resolution approach outlined in Chapter 5, "Engaged Parenting," Anita could sit down with Matt and renegotiate their agreement, adding a consequence for Matt's not replacing the gas when he was using the car—for example, that Matt could not use the car for two weeks. It is a challenge for parents to hold firm to the consequences they decide on with their teenage children, but if you can withstand the inevitable groaning and grumbling, you can have the satisfaction of watching your teenager turn into a responsible adult.

Parents not only need to give their adolescents room to make their own decisions and experience the consequences, but they also need to grant them the freedom to think their own thoughts. This can be a hard challenge when your teenager's thoughts and opinions seem to be radically different from yours.

When Terry's oldest daughter, Lorette, was fifteen, she announced to Terry that she was against abortion and was planning to go to a demonstration at a local clinic. Terry had to bite her tongue to keep from shouting, "No daughter of mine is going to that demonstration." Because she knew that Lorette's best friend's mother was active in the "right to life" movement, she was angry and horrified at the same time. The only worse thing that Lorette could propose doing, as far as Terry was concerned, would be to march against lesbian and gay rights.

In discussion with Lorette, Terry could encourage her daughter to think through her decision. If Terry can stay calm and ask Lorette questions such as "I know some people think abortion is wrong, but why do you think so?" and "What is important to you about participating in the demonstration?" she will be supporting her daughter's thinking for herself and making her own decisions. Because Terry feels so strongly about this issue—a point likely not lost on Lorette—she also needs to acknowledge that fact and the consequences of it. For example, she could let Lorette know that she does support her having her own opinions, making her own decisions and getting involved in community activities. However, there may be times when she does not agree with what Lorette decides. If Lorette's decision is to demonstrate against abortion rights, this will be one of those times.

Many teenagers are interested in community activities and community action. It is true that action, as well as discussion, plays a part in moral development. Encourage your adolescent to get involved in the community, and support her if she is already active. Volunteer activities in social or community service or political campaigns or causes are good ways for adolescents to "feel part of society by taking part in it."[3]

Emotional Growth

Teenagers of all ages get emotional, sometimes very emotional—wracked with pain over a breakup, in the depths of despair over a bad grade, ecstatic about making the team or outraged about toxic waste. Being able to anticipate consequences or to understand another person's perspective helps teenagers to moderate their emotional reactions, and experience can go a long way toward helping an adolescent get a more realistic and balanced perspective on the current situation, whatever it may be. Having survived a breakup or recovered from the disappointment of a bad grade in the past provides a teenager with an experiential reference point and reassurance that he will get through the current crisis, and he can look to the previous experience for possible coping strategies. This does not mean your son will handle every upset with total equanimity, but he will be better prepared to experience his feelings, express them appropriately and take whatever other action may be necessary. For example, he can experience the disappointment of getting a bad grade, talk to his friends and/or you about his disappointment and take whatever action is indicated, whether that's speaking to the teacher if he feels the grade is unfair or if he needs clarification about what was expected, or studying more or getting special assistance.

What about anger? When adolescents erupt into anger, it may seem unpredictable, totally out of proportion, irrational, hateful and even frightening to parents. When adolescents are dissatisfied with themselves or having difficulties, they often look for someone or something else to blame. Parents are a convenient target. Much of their anger may be displaced from someone else onto the parent, such as when a teen angry with his teacher takes it out on his mother. In these situations, as a parent, you need to hold your own emotional center and try to depersonalize the anger; that is, try not to take it entirely personally. Some of it may be about you, much of it may not. As we discussed in the previous chapter, this does not mean that you put up with rudeness and disrespect. It does mean that you need to model responding in a reasonable and relatively calm way, even when your adolescent's emotions are running high. This is not easy, of course. Most people tend to respond to anger and illogical arguments with anger and illogical arguments. If feelings are intense, reason tends to disappear. Recognize your feelings, but resist the temptation to react in ways that would be counterproductive. Model the behavior that you want your teen to learn.

Mothers of adolescent boys may be especially prone to anxiety over their sons' expressions of anger. A boy's size and physical strength combined with what may appear to be, or even actually be, a lack of control can be very scary. This situation will likely have even more emotional intensity if a mother has had personal experience of physical abuse—whether at the hands of her own parent, ex-husband or partner. It is important for a mother to work through her own history of abuse so that she does not react to her sons as if they are or will become like the abusers in her past.

Female adolescents are likely to express their anger with harsh words such as, "I hate you, and I'd rather live anywhere but here," or "You are so stupid," or "You don't care about me; you've never cared about me." This does not mean that adolescent girls never get physical, but they are more likely to slam doors, storm out or throw things at the wall than directly attack their mother. Nor are boys likely to assault their mother physically, but they may either seem to be or actually be more physically threatening than girls are.

◆　◆　◆

Becky and her sixteen-year-old son, Kevin, were going to watch Kevin's younger brother's wrestling match on a Saturday morning. Becky was running late, and they needed to get to the match in a hurry in order not to miss any of it. When Becky told Kevin he couldn't drive because they were in such a rush, he exploded. He screamed obscenities at her and waved his fist in her face. She was shocked and scared. He had never done anything like this before.

In their book *Raising a Son,* Don and Jeanne Elium point out that teenage sons often do not realize their actions can be frightening and threatening to their mothers.[4] They often still see themselves as the little boys that Mommy could pick up and punish and they are not aware their male force may be frightening. For a mother, sometimes the only way out of a struggle with a son is to physically leave the scene until things cool down. Most of the time, she can at least avoid escalating the anger if she acknowledges her son's anger and what he is angry about and also uses "I messages" to let him know how his words and behavior are impacting her. And a mother needs to set firm and clear limits about what behavior toward her is allowed. When teens learn they can feel their feelings *and* control their behavior, they relax. And so do their parents.

The Social Scene

As adolescents move through high school, cliques and crowds become less important while friendship and romance become more important. By the end of high school, adolescents often resemble young adults in having a larger circle of acquaintances and a small circle of intimates.

As they mature, teenagers are more able to stand on their own. Because they are independent, they have less need to prove their independence. They want to be seen as individuals, not as conformists. "I want to do it" replaces "Everyone is doing it." They choose clothes, friends and activities more because they like them than because they want to fit in. Although teens are still influenced by their friends, they are more likely to seek out experts when they need information or assistance. Whereas young adolescents tend to take advice at face value and to favor the opinions of peers over parents, in later adolescence, teenagers realize that different people have different perspectives and that advice may be influenced by self-interest. They are more likely to discriminate concerning who to ask about what. For example, they likely would not ask a parent what to wear to a friend's party but they might ask a parent what to wear to a job interview.

The young adolescent's social life usually revolves around small same-sex cliques. Then these groups of boys and girls may get together for joint activities in place of one-on-one dating. As adolescence progresses, some members of the cliques start dating each other, and the rest follow suit. Parties and group activities are then the center of the social life. Even though they are dating, fourteen- and fifteen-year-olds often find safety in numbers. Toward the end of high school, dating couples become interested in spending more time alone with each other than with a group.

Since parties and other group activities are the hallmark of the teen years, a question for parents is how to exert some control over their adolescent's activities without spoiling the fun. Your primary responsibility as a parent is to know where your teen is going, with whom and what he plans to do. Whether you allow the teenager to do what he plans depends on a number of factors, including:

- Age and emotional and social maturity of your child.
- Participants, that is, who else will be with your child.
- Past behavior.
- Willingness to go along with your guidelines about curfew, driving, alcohol or drugs.
- Supervision, that is, will there be adult supervision at the event?

If your child is gay or lesbian, sexual interest may develop and unfold according to a somewhat different pattern. Some teenagers and even preteens identify as gay or lesbian but others discover their sexual orientation much later.

Leyla didn't define her sexual orientation as bisexual until she was in college. During her high school years, she hung out with the artistic/gay and gay-friendly/slightly punk crowd.

Jay knew he was gay as a young teen and his mothers encouraged him to be "gay and proud." However, they all knew it could be difficult for an openly gay teen in a regular junior high school. They decided that an alternative or even private school might be more supportive and began looking into the various possibilities in their area.

Because society is more accepting or at least more aware of homosexuality and bisexuality than it was previously, and because your teenager has a lesbian family, he or she starts off with advantages that most lesbian and gay kids didn't have in the past. Even so, it's not easy being homosexual, especially as an adolescent. Some larger cities have support groups and even drop-in centers for lesbian and gay teens. Here they can meet each other and have a place where they fit in. But many do not live in areas that have access to these resources. They may not even know another lesbian or gay teen, except perhaps through the Internet. If they have an inkling that someone at school might be homosexual, they may be afraid to ask for fear of rejection and ostracism. The quest for identity that is so critical in the teenage years has special meaning for lesbian and gay youth. For many of them, their sexual orientation is a part of their identity that they deny or at least cover up. They may go along with group activities and parties and even dating, perhaps dating an opposite-sex gay or lesbian teenager, whether they are out to each other or not. It is certainly the teenager's decision whether to remain closeted or not. The great advantage to having a lesbian mother in this situation is the acceptance, affirmation and understanding the teen can find at home, regardless of what he or she experiences in the outside world.

Dating

Remember how you felt as a teenager when the person you thought would never be interested in you showed the slightest flicker of interest—and, on the other hand, how devastating it felt to be turned down, stood up, dumped or dissed! Because teenagers haven't had much experience surviving and recovering from rejection, the pain can be excruciating. Dating in the teens paves the way for developing intimate relationships in adulthood. Yet dating can also reinforce stereotypes of masculinity and femininity or power imbalances if, for example, initiating is the male prerogative and females are left to wait by the telephone hoping he will call. Unless there is room for females to be self-reliant and strong, and for males to be emotional and vulnerable, teens can end up severely limiting themselves.

Parents need not get too anxious over their teen's dating activity unless it is very early or excessive. Those who date very early may miss out on learning who they are and where they are going with their lives because they are too focused on dating. If dating is a teen's whole life, he is missing out on other activities that could help him establish his identity and develop his skills and interests. Parents can use similar guidelines for teen dating as for other activities: know who your teenager is dating; know where they are going on the date and what they plan to do; and clarify when and how often your teenager can go on dates.

As with most issues, negotiation is the most effective approach to resolving conflicts over dating. When you and your adolescent disagree about dating, it is no different than when you disagree about other issues. First you must ask yourself what it is you object to about your teen's dating behavior and why. Is it that he is challenging your authority? Ask yourself if what he is doing or wants to do is dangerous or unhealthy or age-inappropriate. If your answer is "no" to all of these questions, perhaps you are being unreasonable. Then you can sit down with your teenager and try to work out something that is satisfactory to you both.

A note about defiance: most teenagers break the rules sometimes but if your teenager consistently won't abide by reasonable rules, if she lies, sneaks out when she has been grounded, refuses to tell you where she is going or with whom, the problem is not dating, but is defiance, and you should consider seeking professional help.

Many parents are comfortable with the typical short-lived adolescent romance. They may even be amused at the speed with which their teenager's romantic focus changes from one person to the next. However, when there is talk of going together or the relationship seems to be getting serious, parents may have reservations. Worries about premature commitment, premature sex, and narrowing of options arise, particularly if the parents do not like the person with whom their adolescent is involved.

Barbara and Sue were very concerned when their seventeen-year-old son, Shawn, announced that he and his new girlfriend, Pat, were going together, and that he was really serious about her. Shawn had not shown much interest in dating until the previous year and had been heartbroken when his last girlfriend broke off with him. He started dating Pat soon after that.

They had always been pleased with the choices of friends that Shawn made. But neither of them really warmed to Pat. It wasn't that she was rude or wild. It was more that she seemed immature and lacking in direction, particularly compared to his other friends.

What to do?

Unfortunately, there's not a lot you can do when your teenager dates someone you aren't crazy about. If you have ever begun a new relationship and heard your kids say they "don't like" your new partner, you know how much it can hurt. Hence, it's best to keep mum. However, your child may provide an opening for discussion. In Barbara and Sue's case, one day Shawn asked them what they thought of Pat. They replied that they didn't feel they knew her very well and then asked how *he* felt about her. This question was like opening a floodgate: all of Shawn's doubts began to pour out. Shawn ended up admitting he wanted to break up with Pat but didn't know how to go about it. *Now* Sue and Barbara could concentrate on offering much-needed advice instead of criticizing their son's girlfriend.

But what if you believe there is a serious problem? There are situations where, as a parent, you need to intervene. Once again, health and safety are the criteria. Intervening doesn't translate as forbidding your adolescent to see this person—unless this person's behavior endangers your child. If your teenager's boyfriend or girlfriend is abusing your teen verbally, physically or sexually, or is putting your child at risk by behavior such as drinking and driving, drug use or getting in trouble with the law, you need to set limits to protect your child. Also ask yourself why your teenager is seeing this person. Perhaps she is drinking excessively or using drugs as well. Or perhaps she has the fantasy of "saving" her boyfriend.

Other situations that require attention and possible intervention are when your teenager is dating someone considerably older or talking about marriage, or both. Parents first need to consider whether family problems may be a factor in their child's choices. Are tensions so great between your teenager and your partner that your daughter is desperate to get out of the house, and moving in with her boyfriend or getting married seems like the easiest way? If that is what is going on, discussion about the relative merits of her boyfriend as a life partner will get nowhere. His suitability is not the issue—it's the relationships within the family that need to be the focus of your attention.

The Golden Age of Friendship

"Friends for life" was how Alexa, Kim and Lisa described themselves. They had been close friends all through high school, and although they talked about staying together for college, it was beginning to look as if that would not happen. Alexa was offered a math scholarship at a private college on the opposite coast. Lisa was thinking about taking a year off to travel, and Kim was leaning toward the state university because her boyfriend was going there. They assured each other that no matter where they were, their friendship would stay as strong as ever.

As a teenager, Bryan's best friends had been girls. During high school, Renee was his closest friend and confidante. They talked about absolutely everything with each other. If Bryan wanted advice about how to approach a girl he was interested in, he talked to Renee. If Renee was upset about getting a poor grade in French, she cried on Bryan's shoulder. They even exchanged clothes!

Josh and Gavin had played music together since they were thirteen. They started practicing in Gavin's garage with just the two of them—drums and guitar. Pretty soon they had a band. Four years later the band had been through a number of name changes, a few lead singers and what seemed like an army of other musicians. But Josh and Gavin were the force, and the glue, that held it all together. In their music and in life, they were— as they put it—"tight."

Despite all the interest in dating, friends are still the most important people in the adolescent's social world. Friendships based on trust, loyalty, empathy and self-disclosure continue throughout early and middle adolescence. However, as adolescents mature, the pressure to be the same as one's friends and to fit in shifts to allow more individuality. Because they are maturing intellectually, teenagers are more able to tolerate ambiguity and contradictions in people. They understand more clearly than young adolescents do that someone who seems cold may in fact be shy, or that someone who appears self-confident may also feel insecure.

Friendships often deepen in adolescence as teens come to appreciate that friendships need a balance between togetherness and separateness. Platonic friendships between males and females, rare in earlier adolescence, are more common in the later teens. Discovering that they can have room to breathe in their friendships and also be close, and getting to know friends of both the same and opposite sex can contribute greatly to adolescents' learning what to look for and how to be in a serious adult relationship later on.

Adolescents build support networks of friends just as adults do. Their turning to their friends when they are upset or want to talk does not have to mean a breakdown in communication with parents. It may mean, however, that you have to make extra effort to stay connected, for example, staying up past your usual bedtime in order to have a heart-to-heart talk with your teenager after he gets home from a date, or taking a vacation or weekend trip together, away from the distractions of everyday life.

As adolescents gain confidence in themselves, they are more likely to have conversations and relationships with adults, including your friends or their friends' parents. You may also be surprised to find that you make connections and enjoy your relationships with some of your teenager's friends.

Parenting Issues

Is Your Teen's Having a Job Good or Bad?

Most people assume that having a job is good for teenagers. It teaches them responsibility and discipline, and they learn the value of money and get experience in the "real" world. In addition, many adolescents need to work. Their income may be necessary to help support the family or to buy clothes and other items their parents cannot afford to buy for them.

Working may be necessary, but whether it is beneficial or not depends primarily on how much time the teenager spends at a job. There is evidence that working more than fifteen hours a week causes problems;[5] for example, the adolescent may be so busy working that she disengages from school and from family life. Summer jobs, on the other hand, offer a way to earn money and don't interfere with school. Parents can encourage teenagers to look for jobs that will help them acquire skills and knowledge that will be valuable in the future and that will bring them into contact with adults who will be positive role models. For example, if your daughter is thinking about becoming a veterinarian, encourage her to try to get a job in that field.

If teenagers are earning their own money, parents often feel that how they spend it is up to them. But adolescents often need guidance about how to handle their money. Otherwise working may just provide more money for the latest clothes, CD's or whatever, and not teach financial responsibility at all. Don't abdicate your responsibility to provide your adolescent with information and skills about money— where else will she learn them? On the other hand, don't try to *control* what she does with her money.

Money management discussions need to be appropriate to your adolescent's age and can include budgeting, regular saving, consumer savvy and investing. One of the skills you are trying to encourage in this process is long-term planning, so support your teen's saving regularly and learning about investments, such as the other kind of CD's, savings bonds and mutual funds.

Many parents don't want to discuss family finances with their children; however, teenagers are more likely to manage their own money and to accept limitations on family spending if they have some idea of the cost of supporting the family. For example, knowing what the weekly grocery budget is can help adolescents understand why you don't want to waste food or why you can't buy a lot of snack or processed foods.

Sex, Drugs and Rock'n' Roll

Sex

In the teen years, the issues surrounding sexuality are not hypothetical any more. "What if's" may have been replaced by "when's." Many parents would prefer to have their adolescent wait until adulthood to be sexually active, but you really have no control. You can have *influence*, but you are not going to be at the party or in the parked car or at the empty house when your son makes a decision about sexual activity.

A parent's job is to guide teenagers toward healthy sexual attitudes and behavior. Even if you started early in providing information to your adolescent, she likely needs more information at this stage of development.

As parents of teenagers, you can help guide and influence your children's decisions about sex by:

- Talking with them about your values.

- Helping them to anticipate internal and external pressure to have sex and to make responsible decisions.

- Making sure they know how to protect themselves and their partner from pregnancy and sexually transmitted diseases, including AIDS, if they decide to be sexual.

- Letting them know that you love them and will be there for them even if they do become more involved than you hope they will.

- Helping them decide who is a safe sexual partner. What qualities should that person have? How will they know that the person has those qualities?

Providing information does not mean that you are encouraging or condoning sexual activity. Parents can reassure themselves with the knowledge that there is no evidence that sex education of any kind increases sexual activity, but there is a good deal of evidence that it decreases sexual irresponsibility.[6]

In talking with adolescents about making decisions about sex, parents need to remember that teenagers live for the present. Intellectually, teens may know that unprotected sex could expose them to the HIV virus, or that pregnancy would be a disaster or that the person they are involved with is not the person of their dreams. But they may forget these things when they are in the throes of strong emotions or arousal. When you are a fourteen-year-old girl and a handsome senior pays attention to you, or when you are a sixteen-year-old gay teen and the football player you have tried not to stare at in the showers asks you to go to a party with him, it is hard to think clearly, then—or later. Talking with adolescents before they face actual situations helps prepare them to make good decisions.

Parents need to talk with their adolescents about relationships and about right and wrong reasons for being sexual. Parents also need to address the issue of how to say no to sex, because saying no gracefully is one of the most difficult aspects of a relationship for teenagers. Ideally, all an adolescent should have to say is "I'm not ready." However, even if an adolescent has made that decision, it may be hard to stick to it. Talking with adolescents about assertiveness, freedom of choice and self-respect can support them in becoming more confident and more able to say no.

Parents may be relieved to know that sexual abstinence for teenagers seems to be making something of a comeback. Teens are appearing on television shows to promote abstinence, and virgin clubs are emerging at some high schools. Media campaigns and secular as well as religious programs encouraging teenagers to refrain from sex have been inspired in large part by the epidemic of teenage pregnancy—one million teenagers, or one in nine girls ages fifteen to nineteen, becomes pregnant each year in the United States. In addition, the threat of AIDS has spurred education efforts.

Experts who evaluate programs intended to curb adolescent sexual activity report that the most effective efforts are those that combine sex education and the distribution of condoms with lessons in how to resist social and peer pressure. Assertiveness training, role playing and other techniques that allow teens to practice saying no make the difference.[7] These results should speak loudly to parents about talking with their teens about how to resist pressure, including rehearsing "what would you say if..." for different situations.

When she returned home from a date somewhat shaken, sixteen-year-old Megan confided to her mother that the periodic conversations they had had about "what do to if..." had come in handy. To get even with Raoul, her ex-boyfriend, Megan had started going out with Tom, mostly because Raoul disliked him. She ended up getting more than sweet revenge.

This had been their third date. From the moment they got to the house party, Tom had kept pressuring Megan to go up to one of the bedrooms and have sex. Megan was clear that she didn't want to be sexual and told him so, but Tom wouldn't take no for an answer. He kept badgering her verbally and grabbing at her. Finally, she told him that she wanted to go home. Either he could take her, or she would call her mother to come get her. She was fully prepared to follow through with her plan, and Tom knew it. So he brought her home.

Even though she was upset, Megan felt good about how she had handled Tom's behavior. Her mother was thankful she and her daughter had spent time rehearsing what to do in this kind of situation, and she was relieved that Megan was home safe and sound.

Alcohol and Drugs

Like sex education, education about drugs and alcohol needs to begin early in a child's life because through the media, even very young children are exposed to the topic. Parents need to provide information about drugs and drug use that is appropriate to the child's age and level of understanding. Many schools have alcohol and drug education programs, but those do not take the place of the parent's responsibility to inform and set limits for their children.

Studies indicate that the main reason young people *try* alcohol and / or drugs is to fit in, to be part of the group and to be liked. The second most common reason is to feel grown up, and the third is out of boredom. Some try drugs and alcohol out of defiance, and others are simply curious. The reasons young people *continue* to use drugs and/or alcohol are more complex and are often highly related to family histories of alcohol and drug use, abuse and neglect. However, virtually all experts agree that the key to reducing drug and alcohol problems with adolescents is prevention.[8]

The first step in prevention is information. The challenge is for parents to educate their children without alienating them. Lectures and fear tactics don't work. Providing factual information about drugs, including cigarettes, caffeine, alcohol, marijuana, amphetamines, barbiturates and other drugs, does work. Experts advise parents to separate myths from facts and to address issues that are close to adolescents' hearts—their looks, their physical performance and their popularity. In addition, be honest with your child about any history of substance abuse in your family. If, for example, there is alcoholism in your family, the statistical risk of your child becoming alcoholic increases.

The second step is for parents to establish clear rules about alcohol and drugs, their reasons for those rules and the consequences of breaking them. Most authorities advocate a no-alcohol, no-drug policy because growing up is hard enough without having the added complications that these substances involve. Alcohol and drugs are dangerous for young people, they interfere with school, sports and other activities, and they are illegal. Be straightforward and unambiguous about where you stand, and communicate it clearly to your adolescent. Studies show that one of the best predictors of alcohol and drug use in adolescence is the extent to which adolescents believe their parents tolerate their drinking and drugging activities. At the same time that you communicate your expectations and rules about alcohol and drugs, communicate your willingness to discuss the rules and consequences at any time and keep communication about these topics open. You may also want to get involved in school, neighborhood and community drug-prevention programs.

> Regina wasn't sure what to do when she discovered marijuana in her fifteen-year-old daughter's dresser drawer. Tessa had borrowed one of Regina's sweaters the previous week, and Regina was trying to find it when she stumbled upon what looked to her like a stash.
>
> Regina wasn't born yesterday. She figured that Tessa might have tried something, even though Regina made it clear to her daughter that she did not want her using drugs or alcohol. They also had a "no drugs in the house" rule. Tessa always insisted she had not even tried any drugs but here was clear evidence.
>
> When Regina recovered from her initial shock, questions raced through her mind: Did this belong to Tessa? Was she smoking regularly? What about other drugs? Did she have pills hidden somewhere else? In addition, Regina was upset that Tessa had lied to her and had clearly broken the rule by having pot in the house.

Parents need to face facts: certainly by high school, and probably before, your adolescent will likely be offered alcohol or drugs. Surveys indicate that nearly all teenagers will try alcohol before graduating from high school and that a majority will try marijuana once before the end of their senior year. These statistics can help put experimentation in perspective.

If you find out your child is experimenting with drugs or alcohol, a response is appropriate. However, it is important that, in your response, you distinguish between experimentation and regular or frequent use, and between combinations of substances and behaviors in terms of the danger they pose. For example, mixing drinking and driving is more dangerous than sneaking a beer from the fridge and never leaving the house. Intravenous drug use poses more of a risk, including exposure to HIV, than trying marijuana. Your response needs to be appropriate to the situation and to your rules about alcohol and drugs. In addition, your rules may change as your adolescent moves into his late teen years. If you feel, for example, that recreational use of alcohol is acceptable for an older teen of legal age, make the rules for responsible drinking clear and clarify the consequences for irresponsible drinking.

The third step in preventing drug and alcohol problems is helping your child say no. Begin early to help her anticipate situations in which she may be offered alcohol or drugs and rehearse ways to say no that save face. These may vary from a simple "No, thanks" to "I'm in training for the soccer team" to having parents be the bad guy, "If I come home smelling of dope, my mother will ground me for a month." And provide supervision for your child. Younger teens, for example, are often relieved to know they won't have to handle peer pressure all by themselves. And check in with your older teens periodically about their and their friends' attitudes and experiences with alcohol and drugs.

Is This Problem Serious?

It is sometimes difficult for parents to distinguish between normal adolescent problems and ones that are more serious. In the previous chapter we listed signs that indicate a serious problem is at hand and that professional consultation is needed. We also suggested that parents think about the emotional and behavior problems of adolescents as falling somewhere on a continuum from normal to troubled to serious. So a teen's behavior in any of the following areas could be classified as normal, troubled or a serious problem:

- Moodiness
- Eating behavior
- Drug and alcohol use
- School achievement and/or attendance

- Sexual behavior
- Defying authority
- Delinquency
- Running away

Moodiness, suicide and eating disorders were discussed in Chapter 15, on early adolescence. Here we will address evaluating teenage behavior in the other areas on the list. Because adolescents are on their own individual timelines, some parents of older teens may find problems in the chapter on younger adolescents more relevant to their concerns.

Drug and Alcohol Problems

Suppose your fifteen-year-old daughter told you that she felt pressured to drink at a party she attended. Since you can expect that your adolescent will be offered alcohol and even try it sometime during her adolescence, this is a normal problem. That your daughter actually told you about this situation is one indication she is likely not in trouble. Of course you would still want to talk with her about her feelings, about how she handled the situation and how she can deal with future situations.

But what if you suspect that your bottles of liquor are being watered or you notice that your adolescent's speech sometimes seems slurred when he comes home. You may certainly be troubled. But how do you know if your adolescent is in trouble? Teenagers who are regularly using or addicted to drugs or alcohol are highly unlikely to tell their parents that they have a problem. Also, some signs of drug use are similar to symptoms of other problems such as depression, which was discussed in the previous chapter. However, any of the following may indicate a problem:

- Possession of drugs and paraphernalia
- Identification with the drug culture
- Physical deterioration (for example, memory lapses, difficulty in concentration, bloodshot eyes, runny nose, periods of lethargy *and* hyperactivity)
- Changes in behavior (for example, possession of large amounts of money; chronic dishonesty; increasing and inappropriate anger, hostility, irritability and secretiveness)
- Dramatic changes in school performance and/or attendance

If there are indications that your child has a problem, don't pretend that nothing is wrong. Whether you elect to try initially to handle the problem yourself or to seek professional help depends on how deeply involved your adolescent is with alcohol or drugs.

If your teen acknowledges that he is using drugs or alcohol but you don't think he is addicted yet, you may be able to handle the problem yourself. Explain to him why you are concerned and what you expect. Negotiate a contract with him that he will not drink or use drugs, that he will not spend time in places or with people who are drinking or using and that he will keep you informed about where he is and what he is doing. As in all negotiations, you need to ask him what he thinks the consequences should be of violating the contract. This contract needs to be reviewed frequently, for example, weekly. If your son fails to abide by the contract, you need to intervene and set stricter limits (such as cutting his allowance, monitoring his activities, declaring some friends off-limits, and so on). Remind him that health and safety issues are not negotiable.

Expect your teen to be angry and resentful at first. Just remind him (and yourself) that you are not trying to ruin his life, you are trying to get it back on track. During this time your son should not be the only family member held to high standards. Your intervention is likely going to be more successful if everyone in the family is drug-free.

If you have good reason to believe that your child has a serious problem with drugs or alcohol or if your own efforts to handle the problem are not successful within a month or two, get professional help. If an adolescent drug or alcohol problem is detected and treated early, the chances for recovery are good.

The Academic Slide

Children may sail through elementary school and then run into difficulty in middle school or junior high or high school.

Kenyatta was a gifted student who announced, after three weeks in the honors math class in junior high, that she wanted to drop out of it. She insisted, "I just can't do it."

In the tenth grade, Brad's grades dropped noticeably. Never much of a reader, he complained bitterly about the amount of homework he was assigned and the number of papers the teachers demanded. His explanation for the problem was that his teachers expected too much.

Jordan had become very skilled at forging his mother's signature on notes he typed to excuse his frequent absences from school. It wasn't until well into the second semester of this behavior that Dorrie had any idea about her son's truancy. She found out when the school called her because Jordan had been absent so much.

Although these are all examples of school-related problems, very different things are likely going on for each of these adolescents. The most effective approach for all concerned is for the parent to *investigate* the problem. Identifying the underlying reasons for a problem is a process of elimination. Talk with your adolescent about what she thinks is going wrong, and listen to what she says. Don't expect to get to the heart of the matter in one conversation, but communicate concern rather than frustration or disappointment. Future conversations may then lead to more information and pinpointing specific issues. Investigate the factors that the adolescent cannot control:

- *Examine your own attitudes and behavior.*
  Are you expecting too much? Are you taking enough interest? Are you sending mixed messages about achievement? Parental attitudes may have been a factor in the situation with Kenyatta. She may have incorporated her mother's high expectations for her. When she did poorly on a "pop" quiz in class, Kenyatta may have decided the class was too hard for her.

  It is not uncommon for girls to develop feelings of inadequacy in adolescence. Often this happens during the transition from elementary school to junior high, but it can also occur later. Parents need to be especially attentive to helping their daughters maintain their self-esteem during adolescence.

- *Is there a physical problem?*
  Perhaps an easily correctable problem with vision or hearing is interfering with your child's academic performance. Or he might have a learning disability. Some children with learning disabilities are able to compensate in the earlier grades until the reading and comprehension requirements increase beyond their ability to keep up. This may be the case for Brad.

◆ ◆ ◆

- *What about the school?*

  Is your child being challenged enough academically or too much? Does he lack basic study skills? Is a teacher really "picking on" him? Perhaps Jordan is bored by his classes. What is he doing when he skips school? Is he hanging out with other alienated teenagers, or are he and his buddy developing new computer programs?

After some investigation, you should have a better idea whether you are dealing with normal or troubled behavior or with a serious problem. Then you can determine what intervention strategies would be most appropriate.

Other Behavior Problems

It is distressing to parents when their adolescents engage in behaviors such as running away, defying authority, being sexual or violating rules—laws or even school rules. However, just as experimentation with alcohol or skipping class or even a day of school once in a while falls within the normal range of adolescent behavior, so does some behavior in these other categories. For example, if your daughter storms out of the house in anger and goes to a friend's overnight, this is within the normal range as long as it happens once, or very rarely. On the other hand, if she does this more than once in three months, her behavior moves into the troubled zone. And if she runs to the streets, it is a serious problem.

Similarly, occasional arguments with parents are normal, but aggressive outbursts and a pattern of contrariness are an indication of trouble, and defiance that leads to violence or getting suspended or fired is a serious problem.

And while one or two minor (and non-violent) violations of rules or the law is considered within the range of normal adolescent behavior, repeated violations are considered a sign of trouble. Any violent act or crime or solitary delinquent acts are signs of a serious problem.

Some level of sexual behavior is within the normal range but flaunting sexuality and provocativeness may be a sign of trouble, and promiscuity and an excessive interest in sex is serious.

What's a parent to do? The key is to communicate your concern and disapproval of the behavior without rejecting your child. For normal problems, practice your active listening and communicating skills and follow the steps in Chapter 5 for resolving conflicts.

If the behavior is in the troubled zone, do essentially the same thing as with normal problems but with more attention to establishing clear standards for behavior and to monitoring the adolescent's behavior closely. Because the adolescent has shown poor judgment and a lack of responsibility, talk may not be enough. Invoking any agreed-upon consequences for misbehavior promptly and consistently is essential.

If your attempts to resolve the problem with your adolescent do not work, or do not last, or if the problem is serious by the time you become aware of it, it's time to seek professional help. Often an adolescent will agree to see a counselor, especially if he lives in a community where therapy is considered socially acceptable or even "cool." Other adolescents may agree to go to family counseling because they want to tell their side of the story. However, if your adolescent will not go or will not go with you, go yourself. Family therapists are trained to help you get reluctant teenagers involved in counseling.

And don't give up. Even if your adolescent's behavior is driving you to the edge—and beyond—stay engaged. When you feel like giving up, remind yourself that the great majority of teenagers, including ones with problem behaviors, grow up to be responsible and caring adults.

As parents, we sometimes need to have the big picture to sustain us through the highways and byways of parenting adolescents. Remember that your child is on his or her way to becoming a physically, intellectually and emotionally mature adult; someone with a separate identity and the ability to be independent and responsible in his or her work and social life. Your job is to develop trust in yourself and your teenager, to stay calm and patient, to provide support, structure and limits and yet let go in a caring and supportive way, and to maintain an underlying belief that your child will, in time, resolve the issues of adolescence and move into adulthood.

17 Stepping into New Roles:
Our Adult Children

Until she was in her mid-twenties, Eva's daughter, Tiffany, almost never asked her mother for advice or confided in her about what was going on in her life. Eva was disappointed and also wondered if Tiffany kept her at a distance because Eva was a lesbian.

But once Tiffany finished college and was working and living in another city, she started to confide more in her mother. In phone calls, they talked more than they ever had in person. Eva was amazed when Tiffany asked for advice about how to handle a situation at work. Another time she described a fight she had had with her boyfriend and wondered what Eva thought she should do.

When they finally had a conversation about how their relationship had changed, Eva was relieved to hear that Tiffany's previous distance had nothing to do with her mother's lesbianism. She just needed to establish herself and "get her own life" before she could relate to her mother as an individual, rather than as a mother.

Growing up does not have to mean growing apart. In fact, the opposite is often true. Like Eva and Tiffany, parents and children in their twenties and beyond often become closer. Partly this is because adult children are able to see and appreciate their parents as people. They don't need to idealize their parents as was the case in childhood, or de-idealize them as in adolescence. But this process of seeing parents as people, and of parents seeing their children as adults, takes time and may be bumpy.

Young adulthood is a transitional period for parents as well as for their children. While the young adult is shouldering adult responsibilities, leaving home, starting on a career path and perhaps meeting his future partner, his parents are struggling with letting go. For example, if your son goes to college, you may still be providing some financial support but are out of the loop of daily contact. You may have little idea of whether he is dating, who his friends are or if he is getting his assignments in on time. If your child decides to go to the local college, the transition happens more gradually, of course, than if she up and takes a job in another state, but whether she moves across town or across the country, the separation can be difficult. As the mother of one young woman described it, "Just when they become people you would enjoy spending time with, they leave; and it tears your heart out." Any relief you feel about having the house to yourself or not having to hassle about curfews and the like may be offset, at least initially, by the feeling of loss.

Another aspect of this transition is that although it is gratifying for parents to have adult-to-adult relationships with their grown children, they must also confront the fact that they themselves are getting older. You used to be the adult, now you are the "older generation." You may even start to look like your parents once looked to you. No longer are you the only one who has the information or the experience...or the energy. You may find yourself asking your children's advice about VCR's or vacation spots and wanting to go to bed as they are discussing which club to check out. It may be an adult-to-adult relationship, but you are definitely the older of the adults in the equation.

This is just the reality of the situation and, in that sense, just as it should be. However, it is sometimes disconcerting for parents to be not quite with it, or unable to keep up. The "kids" are the ones who know the trendy restaurants and what's happening in local politics, the ones who are bursting with energy for demonstrating and building and changing the world. By comparison, you may feel like a slug, or a pale shadow of your former energetic self. Your children are also likely to be establishing serious intimate relationships that may make you feel even further removed from their universe—and sometimes place you in difficult situations.

In this chapter we look at topics related to adult children, including family occasions, relationships with adult children's partners and in-laws, grandchildren and adult children returning to live at home.

Family Occasions: Fun or Fearful?

Rite-of-passage events and large family occasions can be complicated for lesbian parents. One example is family reunions, where everybody is invited, whether they are homophobic or not. Similarly, as children become adults and host their own family gatherings, their lesbian parents are not in charge of the guest list.

To Winnie, her son Eric's debut as a professional actor was starting to feel like a lesbian soap opera. Besides Winnie, the cast of characters included her mother, her ex-husband, and both her former and her current lesbian partner. And all of them were invited not only to the opening performance, but also to the cast party afterwards. Eric had a close relationship with each of these people, so his wanting them there was understandable, but Winnie herself was speaking to only one of the four.

Strained relationships, with former spouses or partners in particular, can continue for years and turn what might otherwise be happy family occasions into stressful events.

Her daughter Melissa's high school graduation proved to be a tense time for Elaine. When Elaine left her husband to be with a woman, he was furious. A bitter divorce and custody negotiations resulted initially in joint custody of Melissa, but Elaine's ex-husband never let up in his campaign to turn Melissa against her mother and Melissa eventually went to live with him. It wasn't until the beginning of her senior year in high school that Melissa started to have more contact with Elaine, and Elaine was overjoyed to be invited to Melissa's graduation.

As her daughter walked down the auditorium aisle to receive her diploma, Elaine was so proud of her and grateful to share in the moment. But trouble began at the reception afterwards. Melissa was clearly torn. She came over to talk to her mother only briefly and with obvious discomfort. Then, when her father sternly signaled her to join him and his new wife, Melissa hesitated and then told Elaine, "I gotta go." Later she called and apologized for rushing off. Elaine understood, but the brushoff was painful nonetheless.

It is no surprise, of course, that divorced parents do not always have a positive relationship. For lesbian mothers, however, there is the complication of homophobia—on the part of the child, the child's father, the legal system and wherever else it may lurk. Sometimes reconciliation with a lesbian mother can really happen only after a child is grown and on her own. As long as the child is financially, legally and emotionally dependent on a homophobic parent, a lesbian mother may not stand much of a chance. When the child is an adult and has established herself as independent and separate from both of her parents, she may reconnect with her mother.

Whether the interpersonal tensions at family social events are due to homophobia or not, the cure is often communication. Where communicating effectively is not possible, patience, compassion and the hope for change in the future may be the only alternative.

Meeting Your Child's Partner

If your adult daughter joyfully announces that she is in love, or that she and her boyfriend are moving in together or that she is planning to get married, you are likely to be very happy for her. And, parents being parents, you probably also have questions and concerns. Just as you may have done when she was an adolescent, you wonder who this man is and what kind of family he comes from and whether he's good for her and good to her. Depending on your own values—and biases—you may wonder about his religious beliefs, his earning power, his nurturing abilities, his gene pool or his politics. And as lesbian parents you have another concern—being judged by your child's partner. Will he, on one extreme, think of you as "totally weird" or will he fully accept your sexual orientation? All parents may imagine, or try not to imagine, how they are being described by their child as she prepares her boyfriend for the meeting. Just as the boyfriend wants to make a good impression on his girl's parents, the parents want to make a good impression on him.

If your child is lesbian or gay, your sexual orientation will not be a concern in meeting her or his lovers and prospective partners. However, if the statistics are accurate, you can expect that ninety percent of the children of lesbian parents will be heterosexual. Yet nervous as you may be about meeting your child's partner, remember that he, or she, may be just as nervous about meeting you.

When David first met his lesbian in-laws-to-be, he was very scared. He had never, at least to his knowledge, met an actual lesbian. And now he was planning to marry into a lesbian family. Penny assured him that her mothers didn't have fangs, and she was sure they would all like each other a lot. David wasn't convinced. He worried that he might say something wrong or do something that would offend someone.

As it turned out, there was a difficult moment, but it wasn't anything like he expected. Rabid football fans, David and Sue, Penny's co-mother, discovered that their favorite teams were arch rivals. They laugh about it now and figure that if this is the only main tension between them, they have it made.

In his late twenties now, Irene and Paula's son, Jay, had finally met some-one he was serious about. "I think she's the one" were his exact words. His relationship with Gisele was relatively new, and Jay had not talked much with her, until recently, about his family's being a lesbian family. His moth-ers also knew that he took his situation so for granted that he might not even notice if Gisele had a negative reaction. However, he described Gisele as a very open, warm person, and he was sure they would all get along famously.

On their way to dinner with their son and prospective new daughter-in-law, Irene and Paula talked about how they very much wanted to like Gisele and wanted her to like them. When Gisele greeted them with a forced smile and stiff handshake, they were a little concerned. She never relaxed at all during dinner and showed no evidence of the warmth and openness that Jay had described. As they said their good-byes, Paula and Irene exchanged glances that said, "We are definitely not off to a good start here."

A lot of your feelings about meeting your child's heterosexual part-ner and the partner's family will depend on how out or closeted you are. If you are closeted, and choose to remain so, your sexual orienta-tion poses few practical difficulties in meetings with your child's new significant other, and eventually with the other family, because you are assumed to be heterosexual and may simply pass. There is, of course, the high price of pretending to be someone you are not and having to deny and hide your lesbian partner relationship, if you have one.

If you are out, fully accepted and included in the get-togethers, sexual orientation becomes just another ingredient in the family stew, one which your child's partner and family will eventually become accustomed to. Usually, the grown child has come out to his girlfriend long before there are any serious plans. And, ideally, her parents have also been told.

The Challenge of Weddings

For some lesbian parents, weddings can bring up a host of charged emotions. For one thing, you can't legally marry your partner. And given the patriarchal heritage and practice of marriage as an institution, you might not want to if you could. Happy as you may be for your child, your feelings about the institution of marriage may range from resentment to rage. For some lesbian parents, this may mean not even wanting to attend their child's wedding.

Even if your values are not offended by the concept of marriage, there are the challenges raised by your being different from other families. Weddings usually involve relatives and friends, including those on the in-law side. It may not be so obvious that the mother of the bride is a lesbian if she is not partnered. However, if there is a partner, particularly one who has had a parenting relationship with the child, the lesbian couple is likely to be very visible. There are the rituals of meeting the fiancee's parents and of attending, or hosting, rehearsal dinners and all the rituals of the wedding ceremony itself. Do both moms walk their daughter down the aisle—one on either side? Does a son divide the first dance at the reception between his mothers? Can a mom and her daughter share a first dance? Will having his mother's lesbian partner in the receiving line upset relatives of the son's bride?

Depending on whether their child is the bride or the groom, lesbian parents may be more or less involved in the actual wedding plans. Even so, if tradition in these matters is followed, financial and planning responsibilities fall to the parents on each side. Those lesbian parents who still have an ex-husband in the picture have the additional task of working out with him how they will all participate in the event.

Tisha had her heart set on a big church wedding including bridesmaids, flower girls, dinner and dancing at the reception and who knows what else. Her father was financially comfortable and told her that she could have whatever she wanted. The plan was that Tisha would have a wedding consultant who would make the arrangements and her father would pay for them.

Rosemary, the mother of the bride, felt pretty much left out of the process. It wasn't that Tisha didn't keep her informed, but that there really wasn't much of a role for her. Also, Rosemary was concerned about how her partner, Shelly, would fit into the scenario, especially on the actual wedding day. After she had a frank talk with Tisha, Rosemary felt an immense relief. Tisha was very understanding of her mother's concerns, and Rosemary found out what her daughter's thoughts were. For example, she learned that Tisha had decided to use a wedding consultant in part to relieve her mother of feeling burdened by what Tisha described as her "elaborate wedding fantasy." In order for Rosemary to feel more a part of things, they agreed that she would get involved in menu planning and also that Rosemary and Shelly would come over before the wedding to help Tisha get dressed.

Tisha was clear that she would continue to confer with both her parents to make sure they were all satisfied with the plans. Rosemary agreed that this would work. Although they certainly didn't always agree, she and her ex-husband were certainly on good enough terms to be able to manage that. Overall, Rosemary just marveled at what a capable and compassionate adult Tisha had become.

As mentioned earlier in the chapter, sometimes divorced parents, including lesbian parents, do not have a positive relationship with their former partners. If this is the case, it is to be hoped that the parents can rise above any animosity they have for each other. Weddings, like other rites of passage such as bar mitzvahs and bat mitzvahs, graduations and awards ceremonies, belong to the child. A parent's role is to provide support and guidance, and then to stand back and allow the child to have her special moment of celebration.

From Moms to Grandmoms

If lesbian and mother are concepts that supposedly don't fit together, how about lesbian and grandmother? The stereotyped image of a grandmother used to be a little old lady with gray or "blue" hair who wore aprons and dowdy print dresses and knitted by the fire. That image likely does not match us very closely. Adjustments are in order—not in how we are but in how we think, particularly if we have internalized the culture's homophobic message that "grandmother" and "lesbian" are mutually exclusive. When someone told her that she didn't look fifty, Gloria Steinem responded, "This is what fifty looks like." In the same vein, how we look is what grandmothers look like!

Parents of grown children usually look forward to the arrival of grandchildren in their lives. Despite the possible need for an "image adjustment," lesbians are no exception.

> Ever since she was a little girl, Emilia had wanted to be a mother. She thought the only way to do that was to get married. So she did, and at quite a young age. Pregnancy and giving birth to her daughters had been some of the most satisfying experiences of her life.
>
> Now her children were all grown up, and Emilia was expecting her first grandchild. As the due date approached, she was bursting with excitement. Her daughter Lucia was having a home birth and had asked Emilia and her partner, Nancy, to be there. For the last month of the pregnancy, Emilia had rented a beeper so she wouldn't miss the phone call announcing that Lucia's labor had started.

If grandchildren come into a family where the lesbianism of the grandparent(s) is already established and accepted, the adult children are likely to be comfortable providing information to their children about it that is appropriate to the child's age. They themselves have been raised in a lesbian family, so explanations about different kinds of families are very familiar to them. In this open situation you can relax and enjoy your grandchildren, while being aware of the basic guidelines for being a grandparent:

- *Wait to be asked for advice, or at least ask if advice is wanted.*
  Even if you have all kinds of good ideas, you may need to bite your tongue sometimes and hold back your advice if you haven't

been asked for your opinion or if your adult child has made it clear that your advice is not wanted in a particular area, or at all.

- *Be clear about what kind of support is available from you and what the limits are.*
  Time, money and material items are the main areas to consider. How often are you willing to baby-sit, and what kind of notice do you need? Do you want regular time scheduled with the grandchildren, or do you prefer contact on a spontaneous or as-needed basis? Are you willing to loan your adult child money or provide regular financial support? What about material needs? Do you want to be asked if there is something the children need, like shoes for school or a car seat for the baby?

- *Respect your adult children's parenting decisions.*
  Even when you may not agree, it is important to show your adult child the respect due him as a parent, assuming, of course, that the physical or emotional health of your grandchild is not at risk. For example, you may strongly believe that all children should attend public schools but your son is considering sending his daughter to a private elementary school. Or you may think that your grandchildren watch too much television or are too young to start dating, but your daughter doesn't seem concerned about it.

What if the adult children were not raised in a lesbian family or are not accepting of their mother's lesbianism? As discussed in Chapter 4, "Coming Out to Our Children and Families," a parent coming out to her adult children for the first time or her children not being comfortable with her sexual orientation can complicate her relationship with her grandchildren. Adult children may limit or refuse contact with the grandchildren and/or may not want the grandchildren to know that their grandmother is a lesbian. So the grandparent, and her partner if she has one, remain in the closet as far as the grandchildren are concerned. Coming out to the grandchildren may be delayed indefinitely or until they are adults. Depending on the individual woman, the closet may feel worth the price of seeing her grandchildren.

When she was fifty-eight, Jean came out to herself and, shortly thereafter, to her son, John. John's wife was an active member of a very homophobic church. Although John did not share his wife's views, he knew that if she learned about his mother's lesbianism, she would forbid the grandchildren to have any contact with her. So Jean and John decided that Jean would remain in the closet as far as her daughter-in-law and grandchildren were concerned.

Because they lived more than three hours away from each other, and only visited periodically, this did not pose great practical problems. But Jean did not like having to de-lesbianize her house and carefully monitor what she said around her grandchildren. She was also concerned about the impact of this "secret" on her son's relationship with her daughter-in-law, especially if she found out later. She finally decided that their relationship was not her responsibility and if she had to be in the closet, so be it. She felt grateful to her son that she had access to her beloved grandchildren.

For some women, being in the closet is not acceptable, even if it means risking loss of contact with family, including grandchildren. This is a decision that only the individual lesbian can make. For other lesbian mothers, being in the closet is not an option because they are already publicly out. These women can hope their grown children will mellow over time so that contact with the grandchildren becomes possible, or they may have to wait until the grandchildren are themselves adults. It may be only then that the young person will risk violating her parent's wishes and have contact with the "forbidden" lesbian grandmother. But we can certainly hope that by that time being lesbian and a grandmother will be no more unusual than having white hair!

Hey, Mom, I'm Home Again

Just when you thought you could have some private, peaceful, relaxing years with your partner, your adult children may show up on your doorstep. Sometimes they just want to live at home in the summers between college sessions, but other times they will plunge you into their very own, very adult crises. Economic difficulties due to job loss, life events like illness or divorce and a wide variety of changes may bring adult children back home. Sometimes grandchildren come along, too. Although these situations are usually intended to be temporary, they may last longer—and cause more stress—than anyone anticipates.

Even if "temporary" really is for a short time, you as a parent may have adjusted quite nicely to your child no longer being in the house. Your daughter's former bedroom is now the space you use to work on your projects—and you have the luxury of leaving them spread out until you get back to them. You have become used to having the resources, like the car and bathroom, to yourself. Your adult child may also be accustomed to being on her own and not having to answer to anyone. Adjustments are required on both sides.

When her husband of three years suddenly left her, Kristin asked her mother, Bev, if she could come back home to live with Bev and Karen for a while. "Just until I can get on my feet" was how Kristin put it. Given that her husband had left her with a lot of debt and two children under the age of three, Bev knew that it would likely take some time before Kristin was able to be on her feet again. There was no question for Bev and Karen. The answer was yes. However, they were careful to point out to Kristin that it had been a long time since the three of them had lived together and that they would need to talk about how it was going to work. One concern they had was about adjusting to living with babies again. Much as they loved visiting their grandchildren, they had been very happy to go to their quiet home afterwards, leaving the parenting to others.

Joyce was thrilled when her son, Ben, told her that he was going into an inpatient alcohol and drug treatment program. It had taken him until his mid-thirties to acknowledge his addiction to cocaine and alcohol. Although it meant changing her work schedule, she faithfully attended the family sessions at the treatment center and agreed that Ben could live with her after he completed the program.

Looking back, Joyce recalls that things started falling apart about a month after Ben came out of treatment. It started with his taking up with his old friends. He began skipping his twelve-step meetings and coming home at all hours. When she confronted him with her suspicions about his using again, he denied it. Eventually Ben wasn't coming home for days at a time. When Joyce began to notice money missing from her purse, she knew Ben had to move out. Much as she loved her son, she wasn't going to go through the pain of living with a practicing addict all over again.

After two semesters of mediocre to bad grades, Amy decided that she wasn't really motivated to be in college at this point. She wanted to get a job and work for a while until she figured out what she wanted to do. Her plan was to live at home and save money for a place of her own.

When Amy's mom, Lori, heard that her daughter was coming home, many thoughts ran through her mind. On the one hand, she wasn't surprised. She herself had questioned whether Amy was really ready to go to college. Perhaps working for a while was best. On the other hand, she also had experience with Amy's lack of follow-through. Was this just another example? Clearly they were going to need to talk about expectations. As far as Lori was concerned, Amy was an adult and needed to pull her weight financially. After some discussion about their expectations, Lori agreed that Amy could live at home, but she was clear with Amy that she would need to contribute to the household—both financially and by taking on a share of the household chores.

When an adult child returns home, it is important to talk about and agree on ground rules for how things will work. For example, will you function as a family group and have meals together, share chores, and the like? Will the returning child be more like a tenant or boarder than a family member? If grandchildren are involved, agreements about child-care responsibilities need to be clarified. What you decide is not as important as having some kind of agreement. The details can always be renegotiated.

Parents and their adult children need to discuss and agree on what constitutes common courtesy and what is interference in your child's life. For example, it is common courtesy for your son to tell you that he won't be home until the wee hours of the morning so that you won't think someone is breaking into the house in the middle of the night. However, it is interfering for you to lecture him about how he should be getting more sleep because his work will suffer or grill him about where he was and what he was doing. He is an adult and is responsible for his own life. As long as he is living up to the agreements between the two of you, let him be.

Finances are another topic that need to be discussed. If the adult child is working, it is reasonable to ask that she make a financial contribution to the household. If she is not working or working only part-time, you may want to subsidize her living expenses. But if she is not working or going to school and has no immediate plans, you might offer financial support for a limited period of time, specify a cutoff date and expect her to do work around the house that you might otherwise hire out. It is critical to remember that when young adults are drifting, the best thing parents can do is to remain emotionally supportive but also to make real-world demands on them. And the real world *demands* that adults earn their keep. Practice firmness with dignity and respect.

A mother's lesbianism is likely not an issue for an adult child returning to live at home, unless the parent has been closeted or is in the process of coming out during the time that the adult child has returned to live with her. If your adult son or daughter is not accepting of your sexual orientation, it might be quite tense until some accommodation is reached. Ultimately your child may need to become more accepting or find someplace else to live!

The goal is for our children to grow up and become separate and independent adults. Then the opportunity for a parent-child relationship that is more like a friendship really is possible. When children have established themselves as adults who are different and separate from us, they will not be so defensive. They know who they are and are confident about themselves. As parents, our job is to let go of our children and allow them to be adults in their own right. When we accomplish this, we don't need to control their behavior and manage their life for them. Having this kind of relationship, based on mutual liking and respect, is one of the greatest pleasures of parenthood.

NOTES

Chapter One
1. Philip Blumstein and Pepper Schwartz, *American Couples* (New York: William Morrow, 1983), 61, 130.

Chapter Two
1. We particularly recommend Cheri Pies' book *Considering Parenthood* as an excellent resource.

2. Wendell Ricketts and Roberta Achtenberg, "The Adoptive and Foster Gay and Lesbian Parent," in *Gay and Lesbian Parents*, ed. Frederick W. Bozett (New York: Praeger, 1987), 89-111.

3. Wendell Ricketts in *Lesbian and Gay Men as Foster Parents* (Portland, ME: Edmund S. Muskie Clearinghouse, National Child Welfare Resource Center for Management and Administration, University of Southern Maine, 1992), 10-11, cites a case of a lesbian couple who become foster parents in California and references foster placements with couples in Chicago, New York and Philadelphia.

4. In 1985 two openly gay men in Boston were granted a foster-care license and two young boys were placed with them. Two weeks later *The Boston Globe* wrote a story about the placement and set off a public reaction that resulted in the boys' being taken from the home. In spite of a recommendation by the governor's appointed review board to allow case by case evaluation, the state reworked its foster-care guidelines, making it virtually impossible for lesbians or gay men to become foster parents. The National Association of Social Workers, the American Psychological Association and the American Psychiatric Association speak against discrimination toward lesbian and gay foster parents based on sexual orientation alone. In 1986 the two men and other plaintiffs filed suit against the governor and the Massachusetts Department of Social Services saying that the new policy was discriminatory against unmarried couples and single people. In 1990 the state and plaintiffs settled on a policy that did not discriminate as strongly and allowed for the possibility of lesbian and gay foster parents, depending on the individual caseworker's judgment. As we write, the two men once again have foster children and the prospects look better for them to be able to rear these children.

5. Ricketts and Achtenberg, in *Gay and Lesbian Parents*, 95.

6. Ricketts, *Lesbian and Gay Men as Foster Parents*, 91.

7. Ricketts and Achtenberg, in *Gay and Lesbian Parents*, 98.

8. The International Concerns Committe for Children, 911 Cypress Drive, Boulder, Colorado 80303, sends out a newsletter with information on sources for international adoptions.

Chapter Three
1. Judith Wallerstein and Sandra Blakeslee, *Second Chances: Men, Women and*

Children a Decade After Divorce (New York: Ticknor & Fields, 1990), 18.

2. Lenore Weitzman, *The Divorce Revolution* (New York: Free Press, 1985), 266-301.

Chapter Four

1. Joan Sophie, "Counseling Lesbians," *Personnel & Guidance Journal,* 60(6) (1982), 341–345.

2. Suzanne Pharr, *Homophobia: A Weapon of Sexism* (Inverness, CA: Chardon Press, 1988), 16–17.

3. Joy Schulenburg, *Gay Parenting* (Garden City: Anchor Press/Doubleday, 1985), 24.

4. Rip Corley, *The Final Closet* (Miami: Editech Press, 1990), 105.

5. April Martin, *The Lesbian and Gay Parenting Handbook* (New York: HarperCollins, 1993), 290-291.

Chapter Five

1. Haim Ginnott, *Between Parent and Child* (New York: Avon Books, 1956), 25.

2. Morton Deutsch, "Educating for a Peaceful World," *American Psychologist,* 48 (5) (1993), 510–517.

3. John McDermott, *Raising Cain & Abel Too: The Parents' Book of Sibling Rivalry.* Cited in Louise Bates Ames and Carol Chase Haber, *He Hit Me First: When Brothers and Sisters Fight* (New York: Warner Books, 1982), 20-22.

Chapter Six

1. Elisabeth Kübler-Ross, *On Death and Dying* (New York: Macmillan, 1969).

2. Mary Kate Jordan, *Losing Uncle Tim* (Niles, IL: Albert Whitman & Co., 1989).

3. Hope Edelman, *Motherless Daughters* (Reading, MA: Addison-Wesley, 1994), 6-7.

4. Wallerstein and Blakeslee, *Second Chances*, 278-282.

5. Ibid., 282-285.

6. Ibid., 179-182.

7. Ibid., 238.

8. Ibid., 267.

9. Ibid., 289-294.

10. Charles E. Schaefer and Theresa Foy DiGeronimo, *How to Talk to Your Kids About Really Important Things* (San Francisco: Jossey-Bass, 1994).

11. Carol Becker, *Unbroken Ties* (Boston: Alyson, 1988).

12. Constance Ahrons, *The Good Divorce* (New York: HarperCollins, 1994), 138.

Chapter Seven

1. Darlene Powell Hopson and Derek S. Hopson, *Raising the Rainbow Generation*

(New York: Fireside, 1993), 19-20.

2. Ibid., 29.

3. Vickie L. Sears, "Cross-cultural Ethnic Relationships," unpublished manuscript, 1987.

4. D. Merilee Clunis and G. Dorsey Green, *Lesbian Couples* (Seattle: Seal Press, 1988), 131–142.

5. Cheri Register," Answering Nosy Questions," *Adoptive Families,* 27 (4), (1994), 22–23.

6. Peter L. Benson and Anu Sharma, "The Truth About Adopted Teenagers," *Adoptive Families,* 27 (4), (1994), 16-20.

7. Maria P. P. Root, "Multiracial Contribution to the Psychological Browning of America," in Naomi Zack, (Ed.) *American Mixed Races: The Culture of Microdiversity* (Labham, Maryland: Rowman and Littlefield, 1995), 231-236.

8. Maria P. P. Root, personal communication (Seattle, 1995).

9. Maria P. P. Root, from "Bill of Rights for People with Multiracial Identity," *Racially Mixed People in the New Millenium* (Newbury Park, California: Sage, in press).

10. Schaefer and DiGeronimo, *How to Talk to Your Kids About Really Important Things,* 218.

11. Janet E. Helms, ed., *Black and White Racial Identity* (New York: Praeger, 1993), 102–103.

12. *Tools for Diversity Training* (Portland, Oregon: TACS, 1994). For more information, contact TACS, 1903 Ankeny, Portland, Oregon 97214.

13. Hopson and Hopson, *Raising the Rainbow Generation,* 67-73.

14. Joan McNamara, "Growing Up Adopted: Facing Prejudice," *Adoptive Families* 7(6), (1994), 60.

Chapter Eight

1. Becky Butler, *Ceremonies of the Heart* (Seattle: Seal Press, 1990).

2. Elizabeth Berg, *Family Traditions* (Pleasantville, NY: The Reader's Digest Association, 1992), 9.

3. Susan Abel Lieberman, *New Traditions* (New York: The Noonday Press, 1991), 10.

Chapter Ten

1. Frank Caplan, ed., *The First Twelve Months of Life* (New York: Grosset and Dunlap, 1973), 58-73.

2. Jean Ilsley Clarke, *Self-Esteem: A Family Affair* (Minneapolis: Winston Press, 1978), 44.

•   •   •

Chapter Eleven

1. Most of this information on physical development of toddlers is drawn from two books by Frank Caplan and Theresa Caplan, *The Second Twelve Months of Life* (New York: Perigee/Putnam, 1977) and *The Early Childhood Years* (New York: Dell, 1983).

2. Personal communication with David Springer, M.D., February, 1995.

Chapter Twelve

1. Louise Bates Ames and Carol Chase Haber, *Your Three-Year-Old: Friend or Enemy* (New York: Dell Publishing, 1985), 4.

2. Louise Bates Ames and Carol Chase Haber, *Your Seven-Year-Old: Life in a Minor Key* (New York: Dell Publishing, 1985), 14.

3. Caplan and Caplan, *The Early Childhood Years: The 2 to 6 Year Old*. Most of the data we cite on childhood physical development comes from the Caplans' book. We recommend it highly if you are interested in a more thorough discussion of the development of this age group.

4. Melvin Konner, *Childhood: A Multicultural View* (Boston: Little, Brown and Company, 1991), 241.

Chapter Thirteen

1. Carol Tribe as cited by Deborah Lovitky Sheiman and Maureen Slonim, *Resources for Middle Childhood: A Source Book* (New York: Garland Publishing, Inc., 1988), 34.

2. Melvin Konner, *Childhood: A Multicultural View*, 29. Konner researched child development in a variety of cultures, in developed and developing countries, and described some of the constants which occur in this age range. He uses the phrase "rules, reciprocity, and fairness" to describe some universal issues which come into focus in the middle childhood years.

3. Ann Cale Kruger as cited in Konner, *Childhood*, 299.

4. Stella Chess and Alexander Thomas, *Know Your Child: An Authoritative Guide for Today's Parents* (New York: Basic Books, 1987).

5. Erik Erikson, *Childhood and Society* (New York: W.W. Norton and Co., 1963), 258.

6. Sandra Anselemo, *Early Childhood Development: Prenatal Through Age Eight*, (New York: Macmillan, 1987).

7. Sheiman and Slonim, *Resources for Middle Childhood*, 68.

8. Clarke, *Self-Esteem: A Family Affair*, 155.

Chapter Fourteen

1. Laurence Steinberg and Ann Levine, *You and Your Adolescent* (New York: HarperCollins, 1990), 1–3.

2. James Gardner, *The Turbulent Teens* (Los Angeles: Sorrento Press, 1983), 24.

3. Steinberg and Levine, *You and Your Adolescent*, 2.

4. Daniel Offer and K.A. Schonert-Reichl, "Debunking the Myths of Adolescence: Findings from Recent Research," *Journal of American Academy of Child and Adolescent Psychiatry*, 31 (1992), 1003-1014.

5. Ibid., 1010.

6. Carol J. Eagle and Carol Colman, *All That She Can Be: Helping Your Daughter Maintain Her Self-Esteem* (New York: Simon and Schuster, 1993), 66.

7. Anthony Wolf, *"Get out of my life, but first could you drive Cheryl and me to the mall": A Parent's Guide to the New Teenager* (New York: Farrar, Straus and Giroux, 1991).

8. Ibid., 28.

9. American Association of University Women, *Shortchanging girls, shortchanging America*, cited in Eagle and Colman, *All That She Can Be*, 21–23.

10. Mary Pipher, *Reviving Ophelia: Saving the Selves of Adolescent Girls* (New York: Putnam, 1994).

11. AAUW, *Shortchanging girls, shortchanging America*, cited in Eagle and Colman, *All That She Can Be*, 22.

12. Diana Baumrind, "Effective Parenting during the Early Adolescent Transition," in *Family Transitions*, eds. P. A. Cowen and M. Hetherington (Hillsdale, New Jersey: Lawrence Erlbaum Associates), 111-164.

13. Steinberg and Levine, *You and Your Adolescent*, 13.

14. Torey L. Hayden, "Conversations Kids Crave" *Families*, June 1982, cited in Thomas Lickona, *Raising Good Children: From Birth through the Teenage Years* (New York: Bantam, 1985), 255-56.

Chapter Fifteen

1. Adapted from Steinberg and Levine, *You and Your Adolescent*, 106-111.

2. Gardner, *The Turbulent Teens*, 52-65.

3. Thomas Lickona, *Raising Good Children: From Birth Through the Teenage Years* (New York: Bantam, 1985). Cited in Steinberg and Levine, *You and Your Adolescent*, 145-148.

4. Lyn Brown & Carol Gilligan, *Meeting at the Crossroads* (New York: Ballantine Books, 1992), 2–5.

5. Steinberg and Levine, *You and Your Adolescent*, 161.

6. Ibid., 164.

7. Ibid., 165.

8. Pipher, *Reviving Ophelia*, 184-185.

9. American Psychiatric Association. *Diagnostic and Statistical Manual of Mental*

Disorders, Fourth Edition, (Washington, DC: American Psychiatric Association, 1994), 539.

10. Ibid., 543.

11. Pipher, *Reviving Ophelia*, 180.

12. Steinberg and Levine, *You and Your Adolescent*, 226.

13. April Martin, *The Lesbian & Gay Parenting Handbook*, 322.

Chapter Sixteen

1. Erik Erikson, *Identity, Youth and Crisis* (New York: Norton, 1968), 128-135.

2. Steinberg and Levine, *You and Your Adolescent*, 286–287.

3. Lickona, *Raising Good Children*, 57.

4. Don and Jeanne Elium, *Raising a Son* (Hillsboro, OR: Beyond Words Publishing, 1992), 206.

5. Steinberg and Levine, *You and Your Adolescent*, 345.

6. Ibid., 245.

7. Ibid., 240.

8. Ibid., 116.

SELECTED BIBLIOGRAPHY

If you would like more information about specific topics, we recommend the following books. See also our General Bibliography for more.

Adolescence

Bassoff, Evelyn S. *Between Mothers and Sons: The Making of Vital and Loving Men.* New York: Dutton, 1994.

Caron, Ann F. *Strong Mothers, Strong Sons: Raising Adolescent Boys in the 90's.* New York: Henry Holt & Co., 1994.

Caron, Ann F. *Don't Stop Loving Me: A Reassuring Guide for Mothers of Adolescent Girls.* New York: Harper Perennial, 1991.

Eagle, Carol J. and Carol Colman. *All That She Can Be: Helping Your Daughter Maintain Her Self-Esteem.* New York: Simon & Schuster, 1993.

Gardner, James E. *The Turbulent Teens.* Los Angeles: Sorrento Press, 1983.

Levy, Barrie and Patricia Occhiuzzo Giggans. *What Parents Need to Know About Dating Violence.* Seattle: Seal Press, 1995.

McCoy, Kathleen. *Understanding Your Teenager's Depression: Issues, Insights and Practical Guidance for Parents.* New York: Berkley Publishing Group, 1994.

Phillips, Angela. *The Trouble with Boys: A Wise and Sympathetic Guide to the Risky Business of Raising Sons.* New York: Basic Books, 1994.

Pipher, Mary. *Reviving Ophelia: Saving the Selves of Adolescent Girls.* New York: G.P. Putnam's Sons, 1994.

Powell, Douglas H. *Teenagers: When to Worry and What to Do.* New York: Doubleday, 1986.

Silverstein, Olga and Beth Rashbaum. *The Courage to Raise Good Men.* New York: Penguin, 1994.

Slaby, Andrew E. and Lili Frank Garfinkel. *No One Saw My Pain: Why Teens Kill Themselves.* New York: W.W. Norton, 1994.

Steinberg, Laurence and Ann Levin. *You and Your Adolescent: A Parent's Guide for Ages 10-20.* New York: HarperCollins, 1990.

Turecki, Stanley and Sarah Wernick. *The Emotional Problems of Normal Children.* New York: Bantam, 1994.

Wattleton, Faye. *How to Talk to Your Child About Sexuality.* New York: Doubleday, 1986.

Williams, Kate. *A Parent's Guide for Suicidal and Depressed Teens.* Center City, MN: Hazelden, 1995.

Wolf, Anthony E. *"Get out of my life, but first could you drive Cheryl and me to the mall?": A Parents' Guide to the New Teenager.* New York: Farrar, Straus & Giroux, 1991.

Adoption

Arms, Suzanne. *Adoption: A Handful of Hope.* Berkeley: Celestial Arts, 1990.

Bates, J. Douglas. *Gift Children: A Story of Race, Family and Adoption in a Divided America.* New York: Ticknor & Fields, 1993.

Brodzinsky, David M., Marshall D. Schechter and Robin Marantz Henig. *Being Adopted: The Lifelong Search for Self.* New York: Anchor/Doubleday, 1992.

Martin, April. *The Lesbian and Gay Parenting Handbook: Creating and Raising Our Families.* New York: Harper Perennial, HarperCollins, 1993.

Melina, Lois Ruskin and Sharon Kaplan Roszia. *The Open Adoption Experience.* New York: Harper Perennial, 1993.

Register, Cheri. *Are Those Kids Yours?* New York: Free Press, 1990.

Roberts, Colleen Alexander. *The Essential Adoption Handbook.* Dallas, TX: Taylor Publishing Co., 1993.

Van Gulden, Holly and Lisa Bartells-Raab. *Real Parents, Real Children: Parenting the Adopted Child.* New York: Crossroad Publishing Co., 1993.

Wadia-Ells, Susan, ed. *The Adoption Reader: Birth Mothers, Adoptive Mothers and Adopted Daughters Tell Their Stories.* Seattle: Seal Press, 1995.

Adult Children

Adams, Jane. *I'm Still Your Mother.* New York: Delacorte Press, 1994.

Leshan, Eda. *Grandparenting in a Changing World.* New York: Newmarket Press, 1993.

Lieber, Phyllis, Gloria S. Murphy and Annette Merkur Schwartz. *Grown-up Children, Grown-up Parents: Opening the Door to Healthy Relationships Between Parents and Adult Children.* New York: Birch Lane Press, 1994.

Artificial Insemination

Gil de Lamadrid, Maria, ed. *Lesbians Choosing Motherhood: Legal Implications of Donor Insemination and Co-Parenting.* San Francisco: National Center for Lesbian Rights, 1991.

Noble, E. *Having Your Baby by Donor Insemination.* Boston: Houghton Mifflin Co., 1987.

Saffron, Lisa. *Challenging Conceptions: Planning a Family by Self-Insemination.* London: Cassell, 1994.

Books for Adolescents

Garden, Nancy. *Annie on My Mind.* New York: Farrar, Straus & Giroux, 1982.

Klein, Norma. *Breaking Up.* New York: Random House, 1980.

Klein, Norma. *Now That I Know.* New York: Bantam, 1988.

Parker, Roberta N. and Harvey Parker. *Making the Grade: An Adolescent's Struggle with Attention Deficit Disorder.* San Luis Obispo, CA: Impact Press, 1992.

Rafkin, Louise, ed. *Different Mothers.* Pittsburgh, PA: Cleis Press, 1990.

Scoppettone, Sandra. *Happy Endings Are All Alike.* New York: Harper & Row, 1978.

Books for Children

Banks, Ann. *When Your Parents Get a Divorce: A Kid's Journal.* New York: Puffin/Penguin Group, 1991.

Bosche, Suzanne. *Jenny Lives with Eric and Martin.* London: Gay Men's Press, 1981.

Elwin, Rosamund and Michele Paulse. *Asha's Mums.* Toronto: Women's Press, 1990.

Herron, Ann and Meredith Maran. *How Would You Feel if Your Dad Was Gay?* Boston: Alyson Publications, 1991.

Jenness, Aylette. *Families: A Celebration of Diversity, Commitment and Love.* Boston: Houghton Mifflin Co., 1990.

Jordan, Mary Kate. *Losing Uncle Tim.* Niles, IL: Albert Whitman & Co., 1989.

Merriam, Eve. *Mommies at Work.* New York: Simon & Schuster, 1989.

Newman, Lesléa. *Belinda's Bouquet.* Boston: Alyson Publications, 1991.

Newman, Lesléa. *Gloria Goes to Gay Pride.* Boston: Alyson Publications, 1991.

Newman, Lesléa. *Heather Has Two Mommies.* Boston: Alyson Publications, 1989.

Severance, Jane. *Lots of Mommies.* Chapel Hill, NC: Lollipop Power, 1983.

Valentine, Johnny. *Daddy Machine.* Boston: Alyson Publications, 1992.

Valentine, Johnny. *The Duke Who Outlawed Jelly Beans and Other Stories.* Boston: Alyson Publications, *1991.*

Valentine, Johnny. *Two Moms, the Zark, and Me.* Boston: Alyson Publications, 1993.

Willhoite, Michael. *Daddy's Roommate.* Boston: Alyson Publications, 1990.

Willhoite, Michael. *Families: A Coloring Book.* Boston: Alyson Publications, 1991.

Coming Out

Corley, Rip. *The Final Closet: The Gay Parent's Guide to Coming Out to Their Children.* Miami: Editech Press, 1990.

Martin, April. *The Lesbian and Gay Parenting Handbook: Creating and Raising Our Families.* New York: HarperCollins, 1993.

Schulenburg, J. *Gay Parenting.* New York: Anchor Press/Doubleday, 1985.

Communication and Conflict Resolution

Clarke, Jean Illsley and Connie Dawson. *Growing Up Again: Parenting Ourselves, Parenting Our Children.* San Francisco: Harper & Row, 1989.

Clunis, D. Merilee and G. Dorsey Green. *Lesbian Couples: Creating Healthy Relationships for the 90s.* Seattle: Seal Press, 1993.

Faber, Adele and Elaine Mazlish. *How to Talk So Kids Will Listen & Listen So Kids Will Talk.* New York: Avon Books, 1980.

Gordon, Thomas. *P.E.T. Parent Effectiveness Training: The Tested New Way To Raise Responsible Children.* New York: Plume/Penguin Group, 1975.

Nelson, Jane, Lynn Lott and H. Stephen Glenn. *Positive Discipline A-Z: 1001 Solutions to Everyday Parenting Problems.* Rocklin, CA: Prima Publishing, 1993.

Schaefer, Charles E. and Teresa Foy DiGeronimo. *How to Talk to Your Kids About Really Important Things.* San Francisco: Jossey-Bass, 1994.

Weston, Denise Chapman and Mark S. Weston. *Playful Parenting: Turning the Dilemma of Discipline into Fun and Games.* New York: G.P. Putnam's Sons, 1993.

Couple Relationships

Berzon, Betty. *Permanent Partners: Building Gay and Lesbian Relationships that Last.* New York: E. P. Dutton, 1988.

Clunis, D. Merilee and G. Dorsey Green. *Lesbian Couples: Creating Healthy Relationships for the 90s.* Seattle: Seal Press, 1993.

Ulrig, L. *The Two of Us: Affirming, Celebrating and Symbolizing Gay and Lesbian Relationships.* Boston: Alyson Publications, 1984.

Divorce, Death and Loss

Banks, Ann. *When Your Parents Get a Divorce: A Kid's Journal.* New York: Puffin/Penguin Group, 1991.

Blau, Melinda. *Families Apart: Ten Keys to Successful Co-Parenting.* New York: G.P. Putnam's Sons, 1993.

Cole, Diane. *After Great Pain: A New Life Emerges.* New York: Summit Books, 1992.

Jarratt, Claudia Jewett. *Helping Children Cope with Separation and Loss* (rev. ed.). Boston: The Harvard Common Press, 1994.

Nichols, J. Randall. *Ending Marriage, Keeping Faith: A New Guide Through the Spiritual Journey of Divorce.* New York: Crossroad, 1993.

Ricci, Isolina. *Mom's House, Dad's House: Making Shared Custody Work.* New York: Collier/Macmillan Publishing, 1980.

Schaefer, Charles E. and Theresa Foy DiGeronimo. *How to Talk to Your Kids About Really Important Things.* San Francisco: Jossey-Bass, 1994.

Trafford, Abigail. *Crazy Time: Surviving Divorce and Building a New Life.* New York: HarperCollins, 1992.

Wallerstein, Judith S. and Sandra Blakeslee. *Second Chances: Men, Women and*

Children a Decade After Divorce. New York: Ticknor & Fields, 1990.

Early Childhood

Ames, Louise Bates and Frances Ilg. *Your Three-Year-Old: Friend or Enemy.* New York: Delta/Dell Publishing, 1985.

Ames, Louise Bates and Frances Ilg. *Your Four-Year-Old: Wild and Wonderful.* New York: Delta/Dell Publishing, 1976.

Anselmo, Sandra. *Early Childhood Development: Prenatal through Age Eight.* New York: Macmillan, 1987.

Caplan, Theresa and Frank Caplan. *The Early Childhood Years: The 2 to 6 Year Old.* New York: Dell Publishing Group, 1983.

Extended Family

Clark, Don. *Loving Someone Gay.* Millbrae, CA: Celestial Arts, 1987.

Griffin, Carol Welch, Marian J. Wirth and Arthur G. Wirth. *Beyond Acceptance: Parents of Lesbians and Gays Talk about Their Experiences.* New York: St. Martin's Press, 1990.

Rafkin, Louise, ed. *Different Daughters.* Pittsburgh, PA: Cleis Press, 1987.

Rafkin, Louise, ed. *Different Mothers.* Pittsburgh, PA: Cleis Press, 1990.

Infancy

Caplan, Frank, ed. *The First Twelve Months of Life: Your Baby's Growth Month by Month.* New York: Gosset & Dunlap, 1973.

Clarke, Jean Illsley. *Self-Esteem: A Family Affair.* Minneapolis: Winston Press, 1978.

Eisenberg, Arlene, Heidi E. Murkoff and Sandee E. Hathaway. *What to Expect the First Year.* New York: Workman Publishers, 1988.

Ferber, Richard. *Solve Your Child's Sleep Problems.* New York: Simon & Schuster, 1985.

La Leche League. *The Womanly Art of Breastfeeding.* New York: Plume, 1991.

Sears, William and Martha Sears. *The Baby Book: Everything You Need to Know About Your Baby—From Birth to Age Two.* Boston: Little, Brown & Co., 1993.

Spock, Benjamin and Michael B. Rothenberg. *Dr. Spock's Baby and Child Care.* 6th Edition. New York: Pocket Books, 1992.

Lesbian Families

Arnup, Katherine, ed. *Lesbian Parenting: Living with Pride and Prejudice.* Charlottetown, Prince Edward Island: Gynergy Books, 1995.

Benkov, Laura. *Reinventing the Family: The Emerging Story of Lesbian and Gay Parents.* New York: Crown Publishers, 1994.

Martin, April. *The Lesbian and Gay Parenting Handbook: Creating and Raising Our Families.* New York: Harper Perennial, HarperCollins, 1993.

Pies, Cheri. *Considering Parenthood* (second edition). Minneapolis: Spinsters Ink, 1988.

Rizzo, Cindy, Jo Schneiderma, Lisa Schweig, Jan Shafer and Judith Stein, ed. *All the Ways Home: Parenting and Children in the Lesbian and Gay Communities.* Norwich, VT: New Victoria Publishers Inc., 1995.

Weston, Kath. *Families We Choose: Lesbians, Gays, Kinship.* New York: Columbia University Press, 1991.

Legal Issues

Achtenberg, Roberta. *Preserving and Protecting the Families of Lesbians and Gay Men.* San Francisco: National Center for Lesbian and Gay Rights, 1990.

Curry, Hayden and Denis Clifford. *A Legal Guide for Lesbian and Gay Couples.* Berkeley: Nolo Press, 1991.

Hunter, N.D. and N. D. Polikoff. "Custody Rights of Lesbian Mothers: Legal Theory and Litigation Strategy." *Buffalo Law Review,* 25, (1976): 691-733.

Polikoff, N.D. "Lesbian Mothers, Lesbian Families: Legal Obstacles, Legal Challenges." *Review of Law and Social Change,* 14(4), (1986): 907-914.

Rivera, R.R. "Legal Issues in Gay and Lesbian Parenting." In *Gay and Lesbian Parents,* edited by Frederick W. Bozett. New York: Praeger, 1987.

Middle Childhood

Ames, Louise Bates and Carol Chase Haber. *Your Nine-Year-Old: Thoughtful and Mysterious.* New York: Delta/Dell Publishing, 1990.

Ames, Louise Bates and Frances Ilg. *Your Six-Year-Old: Loving and Defiant.* New York: Delta/Dell Publishing, 1979.

Bernstein, Anne C. *Flight of the Stork: What Children Think (and When) about Sex and Family Building.* Indianapolis, IN: Perspectives Press, 1995.

Clarke, Jean Illsley. *HELP! for Parents of School-age Children and Teenagers.* San Francisco: Harper, 1993.

Pregnancy and Childbirth

Eisenberg, Arlene, Heidi E. Murkoff and Sandee E. Hathaway. *What to Expect When You're Expecting.* New York: Workman Publishers, 1984.

Kitzinger, Sheila. *The Complete Book of Pregnancy and Childbirth.* New York: Knopf, 1980.

Kitzinger, Sheila. *Giving Birth: How It Really Feels.* New York: Farrar, Straus & Giroux, 1989.

Perez, Pauline. *Special Woman: The Role of the Professional Labor Assistant.* Seattle: Cutting Edge Press, 1994.

Samuels, Mike and Nancy Samuels. *The Well Pregnancy Book.* New York: Fireside, 1986.

Simkin, Penny. *The Birth Partner.* Boston: The Harvard Common Press, 1989.

Simkin, Penny, Janet Whalley and Ann Keppler. *Pregnancy, Childbirth and the Newborn.* New York: Meadowbrook Press, 1991.

Racism

Comer, James P. and Alvin F. Poussaint. *Raising Black Children.* New York: Plume, 1992.

Golden, Marita. *Saving Our Sons: Raising Black Children in a Turbulent World.* New York: Doubleday, 1995.

Hopson, Darlene Powell and Derek Hopson. *Different and Wonderful: Raising Black Children in a Race-Conscious Society.* New York: Fireside, 1990.

Hopson, Darlene Powell and Derek Hopson. *Raising the Rainbow Generation: Teaching Your Children to be Successful in a Multicultural Society.* New York: Fireside, 1993.

National PTA and Anti-Defamation League of B'Nai B'rith. *What to Tell Your Child About Prejudice and Discrimination.* New York: 1989. Available by writing 700 North Rush Street, Chicago, IL 60611-2571.

Reddy, Maureen T. *Crossing the Color Line: Race, Parenting, and Culture.* New Brunswick, NJ: Rutgers University Press, 1994.

Sibling Rivalry

Ames, Louise Bates and Carol Chase Haber. *He Hit Me First.* New York: Warner Books, 1982.

Faber, Adele and Elaine Mazlish. *Siblings Without Rivalry.* New York: Avon Books, 1987.

Single Parenting

Kennedy, Marge and Janet Spencer King. *The Single Parent Family: Living Happily in a Changing World.* New York: Bantam Books, 1991.

Leslie, Marsha R., ed. *The Single Mother's Companion: Essays and Stories by Women.* Seattle: Seal Press, 1994.

Nelson, Jane, Cheryl Erwin and Carol Delzer. *Positive Discipline for Single Parents.* Rocklin, CA: Prima Publishing, 1994.

Special Needs

Ingersoll, Mary Cahill. *Maybe You Know My Kid: A Parent's Guide to Identifying, Understanding and Helping Your Child with Attention-Deficit Hyperactivity Disorder.* New York: Birch Lane Press, 1990.

Kennedy, Patricia, Leif Terdal and Lydia Fusetti. *The Hyperactive Child Book.* New

York: St. Martin's Press, 1994.

Klein, Stanley and Maxwell J. Schleifer, eds. *It Isn't Fair: Siblings of Children with Disabilities.* Granby, MA: Bergin & Garvey, 1993.

Simons, Robin. *After the Tears: Parents Talk about Raising a Child with a Disability.* San Diego, CA: Harcourt Brace Jovanovich, 1987.

Toddlers

Ames, Louise Bates and Frances Ilg. *Your Two-Year-Old: Terrible or Tender.* New York: Delacorte Press, 1976.

Caplan, Frank and Theresa Caplan. *The Second Twelve Months of Life: A Kaleidoscope of Growth.* New York: Perigee/Putnam Publishing Group, 1977.

Clarke, Jean Illsley and Connie Dawson. *Growing Up Again: Parenting Ourselves, Parenting Our Children.* San Francisco: Harper & Row, 1989.

Eisenberg, Arlene, Heidi E. Murkoff and Sandee E. Hathaway. *What to Expect the Toddler Years.* New York: Workman Publishers, 1994.

Leach, Penelope. *Your Baby and Child: From Birth to Age Five.* New York: Knopf, 1986.

Traditions

Berg, Elizabeth. *Family Traditions: Celebrations for Holidays and Everyday.* Pleasantville, NY: Readers Digest Association, Inc., 1992.

Lieberman, Susan Abel. *New Traditions.* New York: Noonday Press, 1991.

GENERAL BIBLIOGRAPHY

Abbitt, D. and B. Bennett. "Being a Lesbian Mother." In *Positively Gay,* edited by B. Berzon and R. Leighton. Millbrae, CA: Celestial Arts, 1979.

Abbott, Franklin, ed. *Boyhood: Growing Up Male: A Multicultural Anthology.* Freedom, CA: The Crossing Press, 1993.

Achtenberg, Roberta. *Preserving and Protecting the Families of Lesbians and Gay Men.* San Francisco: National Center for Lesbian and Gay Rights, 1990.

Adams, Jane. *I'm Still Your Mother.* New York: Delacorte Press, 1994.

Adelman, Marcy, ed. *Long Time Passing: Lives of Older Lesbians.* Boston: Alyson Publications, 1986.

Afek, Dina. "Sarah and the Women's Movement: The Experience of Infertility." *Women & Therapy: A Feminist Quarterly,* 10(1/2), (1990): 195-203.

Agbayewa, M.O. "Fathers in the Newer Family Forms: Male or Female?" *Canadian Journal of Psychiatry,* 29(5), (1984): 402-406.

Ahrons, Constance R. *The Good Divorce: Keeping Your Family Together When Your Marriage Comes Apart.* New York: HarperCollins, 1994.

Alexander, Shoshana. *In Praise of Single Parents: Embracing the Challenge.* Boston: Houghton Mifflin Co., 1994.

Alpert, Harriet, ed. *We Are Everywhere: Writings by and about Lesbian Parents.* Freedom, CA: The Crossing Press, 1988.

Altman, D. *The Homosexualization of America, the Americanization of the Homosexual.* New York: St. Martin's Press, 1982.

American Association of University Women. *Shortchanging Girls, Shortchanging America.* Washington, DC: AAUW, 1991.

American Psychiatric Association. *Diagnostic and Statistical Manual of Mental Disorders Fourth Edition.* Washington, DC: APA, 1994.

Ames, Louise Bates and Carol Chase Haber. *He Hit Me First.* New York: Warner Books, 1982.

Ames, Louise Bates and Carol Chase Haber. *Your Seven-Year-Old: Life in a Minor Key.* New York: Delta/Dell Publishing, 1985.

Ames, Louise Bates and Carol Chase Haber. *Your Eight-Year-Old: Lively and Outgoing.* New York: Delta/Dell Publishing, 1989.

Ames, Louise Bates and Carol Chase Haber. *Your Nine-Year-Old: Thoughtful and Mysterious.* New York: Delta/Dell Publishing, 1990.

Ames, Louise Bates and Frances Ilg. *Your Two-Year-Old: Terrible or Tender.* New York: Delacorte, 1976.

Ames, Louise Bates and Frances Ilg. *Your Three-Year-Old: Friend or Enemy.* New York: Delta/Dell Publishing, 1985.

Ames, Louise Bates and Frances Ilg. *Your Four-Year-Old: Wild and Wonderful.* New

York: Delta/Dell Publishing, 1976.

Ames, Louise Bates and Frances Ilg. *Your Five-Year-Old: Sunny and Serene.* New York: Delta/Dell Publishing, 1979.

Ames, Louise Bates and Frances Ilg. *Your Six-Year-Old: Loving and Defiant.* New York: Delta/Dell Publishing, 1979.

Anderson, Joan. *The Single Mother's Book: A Practical Guide to Managing Your Children, Career, Home, Finances and Everything Else.* Atlanta: Peachtree Publishers, 1990.

Andrews, Nancy. *Family: A Portrait of Gay and Lesbian America.* San Francisco: Harper, 1994.

Anselmo, Sandra. *Early Childhood Development: Prenatal through Age Eight.* New York: Macmillan, 1987.

Arcana, Judith. *Every Mother's Son: The Role of Mothers in the Making of Men.* Seattle: Seal Press, 1986.

Arent, Ruth P. *Parenting Children in Unstable Times.* Golden, CO: Fulcrum, 1993.

Arms, Suzanne. *Adoption: A Handful of Hope.* Berkeley: Celestial Arts, 1990.

Arnup, Katherine, ed. *Lesbian Parenting: Living with Pride and Prejudice.* Charlottetown, Prince Edward Island: Gynergy Books, 1995.

Banks, Ann. *When Your Parents Get a Divorce: A Kid's Journal.* New York: Puffin/Penguin Group, 1991.

Baptiste, Jr., D.A. "Psychotherapy with Gay/Lesbian Couples and their Children in 'Stepfamilies': A Challenge for Marriage and Family Therapists." In *Integrated Identity for Gay Men and Lesbians: Psychotherapeutic Approaches for Emotional Well-being*, edited by E. Coleman. New York: Harrington Park Press, 1988: 223-238.

Barret, R.L. and B.E. Robinson. *Gay Fathers.* Lexington, Massachusetts: D.C. Heath and Company, 1990.

Barrett, Susan E. and Carol M. Aubin. "Feminist Considerations of Intercountry Adoptions." *Women & Therapy*, 10(1/2), (1990): 127-138.

Bartholet, Elizabeth. *Family Bonds: Adoption and the Politics of Parenting.* New York: Houghton Mifflin Co., 1993.

Bassoff, Evelyn S. *Between Mothers and Sons: The Making of Vital and Loving Men.* New York: Dutton, 1994.

Bates, J. Douglas. *Gift Children: A Story of Race, Family and Adoption in a Divided America.* New York: Ticknor & Fields, 1993.

Baumrind, Diana. "The Influence of Parenting Style on Adolescent Competence and Substance Use." *Journal of Early Adolescence*, 11, (1991): 56-95.

Baumrind, Diana. "Effective Parenting During the Early Adolescent Transition." In *Family Transitions*, edited by P. A. Cowen and M. Hetherington. Hillsdale, NJ: Lawrence Erlbaum Associates, 1991: 111-164.

Becker, Carol. *Unbroken Ties: Lesbian Ex-lovers.* Boston: Alyson Publications, 1988.

Benkov, Laura. *Reinventing the Family: The Emerging Story of Lesbian and Gay Parents.* New York: Crown Publishers, 1994.

Benson, Peter L. and Anu Sharma. "The Truth about Adopted Teenagers." *Adoptive Families,* 27(4), (1994): 16-20.

Benson, Peter L., Anu Sharma and Eugene C. Roehlkepartain. *Growing Up Adopted: A Portrait of Adolescents and their Families.* Minneapolis: Search Institute, 1994.

Berg, Elizabeth. *Family Traditions: Celebrations for Holidays and Everyday.* Pleasantville, NY: Readers Digest Association, Inc., 1992.

Bernstein, Anne C. *Flight of the Stork: What Children Think (and When) about Sex and Family Building.* Indianopolis, IN: Perspectives Press, 1995.

Berzon, Betty. "Sharing Your Lesbian Identity with Your Children." In *Our Right to Love: A Lesbian Resource Book,* edited by G. Vida. Englewood Cliffs, NJ: Prentice-Hall, 1978.

Berzon, Betty. *Permanent Partners: Building Gay and Lesbian Relationships that Last.* New York: E.P. Dutton, 1988.

Bingham, Mindy and Sandy Stryker. *Things Will Be Different for My Daughter: A Practical Guide to Building Her Self-esteem and Self-reliance.* New York: Penguin, 1995.

Blau, Melinda. *Families Apart: Ten Keys to Successful Co-Parenting.* New York: G.P. Putnam's Sons, 1993.

Blumstein, P. and P. Schwartz. *American Couples.* New York: William Morrow and Co., 1983.

Bosche, Suzanne. *Jenny Lives with Eric and Martin.* London: Gay Men's Press, 1981.

Bozett, Frederick W., ed. *Gay and Lesbian Parents.* New York: Praeger, 1987.

Brazelton, T. Berry. *Touchpoints: Your Child's Emotional and Behavioral Development, The Essential Reference.* Redding, MA: Addison-Wesley, 1992.

Briggs, Dorothy Corkille. *Your Child's Self-Esteem: The Key to Life.* New York: Dolphin/Doubleday, 1975.

Brodzinsky, David M. *Adopting the Older Child.* Boston: The Harvard Common Press, 1978.

Brodzinsky, David M., Marshall D. Schechter and Robin Marantz Henig. *Being Adopted: The Lifelong Search for Self.* New York: Anchor/Doubleday, 1992.

Brown, Lyn Mikel and Carol Gilligan. *Meeting at the Crossroads: Women's Psychology and Girl's Development.* New York: Ballantine Books, 1992.

Burke, Phyllis. *Family Values: Two Moms and Their Son.* New York: Random House, 1993.

Butler, Becky. *Ceremonies of the Heart: Celebrating Lesbian Unions.* Seattle: Seal

Press, 1990.

Bush, Richard. *A Parents' Guide to Child Therapy.* Northvale, NJ: Aronson, 1994.

Calladine, Andrew and Carole Calladine. *Raising Siblings.* New York: Delacorte, 1979.

Caplan, Frank, ed. *The First Twelve Months of Life: Your Baby's Growth Month by Month.* New York: Grosset & Dunlap, 1973.

Caplan, Frank and Theresa Caplan. *The Second Twelve Months of Life: A Kaleidoscope of Growth.* New York: Perigee/Putnam Publishing Group, 1977.

Caplan, Theresa and Frank Caplan. *The Early Childhood Years: The 2 to 6 Year Old.* New York: Dell Publishing Group, 1983.

Caron, Ann F. *Don't Stop Loving Me: A Reassuring Guide for Mothers of Adolescent Girls.* New York: Harper Perennial, 1991.

Caron, Ann F. *Strong Mothers, Strong Sons: Raising Adolescent Boys in the 90's.* New York: Henry Holt & Co., 1994.

Chess, Stella and Alexander Thomas. *Know Your Child: An Authoritative Guide for Today's Parents.* New York: Basic Books/HarperCollins, 1987.

Clark, Don. *Loving Someone Gay.* Millbrae, CA: Celestial Arts, 1987.

Clarke, Jean Illsley. *Self-Esteem: A Family Affair.* Minneapolis: Winston Press, 1978.

Clarke, Jean Illsley. *HELP! for Parents from Birth to Five* (rev. ed.). San Francisco: Harper, 1993.

Clarke, Jean Illsley. *HELP! for Parents of School-age Children and Teenagers.* San Francisco: Harper, 1993.

Clarke, Jean Illsley and Connie Dawson. *Growing Up Again: Parenting Ourselves, Parenting Our Children.* San Francisco: Harper & Row, 1989.

Clarke, Jean Illsley, Carole Gesme, Marlon London and Donald Brundage. *HELP! for Kids and Parents about Drugs.* San Francisco: Harper, 1993.

Clunis, D. Merilee and G. Dorsey Green. *Lesbian Couples: Creating Healthy Relationships for the 90s.* Seattle: Seal Press, 1993.

Cole, Diane. *After Great Pain: A New Life Emerges.* New York: Summit Books, 1992.

Comer, James P. and Alvin F. Poussaint. *Raising Black Children.* New York: Plume, 1992.

Corley, Rip. *The Final Closet: The Gay Parent's Guide to Coming Out to Their Children.* Miami: Editech Press, 1990.

Craig, Judi. *Little Kids, Big Questions: Practical Answers to the Difficult Questions Children Ask about Life.* New York: Hearst Books, 1993.

Craig, Judi. *Parents on the Spot: What to Do When Kids Put You There.* New York: Hearst Books, 1994.

Cramer, D. "Gay Parents and their Children: A Review of Research and Practical Implications." *Journal of Counseling and Development*, 64, (1986): 504-507.

Creedy, Kathryn B. "When Kids Ask about Adoption." *Adoptive Families*, 27(4), (1994): 8-12.

Crawford, Sally. "Lesbian Families: Psychosocial Stress and the Family Building Process." In *Lesbian Psychologies*, edited by The Boston Lesbian Psychologies Collective. Urbana, IL: University of Illinois Press, 1987:195-214.

Curry, Hayden and Denis Clifford. *A Legal Guide for Lesbian and Gay Couples.* Berkeley: Nolo Press, 1991.

Deutsch, Morton. "Educating for a Peaceful World." *American Psychologist*, 48 (5), (1993): 510-517.

Di Bella, G.A.W. "Family Psychotherapy with the Homosexual Family: A Community Psychiatry Approach to Homosexuality." *Community Mental Health Journal*, 15(1), (1979): 41-46.

Dreikurs, Rudolf. *Children: The Challenge.* New York: Plume, 1990.

Durrell, Doris D. *Starting Out Right: Essential Parenting Skills for Your Child's First Seven Years.* Oakland, CA: Harbinger, 1989.

Eagle, Carol J. and Carol Colman. *All That She Can Be: Helping Your Daughter Maintain Her Self-Esteem.* New York: Simon & Schuster, 1993.

Edelman, Hope. *Motherless Daughters.* Reading, MA: Addison-Wesley, 1994.

Eisenberg, Arlene, Heidi E. Murkoff and Sandee E. Hathaway. *What to Exepct When You're Expecting.* New York: Workman Publishers, 1988.

Eisenberg, Arlene, Heidi E. Murkoff and Sandee E. Hathaway. *What to Expect the First Year.* New York: Workman Publishers, 1988.

Eisenberg, Arlene, Heidi E. Murkoff and Sandee E. Hathaway. *What to Expect the Toddler Years.* New York: Workman Publishers, 1994.

Elium, Don and Jeanne Elium. *Raising a Son: Parents and the Making of a Healthy Man.* Hillsboro, OR: Beyond Words Publishing, 1992.

Elium, Don and Jeanne Elium. *Raising a Daughter: Parents and the Awakening of a Healthy Woman.* Berkeley, CA: Celestial Arts, 1994.

Elwin, Rosamund and Michele Paulse. *Asha's Mums.* Toronto: Women's Press, 1990.

Erikson, Erik H. *Childhood and Society.* New York: W.W. Norton, 1963.

Erikson, Erik H. *Identity, Youth and Crisis.* New York: W.W. Norton, 1968.

Erlichman, K.L. "Lesbian Mothers: Ethical Issues in Social Work Practice." *Women and Therapy*, 8(1-2), (1988): 207-221.

Estess, Patricia Schiff and Irving Barocas. *Kids, Money and Values: Creative Ways to Teach Your Kids about Money.* Cincinnati, OH: Betterway Books, 1994.

Faber, Adele and Elaine Mazlish. *How to Talk So Kids Will Listen & Listen so Kids Will Talk.* New York: Avon Books, 1980.

Faber, Adele and Elaine Mazlish. *Siblings Without Rivalry*. New York: Avon Books, 1987.

Fairchild, Betty and Nancy Hayward. *Now That You Know: What Every Parent Should Know About Homosexuality*. New York: Harcourt Brace Jovanovich, 1990.

Falco, K. *Psychotherapy with Lesbian Clients*. New York: Brunner/Mazel, 1990.

Falk, P. "Lesbian Mothers: Psychosocial Assumptions in Family Law." *American Psychologist*, 44(6), (1989): 941-947.

Ferber, Richard. *Solve Your Child's Sleep Problems*. New York: Simon & Schuster, 1985.

Fischer, Kurt W. and Daniel Bullock. "Cognitive Development in School-Age Children: Conclusions and New Directions." In *Development During Middle Childhood: The Years From Six to Twelve*, edited by W. Andrew Collins. Washington, DC: National Academy Press, 1984: 70-146.

Flaks, David K., Ilda Ficher, Frank Mastersapqua and Gregory Joseph. "Lesbians Choosing Motherhood: A Comparative Study of Lesbian and Heterosexual Parents and Their Children." *Developmental Psychology*, 31(1), (1995): 105-114.

Fowler, Mary Cahill. *Maybe You Know My Kid: A Parent's Guide to Identifying, Understanding and Helping Your Child with Attention-Deficit Hyperactivity Disorder*. New York: Birch Lane Press, 1990.

Freedman, Marc. *The Kindness of Strangers: Adult Mentors, Urban Youth, and the New Voluntarism*. San Francisco: Jossey-Bass, 1993.

Garden, Nancy. *Annie on My Mind*. New York: Farrar, Straus & Giroux, 1982.

Gardner, James E. *The Turbulent Teens*. Los Angeles: Sorrento Press, 1983.

Gibbs, E.D. "Psychosocial Development of Children Raised by Lesbian Mothers: A Review of Research. " *Women and Therapy*, 8(1,2), (1988): 65-75.

Gil de Lamadrid, Maria, ed. *Lesbians Choosing Motherhood: Legal Implications of Donor Insemination and Co-Parenting*. San Francisco: National Center for Lesbian Rights, 1991.

Gilman, Lois. *The Adoption Resource Book*. New York: Harper Perennial, 1992.

Ginnott, Haim. *Between Parent and Child*. New York: Avon Books, 1956.

Glenn, H. Stephen and Jane Nelsen. *Raising Self-Reliant Children in a Self-Indulgent World*. Rocklin, CA: Prima Publishing, 1989.

Gold, Melanie A., Ellen C. Perrin, Donna Futterman and Stanford B. Friedman. "Children of Gay or Lesbian Parents." *Pediatrics in Review*, 15(9), (September, 1994): 354-358.

Golden, Marita. *Saving Our Sons: Raising Black Children in a Turbulent World*. New York: Doubleday, 1995.

Golumbok, S., A. Spencer and M. Rutter. "Children in Lesbian and Single-Parent Households: Psychosexual and Psychiatric Appraisal." *Journal of Child Psy-*

chology and Psychiatry, 24, (1983): 551.

Gonsiorek, John C. and James D. Weinrich, eds. *Homosexuality: Research Implications for Public Policy*. Newberry Park, CA: Sage Publications, 1991.

Goodman, B. "The Lesbian Mother." *American Journal of Orthopsychiatry*, 43, (1973): 283-284.

Goodwillie, Susan, ed. *Voices from the Future: Our Children Tell Us about Violence in America*. New York: Crown, 1993.

Gordon, Thomas. *P.E.T. Parent Effectiveness Training: The Tested New Way To Raise Responsible Children*. New York: Plume/Penguin Group, 1975.

Gottfried, Adele Eskeles and Allen W. Gottfried, eds. *Redefining Families: Implications for Children's Development*. New York: Plenum, 1994.

Green, G. Dorsey. "Mental Health Considerations of Lesbian Mothers." In *Gay and Lesbian Parents*, edited by Frederick W. Bozett. New York: Praeger, 1987.

Green, G. Dorsey and D. Merilee Clunis. "Married Lesbians." *Women and Therapy*, 8(1-2), (1989): 41-47.

Green, G. Dorsey and Frederick W. Bozett. "Lesbian Mothers and Gay Fathers." In *Homosexuality: Research Implicatons for Public Policy*, edited by J.C. Gonsiorer and J.D. Weinrich. Newbury Park, CA: Sage, 1991.

Green, R. "Sexual Identity of 37 Children Raised by Homosexual or Transsexual Parents." *American Journal of Psychiatry*, 135, (1978): 692-697.

Green, R. "The Best Interests of the Child with a Lesbian Mother." *Bulletin of the American Academy of Psychiatry and the Law*, 10, (1982): 7-15.

Green, R., J.B. Mandel, M.E. Hotvedt, J. Gray and L. Smith. "Lesbian Mothers and their Children: A Comparison with Solo Parent Heterosexual Mothers and their Children." *Archives of Sexual Behavior*, 15, (1986):167-184.

Greene, Beverly. "Sturdy Bridges: The Role of African-American Mothers in the Socialization of African-American Children." *Women & Therapy: A Feminist Quarterly*, 10(1/2), (1990): 205-225.

Greene, Lawrence J. *Learning Disabilities and Your Child: A Survival Handbook*. New York: Fawcett Columbine, 1987.

Greenspan, Stanley I. *Playground Politics: Understanding the Emotional Life of Your School-Age Child*. New York: Addison-Wesley, 1994.

Greydanus, Donald E. (editor-in-chief, American Academy of Pediatrics). *Caring for Your Adolescent (ages 12-21): The Complete and Authoritative Guide*. New York: Bantam, 1991.

Griffin, Carol Welch, Marian J. Wirth and Arthur G. Wirth. *Beyond Acceptance: Parents of Lesbians and Gays Talk about Their Experiences*. New York: St. Martin's Press, 1990.

Hacker, Andrew. *Two Nations: Black and White, Separate, Hostile, Unequal*. New York: Ballantine, 1992.

Hall, M. "Lesbian Families: Cultural and Clinical Issues." *Social Work,* 23, (1978): 380-385.

Hanscombe, Gillian E. and Jackie Forster. *Rocking the Cradle: Lesbian Mothers, A Challenge to Family Living.* Boston: Alyson Publications, 1982.

Harris, M. B. and P.H. Turner. "Gay and Lesbian Parents." *Journal of Homosexuality,* 12(2), (1985/86): 101-113.

Hart, B. "Lesbian Battering: An Examination." In *Naming the Violence: Speaking Out About Lesbian Battering,* edited by K. Lobel. Seattle: Seal Press, 1986:173-189.

Helms, Janet E. *A Race is a Nice Thing to Have.* Topeka, KS: Content Communications, 1992.

Helms, Janet E., ed. *Black and White Racial Identity: Theory, Research and Practice.* New York: Praeger, 1993.

Herron, Ann and Meredith Maran. *How Would You Feel if Your Dad Was Gay?* Boston: Alyson Publications, 1991.

Hochman, Anndee. *Everyday Acts and Small Subversions: Women Reinventing Family, Community, and Home.* Portland, OR: Eighth Mountain Press, 1994.

Hoeffer, B. "Children's Acquisition of Sex-role Behavior in Lesbian-mother Families." *American Journal of Orthopsychiatry,* 51, (1981): 536-544.

Hopson, Darlene Powell and Derek Hopson. *Different and Wonderful: Raising Black Children in a Race-Conscious Society.* New York: Fireside, 1990.

Hopson, Darlene Powell and Derek Hopson. *Raising the Rainbow Generation: Teaching Your Children to be Successful in a Multicultural Society.* New York: Fireside, 1993.

Hotvedt, Mary E. and Jane Barclay Mandel. "Children of Lesbian Mothers." In *Homosexuality: Social, Psychological and Biological Issues,* edited by William Paul, James D. Weinrich, John C. Gonsiorek, and Mary E. Hotvedt. Beverly Hills, CA: Sage, 1982: 287-285.

Huggins, S.L. "A Comparative Study of Self-esteem of Adolescent Children of Divorced Lesbian Mothers and Divorced Heterosexual Mothers." *Journal of Homosexuality,* 18(1,2), (1989):123-136.

Hunter, N.D. and N. D. Polikoff. "Custody Rights of Lesbian Mothers: Legal Theory and Litigation Strategy." *Buffalo Law Review,* 25, (1976): 691-733.

Ilg, Francis, Louise Bates Ames, and Sidney M. Baker. *Child Behavior* (rev. ed.). New York: HarperCollins, 1992.

Ingersoll, Mary Cahill. *Maybe You Know My Kid: A Parent's Guide to Identifying, Understanding and Helping Your Child with Attention-Deficit Hyperactivity Disorder.* New York: Birch Lane Press, 1990.

Jarratt, Claudia Jewett. *Helping Children Cope with Separation and Loss* (rev. ed.). Boston: The Harvard Common Press, 1994.

Jenness, Aylette. *Families: A Celebration of Diversity, Commitment and Love.* Boston: Houghton Mifflin Co., 1990.

Jordan, Mary Kate. *Losing Uncle Tim.* Niles, IL: Albert Whitman & Co., 1989.

Kennedy, Marge and Janet Spencer King. *The Single Parent Family: Living Happily in a Changing World.* New York: Bantam, 1991.

Kennedy, Patricia, Leif Terdal and Lydia Fusetti. *The Hyperactive Child Book.* New York: St. Martin's Press, 1994.

Kirkpatrick, M. "Clinical Implications of Lesbian Mother Studies." *Journal of Homosexuality,* 14(1,2), (1987): 201-212.

Kirkpatrick, M. and D.J. Hitchens. "Lesbian Mothers and Gay Fathers." In *Emerging Issues in Child Psychiatry and the Law,* edited by Benedek and Shetky. New York: Brunner/Mazel, 1985.

Kirkpatrick, M., C. Smith and R. Roy. "Lesbian Mothers and Their Children." *American Journal of Orthopsychiatry,* 51, (1981): 545-551.

Kitzinger, Sheila. *The Complete Book of Pregnancy and Childbirth.* New York: Knopf, 1980.

Kitzinger, Sheila. *Giving Birth: How It Really Feels.* New York: Farrar, Straus & Giroux, 1989.

Kleber, D., R. Howell, and A.L. Tibbits-Kleber. "The Impact of Parental Homosexuality in Child Custody Cases: A Review of the Literature." *Bulletin of the American Academy of Psychiatry and the Law,* 14(1), (1986): 81-87.

Klein, Norma. *Breaking Up.* New York: Random House, 1980.

Klein, Norma. *Now That I Know.* New York: Bantam, 1988.

Klein, Stanley and Maxwell J. Schleifer, eds. *It Isn't Fair: Siblings of Children with Disabilities.* Granby, MA: Bergin & Garvey, 1993.

Knight, R. "Female Homosexuality and the Custody of Children." *New Zealand Journal of Psychology,* 12(1), (1983): 23-27.

Konner, Melvin. *Childhood: A Multicultural View.* Boston: Little, Brown & Co., 1991.

Kreston, J. and C.S. Besko. "The Problem of Fusion in the Lesbian Relationship." *Family Process* 19(3), (1980): 277-289.

Kübler-Ross, Elisabeth. *On Death and Dying.* New York: Macmillan, 1970.

Kweskin, S.L. and A.S. Cook. "Heterosexual and Homosexual Mothers' Self-described Sex-role Behavior and Ideal Sex-role Behavior in Children." *Sex Roles,* 8, (1982): 967-975.

La Leche League. *The Womanly Art of Breastfeeding.* New York: Plume, 1991.

Laskin, David and Kathleen. *The Little Girl Book.* New York: Ballantine, 1992.

Leach, Penelope. *Your Baby and Child: From Birth to Age Five.* New York: Knopf, 1986.

Leshan, Eda. *When Your Child Drives You Crazy.* New York: St. Martin's Press, 1985.

Leshan, Eda. *Grandparenting in a Changing World.* New York: Newmarket Press, 1993.Leslie, Marsha R., ed. *The Single Mother's Companion: Essays and Stories by Women.* Seattle: Seal Press, 1994.

Leslie, Marsha R., ed. *The Single Mother's Companion: Essays and Stories by Women.* Seattle: Seal Press, 1994.

Levy, Barrie, ed. *Dating Violence: Young Women in Danger.* Seattle: Seal Press, 1991.

Levy, Barrie and Patricia Occhiuzzo Giggans. *What Parents Need to Know About Dating Violence.* Seattle: Seal Press, 1995.

Lewin, Ellen. "Lesbianism and Motherhood: Implications for Child Custody." *Human Organization,* 40, (1981): 6-14.

Lewin, Ellen. *Lesbian Mothers: Accounts of Gender in American Culture.* Ithaca, NY: Cornell University Press, 1993.

Lewin, Ellen and Terrie A. Lyons. "Everything in its Place: The Coexistence of Lesbianism and Motherhood." In *Homosexuality: Social, Psychological and Biological Issues,* edited by William Paul, James D. Weinrich, John C. Gonsiorek, and Mary E. Hotvedt. Beverly Hills, CA: Sage, 1982: 249-273.

Lewis, K. "Children of Lesbians: Their Point of View." *Social Work,* 25(3), (1980): 198-203.

Lickona, Thomas. *Raising Good Children: From Birth Through the Teenage Years.* New York: Bantam, 1985.

Lieber, Phyllis, Gloria S. Murphy and Annette Mirkur Schwartz. *Grown-up Children, Grown-up Parents: Opening the Door to Healthy Relationships Between Parents and Adult Children.* New York: Birch Lane Press, 1994.

Lieberman, Susan Abel. *New Traditions.* New York: Noonday Press, 1991.

Loulan, J. "Psychotherapy with Lesbian Mothers." In *Contemporary Perspectives on Psychotherapy with Lesbians and Gay Men.,* edited by T. S Stein and C. J. Cohen. New York: Plenum, 1986.

MacKenzie, Robert J. *Setting Limits.* Rocklin, CA: Prima Publishing, 1993.

MacPike, Loralee, ed. *There's Something I've Been Meaning to Tell You.* Tallahassee, FL: The Naiad Press, 1989.

Mannion, K. *Female Homosexuality: A Comprehensive Review of Theory and Research.* Washington: American Psychological Association. (Catalogue of Selected Documents, 6:44), 1976.

Marks, Jane. *We Have a Problem: A Parent's Sourcebook.* New York: HarperCollins, 1993.

Marshall, Melinda M. *Good Enough Mothers: Changing Expectations for Ourselves.* Princeton, NJ: Peterson's, 1993.

Martin, April. *The Lesbian and Gay Parenting Handbook: Creating and Raising Our Families.* New York: HarperCollins, 1993.

McCoy, Kathleen. *Understanding Your Teenager's Depression: Issues, Insights and Practical Guidance for Parents.* New York: Berkley Publishing Group, 1994.

McDermott, John F. Jr. *Raising Cain & Abel Too: The Parents' Book of Sibling Rivalry.* New York: P.E.I. Books, 1981.

McKay, Matthew, Peter Rogers, Joan Blades, and Richard Gose. *The Divorce Book.* Oakland, CA: New Harbinger Publications, 1984.

McNamara, Joan. "Growing Up Adopted: Facing Prejudice." *Adoptive Families,* 7(6), (1990): 60.

Melina, Lois Ruskin. *Raising Adopted Children.* New York: Harper & Row, 1986.

Melina, Lois Ruskin and Sharon Kaplan Roszia. *The Open Adoption Experience.* New York: Harper Perennial, 1993.

Merriam, Eve. *Mommies at Work.* New York: Simon & Schuster, 1989.

Miller, J.A., R.B. Jacobsen and J.J. Bigner. "The Child's Home Environment for Lesbian v. Heterosexual Mothers: A Neglected Area of Research." *Journal of Homosexuality,* 7(1), (1981): 49-56.

Moses, A.E. and R.O. Hawkins. *Counseling Lesbian Women and Gay Men.* St. Louis: The C. V. Mosely Co, 1982.

Mucklow, B.M. and G.K. Phelan. "Lesbian and Traditional Mothers' Responses to Adult Response to Child Behavior and Self-concept." *Psychological Reports,* 44, (1979): 880-882.

National PTA and Anti-Defamation League of B'Nai B'rith. *What to Tell Your Child About Prejudice and Discrimination.* New York: 1989.

Nechas, Eileen and Denise Foley. *"What Do I Do Now?": Parent-Tested, Expert-Approved Solutions to 100 Common and Uncommon Parenting Problems.* New York: Simon & Schuster, 1992.

Nelson, Jane, Cheryl Erwin and Carol Delzer. *Positive Discipline for Single Parents.* Rocklin, CA: Prima Publishing, 1994.

Nelson, Jane, Lynn Lott and H. Stephen Glenn. *Positive Discipline A-Z: 1001 Solutions to Everyday Parenting Problems.* Rocklin, CA: Prima Publishing, 1993.

Newcomb, M.D. "The Role of Perceived Relative Parent Personality in the Development of Heterosexuals, Homosexuals, and Transvestites." *Archives of Sexual Behavior,* 14(2), (1985): 147-164.

Newman, Lesléa. *Belinda's Bouquet.* Boston: Alyson Publications, 1991.

Newman, Lesléa. *Gloria Goes to Gay Pride.* Boston: Alyson Publications, 1991.

Newman, Lesléa. *Heather Has Two Mommies.* Boston: Alyson Publications, 1989.

Newman, Margaret. *Stepfamilies: How to Overcome Difficulties and Have a Happy Family.* Oakland, CA: New Harbinger Publications, 1989.

Nichols, J. Randall. *Ending Marriage, Keeping Faith: A New Guide Through the Spiritual Journey of Divorce*. New York: Crossroad, 1993

Noble, E. *Having Your Baby by Donor Insemination*. Boston: Houghton Mifflin Co., 1987.

Nungesser, Lonnie G. "Theoretical Bases for Research on the Acquisition of Social Sex-roles by Children of Lesbian Mothers." *Journal of Homosexuality*, 5(3), (1980):177-187.

Offer, Daniel and K. A. Schonert-Reichl. "Debunking the Myths of Adolescence: Findings from Recent Research." *Journal of American Academy of Child and Adolescent Psychiatry*, 31, (1992): 1003-1014.

Ostrow, D. "Gay and Straight Parents: What about the Children?" Unpublished bachelor's thesis, Hampshire College, Amherst, MA, 1977.

Pagelow, M. "Heterosexual and Lesbian Single Mothers: A Comparison of Problems, Coping, and Solutions." *Journal of Homosexuality*, 5, (1980):189-204.

Palmer, Pat. *"I Wish I Could Hold Your Hand . . .": A Child's Guide to Grief and Loss*. San Louis Obispo, CA: Impact Press, 1994.

Parker, Roberta N. and Harvey Parker. *Making the Grade: An Adolescent's Struggle with Attention Deficit Disorder*. San Luis Obispo, CA: Impact Press, 1992.

Patterson, Charlotte J. "Children of Lesbian and Gay Parents." *Child Development*, 63, (1992): 1025-1042.

Patterson, Charlotte J. "Families of the Lesbian Baby Boom: Parents' Division of Labor and Children's Adjustment." *Developmental Psychology*, 1(31), (1995): 115-123.

Patterson, Charlotte J. "Children of the Lesbian Baby Boom: Behavioral Adjustment, Self Concepts, and Sex Role Identity." In *Contemporary Perspectives on Gay and Lesbian Psychology: Theory, Research and Applications*, edited by B. Greene and G. Herek. Thousand Oaks, CA: Sage, 1994.

Penelope, Julia, ed. *Out of the Closet: Lesbians Speak*. Freedom, CA: The Crossing Press, 1994.

Perez, Pauline. *Special Woman: The Role of the Professional Labor Assistant*. Seattle: Cutting Edge Press, 1994.

Pharr, Suzanne. *Homophobia: A Weapon of Sexism*. Inverness, CA: Chardon Press, 1988.

Philadelphia Child Guidance Center. *Your Child's Emotional Health: Adolescence*. New York: Macmillan, 1993.

Phillips, Angela. *The Trouble with Boys: A Wise and Sympathetic Guide to the Risky Business of Raising Sons*. New York: Basic Books, 1994.

Pies, Cheri. *Considering Parenthood* (second edition). Minneapolis: Spinsters Ink, 1988.

Pies, Cheri. "Lesbians Choosing Children: The Use of Social Group Work in

Maintaining and Strengthening the Primary Relationship." *Journal of Social Work and Human Sexuality*, 5(2), (1987): 79-88.

Pipher, Mary. *Reviving Ophelia: Saving the Selves of Adolescent Girls.* New York: G.P. Putnam's Sons, 1994.

Polikoff, N.D. "Lesbian Mothers, Lesbian Families: Legal Obstacles, Legal Challenges." *Review of Law and Social Change*, 14(4), (1986): 907-914.

Pollack, Sandra. "Lesbian Parents: Claiming Our Visibility." *Women & Therapy: A Feminist Quarterly*, 10(1/2), (1990):181-194.

Pollack, Sandra and Jeanne Vaughn, eds. *Politics of the Heart: A Lesbian Parenting Anthology.* Ithaca, NY: Firebrand Books, 1987.

Powell, Douglas H. *Teenagers: When to Worry and What to Do.* New York: Doubleday, 1986.

Rafkin, Louise, ed. *Different Daughters.* Pittsburgh, PA: Cleis Press, 1987.

Rafkin, Louise, ed. *Different Mothers.* Pittsburgh, PA: Cleis Press, 1990.

Rand, C., D.L.R. Graham and E.I. Rawlings. "Psychological Health and Factors the Court Seeks to Control in Lesbian Mother Custody Trials." *Journal of Homosexuality*, 8(1), (1982): 27-39.

Raphael, S. and M. Robinson. "The Older Lesbian: Love Relationships and Friendship Patterns." In *Women-Identified Women*, edited by T. Darty and S. Porter. Palo Alto: Mayfield, 1984.

Reddy, Maureen T. *Crossing the Color Line: Race, Parenting and Culture.* New Brunswick, NJ: Rutgers University Press, 1994.

Reddy, Maureen T., Amy Sheldon and Martha Roth, eds. *Mother Journeys: Feminists Write About Mothering.* Minneapolis: Spinsters Ink, 1994.

Register, Cheri. *Are Those Kids Yours?* New York: Free Press, 1990.

Register, Cheri. "Answering Nosy Questions." *Adoptive Families*, 27(4), (1994): 22-24.

Ricci, Isolina. *Mom's House, Dad's House: Making Shared Custody Work.* New York: Collier/Macmillan Publishing, 1980.

Richardson, D. "Lesbian Mothers." In *The Theory and Practice of Homosexuality*, edited by J. Hart and D. Richardson. London: Routledge and Kegan Paul, 1981.

Ricketts, Wendell. *Lesbian and Gay Men as Foster Parents.* Portland, ME: Edmund S. Muskie Clearinghouse, National Child Welfare Resource Center for Management and Administration, University of Southern Maine, 1992.

Ricketts, Wendell and Roberta Achtenberg. "The Adoptive and Foster Gay and Lesbian Parent." In *Gay and Lesbian Parents*, edited by Frederick W. Bozett. New York: Praeger, 1987.

Rivera, R.R. "Legal Issues in Gay and Lesbian Parenting." In *Gay and Lesbian Parents*, edited by Frederick W. Bozett. New York: Praeger, 1987.

Rizzo, Cindy, Jo Schneiderma, Lisa Schweig, Jan Shafer and Judith Stein, ed. *All the Ways Home: Parenting and Children in the Lesbian and Gay Communities*. Norwich, VT: New Victoria Publishers Inc., 1995.

Roberts, Colleen Alexander. *The Essential Adoption Handbook*. Dallas, TX: Taylor Publishing Co., 1993.

Rohrbaugh, Joanna Bunker. "Choosing Children: Psychological Issues in Lesbian Parenting." In *Lesbianism: Affirming Nontraditional Roles*, edited by Esther D. Rothblum, and Ellen Cole, a special edition of *Women & Therapy*, 8(1/2). New York: Haworth Press, Inc., (1988): 51-64.

Rohrbaugh, Joanna Bunker. "Lesbian Families: Clinical Issues and Theoretical Implications." *Professional Psychology: Research and Practice*, 23(8), (1992): 467-473.

Root, Maria P.P. "Multiracial Contribution to the Psychological Browning of America." In *American Mixed Races: The Culture of Microdiversity*, edited by Naomi Zack. Lanham, Maryland: Rowman and Littlefield, 1995.

Root, Maria P. P. "Bill of Rights for People with Multiracial Identity." In *Racially Mixed People in the New Millenium*. Newbury Park, CA: Sage, (in press).

Rothblum, Esther D. "Introduction: Lesbianism as a Model of a Positive Lifestyle for Women." *Women & Therapy*, 8(1/2), (1988): 1-12.

Saffron, Lisa. *Challenging Conceptions: Planning a Family by Self-Insemination*. London: Cassell, 1994.

Salwen, Laura V. "The Myth of the Wicked Stepmother." *Women & Therapy: A Feminist Quarterly*, 10(1/2), (1990): 117-125.

Samuels, Mike and Nancy Samuels. *The Well Pregnancy Book*. New York: Fireside, 1986.

Sang, B. "Lesbian Relationships: A Struggle Toward Partner Equality." In *Women-Identified Women*, edited by T. Darty and S. Porter. Palo Alto: Mayfield, 1984.

Saphira, M. *Amazon Mothers*. Ponsonby, New Zealand: Papers, Inc., 1984.

Schaefer, Charles E. and Theresa Foy DiGeronimo. *Helping Children Get the Most out of School: How to Instill Essential Learning Skills in Children Ages 6-13*. Northvale, NJ: Aronson, 1994.

Schaefer, Charles E. and Theresa Foy DiGeronimo. *How to Talk to Your Kids about Really Important Things*. San Francisco: Jossey-Bass, 1994.

Schaefer, Charles E. and Howard L. Millman. *How to Help Children with Common Problems*. New York: Plume, 1989.

Schaffer, Judith and Cristina Lindstrom. *How to Raise an Adopted Child*. New York: Plume, 1991.

Schulenburg, J. *Gay Parenting*. New York: Anchor Press/Doubleday, 1985.

Scoppettone, Sandra. *Happy Endings Are All Alike*. New York: Harper & Row,

1978.

Sears, Vickie L. "Cross-cultural Ethnic relationships." Unpublished manuuscript, 1987.

Sears, William and Martha Sears. *The Baby Book: Everything You Need to Know About Your Baby—From Birth to Age Two.* Boston: Little, Brown & Co., 1993.

Severance, Jane. *Lots of Mommies.* Chapel Hill, NC: Lollipop Power, 1983.

Shavelson, E., M. Biaggio, H. Cross and R. Lehman. "Lesbian Women's Perceptions of their Parent-child Relationships." *Journal of Homosexuality,* 5(3), (1980): 205-215.

Sheiman, Deborah Lovitky and Maureen Slonim. *Resources for Middle Childhood: A Source Book.* New York: Garland Publishing, Inc., 1988.

Siegler, Ava L. *What Should I Tell the Kids: A Parent's Guide to Real Problems in the Real World.* New York: Dutton, 1993.

Silver, Larry B. *Dr. Larry Silver's Advice to Parents on Attention-Deficit Hyperactivity Disorder.* Washington, DC: American Psychiatric Press, 1993.

Silverstein, Olga and Beth Rashbaum. *The Courage to Raise Good Men.* New York: Penguin Books, 1994.

Simkin, Penny. *The Birth Partner.* Boston: The Harvard Common Press, 1989.

Simkin, Penny, Janet Whalley and Ann Keppler. *Pregnancy, Childbirth and the Newborn.* New York: Meadowbrook Press, 1991.

Simons, Robin. *After the Tears: Parents Talk about Raising a Child with a Disability.* San Diego, CA: Harcourt Brace Jovanovich, 1987.

Slaby, Andrew E. and Lili Frank Garfinkel. *No One Saw My Pain: Why Teens Kill Themselves.* New York: W.W. Norton, 1994.

Slater, Susan and J. Mencher. "The Lesbian Family Life Cycle: A Contextual Approach." *American Journal of Orthopsychiatry,* 61(3), (1991): 372-382.

Slater, Susan. *Lesbian Family Life Cycle.* New York: Free Press, 1995.

Somerville, M.A. "Birth Technology, Parenting and 'Deviance.'" *International Journal of Law and Psychiatry,* 5(2), (1982): 123-153.

Sophie, Joan. "Counseling Lesbians." *Personnel & Guidance Journal,* 60(6), (1982): 341-345.

Spock, Benjamin and Michael B. Rothenberg. *Dr. Spock's Baby and Child Care.* 6th Edition. New York: Pocket Books, 1992.

Statman, Paula. *On the Safe Side: Teaching Your Child to be Safe, Strong and Street-Smart.* New York: HarperCollins, 1995.

Steckel, A. "Separation-individuation in Children of Lesbian and Heterosexual Couples." Unpublished doctoral dissertation, Wright Institute, Berkeley, CA, 1985.

Steckel, A. "Psychosocial Development of Children of Lesbian Mothers." In

Gay and Lesbian Parents, edited by Frederick W. Bozett. New York: Praeger, 1987.

Stein, T.S. "Homosexuality and New Family Forms: Issues in Psychotherapy." *Psychiatric Annals,* 18(1), (1988): 12-20.

Steinberg, Laurence and Ann Levin. *You and Your Adolescent: A Parent's Guide for Ages 10-20.* New York: HarperCollins, 1990.

Stiglitz, Eloise. "Caught Between Two Worlds: The Impact of a Child on a Lesbian Couple's Relationship." *Women & Therapy: A Feminist Quarterly,* 10,(1/2), (1990): 99-116.

Susoeff, S. "Assessing Children's Best Interests when a Parent is Gay or Lesbian: Toward a National Custody Standard." *UCLA Law Review,* 32(4), (1985): 852-903.

Swigart, Jane. *The Myth of the Bad Mother: Parenting Without Guilt.* New York: Avon Books, 1991.

Taylor, Dena, ed. *Feminist Parenting.* Freedom, CA: The Crossing Press, 1994.

Trafford, Abigail. *Crazy Time: Surviving Divorce and Building a New Life.* New York: Harper Perennial/HarperCollins, 1992.

Turecki, Stanley and Sarah Wernick. *The Emotional Problems of Normal Children.* New York: Bantam, 1994.

Turner, P.H., L. Scadden and M.B. Harris. "Parenting in Gay and Lesbian Families." Paper presented at the First Future of Parenting Symposium, Chicago, IL, March, 1985.

Turner, P.H., L. Scadden and M.B. Harris. "Children in Lesbian and Single Parent Households: Psychosexual and Psychiatric Appraisal." *Journal of Gay and Lesbian Psychotherapy,* 1(3), (1990): 55-66.

Ulrig, L. *The Two of Us: Affirming, Celebrating and Symbolizing Gay and Lesbian Relationships.* Boston: Alyson Publications, 1984.

Valentine, Johnny. *Daddy Machine.* Boston: Alyson Publications, 1992.

Valentine, Johnny. *The Duke Who Outlawed Jelly Beans and Other Stories.* Boston: Alyson Publications, 1991.

Van Gulden, Holly and Lisa Bartells-Raab. *Real Parents, Real Children: Parenting the Adopted Child.* New York: Crossroad Publishing Co., 1993.

Wadia-Ells, Susan, ed. *The Adoption Reader: Birth Mothers, Adoptive Mothers and Adopted Daughters Tell Their Stories.* Seattle: Seal Press, 1995.

Wallerstein, Judith S. and Sandra Blakeslee. *Second Chances: Men, Women and Children a Decade After Divorce.* New York: Ticknor & Fields, 1990.

Watkins, Mary and Susan Fisher. *Talking with Young Children About Adoption.* New Haven, CT: Yale University Press, 1993.

Wattleton, Faye. *How to Talk to Your Child About Sexuality.* New York: Doubleday, 1986.

Webster-Stratton, Carolyn. *The Incredible Years: A Trouble Shooting Guide for Parents of Children Aged 3–8.* Toronto: Umbrella Press, 1993.

Weeks, R.B., A.P. Derdeyn and M. Langmon. "Two Cases of Children of Homosexuals." *Child Psychiatry and Human Development,* 6, (1975): 26-32.

Weitzman, Lenore J. *The Divorce Revolution: The Unexpected Social and Economic Consequences for Women and Children in America.* New York: Free Press, 1985.

Weston, Denise Chapman and Mark S. Weston. *Playful Parenting: Turning the Dilemma of Discipline into Fun and Games.* New York: G.P. Putnam's Sons, 1993.

Weston, Kath. *Families We Choose: Lesbians, Gays, Kinship.* New York: Columbia University Press, 1991.

Whittlin, W.A. "Homosexuality and Child Custody: A Psychiatric Viewpoint." *Conciliation Courts Review,* 21(1), (1983): 77-79.

Willhoite, Michael. *Daddy's Roommate.* Boston: Alyson Wonderland, 1990.

Willhoite, Michael. *Families: A Coloring Book.* Boston: Alyson Wonderland, 1991.

Williams, Kate. *A Parent's Guide for Suicidal and Depressed Teens.* Center City, MN: Hazelden, 1995.

Wolf, Anthony E. *"Get out of my life, but first could you drive Cheryl and me to the mall?": A Parents' Guide to the New Teenager.* New York: Farrar, Straus & Giroux, 1991.

Wolf, Anthony E. *"It's not fair, Jeremy Spencer's parents let him stay up all night": A Guide to the Tougher Parts of Parenting.* New York: Farrar, Straus & Giroux, 1995.

Woodman, N.J. and H.R. Lenna. *Counseling with Gay Men and Women.* San Francisco: Jossey-Bass, 1980.

Wyers, N. "Homosexuality in the Family: Lesbian and Gay Spouses." *Social Work,* 32(2), (1987): 143-148.

RESOURCES

Organizations experienced in legal and research issues related to lesbian and gay parenting:

National Gay and Lesbian Task Force
Family Issues Project
1517 U Street NW
Washington, DC 20009
(202) 332-6483

Lambda Legal Defense and
Education Fund
666 Broadway
New York, NY 10012
(212) 995-8585

Lesbian and Gay Parenting Project
c/o Lyon-Martin clinic
2480 Mission Street, Suite 214
San Francisco, CA 94110
(415) 525-7312

Lavender Families Resource Network
(previously Lesbian Mothers' Defense
Fund)
P.O. Box 21567
Seattle, WA 98111
(206) 325-2643

Organizations for lesbian and gay parents:

CenterKids
The Family Project
Lesbian/Gay Community Services
Center
208 West 13th Street
New York, NY 10011
(212) 620-7310

Love Makes a Family, Inc.
P.O. Box 11694
Portland, OR 97211
(503) 228-3892

National Gay and Lesbian Parents
Coalition
Post Office Box 50360
Washington, DC 20004
(202) 583-8029

Alternative insemination:

The Sperm Bank of California
Telegraph Hill Medical Plaza, Suite 2
3007 Telegraph Avenue
Oakland, CA 94609
(415) 444-2014

For information on adoption:

National Adoption Information
Clearinghouse
Suite 600
1400 I Street NW
Washington, DC 20005
(202) 842-1919

International Concerns Committee for
Children
Report on Foreign Adoption
911 Cypress Drive
Boulder, CO 80303
(303) 494-8333

For information on breastfeeding:

La Leche League International
P.O. Box 1209
Franklin Park, IL 60131
(800) LA LECHE
(708) 455-7730

For information on eating disorders:

Anorexia & Related Disorders, Inc.
P.O. Box 5102
Eugene, OR 97405
(503) 344-1144

American Anorexia & Bulemia
Association, Inc.
418 East 76th Street
New York, NY 10021
(212) 734-1114

For information on overeating support groups:

Overeaters Anonymous
World Service Office
P.O. Box 92870
Los Angeles, CA 90009
(310) 618-8835
(or check in your local telephone directory for the nearest OA branch)

For information on sexually transmitted diseases, contraception, and other reproductive issues:

Public Health Service AIDS Hotline: 1-800-342-AIDS

Teens Teaching Teens AIDS Prevention: 1-800-234-TEEN

Planned Parenthood
National Headquarters
810 Seventh Avenue
New York, NY 10019
(212) 541-7800
(check your telephone directory for a local branch)

For information and/or questions about alcohol and drugs:

The American Council for Drug
Education
5820 Hubbard Drive
Rockville, MD 20852

National Clearinghouse for Alcohol
Information
1776 Jefferson Street, 4th floor
Rockville, MD 20852

Mothers Against Drunk Driving
(MADD)
P.O. Box 18200
Fort Worth, TX 76118

Self-help groups:

Alcoholics Anonymous World
Services
Box 459, Grand Central Station
New York, NY 10163
(or check your local telephone
directory for nearest group)

Al-Anon & Alateen
P.O. Box 182
Madison Square Station
New York, NY 10159
1-800-344-2666 (U.S.)
1-800-443-4525 (Canada)

Narcotics Anonymous World Services
Office, Inc.
P.O. Box 622
SunValley, CA 91352

Hotlines:

Alcohol and Drug Helpline: 1-800-252-6465

Cocaine (and crack): 1-800-COCAINE

NIDA Prevention Information Line: 1-800-638-2045

For information about learning disabilities/ADD/ADHD:

A.D.D. Warehouse
300 Northwest 70th Avenue, Suite 102
Plantation, FL 33317
(call for catalog 305-791-8944)

Association for Children with
Learning Disabilities
4156 Liberty Road
Pittsburgh, PA 15234

Foundation for Children with
Learning Disabilities
99 Park Avenue
New York, NY 10016

For referrals for therapy and/or counseling, contact your:

- local mental health association or agency
- State Psychological Association
- State Association of Social Workers
- State Psychiatric Association
- American Association of Marriage and Family Therapists
  1717 K Street, Suite 407
  Washington, DC 20006
  (202) 429-1825

Videos

Choosing Children
Cambridge Documentary Films
P.O. Box 385
Cambridge, MA 02139

In the Best Interests of the Children
Women Make Movies
225 Lafayette Street
New York, NY 10012

Love Makes a Family
Fanlight Productions
47 Halifax Street
Boston, MA 02130

Love Makes a Family
(a film about lesbian and gay
Quaker families)
P.O. Box 11694
Portland, OR 97211

Other Families
BASHT Productions
P.O. Box 578712
Chicago, ILL 60657

Not All Parents Are Straight
Cinema Guild
Suite 802
1697 Broadway
New York, NY 10019

Sandy and Madeleine's Family
Multi-focus, Inc.
1525 Franklin Street
San Francisco, CA 94109

We Are Family
WGBH-TV
125 Western Avenue
Allston, MA 02134

APPENDIX A: SECOND-PARENT ADOPTION

A "second-parent" adoption is the process by which a lesbian may adopt and become a legally recognized parent of her partner's birth or adopted child. Currently only a very few states (approximately six at the present time) provide this legal means of protecting the relationship between the non-biological or non-adoptive lesbian parent and the child of her partner. In those few jurisdictions where "second-parent" adoptions are available, the legal status of "second parent" provides critical legal protection to the non-biological or non-adoptive lesbian parent in the event of the death or disability of the child's biological or adoptive mother or in the event of the termination of the lesbian partnership.

In the few jurisdictions which provide for "second-parent" adoptions, the procedure is often similar to the fairly routine procedure established for heterosexual "step-parent" adoptions. A "step-parent" adoption permits a spouse to adopt legally the child of his or her new spouse. In such adoptions the other parent's relationship with the child must be legally terminated in order for the step-parent to adopt. Typically a "step-parent" adoption occurs as a result of the death of the other parent or as a result of the other parent's willingness to give up parental rights.

Similarly, in order for a lesbian to adopt and become a "second-parent" to her partner's child, it is necessary that the parental rights of the biological father be terminated. This is often done by the father's willingness to sign a Consent to the termination of his parental rights. When a sperm bank is used in alternative insemination, the "second-parent" adoption process is often simplified. Many states have laws that the donor to a sperm bank will not be a legal father, thus eliminating the need for a signed Consent to termination of parental rights.

Contact an attorney to coordinate the process. She or he should be familiar with the forms and procedures necessary to complete the adoption. Generally speaking, the mothers fill out an application for the adoption. This is submitted to the court, probably county, and sent to the agency responsible for screening the family. The screening can include interviews and home visits or can simply be interviews with parents and child at the agency's office. The case worker will want to know that the relationship between parents is and has been stable and that adequate living space is available for the family. She or he may ask questions about the child's happiness, schooling, parenting philosophy, etc. In places where there have been a number of such adoptions the process may be purely routine, in other areas a family may be scrutinized carefully.

The legal or biological father needs to sign a Consent to the termination of his parental rights or the mothers need to provide proof of his death or the fact that a sperm bank was used.

In King County, Washington, the state issues a new birth certificate when the adoption is final. The certificate lists both women as the child's parents and has no mention of a father. This means that both women are legal parents and in the event of death of one of the mothers the surviving parent becomes sole parent. Again, this information may not be accurate for your location; be sure to consult an attorney for the options in your county and state.

APPENDIX B: ALTERNATIVE INSEMINATION
AND INFERTILITY WORKUPS

The following information is based on a discussion with an obstetrician/gynecologist in Seattle, Washington. Women who suspect they may have an infertility problem should consult a physician for information specific to their condition.

Statistically speaking, women under 34 years of age who use fresh sperm have the best chance of getting pregnant. Women in this category whose menstrual cycle is regularly more than 25 days long and are ovulating and who use BBT's (Basal Body Temperature charts) or an ovulation predictor kit usually get pregnant within six cycles. Women who do not get pregnant in this time frame should begin to consider seeking medical consultation. The use of frozen sperm or being over 34 years old decreases the chances of getting pregnant. Generally speaking, the frozen sperm pregnancy rate is 20–40% (for five cycles) at two inseminations per month. At 34 a woman's fertility declines, ovulation is less predictable, and the eggs are older. There is also a slight increased miscarriage rate. Women in this category should also try to get pregnant for six cycles but they should start an infertility workup after the six cycles because fertility lessens after 34 and something may be wrong with their ability to conceive. This may apply particularly to prospective lesbian mothers because many lesbians are in the almost over or over 35 years old category when they decide to have a child.

A woman who is wondering if she may have an infertility problem should consult a D.O. or M.D. Ob-Gyn or Reproductive Endocrinologist. The physician will usually review the past history to make sure the woman has been trying to get pregnant the most efficient ways. If everything looks good the physician will likely ask for a semen analysis first. The physician will also evaluate the BBT's and look at ovulation prediction. She or he may then do a hormone profile, an evaluation of the pituitary gland and the thyroid. These tests are done to assess how well the woman's body is functioning in terms of the chemicals which regulate ovulation. The physician may then do a Hysterosalpingogram, a test where dye is pushed into the cervix and is watched by fluoroscopy to assess tubal patency, i.e., whether the fallopian tubes are clear.

If everything checks out and the woman does not have blocked tubes the problem may be that she is not ovulating or not ovulating regularly. A first line intervention would be to give clomiphene citrate tablets orally for five days early in the month. The woman would also be instructed to use BBT and ovulation predictors and occasionally ultrasound to monitor ovulation. The physician would then inseminate with sperm that had been "washed." "Washing" concentrates the sperm and selects out the best sperm in terms of morphology (shape of sperm) and motility (ability to move). That sperm is injected via a catheter that is placed in the uterine cavity. This procedure is called Intrauterine Insemination or IUI. Assisted Reproductive Technologies (ART) is the umbrella name for all the methods used to help women get pregnant who cannot conceive by intercourse or A.I.

The second line of attempts of IUI to impregnate a woman is usually to use injectable drugs, menotropins for injections. The woman is monitored by blood tests and ultrasound with vaginal probes. This is usually done daily or every other day in order to monitor when an egg develops and is ready for ovulation. At ovulation the physician uses IUI to place the sperm in the uterine cavity. Individual physicians will tell you how many cycles of the above two methods a woman should go through. Generally, clomiphene with IUI is up to six cycles and can cost up to $350 per cycle. Injectables with IUI is usually used up to 2–3 cycles and can cost up to $2,000 per cycle. Cost estimates are based on data available in Seattle at the time of our writing; you will need to find out current costs in your area.

Before you choose a center with which to do fertility work it is important to ask to see the statistics for babies produced at that center. Since rate of pregnancy and children-born rates differ from center to center and within centers it is important to find out what the percentage of children born is at the particular centers you are considering. It can be as high as 16% per cycle of the women treated with IUI.

If the fallopian tubes are blocked this may have been due to Pelvic Inflammatory Disease (PID), Intrauterine Device (IUD) use or history of ruptured appendicitis and peritonitis (infection in the peritoneal cavity in the abdomen). There are several ways of dealing with blocked tubes. Historically, physicians performed micro surgery to unblock the fallopian tubes. Now they do more in vitro fertilization (IVF) as the first method of dealing with blocked tubes.

There are three options for IVF. Usually a woman chooses one and follows it rather than trying all three. The most common has a series of steps. The first is to use an injectable drug as in IUI, including blood and ultrasound monitoring. The physician then aspirates eggs transvaginally (through the vagina) from the woman's ovaries when they are ready for ovulation and monitors that procedure by ultrasound. This is performed under intravenous sedation, usually at the lab. The eggs are inseminated with washed sperm and if the eggs are fertilized they are incubated in the laboratory. If the eggs develop to a certain stage, usually within a week, up to four embryos are transferred and placed in the uterus. The woman needs to stay flat on her back for eight hours. With this procedure the laboratory can do prenatal diagnosis and so avoid having to do an amniocentesis (a procedure whereby the physician uses a long syringe to draw out some amnionic fluid from the placental sac) when the woman is pregnant. The laboratory can freeze the embryos if more than four survive the fertilization process and save the woman from repeating the aspiration and insemination process. There is approximately a nine to ten per cent "take-home-baby rate" with this procedure and a 25% pregnancy success rate but rates are variable center to center. It costs approximately $5,000–6,000 per implantation as of this writing.

The second IVF process is called Gamete Intrafallopian Transfer or GIFT. The development of eggs is done in the same way as the above process. The eggs are aspirated through a laparoscope instead of transvaginally. A laparoscope is a small scope inserted through the abdominal wall under general anesthesia. An endocrinologist present at the surgery looks at the eggs and washed sperm and if all is well she/he mixes them and puts them into a syringe. The surgeon places the mixed eggs and sperm into the fallopian tube(s) via catheter. This procedure has as high as a 35% success rate per cycle for pregnancy.

The third IVF procedure is called Zygote Intrafallopian Transfer or ZIFT. ZIFT begins the same way as the above two procedures and the eggs can be aspirated transvaginally or by laproscope. Instead of placing the newly mixed eggs and sperm in the fallopian tubes the physician places fertilized embryos in the fallopian tube(s) via laproscopy. This requires the woman to come in for surgery perhaps a second time under general anesthesia, depending on which aspiration process was used. This procedure is the most expensive of the three IVF's with

GIFT being the middle range. Technically, a woman can go through as many of these procedures as she can afford but three cycles is a reasonable test of her ability to bear a child.

Ovum Donation and Other Options

There are other options besides getting pregnant for a woman who wants a child. Surrogate motherhood, in which another woman gets pregnant and bears the child, is one possibility. Ovum donation occurs when one woman's eggs are fertilized and placed in another woman's fallopian tubes. This may be of particular interest to lesbian couples as one woman could bear her partner's biological child.

APPENDIX C: SAMPLE PARENTING AGREEMENT

This is not a legal document and should not be used in place of consultation with an attorney. This sample includes both legal and more mundane issues, and is intended to provide the reader with ideas only.

1. Joan Washington and Kelly Greenberg agree to parent their child, Tamara, together as equal parents. Tamara's name reflects this and is: Tamara Washington-Greenberg.

2. Kelly agrees to allow Joan to become a second legal parent if the courts permit it. Both women agree to pay for the legal fees out of joint household funds.

3. Both parents agree that Kelly will stay home full-time for one year and Joan will continue her job. Kelly will be responsible for cooking on the weekdays, childcare during work hours and nightime feedings, grocery shopping and cleaning the living and dining rooms. Joan will be primarily responsible for afterwork childcare, cooking on weekends, cleaning bathroom and bedrooms. Parents can negotiate trades or favors with both women's consent. All other household jobs will be divided by interest and energy.

4. After the first year Kelly will work full-time and Joan will stay home full-time. They will trade responsibilities as well.

5. When Tamara is two years old the parents will find childcare for Tamara and both women will work.

6. All child related expenses will be paid out of joint household funds. During the first two years when only one parent is working for pay, all of her earnings go into the joint account. When both women are working full-time again they return to their earlier agreement of paying a mutually agreed upon amount into the joint account, depending on the financial needs of the family, and reserving any left over money for personal savings or entertainment.

7. In the event that Joan and Kelly divorce they agree to the following:

    A. Both women are equal parents and must agree on decisions which affect Tamara. This includes but is not limited to whether one mother wants to move from their home city, where Tamara goes to school, medical issues, religious affiliations and vacation dates.

    B. Both women agree to see a counselor for help in resolving issues between the two of them as they co-parent together.

C. Both agree to see a counselor if they are unable to help Tamara resolve behavior problems such as acting out or skipping school.

D. Both parents intend to share custodial responsibilities. At times this may be having Tamara go back and forth between homes a week at a time or every three days or a year at one and then a year at the other parent's house. Both women need to agree to the arrangement and will seek counseling or mediation if they are unable to find agreement on their own.

E. Each parent is responsible for half of Tamara's expenses, including education until she is twenty-one.

F. Both parents agree that in the event of the death or incapacitation of the other it is in the best interests of their daughter that she remain with the surviving or competent parent.

Signed: _____

_____

Date: _____

INDEX

A.I. (alternative insemination), 21-28. *See also* Appendix B
abstinence, sexual, 303
academic achievement, 282, 306, 308-310
active listening, 82-85
activities, group, 295
addiction, drug, 162, 307-308
adolescents, 260-285, 286-311. *See also* preteens; teenagers
  coming out to, 71-72
  control of, 246
  development, 246-248, 261-273, 289-300
  parenting, 97-104, 244-259, 260-285, 286-311
  reaction to divorce, 117
  resolving conflicts, 97-104
  transracial adoption, 135-136
adoption, 4, 20, 29, 32-38. *See also* Appendix A
  agencies, 35-36
  international, 37-38, 222-223
  interracial, 34-35, 222-223
  parents-to-be, 167
  second-parent, 4, 36, 125. *See also* Appendix A
  transracial, 130-136
Adoptive Families of America, Inc., 167
adult children
  coming out to, 72-75, 324
  parenting, 312-324
AFP (alpha-fetoprotein screening), 163-164
After Great Pain: A New Life Emerges, 177
agencies, adoption, 35-36
agreement, parenting, 125. *See also* Appendix C
Ahrons, Constance, 123

AIDS, 112-113
  children with, 30, 39
  semen, 23-24, 26
alcohol, 162, 274-275, 304-306, 307-308
alpha-fetoprotein screening (AFP), 163-164
alternative insemination (A.I.), 21-28. *See also* Appendix B
amniocentesis, 163-164
anger, adolescent, 293
anorexia nervosa, 277
anti-sodomy laws, 31
artificial insemination. *See* alternative insemination (A.I.)
authority, defying, 274-275, 297, 306
babies. *See also* adoption; childbirth; pregnancy
  development, 179-181
  impact on relationship, 20, 181-182
  parenting, 179-191
  sharing parenting of, 182-185
  support systems, 185-187
banks, sperm, 24-25
basal body temperature (BBT), 22-23
behavior
  modeling, 92, 139-140, 144-145
  problems, 310-311
  troubled, 274-277
Berg, Elizabeth, 147
Beyond Acceptance, 78
bias-free children, 138-145
Big Sisters, 39
biological
  father, 25-26, 28-29, 48-55, 221
  parent, role of, 41-48
Birnbaum, Nan, 114
birth, 169-176

birthdays, 155-156
birthing center, 174-175
Black and White Racial Identity, 139
Blakeslee, Sandra, 115-118
blended families, 45-48
body temperature, basal (BBT), 22-23
bonding, 183
Boys Clubs, 39
breastfeeding, 182-183
brothers. *See* siblings
Brown, Lyn, 272
Bruner, Jerome, 233
bulimia nervosa, 277
Camp Fire Girls, 39
care, baby, 179-191. *See also* babies
celebrations, family, 147-158
center, birthing, 174-175
ceremonies, 147-158
child care, 189-191, 202-203
childbirth, 169-176
children. *See also* adolescents;
    development; middle
    childhood; preteens; teenag-
    ers; young children
  AIDS, 30, 39
  bias-free, 138-145
  blended families, 47-48
  coming out to, 62-72
  death of, 114-115, 177
  decision to raise, 19-21, 38-40
  experiencing racism, 142-144
  father fantasies, 54-55
  gay, 263-265, 295-296, 315-316
  impact on relationship, 20, 206-
    207, 223-224
  lesbian, 263-265, 295-296, 315-
    316
  partners of, 315-317
  racist behavior, 141-142
  reaction to divorce, 117
  resolving conflicts, 92-96
  sex of, 21, 23
chlamydia and semen, 26

chorionic villi sampling (CVS),
    163-164
chromosomes, 23
cigarettes, impact on health, 162
Clarke, Jean Ilsley, 236
classes, birth preparation, 172-173
co-parenting with fathers, 52-54
coaching youth sports, 40
cognitive development. *See also*
    intellectual development
  adolescents, 247-248
  babies, 180-181
  child, 211-213
  middle children, 226-229
  toddlers, 194-195
Cole, Diane, 177
coming out. *See also* homophobia
  adolescents, 71-72
  as grandparents, 320-321
  as parents, 60-80, 203-206, 238-
    241
  custody rights, 13-14
  decision to, 12-14
  heterosexism, 61-62
  homophobia, 62
  school, 283
  to adult children, 72-75, 324
  to children, 62-72
  to family of origin, 75-80
  to young children, 70-71
communication skills, 81-90, 216-
    219
community, 187-188
community, religious, 187-188,
    221-222, 242
compulsive eating, 277
conception. *See* alternative
    insemination; Appendix B
  problems with, 29-30
concrete logical operations, 226-
    227
conflict resolution, 91-106
  adolescents, 97-104
  siblings, 96-97

young children, 92-96
confronting racism, 140-142
conscience, development of, 228-229
constructive play, 233
control of adolescents, 246
control of teenagers, 288-289
Corley, Rip, 72
counseling, 107, 274
court system, 4, 39
    biological father, 28-29
    sperm donor, 26
cravings, food, 162
custody rights, 78-79, 118, 121-125
    and coming out, 13-14
    biological father, 28-29
    sperm donor, 26
CVS (chorionic villi sampling), 163-164
dating, (adolescent), 296-299
day care, 189-191
death
    dealing with, 108-115, 177
    of child, 114-115, 177
    rituals, 157-158
decision making, 290-292
decision to raise children, 19-21, 38-40
defying authority, 274-275, 297, 306
delinquency, 274-275, 306
demographics, racial, 126
depression, 275-276, 277
development. See also cognitive development; emotional development; moral development; physical development; psychological development; social development
    adolescents, 246-248, 261-273, 289-300
    babies, 179-181
    child, 209-216
    middle childhood, 226-234

preteens, 261-273
puberty, 261-273
teenagers, 261-273, 289-300
toddlers, 193-196
DiGeronimo, Theresa Foy, 138
disabilities, 21, 33-34, 232-233
    learning, 231-232, 282, 309
discipline, 198-202
discrimination, defined, 127-128
disequilibrium, developmental, 209-210
disorders, eating, 274-275, 277, 306
divorce
    dealing with, 115-125
    fathers from, 49-51, 315, 318
    lesbian, 121-125
donation, ovum, 22. See also alternative insemination
donor semen and STDs, 23-24, 26
donor sperm sources, 24-26
donor, sperm
    parental rights of donor, 25-26
    role of, 51-52
Down syndrome, 163
drinking, 162. See also alcohol; drugs
drugs, 39, 162, 274-275, 304-308
eating disorders, 274-275, 277, 306
Edelman, Hope, 113-114
education, sex, 241-242
educators, 134
Elium, Don and Jeanne, 294
emissions, nocturnal, 262-263
emotional development. See also psychological development; social development
    adolescents, 272-273, 292-294
    child, 214-215
    middle children, 230-232
    preteens, 272-273
    puberty, 272-273
    teenagers, 272-273, 292-294
employment, teenage, 300-301

engaged parenting, 81, 254-259

equilibrium, developmental, 209-210

Erikson, Erik, 231, 286

everyday rituals, 148-150

exercise during pregnancy, 162-163

experiencing racism, 142-144

extended families, 57, 224-225

extracurricular activities, 284-285

failure, fear of, 231-232

families, blended, 45-48

families, extended, 57, 224-225

families, lesbian, 4-5
   creating traditions, 146-158
   gender roles, 15-16
   multiracial, 129-138
   research, 4, 11
   roles, 12, 15-16, 17-18, 41-59, 90-91
   strengths, 14-18, 251
   structure, 12, 16, 17-18, 41-59, 218

family
   finances, 301, 323-324
   meetings, 105-106
   occasions, 314-318
   of origin, coming out to, 75-80

Family Traditions, 147

FAS (Fetal Alcohol Syndrome), 162

father fantasies, 54-55

father, biological, 25-26, 28-29, 48-55, 221, 315, 318

fear of failure, 231-232

female (X) chromosome, 23

fertility, 29-30

fertilization, in vitro, 22. *See also* alternative insemination

Fetal Alcohol Syndrome (FAS), 162

finances, family, 301, 323-324

first trimester, 162-163, 164

foster-adoptions, 36-37

foster-parenting, 20, 29, 30-32, 36-37

friendship, 242-243, 299-300

game-playing, 233-234

Gardner, James, 245

gay children, 263-265, 295-296, 315-316

Gay Parenting, 67

gender identity, 215-216, 217, 230-231, 248-252

gender roles, 15-16

"Get out of my life, but first could you drive Cheryl and me to the mall": A Parent's Guide to the New Teenager, 248

Gilligan, Carol, 272

Girl Scouts, 39

Girls Clubs, 39

goddess-parents, 57

gonorrhea and semen, 26

Good Divorce, The, 123

grandmothering, 319-321

grandparents, 57, 75-80

grief, stages of, 108-111

group activities, 295

guardian ad litem, 39

Health Maintenance Organizations (HMOs), 4

Helms, Janet, 139

help, parenting, 106-107

heterosexism, 20, 62, 187-188, 220, 250-252

HIV infection and semen, 23-24, 26

HMOs (Health Maintenance Organizations), 4

holiday celebrations, 151-153

home
   births, 175-176
   insemination, 27-28
   adult children living at, 321-324

homophobia
   adoption, 20, 36
   coming out, 62, 187-188, 220,

324
family relations, 314-318
father, 50, 315
foster-parenting, 20, 31
grandmothering, 319
impact on children, 20, 87-88
internalized, 62, 129, 264-265
parenting against, 17
Hopson, Darlene and Derek, 141
hospital births, 172-174
hospital volunteering, 40
*How to Talk to Your Kids About
    Really Important Things*, 138
hypodescent, 137
"I"-messages, 89-90
identity
    development, 61, 195, 281, 286-
        289
    gender, 215-216, 217, 230-231,
        248-252
    racial, 130-145, 217
imaginary play, 233
in vitro fertilization, 22. *See also*
    alternative insemination
independence
    adolescents, 278-281
    teenage, 286-306
    toddlers, 196
independent adoptions, 37
indicators, ovulation, 23
infancy, 179-180. *See also* babies;
    childbirth; pregnancy
infant care volunteering, 40
infertility, 29-30. *See also* Appen-
    dix B
insemination, alternative (A.I.),
    21-28. *See also* Appendix B
intellectual development, 267-272,
    289-292. *See also* cognitive
    development
intercourse and pregnancy, 28-29
internalized
    homophobia, 62, 129
    racism, 128-129

international adoption, 37-38, 222-
    223
interracial
    adoption, 34-35, 222-223
    couples, 136-138
intrauterine insemination, 22. *See
    also* alternative insemination
jobs, teenage, 300-301
Jordan, Mary Kate, 113
Kegel exercises, 162-163
kindergarten, 220-221
known donor
    role of, 52
    sperm sources, 26
Kruger, Ann Cale, 229
Kubler-Ross, Elisabeth, 108
labor, 169-176
language
    and family roles, 12-14, 41-46
    learning, 181, 194, 211-213
laws
    anti-sodomy, 31
    biological father, 28-29
    sperm donor, 26
learning disabilities, 231-232, 282,
    309
learning language, 181, 194, 211-
    213
legal system. *See* court system;
    custody rights; laws
lesbian adoption, 4
*Lesbian and Gay Parenting Hand-
    book*, 77
lesbian children, 263-265, 295-296,
    315-316
Lesbian Couples, 129
lesbian divorce, 121-125
lesbian families, 4-5
    creating traditions, 146-158
    gender roles, 15-16
    multiracial, 129-138
    research, 4, 11
    roles, 12, 15-16, 17-18, 41-59, 90-
        91

strengths, 14-18, 251
structure, 12, 16, 17-18, 41-59,
  90-91, 218
Lickona, Thomas, 271
Lieberman, Susan Abel, 148
limits, setting, 90-91, 255-256, 280
listening, active, 82-85
living at home, adult children,
  321-324
logical thinking, 226-227
Losing Uncle Tim, 113
loss, dealing with, 108-125, 177
Loving Someone Gay, 78
mail-order sperm banks, 25
male (Y) chromosome, 23
male role models, 55-56, 215-216
marriage, 317-318
  ending, 115-125
  fathers from, 49-51, 314-315, 318
Martin, April, 77
masturbation, 266
meetings, family, 105-106
memorials, 157-158
menstruation, 262-263
middle childhood, parenting, 226-
  243
midwives, 173, 175-176
mirroring, 216-217
miscarriage, 163, 177
modeling behavior, 92, 139-140,
  144-145
money management, 301
moodiness, (children's), 272-273,
  274-275, 306
moral development, 228-229, 267-
  272, 289-292
mother, concept of, 42-44
mother, single
  dating, 206
  discipline, 201-202
  pregnancy, 165-166
  support, 202-203
motherhood, surrogate, 22. *See
  also* alternative insemination

Motherless Daughters, 114
motor skills. *See* physical development
moving, 242-243
multiracial lesbian families, 129-
  138
myths re: adolescents, 245-246
nannies, 190-191
neural tube defects, 164
New Traditions, 148
nocturnal emissions, 262-263
non-biological parent, role of, 12,
  41-48, 165, 168-169, 171-172,
  182-185
non-legal parent, rights of, 46-47,
  221
non-verbal communication, 82
Now That You Know, 78
nutrition during pregnancy, 161-
  162
  systematic, defined, 128
outing, accidental, 203-204
overidentification, 288
ovulation, 23
ovum donation, 22. *See also*
  alternative insemination
P-FLAG (Parents, Families and
  Friends of Lesbians and
  Gays), 78
parent
  biological, role of, 41-48
  legal, 4
parental rights, 28-29
  non-legal parent, 46-47
  sperm donor, 25-26, 51-52
parenting
  active listening, 82-85
  adolescents, 97-104, 244-259,
    260-285, 286-311
  adult children, 312-324
  agreement, 125. *See* Appendix C
  babies, 179-191
  children, 208-225
  coming out, 60-80, 203-206, 238-

241

communication skills, 81-90
conflict resolution, 91-106
death, dealing with, 108-115
discipline, 198-202
divorce, dealing with, 115-125
engaged, 81, 254-259
family meetings, 105-106
foster, 20, 29, 30-32, 36-37
help, 106-107
"I"-messages, 89-90
limit-setting, 90-91
loss, dealing with, 108-125
middle childhood, 226-243
modeling behavior, 92
preteens, 260-285
problem ownership, 88-89
puberty, 260-285
racism, 126-145
resources, 106-107, 274
sharing with partner, 41-48,
    182-185, 198-202. *See also*
    Appendix C
siblings, 96-97
support groups, 187, 202-203
talking, 85-88
teenagers, 97-104, 260-285, 286-
    311
toddlers, 192-207
work, 188-191, 205-206
young children, 92-96
parents, coming out to, 75-80
Parents, Families and Friends of
    Lesbians and Gays (P-FLAG),
    78
partners
    child's, 315-317
    impact of children, 20, 181-182,
        206-207, 223-224
    interracial, 136-138
    role of, 12-14, 165, 168-169, 171-
        172, 221
    sharing parenting with, 41-48,
        182-185, 198-202. *See also*

Appendix C
past, dealing with own, 252-253
paternal rights, 28-29
    sperm donor, 25-26
peers
    involvement with, 230-231
    pressure, 246, 270-272, 303
Perez, P., 173
physical development
    adolescents, 247-248, 261-263
    babies, 180-181
    child, 211
    middle children, 232-234
    preteens, 261-263
    puberty, 261-263
    teenagers, 261-263
    toddlers, 193-194
physical punishment, 257
Piaget, Jean, 226-227
Pipher, Mary, 250
play groups, 202-203
play, importance of, 233-234
potty training. *See* toilet learning
predictor kit, ovulation, 23
pregnancy, 161-172. *See also*
    Appendix B
    alternative insemination (A.I.),
        21-28
    intercourse, 28-29
prejudice, 17, 127-128. *See also*
    discrimination; homophobia
prenatal care, 163-164, 169-170
prenatal testing, 163-164
preschool, 220-221
preteens, parenting, 260-285. *See*
    also adolescents; teenagers
private adoption agencies, 36
problems, serious, 274-277, 306-
    311
psychological development. *See*
    also emotional development;
    social development
    adolescents, 247-248
    child, 214-215

middle children, 230-232
toddlers, 195-196
puberty, 260-285
public adoption agencies, 36
punishment, physical, 257
racial demographics, 126
racial identity, 130-145, 217
racism, 17, 20-21, 34-35
  behavior of children, 141-142
  confronting, 140-142
  children experiencing, 142-144
  parenting against, 126-145
Raising a Son, 294
raising children, decision to, 19-21, 38-40
Raising Good Children: From Birth Through the Teenage Years, 271
Raising the Rainbow Generation, 141
rehabilitation, drug, 39
relationship, impact of children, 20, 181-182, 206-207, 223-224
relaxation during pregnancy, 162-163
religious community, 187-188, 221-222, 242
research on lesbian families, 4, 11
Resolve, 167
resources for parenting, 106-107, 274
returning home, adult children, 321-324
reunions, family, 314
Reviving Ophelia: Saving the Selves of Adolescent Girls, 250
Rise 'N Shine, 39
rites of passage, 155-156
rituals, 147-158
rivalry, sibling, 96-97
role models, 55-56, 139-140, 144-145
roles
  in lesbian families, 12, 15-16, 17-18, 41-59, 90-91
  gender, 215-216

rules, learning, 228-229, 233-234, 235-237
running away, 39, 274-275, 306
safety issues, 258
Schaefer, Charles E., 138
school, 220-221, 239-241, 281-285
  problems, 274-275, 301, 306, 308-310
  volunteering, 40
Schulenburg, Joy, 67
seasonal rituals, 150-151
Second Chances, 115
second trimester, 162-163, 164
second-parent adoption, 4, 36, 125. *See also* Appendix A
self-esteem, 64, 139-140, 217, 249-252, 272-273
Self-Esteem: A Family Affair, 236
semen. *See also* sperm
  HIV infection, 23-24
  STDs, 26
setting limits, 90-91, 255-256, 280
sex of child, 21, 23
sexuality
  abstinence, 303
  adolescence, 241-242, 248-252, 263-267
  children, 215-216
  pregnancy, 169
  preteen, 241-242, 248-252, 263-267
  problem behavior, 274-275, 306
  puberty, 241-242, 248-252, 263-267
  teenagers, 274-275, 301-304, 306
shower, baby, 165
siblings, 57-58, 96-97
Simkin, Penny, 173
single mothering
  dating, 206
  discipline, 201-202
  pregnancy, 165-166
  support, 202-203
sisters. *See* siblings

smoking, 162
social development. *See also*
    emotional development;
    psychological development
    adolescents, 247-248, 272-273,
        294-296
    child, 214-215
    middle children, 230-232
    preteens, 272-273
    puberty, 272-273
    teenagers, 272-273, 294-296
    toddlers, 195-196
social events, family, 314-318
social life, 281-285
Sophie, Joan, 61
sources of donor sperm, 24-26
Special Olympics, 232
Special Woman: The Role of the
    Professional Labor Assistant,
    173
sperm. *See also* semen
    AIDS, 23-24
    donor, role of, 51-52
    HIV, 23-24
    parental rights of donor, 25-26
    sources, 24-26
    X or Y bearing, 23
spina bifida, 163-164
sports, 40, 233-234, 238-239
stages of grief, 108-111
state laws, 31
    sperm donor, 26
STDs and donor semen, 23-24, 26
stillbirth, 177. *See also* death of
    child
strengths of lesbian families, 14-
    18, 251
structure of lesbian families, 12,
    16, 17-18, 41-59, 218
structured games, 233-234
substance abuse. *See* alcohol;
    drugs
suicide, 275, 276, 277
summer jobs, teenage, 301

support during pregnancy, 164-
    167
support groups, 187, 202-203
support systems, 16-17, 185-187
surrogate motherhood, 22. *See also*
    alternative insemination
syphilis and semen, 26
systematic oppression, defined,
    128
talking to children, 85-88
    about sex, 262-267
teaching tolerance, 138-145
teenagers, 253-254. *See also*
    adolescents; preteens
    control of, 288-289
    development, 261-273, 289-300
    parenting, 97-104, 260-285, 286-
        311
    reaction to divorce, 117
    resolving conflicts, 97-104
    runaway, 39
    transracial adoption, 135-136
temperature, basal body (BBT),
    22-23
Terrible Twos, 195
testing, prenatal, 163
The Birth Partner, 173
The Final Closet, 72
The Turbulent Teens, 245
third trimester, 164-165
time with family, 254-255
toddlers
    development, 193-196
    discipline, 198-202
    independence, 196
    outings, 203-204
    parenting, 192-207
    toilet learning, 197-198
toilet learning, 197-198
tolerance, teaching, 138-145
traditions, creating, 146-158
transracial adoption, 130-136
trimesters, pregnancy, 162-163,
    164-165

troubled behavior, 274-277
trust, 86, 255
tutoring, 40
Twos, Terrible, 195
ultrasound, 163-164
values, learning, 237-238
vegetarianism during pregnancy, 161
visitation rights, 28-29
  sperm donor, 26
volunteering, 39-40
Wallerstein, Judith, 115-118
weddings, 317-318
weight gain during pregnancy, 163
Wicca, 222

Wolf, Anthony, 248
work and parenting, 188-191, 205-206
work, teenage, 300-301
X (female) chromosome, 23
Y (male) chromosome, 23
YMCA, 39
young children
  coming out to, 70-71
  parenting, 92-96
  reaction to divorce, 117
  resolving conflicts, 92-96
  transracial adoption, 132-136
youth sports, coaching, 40
YWCA, 39

ABOUT THE AUTHORS

D. Merilee Clunis, Ph.D., and G. Dorsey Green, Ph.D., are the authors of the bestselling *Lesbian Couples: Creating Healthy Relationships for the 90s* (Seal, 1993). Both are lesbian psychologists in private practice with extensive experience in counseling lesbian parents; they also have published professional papers and led workshops and trainings on the topics of communication, couple relationships and parenting. They live with their families in Seattle.

OTHER TITLES FROM SEAL PRESS

LESBIAN COUPLES: *Creating Healthy Relationships for the 90s* by D. Merilee Clunis and G. Dorsey Green. $12.95, 1-878067-37-0. The definitive guide for lesbians that describes the pleasures and challenges of being part of a couple. Also available on audiocassette. $9.95, 0-931188-85-7.

THE LESBIAN HEALTH BOOK: *Caring for Ourselves* edited by Jocelyn White, M. D. and Marissa C. Martínez. $18.95, 1-878067-31-1. The first comprehensive health book for lesbians.

THE SINGLE MOTHER'S COMPANION: *Essays and Stories by Women* edited by Marsha R. Leslie. $12.95, 1-878067-56-7. The single mothers in this landmark collection explore both the joys and the difficult realities of raising children alone. Contributors include Barbara Kingsolver, Anne Lamott, Linda Hogan, Julia A. Boyd and Senator Carol Moseley-Braun.

CEREMONIES OF THE HEART: *Celebrating Lesbian Unions* edited by Becky Butler. $16.95, 1-878067-87-7. An anthology of twenty-five personal accounts of lesbian ceremonies of commitment.

LOVERS' CHOICE by Becky Birtha. $10.95, 1-878067-41-9. Provocative stories charting the course of women's lives by a Black lesbian feminist writer.

THE BLACK WOMEN'S HEALTH BOOK: *Speaking for Ourselves* edited by Evelyn C. White. $16.95, 1-878067-40-0. A pioneering anthology addressing the health issues facing today's Black women. Contributors include Faye Wattleton, Byllye Y. Avery, Alice Walker, Audre Lorde, Toni Morrison, Angela Y. Davis.

PAST DUE: *A Story of Disability, Pregnancy and Birth* by Anne Finger. $10.95, 0-931188-87-3. In this riveting account of her pregnancy and childbirth, a writer disabled by polio explores the complexities of disability and reproductive rights.

THE ME IN THE MIRROR by Connie Panzarino. $12.95, 1-878067-45-1. The memoir of writer, lesbian and disability rights activist and artist Connie Panzarino, who has been living with a rare muscular disease since birth.

ALMA ROSE by Edith Forbes. $10.95, 1-878067-33-8. A brilliant lesbian novel filled with unforgettable characters and the vibrant spirit of the West.

OUT OF TIME by Paula Martinac. $9.95, 0-931188-91-1. A delightful and thoughtful novel about lesbian history and the power of memory. *Winner of the 1990 Lambda Literary Award for Best Lesbian Fiction.*

SEAL PRESS publishes many books by women writers under the categories of women's studies, fiction, translations, young adult and children, parenting, self-help, recovery and health, and women in sports and the outdoors. To receive a free catalog or to order directly, write to us at 3131 Western Avenue, Suite 410, Seattle, Washington 98121. Please include 16.5% of total book order for shipping and handling; Washington residents add 8.6% sales tax.